International Perspectives on Research in Early Childhood Education

a volume in
Contemporary Perspectives in Early Childhood Education

Series Editors:
Olivia N. Saracho, *University of Maryland*
Bernard Spodek, *University of Illinois*

Contemporary Perspectives in Early Childhood Education

Olivia N. Saracho and Bernard Spodek, Series Editors

Contemporary Perspectives on Families, Communities and Schools for Young Children (2004)
  edited by Olivia N. Saracho and Bernard Spodek

Contemporary Perspectives on Play in Early Childhood Education (2003)
  edited by Olivia N. Saracho and Bernard Spodek

Studying Teachers in Early Childhood Settings (2003)
  edited by Olivia N. Saracho and Bernard Spodek

Contemporary Perspectives on Curriculum in Early Childhood Education (2002)
  edited by Olivia N. Saracho and Bernard Spodek

Contemporary Perspectives on Literacy in Early Childhood Education (2002)
  edited by Olivia N. Saracho and Bernard Spodek

Contemporary Perspectives on Language Policy and Literacy Instruction in Childhood Education (2002)
  edited by Olivia N. Saracho and Bernard Spodek

International Perspectives on Research in Early Childhood Education

Edited by

Bernard Spodek
University of Illinois

and

Olivia N. Saracho
University of Maryland

INFORMATION AGE
PUBLISHING

Greenwich, Connecticut • www.infoagepub.com

Library of Congress Cataloging-in-Publication Data

International perspectives on research in early childhood education /
edited
by Bernard Spodek and Olivia N. Saracho.
    p. cm. — (Contemporary perspectives in early childhood
education)
  Includes bibliographical references.
  ISBN 1-931576-66-1 (pbk.) — ISBN 1-931576-67-X (hardcover)
  1. Early childhood education--Cross-cultural studies. I. Spodek,
Bernard.
II. Saracho, Olivia N. III. Series.
  LB1139.23.I69 2005
  372.21—dc22
                                          2005013178

Printed in the United States of America

CONTENTS

Introduction: Early Childhood Education Research and Practice in
International Perspective
Bernard Spodek and Olivia N. Saracho   *ix*

1. Early Childhood Education in Australia
   Approaches, Issues, Policies and Research
   Wendy Schiller   *1*

2. Contemporary Early Childhood Education and
   Research in China
   Jiaxong Zhu and X. Christine Wang   *55*

3. How Finland is Researching Early Childhood Education
   Mikko Ojala   *79*

4. Contemporary Perspectives in Early Childhood Education:
   The Case of Greece
   Demetra Evangelou and Hara Cortessis-Dafermou   *119*

5. Research and Policy Issues in Early Childhood Care and
   Education in Japan.
   Yoko Shirakawa and Sachiko Kitano   *137*

6. Early Childhood Care and Education in Korea:
   Current State and Research
   Unhai Rhee, Won Young Rhee, and Young-Ja Lee   *161*

7. A Global Perspective on Early Childhood Education:
   Characteristic Traits and Research in Norway
   Ole Fredrik Lillemyr   *191*

8. Elementary Education in Poland: A Brief History and
   Current Research
   Barbara Muraska   233

9. Research in Early Childhood Education in Portugal
   Teresa Vasconcelos   259

10. Early Childhood Education Research in Spain
    Miguel A. Zabalza   293

11. Early Childhood Education in Turkey: An Overview
    Sevda Bekman   335

12. Early Childhood Education: An International and
    Contemporary Perspective
    Bernard Spodek and Olivia N. Saracho   355

About the Authors   *361*

INTRODUCTION

Early Childhood Education Research and Practice: An International Perspective

Bernard Spodek and Olivia N. Saracho

Even before the development of the Froebel kindergarten more than 150 years ago, curriculum models had been transported over the world. The first models of early childhood education came from Britain, Germany, and Italy. These were transported from their places of origin to other countries by various means. Sometimes books written in one country were read in other countries, thus spreading the world about educational models. Sometimes women trained in early childhood education in one country emigrated to other countries bringing the practices they learned with them. Sometimes commissions or individuals traveled abroad specifically to study a new early childhood program to be disseminated back in their home country. Whether by slow boat, by more rapid transportation and communication, or by the exchange of ideas through various media, approaches to early childhood education have spread beyond their places of origin. They were studied and adopted in countries that were often halfway around the world from where they originated. Once adopted, they were quickly adapted to the local culture. Thus, not only were these

International Perspectives on Research in Early Childhood Education, ix–xxii
Copyright © 2005 by Information Age Publishing
All rights of reproduction in any form reserved.

programs developmentally appropriate in their dissemination, they also became culturally appropriate (Woollens, 2000a). We want to explore here the roots of early childhood practice as it has developed internationally. Then we shall explore research in early childhood education in the same way. While our emphasis is on the United States, we take into account developments in the field abroad.

In the chapters that follow, the history and current status of early childhood education in selected countries, along with a review of current research that is being conducted in these countries will be presented. In essence this will provide a glimpse of the intellectual base of early childhood education in many parts of the world

ROOTS OF EARLY CHILDHOOD EDUCATION PRACTICE

The first educational programs in the United States that were specifically designed for young children were *infant schools*. This program was based on the ideas that Robert Owen had developed in Scotland (Owen, 1824). Even before Owen himself came to America, his ideas had crossed the ocean. Infant schools were established in a number of communities in the eastern United States during the first quarter of the nineteenth century. These programs did not flourish for long in America. The infant school educated young children separately from their families. The idea of educating young children outside the home was counter to the family ethic of the time (Strickland, 1982).

The next approach to early childhood education that was established in America was the kindergarten, created by Freidrich Froebel in Germany. It was originally brought to the United States by German immigrants in the middle of the nineteenth century. Margarethe Schurz, who studied to be a kindergartner in Germany, emigrated to the United States in the 1850s. She established the first American kindergarten in Watertown, Wisconsin in 1856. It was a German speaking kindergarten that served the Schurz' children and those of the extended family

The kindergarten slowly expanded in the United States, first in German American communities and then in mainstream communities. Kindergartners, as kindergarten teachers were called then, were brought to America to start programs for children and to train teachers. These kindergartens, originally private, were sponsored by various organizations to serve a number of purposes in addition to educating young children. By the late nineteenth century, kindergartens began to be incorporated into public school systems (Shapiro, 1983). Today, kindergartens are part of public elementary schools throughout the United States and almost all 5-year-olds go to kindergarten

Other approaches to early childhood education were imported to the United States in the first quarter of the twentieth century and kindergartens themselves changed drastically during that time. The nursery school, which originated in England with Margaret Macmillan at the beginning of the twentieth century to serve low-income children and their families, was soon established in America. Americans read about nursery schools and visited nursery schools in England. They then established nursery schools in America where they slowly spread. The concept of *nurturance* advocated by the Macmillan's—which can roughly be translated as "dealing with the whole child"—seemed less important in America, though, as the children enrolled in these schools came from families with greater resources.

The Montessori method originated in Italy. Here, too, Americans read about the method, went to observe this approach, and invited Maria Montessori to lecture in the United States. The books Maria Montessori wrote on her approach to early education were translated into many languages and she trained women from many countries to become Montessori directresses. By the 1920s Montessori schools were being established in the United States. The Montessori schools that were established after World War I, however, closed during the Great Depression of the 1930s, as did many other private educational institutions. At the same time, the nursery school took hold, supported by federal funds, partly to provide work relief for unemployed teachers. The Montessori approach was not firmly established in America until it was resurrected in the late 1950s and early 1960s. Nancy Rambusch, an American, became aware of Montessori education in Europe and brought the approach to the United States again.

In time, all these approaches to early childhood education became firmly established in the United States. A similar pattern of importing early childhood education could be told about many other countries—Australia, Japan, Korea, China, to name but a few. In a sense, by thinking globally, approaches to early childhood education were helped to spread from their countries of origin to become established throughout the world. While each of the programs set down firm roots in American soil, none of them remained as they first appeared on the scene. While first adopted in their original form, the process of adaptation made them truly American.

Thus, kindergartens, which were first taught in German, made the transition and translation into English-speaking kindergartens in the United States. The nature of the kindergarten program changed as well as its language. While they were originally Froebelian, kindergarten was influenced by American progressive education and reconstructed to become the American kindergarten we can observe today. They became more child centered, more play oriented, and more reflective of American life. While some early childhood educators have noted that the spirit of the Froebelian kindergarten remained, the content, methods, and activities look nothing like the kindergarten that Froebel envisioned. Even now changes are taking place. With kindergartens essentially part of the elementary school in America, it has been influenced by the program of the primary grades, at the same time as it influenced the program of the primary grade. Today, American kindergartens are more academically oriented, especially since the recent Federal No Child Left Behind Act (2001) was passed.

Similarly, the nursery school, which was designed in England to serve the children of the poor, was reconstructed in America to serve a middle-class population. Today, even the name has changed. It is called a pre-school more often than it is called a nursery school.

The Casa di Bambini of Maria Montessori was also originally designed to serve low-income children. Today, it primarily serves the most affluent in America. In addition, the Montessori movement split in two, offering both a traditional approach and an American version of Montessori education, which has become increasingly popular. The earliest form of early child-hood education, which is the infant school, faded from the scene early and never recovered here. However, infant schools have flourished in England.

Just as Americans imported approaches to early childhood education from abroad, American approaches to early childhood education have been exported to other countries. Early on, the Progressive Education approach was studied by many educators abroad and brought to their country. Chen He-Chin studied progressive early childhood education in the United States and brought these progressive ideas to China where he recreated that approach within the Chinese social context in the Gulou kindergarten in Nanjing (Spodek, 1989). Helen Heffernan was brought to Japan after World War II to establish American-style kindergartens in Japan (Oda, 2004). Annie Howe, a missionary from Chicago, had influenced Japanese kindergartens earlier (Woollens, 2000b). American influences, brought by educators, missionaries, and others, also influenced early childhood education in other countries, including Australia, which has been influenced both by American and British early educators. As the process of adoption and adaptation takes place, the approaches become less American and take on the characteristic of education in that particular country.

There are times when approaches to early childhood education that have been exported from America returned to the United States in a modified form. Progressive education was exported to England before World War II as it was to many other countries. There it was adapted into the Integrated Day infant school approach. This approach returned to the United States in the late 1960s and early 1970s and again was adapted, as it became the Open Education movement in America.

SEEKING THE ROOTS OF
EARLY CHILDHOOD EDUCATION RESEARCH

Research in early childhood education has had a much shorter history than practice. It also does not seem to demonstrate the same processes of adoption and adaptation. Is it that science is more universal than practice and thus less influenced by local culture? Perhaps, but it also has a much shorter history.

Until about 50 years ago the only research on young children was research in child development, even though the field of early childhood education is older than the field of child development. The one exception to this might be the work of Dr. Montessori in developing her method. She began with the work of Sequin, modifying his materials and observing children using them. Her research method was more anthropological than psychological. For 2 years she modified materials and activities and observed children. She then concluded that she had perfected her method and stopped further testing and observation. Unfortunately, while her work contained some elements of research, it would not be considered as valid research today. Only her conclusions were made public and others were not able to replicate her work. Only Dr. Montessori herself was allowed to conduct the tests and observations.

In the United States, nursery schools were often established in universities as *laboratories*. Too often these laboratory nursery schools essentially served as corrals for subject for the psychological study of young children. The children were taken from the classroom as needed and sent to testing rooms. The nursery schools also served to provide *laboratory experiences* for students in child development, home economics, and education. College students would be brought in to observe what young children were like and to practice being with young children as preparation for becoming a teacher or a homemaker. But seldom were these laboratory nursery schools used as a means of inquiring into the nature of the educational process for young children or as a way of testing new curriculum ideas in early childhood education.

Only in the late 1950s and early 1960s did we see moves toward establishing a research base that was purely in early childhood education. The impetus came from two major changes: one in developmental psychology and the other in concerns for social justice.

For years in America, the maturationist theory was the accepted theory in child development: human intelligence, as well as other attributes, was fixed—determined at birth by genetics. It was believed that you could no more increase a person's intelligence or modify any other such attribute than make her or him taller. Thus, any attempt to increase the intelligence of individuals was futile. The nursery school and kindergarten were designed to keep children healthy and safe so that their genetic makeup would unfold. Real education, it was believed, began in the primary grades when children were taught to read.

This changed when new English translations of the work of Jean Piaget reached our shore. The arguments regarding the impact of environment were further supported when J. McVicker Hunt, an American psychologist, pulled together a range of studies supporting this notion in a book that had a major impact on psychology and education: *Intelligence and Experience* (1964). Others further argued that preschool experiences could have a greater impact on human development than experiences provided to children later in life (Bloom, 1964). In addition, behavioral psychologists were arguing that environmental conditions could shape human development. It was further found that children growing up in poverty suffered from significant environmental deficiencies. By offering these children early educational experiences, it was argued, society might be able to ameliorate the consequences of poverty—and ultimately even eliminate poverty.

A number of research projects were established testing the value of new approached to early childhood education. They were based on different assumptions about what might be considered an effective early education. (See Spodek, 1973, for a description of these program assumptions.) These research projects predate Head Start and were the basis later for a major national study of Head Start programs called the Planned Variations project—an attempt to compare the outcomes of different approaches to early education in terms of children's intelligence and school success. These outcomes were to prove which curriculum was most effective for young children. Unfortunately, the evaluation of the outcomes of these various projects were controversial and no "one best system" prevailed. However, the idea that various early educational curriculums can be tested in practice and that various aspects of early childhood education are worthy of study led to a growth in research relating to early education in the United States. It can be argued that this was the beginning of early childhood educational research in the United States.

CONDITIONS THAT SUPPORT EARLY CHILDHOOD EDUCATION RESEARCH

There are a number of conditions that are necessary for research in a field to flourish. There needs to be a cadre of well-trained researchers who are knowledgeable of their field. There needs to be financial support for research to be conducted. There needs to be a place where research will be nurtured or at least allowed to develop. And there needs to be a way for researchers to share their work—to communicate with one another and with others—practitioners, administrators, and policymakers. These conditions would slowly develop in America.

Early childhood education was a small field in the 1960s. There were no public kindergartens for children in the southeast or the central parts of the United States. There were few early childhood teacher-training programs in colleges or universities at that time nor were community colleges yet established. When the National Association for Nursery Education (NANE) became National Association for the Education of Young Children (NAEYC) in 1964, it had fewer than 1,500 members throughout the United States, though there were many more members of local and regional groups that later became affiliates of NAEYC. The other national association that devoted attention to early childhood education was the Association for Childhood Education International (ACEI). This organization had tens of thousands of members then, but was concerned with the education of children in nursery schools, kindergartens, and elementary schools, with its special focus on kindergarten and primary education. The World Organization for Early Childhood (OMEP) also functioned on an international level with national committees functioning in many of the 70 countries represented in the organization. The U.S. Committee for OMEP functioning in the United Sates was a small organization then and continues to be relatively small

Because there were few early childhood education teacher education programs in those days, there were few early childhood education positions available in colleges or universities. The only doctoral program specifically in early childhood education at that time was at Teachers College, Columbia University. In other universities, students interested in early childhood education pursued advanced degrees in curriculum studies, child development, or a similar related field. Nor was there an expectation that graduates of doctoral programs would conduct much research beyond their dissertation. They were primarily trained as teacher educators. While the preparation of early childhood education teachers was limited, there were also programs in child development, primarily in the Midwest, which trained teacher for nursery schools.

Thus, when the expansion of early childhood education programs took effect in the late 1960s and 1970s, the U.S. Office of Education established a program to train individuals from other fields to become early childhood educators. Individuals with doctorates in related fields were given a special 1-year program that retrofitted them as early childhood educators. Many of the graduates of this program went on to make significant scholarly contributions in early childhood education.

Since that time, many universities have established early childhood education programs, both at the undergraduate and graduate levels.

Many individuals have received PhDs in programs in education or human development that are related to early childhood education. And many university professors have been conducting research into early childhood education.

While the production of research in early childhood education increased in the United States, the vehicles for disseminating that research were limited. Both NAEYC and ACEI were essentially practitioner oriented, as has been OMEP. Their journals have reflected that and so have their conferences. *Young Children* was the only journal that was sponsored by NAEYC. While it had a "research in review" column which appeared in each edition, this was generally an attempt to provide an integrated review of research related to one facet of early childhood education at a time. Actual studies were not presented. The same was true of *Childhood Education*, the journal sponsored by ACEI and OMEP's *International Journal of Early Childhood*.

Over the past years, both American organizations began to sponsor research journals: The *Early Childhood Research Quarterly* was sponsored by NAEYC and published originally by Ablex and currently by Elsevier and the *Journal of Research in Childhood Education* published by ACEI. Additional journals related to research in early childhood education have developed over the years, such as *Early Education and Development* while other journals, such as *Early Childhood Education*, have become more scholarly and research oriented.

There were two other organizations that have served to disseminate research in early childhood education. One of these is the Society for Research in Child Development (SRCD). This organization focuses primarily on child development research and has paid less attention to early childhood education in recent years, both in its journal and in its conference programs. The other organization is the American Educational Research Association (AERA). In addition to sponsoring a number of journals, AERA holds an annual conference. Its divisions and its Special Interest Groups (SIGs) determine the content of that conference. Many early childhood studies are presented in sessions sponsored by divisions B and C (Curriculum Studies and Learning and Instruction) of the organization. Most important, there are two SIGs that are specifically devoted to early childhood education: the Early Education and Child Development SIG and the Critical Perspectives in Early Childhood Education SIG.

The research that is done in the United States, and to a lesser extent, in other English speaking countries like Canada, Britain, and Australia, is disseminated in the United States through the journals and conferences. A review of the *Current Index of Journals in Education*, and the American conferences and journals, gives the impression that the only significant research that is being done in early childhood education is done, or at least is reported, in the United States and, to a lesser extend, in other English speaking countries, such as Australia, Britain, and Canada. This suggests that there is no need to look further into the research literature in early childhood education. The *Handbook of Research in Early Childhood Education* (Spodek, 1982) and the *Handbook of Research on the Education of Young Children* (Spodek, 1993) reinforced the impression that research in early childhood education was predominantly conducted in the United States.

While this may have been true at one time, this situation has been changing. There are early childhood research institutes, early childhood research journals and early childhood research associations being established nationally and regionally in many parts of the world. And research is being conducted and reported in many different languages. But the issue remains: How do we access this important information?

New journals devoted to research in early childhood education have been developed and are being published in many areas of the world. Most of them are being published in English or at least an abstract of each article is presented in English. New regional associations designed to disseminate research in early childhood education have been established in many areas. The European Early Childhood Education Research Association (EECERA) is one, which publishes the *European Early Childhood Education Research Journal*. The Pacific Early Childhood Education Research Association (PECERA) is another such organization. While PECERA has no journal, selected papers from its conferences have been published in the *International Journal of Early Childhood Education*, a research journal published by the Korean Society for Early Childhood Education. Countries like Portugal are establishing their own early childhood education associations as well. Australia also has one and so does Japan. Possibly there are others. Unfortunately, these national associations are not well known and the content of their conferences and journals are not spread beyond the country's boundaries.

INTRODUCING THE CHAPTERS THAT FOLLOW

The following chapters in this book each describe the early childhood situation in one country. In each, a brief history of early childhood education in that country is presented. The current status of early childhood education is also presented as well as a discussion of the critical issues facing the field at this time. The authors then present the significant contemporary research that is being conducted in each country along with a list of references. The reader needs to be reminded that since the consumers of this research are scholars and practitioners in that country, most of the references are to material that is not written in English.

In her chapter, "Early Childhood Education in Australia: Approaches, Issues, Policies and Research," Wendy Schiller describes early childhood education and care services for children under 8 years of age. Care became institutionalized quite early in Australia's history with long day-care serving children from birth to 3 years from working class families, kindergarten serving children 3 to 5 years of age from middle class families, and compulsory school education serving children over 5 years of age. These three systems have differential staffing qualifications, programs, operations, policies, and funding sources.

Early childhood educators in Australia did not engage in much research into early childhood services until about 1990. Since then, there has been an increase in collaborative research studies, especially in interdisciplinary areas affecting young children and their families, and studies combining qualitative and quantitative methods. Topics for research have included feminist pedagogy and reconceptualization of childhood, new ways of constructing curriculum, parent-child-teacher/caregiver interactions and relationships, and children's health and well-being.

Formal early childhood education plays an important role in Chinese society as well as in their children's development. The chapter, "Contemporary Early Childhood Education and Research in China," by Jiaxong Zhu and Christine Wang, provides an overview of contemporary early childhood education practice and research in China. A brief history is provided of the three major early childhood education reforms of the past century. These reforms are closely aligned with the sociocultural changes that occurred during the period and reflect different cultural values. The current state of early childhood education in China is described, including the three types of programs available, administrative institutions, policy and legislation, budgets and financing, and teacher education. It also discusses the research infrastructure and reviews the major studies that have been conducted in the past 2 decades, focusing on six major research and policy issues. The authors also offer suggestions for future research in China and what we can learn from Chinese experience.

Mikko Ojala describes how Finnish research on early childhood education reflects both social and pedagogical importance in his chapter, "How Finland is Researching Early Childhood Education." These two aspects have their historical roots in the early start of public education and kindergartens from the mid nineteenth century. The forms and basic philosophy for modern Finnish early childhood education were created in 1970s. In 1973 the public daycare service was established, offering families options to educate and care for their children in daycare centers, family daycare homes, or in their own homes supported by child home care allowances. Since 2000 all children can have free public preschool education starting at age 6, one year before their start of school. The national core curriculum for preschool education (serving 6-year-old children), established in 2000, and the new core curriculum for comprehensive schools established in 2002 (7-8-year old children) are important pedagogical guidelines for modern Finnish early childhood education.

The most important topics in current research related to early childhood education in Finland are: (1) cross-cultural comparison, (2) leadership and expertise, (3) children in connection with modern information and communication technology (ICT), (4) language immersion, (5) intervention of learning problems, (6) historical research, and (7) developmental activities for preschool education and transition to school.

Systematic research efforts in the field of early childhood education in Greece are relatively new. They are described by Demetra Evangelou and Hara Cortessis-Dafermoun in their chapter, "Contemporary Perspectives in Early Childhood Education: The Case of Greece." These efforts in Greece are supported by several European Union initiatives and a growing awareness of the importance of research for informing national policy and best practices. Although the Greek educational system is highly centralized and educational research is rather nascent, the need to establish coordinating research agencies is widely recognized. The chapter describes the historical antecedents of early childhood education in Greece and explores emerging research practices and needs, including the urgent need for training qualified researchers in the university system. It also offers perspectives on future trends, particularly on the role of the European Union as an engine for institutional development in early childhood education research in Greece.

The chapter, "Research and Policy Issues in Early Childhood Care and Education in Japan," by Yoko Shirakawa and Sachiko Kitano examines the historical development, the recent changes in society, particularly in family relationships that have influenced early childhood policy making, the current systems and the present state of research and research related issues. Research has strongly been influenced by government policy from the beginning. Research that promotes high quality early childhood care and education has just started to bloom as the number of kindergartens, university programs, and research institutions in the field is decreasing in response to a declining birth rate that is seen as a national crisis. Many governmental measures have affected early childhood education and care. Unfortunately, the authors suggest, the research in the field does not match the interest in practice.

Education and care services for young children in Korea started early in 1900 with the establishment of a kindergarten and a childcare center. This is described by Unhai Rhee, Won Young Rhee, and YongJa Lee in their chapter, "Early Childhood Care and Education in Korea: Current State and Research." Since that time, kindergartens and child-care centers have grown as the two separate systems for early education and care. Both systems have experienced a tremendous growth in enrollment since 1980.

The overall trend in research in early childhood education in Korea during the past 15 years indicates a sharp increase in the number of research publications since 1990, an increase in collaborative research, and a predominance of empirical and quantitative studies with some recent attention paid to qualitative approaches. Research topics and areas have been expanded and diversified to include child development, early childhood curriculum, and parent-child relationships. Some of the research has been concerned with improving the quality and availability of early education and care service for all children.

In Norway the history of early childhood education and care institutions (ECECs) originated in the early children's asylums and Froebelian kindergartens. Early childhood education and care was first established in Trondheim in 1837. Today early childhood education and care for children ages 1 to 5 is offered for almost everyone that wants them. At 6 years of age children start in a 10-year comprehensive school. The chapter, "A Global Perspective on Early Childhood Education: Characteristic Traits and Research," by Ole Fredrik Lillemyer, describes this and discusses the different issues that drive early childhood research in Norway. These include preschool quality, influences of play and social interaction, early childhood education and care and special education, the challenges of preschool-primary school transition, and play and free activities versus teaching the formal subjects in primary school. Research indicates that children's time in early childhood education and care is important to learning. Lillemyer views the integration of the preschool and school traditions as the important issue for the future.

Barbara Muraska's chapter, "Elementary Education in Poland: A Brief History and Current Research" is concerned with early childhood education. The term "elementary education" is defined in Poland as educating and bringing up children between 3 and 9 years of age. It comprises two levels of school organization: the preschool level for children between 3 and 7 years of age and the first 3 years of the elementary school education, called early education, for children between 7 and 9 years of age.

The end of the 1980s brought the beginning of systemic changes in education in Poland. Nonstate kindergartens and schools were established alongside state institutions. Educational decentralization also brought some changes in the state school system. A uniform curriculum was abandoned and many new curricula were introduced. The research projects on young children in Poland over that time have been interesting but few in numbers. There are no well-defined research domains. The majority of the research has little chance of influencing the shape of education at the national level. Rather, it is a stimulus to the revision of teachers' opinions and a demonstration of ways of proceeding methodologically in contacts with children.

The chapter, "Research in Early Childhood Education in Portugal" by Teresa Vasconcelos, provides a description of research in early childhood in Portugal. After presenting the history of the field, especially from the standpoint of women's issues and the struggle for democracy, information is given about recent developments in the field. This includes a description of services for 0-3 year olds and 3-5 year olds. There was a significant effort put into the expansion of the field from 1996-2002. The main research threads are then presented within the framework inspired by Bronfenbrenner's ecological theory: macro level, meso level, and micro level. Finally, trends and challenges for the future are discussed.

Beginning with a short description of the current political structure of Spain and its influences on education, this chapter, "Early Childhood Education Research in Spain" by Miguel A. Zabalza, focuses on the strength and weakness of early childhood education in Spain from its origins 150 years ago until now. The chapter is organized into three main sections. First, a short review of the history of social services and resources offered to children in Spain is presented. Mention is made of the pioneers in early childhood education and their contributions to the field in Spain. The main approaches to early childhood education during this period are also analyzed. The next section focuses on curricular dilemmas that Spanish early childhood education is dealing with: care versus education, free play versus pre-academic subjects, and generic versus specialist educators. The final section is centered on research: the most important research in the field conducted in Spain during the last decade is classified into thematic categories.

It was only in the 1990s that early childhood education began to receive the attention it deserved in Turkey. This is a key point made by Sevda Bekman in her chapter, "Early Childhood Education in Turkey: An Overview." A large number of studies, projects, and programs have been conducted since then. Turkey does not have a standardized widespread system of early childhood education programs. Services in early childhood education either belong to or are under the supervision of the Ministry of National Education (MONE) or the General Directorate of Social Welfare and Child Protection Agency (SSCPA). In addition, a few nongovernmental organizations provide services alternative to center-based early childhood education, including home-based programs, television programs, and summer schools for preschool age children.

The early childhood education services fall into the following three categories: nursery classes (kindergartens) for children 5-6 years of age in the year before they begin formal schooling; preschool centers (daycare centers, children's houses) for children between 3-6 years of age; and crèche and daycare centers for children from 0-6 years of age. Presently early childhood education programs are divided into two services with respect to their aims: custodial and educational. Unfortunately, the numbers of custodial centers far outweigh the number of educational ones. Although the current research in the area is limited in coverage, it has addressed some of the significant concerns in the area.

These chapters provide a snapshot of early childhood education in the various countries covered in this volume. They describe a vibrant intellectual community concerned with improving the quality of services for young children as well as with exploring the knowledge base of early childhood education.

REFERENCES

Bloom, B. S. (1964). *Stability and change in human characteristics*. New York: Wiley.

Hunt, J. M. (1964). *Experience and intelligence*. New York: Roland Press

No Child Left Behind Act of 2001, Pub. L. No. 107-110, 115 Stat. 1425 (2002).

Oda, Y. (2004). Tracing the development of Japanese kindergarten education—Focusing on changes of content and curriculum. *National Institute for Educational Policy Research Bulletin, 133*, 77-84.

Owen, R. D. (1824). *Outline of the system of education in New Lanark*. Glasgow, Scotland: Wardlaw & Cunningham.

Shapiro, M. S. (1983). *Child's garden: The kindergarten movement from Froebel to Dewey*. University Park, PA: Pennsylvania State University Press

Spodek, B. (1973). *Early childhood education*. Englewood Cliffs, NJ: Prentice-Hall.

Spodek, B. (Ed.) (1982). *Handbook of research in early childhood education*. New York: Free Press.

Spodek, B. (1989). Chinese kindergarten education and its reform. *Early Childhood Research Quarterly, 4*, 31-50.

Spodek, B. (Ed.). (1993). *Handbook of research on the education of young children*. New York: Macmillan.

Strickland, C. E. (1982). Paths not taken: Seminal models of early childhood education in Jacksonian America. In B. Spodek (Ed.), *Handbook of research in early childhood education* (pp. 321-340). New York: Free Press.

Woollens, R. (Ed.). (2000a). *Kindergartens and cultures*. New Haven, CT: Yale University Press.

Woollens, R. (Ed.). (2000b). The missionary kindergarten in Japan. In *Kindergartens and cultures* (pp. 113-136). New Haven, CT: Yale University Press.

CHAPTER 1

EARLY CHILDHOOD EDUCATION AND CARE IN AUSTRALIA

Approaches, Issues, Policies, and Research

Wendy Schiller, Ann Veale and Jane Harper

In Australia, early childhood education and care (ECEC) is a generic term for an extensive network of children's services for young children (from birth to 8 years of age) and their families, which includes all forms of child care, preschool/kindergarten, school (and after-school-hours care) and specialized services for children. Most services integrate health, welfare, and education. Innovative services have been developed to respond to Australian conditions such as the needs of remote and isolated communities. This network of services reflects some of the complexities and characteristics of Australia's legacy from the past. The next section will outline briefly the history of ECEC in Australia and highlight some longstanding issues.

International Perspectives on Research in Early Childhood Education, 1–53
Copyright © 2005 by Information Age Publishing

HISTORY OF EARLY CHILDHOOD
EDUCATION AND CARE IN AUSTRALIA

Australia is an island continent in the southern hemisphere. Most of the population is located in towns and cities around the coastline, while inland areas are arid and sparsely populated (see Figure 1.1).

Indigenous communities have lived in Australia for thousands of years, so Australia was "occupied by Aboriginal peoples" (Milroy, 1996, p. 2) prior to White settlement. Aboriginal people managed and moved across their lands according to the seasons. They saw the earth as plentiful. It provided everything they needed. Integral to Indigenous communities were complex kinship systems and traditional child rearing practices. Children learned about culture, values, beliefs, and family from everything around them. Their education was embedded in the cultural life of the community, the dreaming, the law, and the land (Priest, 2002; Warrki Jarrinjaku Aboriginal Childrearing & Associated Research Project Team, 2002).

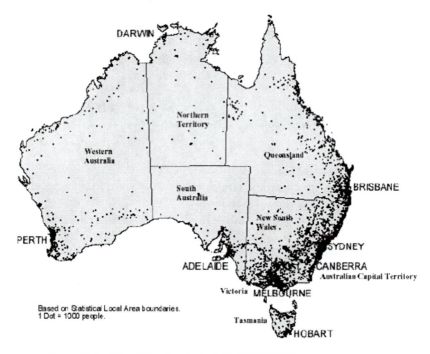

Source: Regional Population Growth, Australia 1998 (3218.0)

Source: Press and Hayes (2000; Copyright Commonwealth of Australia, reproduced by permission.

Figure 1.1.   Population distribution in Australia.

The first permanent White settlement of Australia began in 1788 when Britain sent a fleet of ships carrying convicts, settlers, and military personnel to Sydney, New South Wales (NSW). The new arrivals included 26 children, pregnant women, and convict women with babies born en route to Australia (Flannery, 2000), but no plans had been made to provide facilities for children in the colony. This situation raised issues (Brennan, 1998; Clyde, 2000; Kelly, 1988) which have endured in ECEC in Australia ever since:

- Who is responsible for children's health, welfare, and education?
- What is the role and responsibility of parents? If they cannot provide for their children, who should?
- What services are needed for children and who should implement these?
- What forms of services could be offered—care, education, or both?

The Development of Early Schooling for Children Under 8

By 1800, ragged and destitute children roamed the streets of Sydney. Concerned citizens appealed to churches and the government to provide for these latch-key, orphaned, and destitute children (Mellor, 1990). In 1803 Anglican and Roman Catholic schools were opened, funded by the government and administered by churches. These were the "first organised children's services in Australia" (Clyde, 2000, p. 88). By 1824, infant schools had been established by church organisations for children under 6 years of age. The NSW Department of Public Instruction had set a curriculum of reading, writing, and religion. Fort Street Model School in Sydney was a government school for children 6 years of age and over, and served as a training center for teachers who were given a 6-month preparatory course for teaching (Harrison, 1985). In 1850, public school inspectors found underage children at school to be an impediment to the "progress of instruction" (Clyde et al., 1994, p. 191). Classes for 2- to 5-year-olds were set up in one corner of public school classrooms supervised by young pupil teachers (Turney, 1975) to teach "technical education skills," sensory training, and keep children "happy and busy" (Clyde, 2000, pp. 92-93). The 1860s also saw an increase in orphanages, industrial schools, and schools for mentally defective children, run by church groups and nongovernment organizations as part of the child rescue movement.

Although 60% of all children from 3 to 5 years of age were at school by 1874 (Clyde et al., 1994), critics saw this as childminding "maintained at the expense of the state" (Mellor, 1990, p. 61) rather than education as a high priority for the young. In 1881, the NSW Public Instruction Act provided state-controlled education for children from 6 to 14 years of age (Harrison, 1985) but in response to pressure from church and voluntary organizations, the government opened the first kindergarten (using Froebelian principles) in Australia at Crown Street Public School, Sydney, for children under 6 years of age.

The imperatives of social reform, cohesion, and universal schooling for the young could only be met by having centrally run, state-based structures given Australia's population distribution. By Federation in 1901, these structures were in place and the imperatives had largely been achieved.

Today there is still a mix of school providers; government, nongovernment, and religious schools. Federal and state governments support school education but the federal government also funds matters of national importance such as curriculum, literacy, and numeracy initiatives and science/technology education. The range in provision of education reflects Australia's multicultural diversity and parental choice for children's education.

Indigenous Communities

By 1860, denied ownership of their land and ravaged by disease, Indigenous people were living at the edge of White communities, dependent on charity and casual employment. Family systems had broken down (Milroy, 1996). Volunteer organizations and church groups, concerned about children's welfare, sought drastic solutions to "rescue children from bad homes" (Mellor, 1990, p. 9). For example, in South Australia, the Legislative Council of 1860, concerned about apparent degradation of Aborigines through contact with Whites, urged that "Aboriginal children be removed from their tribes and reared in schools" (Mellor, 1990, p. 9). In the 1870s Aboriginal half-caste children were also adopted by White families to be raised in "good" homes (Davey, 1960). These measures were a total denial of indigenous families' rights and emotional bonds which are the foundation of kinship and community.

Though proclaimed to be for "care and protection of Aboriginal people" (Milroy, 1996, p. 3), restrictive government legislation affected all areas of their lives and controlled employment, education, freedom of movement, the right to marry, and guardianship of children. This approach perpetuated animosity for generations and strained relations between Indigenous families and government organizations for more than a century. The removal of Aboriginal children, one of the most devastating consequences of social reform, continued in Australia until the 1960s, when Aboriginal people were granted Australian citizenship.

After 1970, special initiatives were introduced to train Aboriginal early childhood teachers (Palmer & Ebbeck, 1990). Some Aboriginal groups were given ownership of their early childhood facilities, schools, preschools, and programs. Today these are successfully administered and organized by Aboriginal groups with Indigenous staff, and for Aboriginal communities. In the words of Yunupingu (2002) "the best results come when services to Aboriginal people are owned, run and managed by Aboriginal people" (cited in Priest, 2002, p. 1). This is best achieved by "indigenous people owning and managing their own institutions. The significant role that governments play, in strengthening or undermining community capacity is undeniable" (cited in Priest, 2002, p. 1).

The Birth of Kindergartens and Preschools

The worldwide depression in the 1890s forced governments to take measures to alleviate the poverty and suffering of urban and rural families. Philanthropic organizations in Australia, influenced by the work of Pestalozzi, Froebel, and Dewey, sought establishment of "free" kindergartens as a partial solution to the problem of caring for children where both parents had to work. Free meant independent, nongovernment funded kindergartens. The Kindergarten Union of New South Wales formed in 1895, opened the first free kindergarten in Woolomooloo, Sydney, in 1896 and the Sydney Kindergarten Training College for early childhood teachers in 1897. Within 20 years (see Table 1.1) similar organizations were established in all states of Australia and they remained the main providers of early childhood education until the 1950s (Kelly, 1988; Spearritt, 1979). Early childhood education in Australia owes much to the handful of strong women who used their political influence to good effect and who embraced this new field of "charitable endeavour" with "time, goodwill and finance" (Spearritt, 1979, p.11).

Free Kindergartens were established in poor, working-class areas and operated from 9 a.m. to 3:30 p.m. daily. With educationally sound programs, qualified teachers, and an agenda of social reform (Brennan 1998), kindergartens were seen as more than child-minding centers and until the introduction of government subsidies after World War II, provided programs, facilities, and trained teachers at very little cost to participating families. However, operating hours for kindergartens made them

Table 1.1.   Foundation of Voluntary Agencies and Kindergarten Teachers Colleges

State	Year	Organization	Year	College
New SouthWales	1896	Kindergarten Union of New South Wales	1897	Sydney Kindergarten Teachers College
New South Wales	1905	Sydney Day Nursery and Nursery Schools Association	1932	Nursery School Teacher's College
South Australia	1905	Kindergarten Union of South Australia	1907	Adelaide Kindergarten Teacher's College
Queensland	1906	Crèche and Kindergarten Association of Queensland	1911	Brisbane Kindergarten Teachers College
Victoria	1908	Free Kindergarten Union of Victoria	1916	Melbourne Kindergarten Teacher's College
Tasmania	1910	Kindergarten Union of Tasmania		(No kindergarten teachers college)
Western Australia	1912	Kindergarten Association of Western Australia	1912	Perth Kindergarten Teachers College

Source: Commonwealth of Australia (1974, p. 15). Copyright Commonwealth of Australia, reproduced by permission.

unsuitable for working class families and shift workers who required different patterns of care.

Shortly after World War II, middle-class families initiated community-managed kindergarten/preschools. During the 1960s and 1970s, some state governments also became involved with preschool service provision. Tasmania incorporated preschools into the Education Department; the Western Australian government established preprimary programs and took over administration of preschools; the Queensland government was involved with administration of some preschools and establishing of preschools within primary schools. Victoria and South Australia (SA) relied on voluntary organizations for preschool provision. NSW had government and voluntary agency support for preschools (Brennan, 1998).

Kindergarten unions in each state were instrumental in sponsoring innovative delivery of services using radio, television and "School of the Air" broadcasts, and providing mobile preschools for new housing areas, small communities, or rural and remote areas which could not sustain a preschool. Based on Head Start in the United States, Aboriginal preschools opened in the 1960s with support of international agencies such as Save the Children Fund and the Bernard van Leer Foundation in the Northern Territory (NT), NSW, Victoria, and SA. In this way, Australia benefited from European and North American ideas and practices, implemented in distinctive ways for Australian conditions.

Looking back, it is easy to be critical of the educational and the social reform agenda of kindergartens, but they were the backbone of the early childhood movement in Australia and their emphasis on quality programming has given generations of children a strong and distinctive educational grounding (McLean, Piscitelli, Halliwell, & Ashby, 1992).

Early Childhood Teacher Education in Australia

Australia's first Kindergarten teacher was University of Chicago-trained, but demand for local kindergarten teacher training increased with the expansion of the kindergarten movement. Between 1897 and 1916, all states of Australia had established kindergarten teachers colleges (see Table 1.1).

The independently funded Sydney Kindergarten Training College offered a 3 year kindergarten teacher's course. Trainee teachers worked in makeshift crèches and kindergartens in inner city areas to learn about children's development and experience the need for social and educational reform (Harrison, 1985). Lectures were given on Dewey, Froebel, and the importance of the early formative years of a child's life by staff from the United Kingdom and the United States. Links with early childhood educators in the United Kingdom and the United States continued for many years, raising Australian standards of ECEC and improving international understanding. For example, British educator and psychologist Susan Isaacs toured Australia in 1937. Isaacs' emphasis on "child development as the basis for curriculum became the core of Australian early education" (McLean et al., 1992, p. 51).

Lillian de Lissa was one of the few early childhood educators who reversed this trend by leaving Australia for a senior academic position at Gipsy Hill, England in 1917 (Jones, 1975) after an outstanding career in early childhood education in Australia. A Sydney-trained graduate, Lillian de Lissa, moved to Adelaide, SA and began a new training college in 1907 (at 21 years of age). She was an outspoken and influential advocate for the free kindergarten movement and for teacher training and saw kindergarten teachers as "social pioneers" (Dowd, 1983, p. 30). Her vision was for welfare, health, and education to be integrated and she recognized the importance of play in the kindergarten curriculum. She advocated inclusion of children with physical and intellectual disabilities in kindergartens long before the Education Act was passed in South Australia making such a policy mandatory.

Lillian de Lissa wanted kindergarten teacher training colleges to be separate from primary school teacher training in government-run colleges. Critics saw this as limiting kindergarten teacher training to those students who could pay for tuition and "effectively placed kindergartens outside the mainstream of education" (Mellor, 1990, p. 24). Others saw it as a "bold decision and a powerful statement by voluntary groups to retain their status as independent organisations, offering a service that was not governed by politicians or bureaucrats" (Brennan, 1994, p. 28). It highlighted the dichotomy between state government-controlled training colleges and independent training colleges. Kindergarten teachers colleges remained independent until the 1970s when the small private colleges were merged with the federated system of Colleges of Advanced Education, which in turn in the 1990s amalgamated with Schools of Education in universities (Schiller & Lewis, 1996). Therefore, vocationally oriented teacher education had become embedded in research-oriented universities. Today, early childhood students complete a 4 year Bachelor of Early Childhood Education degree to qualify as early childhood teachers or day care directors. Technical and Further Education (TAFE) college programs enable students to become directors of small centers or childcare assistants with associate diplomas or diplomas in child care. Articulation programs between TAFE and universities are in place to enable upgrading of qualifications. Australian ECEC degree programs are also offered in the Pacific, Asia, India, and Papua New Guinea, and student/staff exchanges with Europe, the United States, and Asia are encouraged.

Day Nurseries and the Birth of Long Day Care

Day Nursery Associations were formed to care for children of the working class because kindergartens were reluctant to enrol children younger than 3 years of age as kindergarten staff were "teachers not nurses" (Kelly, 1988, p. 55). "For a small sum of threepence a day, children from 15 days to 3 years of age are taken charge of from 7am to 6.30pm" (Sydney Day Nursery School Association Report, 1905, as cited in Kelly, 1988).

In Queensland, the policy was not to allow babies access to crèches unless the mother was working, but the Depression caused crèches/nurseries to modify their stance in order to take babies of mothers who were unable to find work. This change was made to give the children "nourishing food and healthy surroundings" (Spearritt, 1979, p. 20). The Day Nurseries Association was dependent on voluntary assistance and financial contributions but standards of health, cleanliness, care, and education in centers were very good. Although less influential than the kindergarten movement, the Day Nurseries Association opened Sydney Nursery School

Teacher's College in 1932. Queensland was the only state of Australia to have one organization responsible for kindergarten and day care—the Crèche and Kindergarten Association of Queensland (formed in 1906 and operational today).

The dichotomy between care and education was that 4-year-olds required education, care, and a teacher, but birth to 3-year-old care focussed on physical health and well-being requiring a lesser nursing or child care qualification as "two years of intensive specialised training was a pretentious waste of time (when) anybody could mind a baby" (Dowd, 1983, p. 22). This issue has resonated through the debates and policy initiatives which have shaped early childhood provision in Australia (Press & Hayes, 2000), but also is reflected in the ECEC debates of many other countries.

State and National Initiatives 1930-2000

A feature of Australian education has been that funding for education comes from the federal government, but the delivery of public education is a state government responsibility. Therefore, early childhood voluntary organizations had a state rather than a national focus until a national professional body (forerunner of Early Childhood Australia) was formed in 1938 to advocate for preschool education (Waters, 2000). Some financial assistance was then provided to kindergartens by the federal government and states assumed some responsibility for monitoring and subsidizing the services (McLean et al., 1992).

A federally funded initiative in 1938 was the establishment of Lady Gowrie Centres throughout Australia. In 1930 (during the Depression) children's health became a national concern. One third of kindergarten children in Victoria were suffering from malnutrition, and dental checks revealed that 95% were "not dentally fit." The infant mortality rate had risen, and children in South Australia showed evidence of rickets and malnutrition on school entry (Brennan, 1994; Waters, 2000). Kindergarten was seen as one means of alleviating these health and poverty-related problems. The Commonwealth government (through the National Health and Research Council) released funds in 1939/40 to establish one Demonstration Child Centre in each state capital. These child education and health centers for disadvantaged children were called Lady Gowrie Centres. Establishment of these Demonstration Centres was controversial (Brennan, 1994), but they have remained true to their mission continuing to give priority to the poor, the underprivileged, and the disenfranchised. They offer leadership to the early childhood field through inservice and specialist programs, research projects, and consultation with universities.

They demonstrate sound early childhood educational practice in Australia with emphasis on health, nutrition, and children's physical well-being. However, there was concern that conduct of research and data gathering were replacing the child-saving mission of the early kindergartens (Spearritt, 1979).

Not-for-profit child care services saw modest growth in the 30s and 40s as expanded child care services were necessary for women to return to the workforce to supplement the labour market. The Federal Department of Labour and National Service made small grants available for child care. This was the earliest acknowledgement of links between employment and child care in Australia. Because preschools had not met the needs of working parents, a coalition of feminist women advocated for the expansion of child care as part of women's right to employment. This was a powerful incentive for governments to treat child care seriously (Press & Hayes, 2000) and led to strong growth in service provision. For the first time, the nexus between private and public funding had been pushed to one side in favor of universal children's service provision for children from birth to 5 years.

The Child Care Act of 1972 heralded the federal government's involvement with funding child care programs (in addition to Lady Gowrie centres). Emphasized in the Child Care Act was provision of good quality care to meet children's needs at a cost parents could afford, so additional federal government funding was made available to employ more teachers and nurses in day care centers for children. This focus has shifted to meet the needs of workforce participation under subsequent federal governments. The Fry report (Commonwealth of Australia, 1974) pinpointed the overall problem with ECEC in Australia as "lack of a national plan which provides for adequate funding and recognised standards" (p. 11) and overreliance on voluntary/community organizations to raise funds and maintain standards.

The Fry report also highlighted the need for special services for families with preschool children in remote areas of Australia, known as *the outback*. Innovations such as the federal/state funded Remote and Isolated Children's Exercise (RICE) in SA and Contact Incorporated in NSW were introduced to combat social isolation and loneliness of remote families, using road, rail, and air services. Mobile units and vans were also a solution to taking children's services to Australia's sparsely populated areas, to itinerant populations, and caravan park communities (Bernard van Leer Foundation, 1987). By the 1980s, most states of Australia had mobile vans or units. They enjoyed widespread community support as they offered flexibility and diversity in provision of children's services.

The Federal Labor government 1983-1990 saw child care as a government benefit related to wage restraint agreements with unions. New services were established on assessed need and there was a rise in multiple care settings located in one centre to cater for family needs. Fee subsidies for parents were only available for not-for-profit services and these were largely parent-run or community- based services, or large organizations such as the Kindergarten Union. Local councils administered family day care schemes, with licensed providers caring for children in their homes.

In 1989, Australia ratified the United Nations Convention for the Rights of the Child. In 1990, the Australian Early Childhood Association (AECA) developed a voluntary code of ethics for early childhood person-nel to establish professional standards and guide behavior (Australian Early Childhood Association, 1990). As children spent increased hours in out-of-home care, professional groups, unions, parents, and councils advocated the setting up of a national accreditation scheme to assess the quality of children's experiences in various day care settings. In 1993 the Quality Improvement and Accreditation System (QIAS) for long day care centers was introduced and was similar to that established in the United States, with long day care services participating in the process, eligible for fee subsidy from the government if accredited. For-profit centers were also eligible for fee subsidy under this scheme. In 2003, quality assurance systems were established for family day care programs across Australia and out-of-school-hours care.

Return of a federal (Coalition) conservative government has again seen a pendulum swing, with removal of direct-fee subsidies (operational subsi-dies) to not-for-profit long day care centers and out-of-school-hours care in 1996. Only indigenous special needs services, family day care and occa-sional care now receive operational funding. The trend is to more private sector involvement and investment in provision of child care services. New places for family day care and out-of-school-hours care are likely to open for private sector investment in the near future.

Summary

The history of ECEC for children under 8 years of age in Australia needs to be seen in the light of the massive social experiment by the Brit-ish government in establishing penal colonies on Australian soil in the 1800s. This necessitated social reform responses by churches, govern-ments, and concerned citizens, with disastrous consequences for indige-nous communities.

These events shaped the formation and spread of kindergartens by philanthropic groups, with day care centers to provide support for the poor and disenfranchised. The reform movement which began with schools saw the participation of state and federal governments, church organizations, professional bodies, and community-based alliances, and all of these aspects remain part of ECEC today. Thus, Australia reflects international trends in ECEC as well as distinctive services for Australian conditions, but advocacy for young children, establishment of contextually-appropriate care and support for families, balancing policy initiatives and funding are as important today as they were in 1788. Today there is more flexibility in services available but still the expectation is that the user pays, so ECEC provision is neither free nor universal.

THE CURRENT STATE OF EARLY CHILDHOOD EDUCATION AND CARE IN AUSTRALIA

Similarities and differences between school, kindergarten, and child care provisions including administration, funding, curriculum and staff qualification, will be explained in this section. Attention will also be given to services for remote, rural, and isolated families and Indigenous communities. Similarities are found in the increasing number of children accessing services in Australia and the initiative to develop a cohesive approach to curriculum for children from birth to 8 years of age (and beyond) in each state. In each state's curriculum there is an integrated approach to learning and development in the early years, and for very young children the emphasis is on development of positive relationships and learning experiences within social and cultural contexts. The family is recognized as the most important social context within which a young child learns.

Differences are reflected in the foci of the programs, the age of the children enrolled in the services, the governance of services (including differing regulations and operational requirements), and employment and workplace conditions for staff. Differential funding is provided for ECEC services by the state or federal government, and jurisdiction for ECEC services may be within different government departments at state and federal levels.

Universal Schooling

Schooling is compulsory in every Australian state and territory. Legally, children are required to attend school from 6 years of age, but normally children commence school at 5. Ages of entry vary in each state (see Table 1.2).

As previously noted, funding for education comes from the federal government but delivery of public education is a state responsibility. State

Table 1.2.   Comparison of Ages of Entry into School-based Programs in Australia

State/Territory	Entry Age into Program 2 years before Yr 1	Entry Age into Program 1 Year before Yr 1	Entry Age into Yr 1	Compulsory Starting Age
Western Australia	4 by December 31 *From 2001 4 by June 30	5 by December 31 *From 2002 5 by June 30	6 by December 31 *From 2003 6 by June 30	6th birthday *From 2003 from the beginning of the year the child turns 6 years and 6 months
New South Wales	4 by July 31	5 by July 31	6 by July 31	6th birthday
Victoria	4 by April 30	5 by April 30	6 by April 30	6th birthday
Queensland	4 by December 31	5 by December 31	6 by December 31	6th birthday
South Australia	Continuous entry after 4th birthday	Continuous entry into Reception class after 5th birthday	Single entry in January after 2-5 terms in Reception depending on initial entry	6th birthday
Tasmania	4 by January 1	5 by January 1	6 by January 1	6th birthday
ACT	4 by 30 April	5 by 30 April	6 by 30 April	6th birthday
Northern Territory	Continuous entry after 4th birthday	5 by June 30 Continuous intake after 5th birthday into Transition	Continuous entry after minimum of two terms in Transition	6th birthday

Source: Press and Hayes (2000). Copyright Commonwealth of Australia, reproduced by permission.

and territory governments are required to ensure provision of school for all children 5 to 16 years of age, and this is achieved through Catholic (17%) and independent providers (10%) and government schooling (72%) (Ministerial Council on Education, Employment, Training and Youth Affairs, 1998). Since the federal government began to fund non-government schools in 1997 there has been a definite move by families to change their children's schooling from government to independent schools (Ministerial Council on Education, Employment, Training and Youth Affairs, 2003), and this drift is causing state governments to focus on new policies to improve facilities, and lower teacher student ratios in a bid to retain family support for the government school system.

Education is centrally administered through state departments of education and curricula are determined at the state level. Recently, states have moved to a more generic and integrated framework to guide curriculum approaches and content and to provide for smooth transitions for children between grade levels. In the last 3 years, an early childhood curriculum for birth to 8 years of age has been prepared in most states. However, in South Australia, there is a curriculum framework for children from birth to 18 years of age (Organization for Economic Cooperation and Development, OECD, 2001) and early childhood services are within the jurisdiction of the Department of Education and Children's Services. This umbrella organization enables integration of a curriculum framework across children's services. There has also been federal government support for monitoring the quality of early schooling and outcomes through national student assessment. Tests are undertaken by children in years three, five and seven of schooling to achieve benchmarking across Australia for literacy and numeracy standards, and improve literacy and numeracy skills.

Teachers in schools are required to hold a Bachelor of Early Childhood Education (for lower primary grades) or a Bachelor of Education degree to teach children aged 5 to 12 years. Each state requires notification training for reporting child abuse as a condition of teacher employment. Some states also require a formal police clearance.

Preschool–Kindergarten

Preschool provision is not universal or mandatory in Australia. States have been responsible for funding preschool education since 1985, but the federal government provides supplementary funding for Indigenous children and children with disabilities. Preschools or kindergartens may be stand alone services, located in schools or long day care centers, privately run or part of rural and remote mobile services. They provide daily 3 hour or 6 hour programs during school terms with educational and social experiences for 3- to 5-year-old children prior to school entry. Most 4-year-olds in Australia attend a preschool or kindergarten service. Attendance varies from 80% in WA, to 96% in Queensland (OECD, 2001). For children attending a preschool service at 3 years of age (that is 2 years prior to school entry), the pattern of organization will vary as services may be administered by different departments or agencies (see Table 1.3). This makes for a fragmented pattern of ECEC for preschool children across the states and territories of Australia. A 3- or 4-year degree in early childhood education is required to be a preschool director or a teacher unless the preschool has less than 15 children. Then a child care qualifica-

Table 1.3.   Comparison of Preschool Programs across Australia

2002: Program by State 1 Year Prior to School Entry in Australian States and Territories

State/Territory	Name of Program	Days Attended	Provider
Western Australia	Preprimary	5	Education Department
New South Wales	Kindergarten	5	Department of School Education
Victoria	Preparatory	5	Department of Education
Queensland	Preschool	5 half days	Department of Education
South Australia	Reception	5	Department of Education, Training and Employment
Tasmania	Preparatory	5	Department of Education
ACT	Kindergarten	5	Department of Education and Training
Northern Territory	Transition	5	Department of Education

2001: Program by State 2 Years Prior to School Entry in Australian States and Territories

State/Territory	Name of Program	Hours Attended	Provider
Western Australia	Kindergarten	11hrs a week	Education Department
New South Wales	Preschool	12hrs 30 mins a week	Department of School Education; Department of Community Services
Victoria	Preschool	10hrs a week	Department of Human Services
Queensland	Kindergarten	Up to 12hrs 30 mins a week	Community preschools, crèche providers, child care providers.
South Australia	Kindergarten	10 hrs 30 mins a week	Department of Education, Training and Employment
Tasmania	Kindergarten	10 hrs a week	Department of Education
ACT	Preschool	10 hrs 30 mins a week	Department of Education and Training, Children's Services Branch
Northern Territory	Preschool	12 hrs a week	Department of Education

Source: Press and Hayes (2000). Copyright Commonwealth of Australia, reproduced by permission.

tion is acceptable (see Table 1.4). The staff to child ratios vary depending on the size of the group and the age of the children (see Table 1.4) and regulations vary from state to state (see Table 1.5).

CHILD CARE SERVICES—LONG DAY CARE CENTERS, FAMILY DAY CARE, OCCASIONAL CARE

Establishing and maintaining a national child care program has been the responsibility of various federal departments including Family and Community Services (FACS), Health, and Education through the Department of Education, Training and Youth Affairs (DETYA). Often there is variation between state government portfolios and responsibilities and those of the federal government or they share responsibility in a *mix and match* fashion. Currently, there are Labor governments in all states, but the federal government is conservative—a Coalition government. This means that in relation to child care provision the Labor states are mindful of service provision for parents in the workforce and offer flexible hours of care to afford women access and equity in the labor market. Long day care centers, family day care schemes, and out-of-school-hours care services have been supported by governments, primarily to assist working parents. These services can also be accessed by parents who are not working or who require respite or occasional care for their children. The federal government however, has placed children's services in the Family and Community Service portfolio offering tax relief to parents for child care services and favoring user-pays schemes and private investment in out-of-home care for children under 5. Currently most center-based, long day care is provided by the private sector (73%). Other ECEC services are provided by state governments, local government, and the not-for-profit sector. Thus, the ambivalence of government attitudes to funding and provision of child care (particularly for children under 3 years of age) is ongoing.

Long day care centers are usually purpose-built, stand alone facilities which can cater for up to 60 children from 2 weeks to 5 years of age. They operate all year round and have extended hours care from 7 a.m. to 6 p.m. in most states. Therefore, meals are provided for children who attend these centers. Complex regulations apply (see Table 1.5) and staff qualification requirements vary from state to state (see Table 1.4). Staff work in 7 hour shifts and staff turn over is a problem as the work is physically and emotionally demanding and leave conditions are less favorable than those for preschool staff. Child to staff ratios in long day care are 5:1 for birth to 2-year-olds, 8:1 for children 2 to 3 years, and 10:1 for children 3 to 6 years (see Table 1.4). In general, there is one qualified staff member for every 20 to 25 children. Improved infrastructure, firmer regulations and increased numbers of trained staff in long day care would improve the quality of care but affect service affordability. Four percent of children under 1 year of age are enrolled in regulated services but parent and informal care are most common (OECD, 2001). Forty percent of children

**Table 1.4.   Staffing Requirements for
Long Day Care Centers in Each State and Territory**

State/ Territory	Supervisor of Center Program	Qualifications Specified by Regulations	Age of Children	Staff to Child Ratios	Numbers of Qualified Staff
New South Wales	3 year full-time university course in early childhood studies or Child Care Certificate: a Certificate of Child Care Studies or Associate Diploma of Social Science (Child Studies) from TAFE or Other qualifications approved by the Minister NB: Must have minimum of 12 months experience in providing childcare services as a member of primary contact staff.	3 year university course in early childhood studies Child Care Certificate: a Certificate of Child Care Studies or Associate Diploma of Social Science (Child Studies) from TAFE	0-2 2-3 3-6	1:5 1:8 1:10	An authorized supervisor with a minimum of a child care certificate for less than 30 children • 1 teaching or nonteaching staff for 30 to 39 children • 2 teachers for 40 to 59 children • 3 teachers for 60 to 79 children • 4 teachers for 80 to 90 children • 1 enrolled or registered nurse with a child care certificate or diploma if these children are under 2 years of age
Victoria	Diploma of Children's Services or equivalent	Diploma of Children's Services. 2 year postsecondary qualification in early childhood education.	0-3 3-6	1:5 1:15 with a minimum of 2 staff	1 trained staff for • 15 children aged under 3 years • 30 children aged 3 years and over
Tasmania	3 years tertiary study in early childhood education or equivalent (plus experience)	Diploma of Children's Services or equivalent 3 years tertiary study in early childhood education	0-3 3-5	1:5 1:10	1 trained staff for • 10 children aged under 3 years • 20 children aged over 3 years • or for mixed age group

(Table continues)

Table 1.4.   Continued

State/ Territory	Supervisor o Center Program	Qualifications Specified by Regulations	Age of Children	Staff to Child Ratios	Numbers of Qualified staff
South Australia	Director of LDC – no qualification required	2 year Associate Diploma in Children's Services or 3 year Early Childhood Teaching qualification	0-2 2 and over	1:5 1:10	1 trained staff for • 20 children aged under 2 years • 35 children aged 2-6 years
Western Australia	Degree in early childhood care or education or Diploma of Children's Services or Mothercraft Nurse Certificate	Education degree (4 year) (Teacher registration required to work in pre-school) 2 year TAFE Associate Diploma	0-2 2-3 3-6	1:4 1:5 1:10	1 trained staff for • 12 children aged under 2 years • 15 children aged 2 – 3 years • 30 children aged 3 years and over
Northern Territory	2 year postsecondary qualification or 3 years experience in childcare	2 year post secondary qualification	0-3 3 and over	1:5 1:11	1 trained staff for • 10 children aged under 3 years • 22 children over 3 years • 16 children in mixed age groups
Queensland	3 years tertiary study in early childhood (status of advanced diploma yet to be determined) for centers with more than 30 children. 2 years tertiary study for centers with less than 30 children	Diploma of Children's Services Or Endorsement of Chief Executive	0-2 15m-2.6yrs 2-3 2.6-3.6 3-5	1:4 1:10 1:12 1:16 1:24	1 trained staff for • 8 children aged under 2 years • 10 children aged 15mths – 2.6 years • 12 children aged 2 – 3 years • 16 children aged 2.6 – 3.6 years • 24 children aged 3 – 5 years
Australian Capital Territory		2 year tertiary qualification	0-3 3 and over	1:5 1:11	1 trained staff for • 10 children aged under 3 years • 22 children over 3 years • 15 for mixed age groups

from birth to 4 years of age are enrolled in full-day or part-time formal care in Australia (Commonwealth Task Force on Child Development, Health and Wellbeing, 2003) but day care places needed for children under 3 years exceed the quota set by the federal government. Provision of private child care has increased and child care companies listed on the stock market have made strong gains in just 2 years (Horin, 2003). Similar private sector investment and growth is expected in provision of family day care and out-of-school-hours care with the federal government's announcement that the cap on child care places in these areas will be lifted in 2004 (Denholm, 2003).

Occasional care services provide limited casual care for children under 5 years of age and are located in shopping centers, gym clubs, and community centers and usually administered by local councils. Long day care and preschool centers may offer a limited number of occasional care places if licensed to do so. Staff working in occasional care are not required to hold formal qualifications.

Family day care schemes offer flexible hours of care for up to 7 children (0 to 12 years) within the home of a licensed day care provider (see Table 1.5). These are usually authorized by local council authorities and linked with local playgroup attendance for young children and afterschool hours care for older children. Family day care is often preferred by parents in rural areas, parents who are shift workers, or those seeking the intimacy of a home environment for very young children. Family day care is often used for respite care or to supplement other child care services. Only the family day care coordinator is required to have a formal qualification. Licensed carers hold a first aid certificate. Increased inservice training and more ECEC qualified staff would improve the quality of care. Family day care became part of the national QIAS accreditation scheme in 2003, a world first, and a boost for family day care in Australia.

Mobile and Integrated Services

Mobile services are widely used to provide a diverse range of ECEC in communities which are itinerant, isolated, in rural, and remote areas, or new housing areas without adequate service provision for children and families. The flexibility of service provision includes toy and book libraries, preschool sessions, health services for parents and babies, and activity days for families with children from birth to 12 years of age. Often, mobile services link with local radio broadcasts, "School of the Air" or correspondence schools and local television stations for educational programs, or the Royal Flying Doctor Service and health organizations to provide special health checks and programs (Jeremy, 1996). For example,

SA has 273 families enrolled in the Remote and Isolated Children's Exercise (RICE). The RICE team visit lighthouse keepers' families (note that lighthouses are soon to be fully automated) and they connect families on remote cattle and sheep stations, and Aboriginal communities who may have previously only had access to School of the Air facilities (Reynolds, 2001). The School of the Air in Port Augusta, SA closed on April 12, 2003, after 45 years of operation, so these remote families were the first in Australia to switch to a virtual classroom using Internet video-conferencing technology (Ker, 2003). The coordinator of a mobile service generally holds a teaching qualification and the assistant a health qualification, but this varies in each state, in accordance with service regulations and functions of the mobile service (see Table 1.5).

Out of School Hours Care

Out of school hours care (OSHC) programs for children from 5 to 12 years are provided throughout Australia, by community organizations, local government authorities, and some departments of education. Located in schools, multipurpose centers, or neighborhood centers, out-of-school-hours care supplements other child care services. There is pressure to extend the program to include both younger and older children, and for state regulations in addition to national standards (see Table 1.5). Coordinators are not required to hold formal qualifications, but many have tertiary leisure or teaching degrees/diplomas.

Aboriginal Services

Indigenous ECEC services attract federal and state funding. In the last 5 years, exciting initiatives have seen adult employment programs linked with ECEC provisions in community employment development programs (CEDP) in all states. Child and Youth Health have a $3 million program to promote sustainable home visiting programs in Aboriginal communities, and preschools (recently granted more flexible hours of provision) are enjoying increased enrolment and participation rates. Multifunctional centers (with cultural programs), "safe" houses for children (from birth to 12 years), and TAFE child care upgrading courses in preschools in remote areas, are encouraging communities to use and value ECEC programs. Families are accessing family day care programs in rural and metropolitan areas where there are Aboriginal fieldworkers. Parents who have had access to higher levels of education now value education for their children and therefore want their children to participate in ECEC services. Community management of services with qualified local Aboriginal staff is being encouraged and supported at state and federal levels. In some schools, to ensure adequate nutritional intake by Aboriginal children, kitchens are built adjacent to classrooms and cooking is part of the curriculum.

Children's Health and Well-Being

Concern at federal and state government levels about a decline in children's health has led to new initiatives and cooperative ventures. The increase in childhood asthma as a long-term condition affects one in five school-aged children (Australian Institute for Health and Welfare, 2002). The increase in obesity of young children and declining health of Aboriginal children has led to each state government's resolve to take action on children's health (MacDougall, Schiller, & Darbyshire, 2004; Nossar, 2003). For example, South Australia has a five-minister forum on child and family health and an $18 million government commitment to fund "Be Active," a 4-year strategy to promote increased levels of physical activity and participation in schools and communities and to improve the quality of community health.

Where Does Responsibility Lie for Child Care?

Federal departments responsible for ECEC are Family and Community Services (FACS) and the Department of Education Training and Youth Assistance (DETYA). The federal government has also appointed a Child Care Advisory Council to the minister for FACS. FACS administers the regulations and the Child Care Act 1972 (see Table 1.5), and has responsibility for family programs and ECEC (excluding schools and preschools). This includes policy and funding for long day care, family day care, multifunctional centers, and Aboriginal services as well as occasional care, mobile units in remote, rural areas, and some out-of-school-hours care. Funding is available for training and in-service provision to centers, agencies, and management committees, and to facilitate inclusion of children with special needs. Playgroup associations also attract subsidies from FACS in most states. There are strong links between workforce participation and funding of children's services in a "Strengthening Families" initiative to assist families and communities in capacity building through the provision of affordable child care. All services must comply with state and territory regulations and participate in the QIAS accreditation scheme to be eligible for assistance. DETYA provides funding for national strategies or priorities such as literacy and numeracy or special-purpose, targeted programs, and financial assistance for state and territory school education authorities and nongovernment organizations. DETYA plays an important role in the development of indigenous education and services (including preschool). DETYA exerts a strong influence on child care through national agenda setting, and quality issues addressed through the QIAS system (OECD, 2001).

State and Territory Governments

Each state or territory sets its own priorities in relation to ECEC funding and regulation. In several states, all ECEC services—preschool, school, occasional care, family day care, out-of-school-hours care, and playgroups—come under one department. In other states, ECEC service provision is by state and local government and not-for-profit organizations. NSW has an explicitly child-centerd policy framework for ECEC, which was developed with reference to the United Nations Convention on the Rights of the Child (1989). In Queensland and NSW the Department of Community Services has the major responsibility for legislation, funding, and policies for ECEC through the Office of Child Care while the Department of Education (DET) is concerned with preschool and school provision. Northern Territory has ECEC services within the Health Department, and preschool and school within the Department of Education. Currently, a whole of government approach for implementation of ECEC policy is being developed in the NT (Crawford, 2002; Creswick, Fasoli, & Hazard, 1999). Victoria's Department of Human Services has main carriage of ECEC policy and programs (other than schools) but there are strong links from the past with maternal and child health services. South Australia has all ECEC services and programs within the Department of Education and Children's Services, but is developing strong links with Health. In Tasmania and the Australian Capitol Territory (ACT) all services are integrated within the Department of Education.

Local Government, Nongovernment Organizations

Local governments are involved in diverse services which support families and ECEC programs. These include playgrounds, parks and recreation facilities, libraries, and galleries/museums. Often they provide parenting programs and immunizations services. Many local governments (councils) are directly involved in provision of ECEC programs

Table 1.5. ECEC Regulations by Service Type

State/ Territory	Preschool	Long Day Care Center	Family Day Care	Home-Based Care	Mobile Children's Services	Outside School Hours Care
Australian Capital Territory	Mainly operated by Department of Education. Otherwise Children's Services Amendment Bill 1999. Licence Conditions Handbook (No regulations—power stems from Act)	Children's Services Amendment Bill 1999. Licence Conditions Handbook (No regulations—power stems from Act)	No territory regulation if less than 5 children who have not enrolled in school or 8 children under age 12	No territory regulation if less than 5 children who have not enrolled in school or 8 children under age 12	No mobile children services	Children's Services Act
New South Wales	Center based and Mobile Child Care Regulation (No2) 1996	Center based and Mobile Child Care Regulation (No2) 1996	Family Day Care and Home-based Child Care Services Regulation 1996	Family Day Care and Home-based Child Care Services Regulations 1996	Center based and Mobile Child Care Regulation (No2) 1996	No state regulations
Northern Territory	Mainly operated by Department of Education. Otherwise Community Welfare (Child Care) Regulations 1987: Standards NT Child Care Centers 1997	Community Welfare (Child Care) Regulations 1987: Standards NT Child Care Centers 1997	None if less than 6 children under 6 years.	No territory regulation if less than 6 children under 6 years of age. Guidelines for Home Based Child Care —published but legislated.	No	No territory regulations
Queensland	Child Care (Child Care Centers) Regulation 1991	Child Care (Child Care Centers) Regulation 1991	Child Care (Family Day Care) Regulation 1991	Care in a private home not specifically prescribed by regulation.	Child Care (Child Care Centers) Regulation 1991	No state regulations

(Table continues)

Table 1.5.   Continued

State/ Territory	Preschool	Long Day Care Center	Family Day Care	Home-Based Care	Mobile Children's Services	Outside School Hours Care
South Australia	Mainly operated by Department of Education Training and Employment (DETE). Otherwise Children's Services (Child Care Center) Regulations 1998	Children's Services (Child Care Center) Regulations 1998	FDC National Standards in service agreements. DETE must approve services.	No state regulation if less than 4 children. If more than 4 children requires a licence under Children's Services Act	Licensed under the Children's Services Act as a babysitting agency.	OSHC National Standards in service agreements
Tasmania	Mainly operated by Department of Education. Otherwise Child Welfare Act 1960 and Regulations 1961. Center Based Child Care Licensing Guidelines 1998	Child Welfare Act 1960 and Regulations 1961. Center Based Child Care Licensing Guidelines 1998	Child Welfare Act 1960 and Regulations 1961. Department of Community and Health Services' Outcome Standards	Child Welfare Act 1960 and Regulations 1961: Department of Community and Health Services' Outcome Standards	No mobile children services	No state regulations if children over 7 years regulations
Victoria	Children's Services Regulation 1998	Children's Services Regulation 1998		No state regulation if less than 5 children under 6 years of age	Children's Services Regulation 1998	No state regulations
Western Australia	Community Services (Child Care) Regulations 1988 or Education Department: School Education Act and Regulations, 1999	Community Services (Child Care) Regulations 1988	Community Services (Child Care) Regulations 1988	Community Services (Child Care) Regulations 1988	Mobile Kindergarten: School Education Act and Regulations, 1999	Guidelines for OSHC but these are not legislated.

such as family day care schemes, out-of-school-hours services and vacation care programs. Local councils usually employ a children's services coordinator and specialized staff to manage and resource local children's services.

Not-for-profit nongovernment organizations (NGOs) originated in the early philanthropic kindergarten movement. Community-based services and parent management remain a priority in these services. The not-for-profit sector now includes parent associations and large sponsoring organizations such as the Uniting Church, Kindergarten Union Children's Services, Day Nursery Children's Services, and the Creche and Kindergarten Association (in Queensland).

Summary

ECEC provision is a complex mosaic in Australia and highlights the need for a national plan and agenda. The lack of clarity in regulatory and monitoring mechanisms mirrors the dispersal of responsibility for regulations, support, and funding (Raban, 2003). Demand for service exceeds supply in center-based, long day care provision for birth to 3-year-olds, and private sector investment is being encouraged by the federal government. Most other ECEC services are provided by state governments, local governments and the not-for-profit sector. However, many families do not have access to ECEC options for their children, particularly poor, remote and isolated famlies.

RESEARCH AND POLICY ISSUES IN EARLY CHILDHOOD EDUCATION AND CARE IN AUSTRALIA

In this section, research and policy issues in ECEC will be discussed. Many policy issues relate to the quality of ECEC being provided in Australia and how to access appropriate care and education services. Research issues may well include policy issues, but research specifically on policy is less likely to be funded as government priorities help shape national research funding.

Reconceptualisation of childhood and international research findings about the importance of the child's earliest years as a foundation for future learning, wel-lbeing, and citizenship, have influenced governments to reassess their responsibilities toward young children. In Australia too, the National Childcare Accreditation Council, the Childcare Advisory Council, and national lobby groups for children and families have put pressure on the federal government to invest in young children's health, care, and education, to set a national agenda for early childhood, and to implement a coordinated, sustainable approach to policy and service provision across Australia. The question remains, why is there no national policy framework for ECEC? What does this say about the valuing of young children in Australia today?

Three recent documents that identified key policy and research issues for ECEC in Australia and provided impetus for change are the Organization for Economic Cooperation and Development (OECD) report Starting Strong: Early Childhood Education and Care (OECD, 2001), the OECD thematic review of early childhood education and care policy; Australian background report (Press & Hayes, 2000); and the Australian Economic Review "Issues in Child Care Policy in Australia" (McDonald, 2002). The OECD (2001) report of ECEC policy in 12 countries (including Australia) made it possible to share a world view of ECEC policy, to see care and education in Australia within a global context, and to shape future policy directions. Policy issues identified in each of the reports have been summarized in Table 1.6.

One of the policy lessons learned from the OECD (2001) report is that countries which have developed strong systems have focussed on "children as a social group with rights" (p.127) thereby changing the focus of ECEC policy. Each report raised the issue of integration of children's services into one system under one Ministry. Sweden has fully integrated children's services into the education system under the Ministry of Education (OECD, 2001). In Australia, SA, ACT and Tasmania have fully integrated ECEC services (as previously discussed). McDonald (2002)

Table 1.6.   Summary of Issues Raised in Reports on ECEC Policy in Australia

	Press and Hayes (2000)	*OECD (2001)*	*McDonald (2002)*
Views of childhood	Fundamental principles underlie policy approaches of government departments to ECEC services. How does policy reflect the intrinsic value of children and the relationship between care and education?	ECEC reveals a range of beliefs and directions depending on government philosophy, jurisdiction, type of setting and community perception. Clearer vision (including a strategy framework of ECEC policy) should be generated, drawing on views and interests of children, families, communities, professionals and researchers.	The impact of European and North American research necessitates a cultural shift by government in relation to ECEC policy. A strong and equal partnership with education is needed (as in Sweden).

(Table continues)

Table 1.6.   Continued

	Press and Hayes (2000)	OECD (2001)	McDonald (2002)
Policy coherence and coordination	The mix of approaches is reflected in variety of service types, targeted funding, staff requirements and program structure and content.	Complexities of multi-layering of administration and regulation, size of country and dispersal of population cause difficulties in system coherence and coordination.	A coordinated policy framework at centralised and decentralised levels is necessary.
Standards and quality of care	Community concerns relate to flexibility, education, quality of staff/child interaction. Are quality assurance systems appropriate and effective ?	Low pay, low status and training of staff undermines quality. ECEC has poor working conditions in relation to other education sectors. Gender pedagogy also needs to be addressed.	A participatory approach to quality improvement and assurance is required.
Access and equity	Issues include access to ECEC for children who do not currently benefit from such services and appropriate provision for children with additional needs (rural, remote, indigenous, poor).	The most acute needs are for indigenous communities and relate to respect, self determination, cultural ownership and language.	A universal approach to access with particular attention to children in need is required (as used in France).
Funding issues	With funding changes and privatisation of long day care, there is tension between financial viability, affordability and quality.	Pedagogical needs are important and require adequate resource allocation (e.g. staff:child ratios).	Substantial public investment in services and infrastructure are needed in ECEC
Staff selection and training	Issues of staff development, training, qualifications, recruitment, retention and workplace conditions are all policy concerns.	Firmer regulations for staff training and adequate staff numbers in long day care and family day care will improve quality of service. Inservice training and recruitment of ethnically diverse, bilingual staff is necessary.	Appropriate training and working conditions for staff must be implemented.
Monitoring and evaluation	Improve transitions between ECEC environments, multiple care arrangements and transition to school.	QIAS is well regarded and birth to eight years curricula are highlighted as a seamless guide to development.	Systematic attention to monitoring and data collection is required.
Data collection and research	Policy foci on literacy and numeracy at school are outcomes based and show literacy problems for boys and indigenous students.	Excellent resources of professional staff and staff in research universities could be utilized.	A long term agenda for research and evaluation is needed.

Developed from Press and Hayes (2000), OECD (2001) and McDonald (2002).

supports this move to education (if it is an equal partnership) as it offers parity in status for ECEC, better conditions for ECEC staff and smooth transition between ECEC services. Press and Hayes (2000) have reservations because, while there are advantages in pedagogical continuity, there is potential for ECEC services to become isolated from child welfare, health and other policy areas unless strong interdepartmental links are developed.

Curriculum Frameworks

A pedagogical framework has the potential to "improve the educational focus of ECEC settings" and "support an integrated approach for all children under compulsory school age" (OECD, 2001, p. 112). A number of states in Australia have created integrated curricula frameworks which are optional rather than mandated. Tasmania has a curriculum for birth to 5-year-olds (Hughes & MacNaughton, 2002; MacNaughton, 1999); NSW has developed an early childhood curriculum for nonschool settings (Stonehouse, 2002) and SA has developed an integrated curriculum framework from birth to 18 years with transitions and continuity as key elements (Department of Education, Training and Employment, 2001). This process of collaboration at all levels can lead to a "synergy of cultures" (OECD, 2001, p. 113) and strengthen children's learning as long as there is equal emphasis and value given to each age group. These state curricula frameworks will need to be reviewed systematically providing excellent opportunities for research.

Policy Shifts in Funding

Press and Hayes (2000) assert that "the policy shift from funding ECEC services to funding parents as service consumers has seen reconceptualisation of ECEC services as businesses and put pressure on services to strengthen business plans and financial management processes" (p. 59). This shift has seen the demise of the not-for-profit community-based centers with qualified staff, lower child to staff ratios and emphasis on care and the pedagogical needs of children under 5. Now, a delicate balance is required between providing quality care and service affordability, that is, the capacity of parents to pay for services: Improving facilities and increasing trained staff might raise the quality of care offered, but the extra costs incurred may lead to restricted hours of service provision. Private care providers trying to minimize staff costs will tend to meet only minimum standards in order to maximize returns to their shareholders. For example, one private child care company has been so successful commercially that it is one of the strongest performers on the stock market and is returning record profits to investors. The company has acquired 200 centers across Australia, and encouraged staff to sign individual employment contracts and complete training within the company rather than at TAFE or university (Horin, 2003). What does this mean for policy? "With 60% of all revenue for child care centres coming from government subsidies, within these corporatised services, shareholder profits are directly supported by taxpayer funds" (Griffiths, 2003). Currently, thousands of children are on waiting lists for center-based long day care and out-of-school-hours care and parents cannot return to work because child care is unavailable. Expansion of places through private providers would mean that parents could use their Child Care Benefits allowance (A\$137 per week) to pay for care in accredited ECEC services (Denholm, 2003) but when options are limited and what is available may not constitute good quality care, parents have no real choice. The Australian federal government's reluctance to invest in child care infrastructure or raise government expenditure on child care, combined with their preference for user pays private child care provision in ECEC, is rapidly changing child care from a service to a commercial enterprise (McDonald, 2002). "If ECEC is to be treated as a vital public service.... It cannot be funded largely by the parents who use it" (OECD, 2001, p. 130).

Quality Assurance and Control

When licensing issues are separately determined by state government regulations (see Table 1.5) consistency of quality remains an ongoing priority, so the federal government has established a means of quality control through the Quality Improvement and Accreditation system (QIAS). The National Childcare Accreditation Council (NCAC) (established in 1993) administers the QIAS and accreditation for day care across Australia. Quality systems are defined as those providing quality outcomes for children. Subdivided into elements and principles, the QIAS covers interactions and communications; program experiences and activities for children; nutrition, health, safety and child protection; service management and staff development. Accreditation requires a five-step process and services are accredited for 2.5 years. One of the strengths of the process is the requirement to address plans for continuing improvement (National Childcare Accreditation Council, NCAC, 1993, 2001a). In 2003 a family day care quality assurance system was introduced. This is the first quality assurance scheme for family day care in the world to be linked to child care funding through legislation and to be funded and supported by a federal government (NCAC, 2001b). In June 2003 an outside school hours care quality assurance system was launched (NCAC, 2003). Quality improvement and accreditation systems, while impressive and standard across Australia, are not a panacea for maintaining quality of care. They will need to be evaluated constantly and other monitoring strategies put in place in order to maintain quality in ECEC services.

Employment, Maternity Leave and Care

Changing employment patterns of women have meant that some women delay the age when they choose to have children. Women with established careers want to maintain continuity in the workforce. Wooden (2002) highlighted the growing conflict between employment opportunities for women and childbearing concluding that "current government incentives for women to remain out of the workforce, appear to be out of step with other changes in society"(p. 177). Forty-seven percent of women with children under 3 years of age are working but maternity leave provisions in Australia are only available to 17% of these women (this is one of the lowest rates in the developed world). Currently, the Office of the Status of Women is challenging the federal government over these issues in a bid to increase maternity leave provisions (Jackman, 2003). Consequently, Australia lags behind most OECD countries in the amount of money allocated for care (OECD, 2001).

Multiple Care Arrangements

A pressing concern is children in multiple care arrangements because of cost of care, hours of operation of centers, and reluctance of the federal government to look at maternity leave arrangements or expand employment-based care for working parents. Consequently informal care arrangements account for most of the care in Australia. Australia is not alone in this. In their analysis of recent trends in early childhood practice in the United States, Saracho and Spodek (2003) note the management of horizontal and vertical transitions for children as an issue. Australian Bureau of Statistics (ABS) figures show that in 1999, 66% of children from birth to 4 years used some form of informal child care. This means that the care was unregulated (i.e., took place at home, or was out-of-home care by family members, friends, neighbors or babysitters). These figures were recorded 1 year after government fee subsidies for service were withdrawn from not-for-profit long day care centers across Australia. Forty percent of children from birth to 4 years were in formal care services (i.e. government approved child care) except for Indigenous populations where in 2002 only 12% of Indigenous children from birth to 5 years used formal care, but many children in remote communities had no service available so informal care was the only option (Commonwealth Task Force on Child Development, Health and Wellbeing, 2003). The figures are not mutually exclusive, so some children may have been in formal care for a few days a week and informal care arrangements for other days of the week. Bowes et al. (2003) are currently researching this area nationally but have only released results from the first year of their 3-year study. Margetts (2003) is undertaking similar research in Victoria.

Staff Training

All three reports raised issues about appropriate training and working conditions for ECEC staff. The OECD (2001) study found that countries such as Australia, the United Kingdom, and the Unites States, with large private and voluntary sectors, have "low-trained and untrained staff working in ECEC, particularly with infants and toddlers" (OECD, 2001, p. 99) whereas in Sweden, 98% of ECEC staff have specific training in working with young children. The OECD (2001) report identified staff training gaps in working with parents; working with infants/toddlers; in bilingual/multicultural and special education, research, and evaluation (p. 96). In the Australian federal system there are currently no agreed national frameworks for staff qualifications (see Table 1.4) and a complex system of staff roles and responsibilities in relation to service regulations (see Table 1.5). Annual staff turnover can reach over 30% in center-based care so retention of staff is a serious problem causing a lack of continuity in programs. Press and Hayes (2000) mentioned the need to "improve status and retention rates of staff" (p. 62) because early childhood staff with teaching qualifications could enhance quality in programming for children in care. McDonald (2002) supports this, reporting that "tertiary institutions today produce graduates who see themselves as early childhood educators and carers. Caring for children is part of their education and part of their philosophy" (p. 197). This favorable cultural shift comes at a time when more graduates are available to work in the full range of ECEC services, but increasing the number of qualified staff is not economically viable in user pays ECEC environments (Press & Hayes, 2000).

Gender equality in ECEC services needs to be reviewed. Some people view the feminization of the workforce in places like Australia as a continuation of what was considered "women's work" while others see this as short sighted. In Norway and Denmark there is a public commitment to children having a right to have both men and women in their lives and this is discussed as a part of gender pedagogy. If there is community concern about the possibility of child sexual abuse in child care, this should be resolved by routine police checks for both men and women. Children benefit from having both male and female role models in their lives, and there is a need for ECEC in Australia to strive for this situation in ECEC services.

Child abuse is a matter of concern in Australia and in most states and territories, ECEC staff are required by law to report suspicions and signs of child abuse. It is also important to provide children with a child protection/personal safety curriculum and NSW has prepared extensive teaching resources for child protection to use with children and students of all ages, including those with special needs (Briggs, Broadhurst, & Hawkins, 2003).

Long Day Care for Birth to 3-Year-Olds

A controversial policy issue is the inclusion of birth to 3-year-olds in center-based long day care. The staff to child ratio for under 2-year-olds is 1:5 in most states and territories (see Table 1.4) but recent research relating to social attachment, early brain development, and stimulation suggests that this is too high (Winter, 2003) and does not allow sufficient time for individual attention and meaningful interaction. Instead, there are stressful work demands and too little time for staff reflection and planning because time is taken up with routine chores and health requirements. In Australia, there is no requirement to employ trained staff unless numbers of children exceed a specified limit. How services are provided for younger children is an important policy issue as low-quality service can be harmful for children (Vandell & Wolfe, 2000).

These issues need research, but this is expensive and funding is difficult to obtain in the current financial climate. Private providers are unwilling to fund such research because findings may affect their franchise arrangements and profit margin if results show, for example, that extra, qualified staff need to be employed. The federal government, through its Australian Research Council, is unlikely to fund research on long day care because early childhood is not a recognized research discipline, it is seen as a low priority, and research outcomes may have costly implications requiring policy changes. Consequently, such research is left to independent researchers, doctoral students, or university/industry consortia with access to project funds. Governments through DETYA and industry are most likely to jump-start early childhood research initiatives in the policy area if sufficient pressure can be brought to bear on the government to put this issue on a national agenda.

Assessment and Standards

Policy focusing on emergent literacy and numeracy skills and their enhancement in early childhood has been shown to relate to school retention and participation rates at the secondary school level (Commonwealth Task Force on Child Development, Health and Wellbeing, 2003). Recent literacy assessments have shown that 86.9% of Year 3 children (8-year-olds) in Australia in 1999 achieved the agreed minimum standard for reading. However, there was a 5% gap in performance between girls and boys (with girls achieving higher scores) and approximately one third of Indigenous students were below the agreed minimum standards (Press & Hayes, 2000). On local test results in 2000, 92.5% of students in Year 3 met the national benchmark for literacy with 92.7% achieving the numeracy benchmark. Again, the poorer performance of boys was noted (Commonwealth Task Force on Child Development, Health and Wellbeing, 2003). Since 2000, there has been a flurry of activity and research sponsorship by governments through the Department of Education, Training and Youth Affairs (DETYA) and the Office for Child Care (NSW) in the areas of transition, education for boys, literacy and numeracy, and technology, but little more than recognition and acknowledgment of the problems facing Indigenous children in early childhood schooling. It is clear that research in this area is needed urgently.

Children with Additional Needs

Each report drew attention to children with special educational needs including children with disabilities. Australia has a policy of social inclusion of children with disabilities in ECEC services and statistical analysis suggests that between 15% to 20% of children have special educational needs (OCED, 2001; Press & Hayes, 2000). Recent research in WA has shown that 26% of urban children "have developmental difficulties, with potential for life-long impact by age five" (Nott, 2003, p. 1).

While the inclusion policy has many advantages, staff in ECEC settings, particularly long day care and family day care, are likely to need extra support to fulfil their roles effectively. There are not many permanent staff within care settings who have specialized training in this area so staff development is required. Certainly a concerted research effort is needed to establish how the policy of inclusion is being implemented. It is important that children have "equitable access" to ECEC services (OECD, 2001, p. 48) from birth because early identification and intervention through special programs are critical for children under three years (McDonald, 2002).

The urgent issue of refugees and asylum seekers has been brought to public attention by the plight of so called "boat people" who fled from conflict in their homelands seeking asylum in Australia. Without the necessary permits for residence in the country, families are required to spend lengthy periods in detention waiting for their applications to be processed. Community opposition to the federal government's actions has brought pressure to bear for women and children seeking asylum in Australia to live in the community until their application for asylum has been processed. It has been shown that young children's physical and mental health is deteriorating in detention centers, and some children have been self-harming as a result (Cologon, 2003). However, there is little that ECEC services can provide until the federal government declares people's status to be other than asylum-seekers under current law. As the OECD report suggests these families "are often traumatised, yet because of their ambivalent status are among the least likely to access benefits and services" and "it is of great policy concern that the most vulnerable children are either likely to miss out on ECEC services, or find that the services are insensitive to their needs" (OECD, 2001, p. 37).

A second issue is that the proportion of "ethnic minority children is growing more rapidly than the ethnic majority population in countries such as Australia" (OECD, 2001, p. 24) and this diversity presents a challenge for staff in ECEC services in valuing and responding to the needs of ethnically, culturally, and linguistically diverse families. An ethnically diverse staff profile which matches the diversity in the families using the program would be desirable. Australian states have begun to employ bilingual assistants to help to support a child's home languages (Makin & Spedding, 2003), to enable improved interactions with parents, and to increase understanding of cultural diversity by all of the children and families in the ECEC services. New South Wales is the only state which has made this practice a staff selection policy in ECEC.

The OECD (2001) report found that Indigenous people were "the most disadvantaged in the country" (p. 35). There is inadequate inclusion of Indigenous cultural needs, values, and backgrounds in educational settings. It has been difficult to staff schools in remote and isolated areas and Bachelor Institute of Indigenous Tertiary Education in the NT has played an important role in creating early childhood courses for Aboriginal students and in facilitating community development in remote indigenous communities. Still, there is limited access to educational services for children in some remote locations and for many children English is not their primary language (OECD, 2001). Poverty is endemic in Indigenous communities and while 40% of the Indigenous population is under age 15 their anticipated life expectancy is nearly 20 years less than for the White population of Australia. Of great concern in Aboriginal communities, is the health issue of children from poor and remote Indigenous communities spending their days petrol-sniffing which can lead to early death or brain damage and children affected may be as young as 5 or 6 years of age. This terrible issue which communities and governments are grappling with in Australia has no apparent solution nor strategies to lessen the destructive practices.

Research and Policy Issues

In 2003, the federal government announced early childhood as a priority for its term of office in the next 3 years and launched a consultation paper toward the development of a national agenda for early childhood produced by the Commonwealth Task Force on Child Development, Health and Wellbeing (2003) with a focus on children under 5 years of age. The paper acknowledges lack of integration of services for children and families and the need for a plan to guide future progress. It promises much but it is clear that there is no intention of changing the current balance of responsibilities between federal and state jurisdictions; rather on finding ways to coordinate effort and work more effectively for families and children to improve health and well-being. No information has been released on the agenda since the launch. What is revealing is the foreword to the national agenda consultation paper by Professor Fiona Stanley, stating that a joint effort is required from all levels of government, stakeholders, communities, and service providers based on sound evidence. She then challenges the researchers! "For too long, researchers and policy makers have been working in their own silos. The coming together of these two groups to tackle the challenge of improving the health and well-being of Australian children is truly historic" (Commonwealth Task Force on Child Development, Health and Wellbeing, 2003, p.ii).

How can researchers comment on the efficacy of the changes to ECEC and contribute to policy formation in ECEC? As policy analyst McDonald (2002) suggests data availability is problematic. The data from the 1999 Australian Bureau of Statistics Child Care survey has not been made available to researchers and the regular FACS census of child care providers has been postponed for more than a year. McDonald proposes that a cultural shift on the part of the Australian federal government is needed in relation to child care and research as a "research agenda that is more evaluative and arm's length from the government is desirable, but largely non-existent" (p. 202). The OECD (2001) report suggested that a national emphasis on learning outcomes, (especially on literacy and numeracy skills in education), and state government commitment to improving the quality of ECEC through the development of curriculum frameworks and standards, provide excellent opportunities for the research agenda to contribute to the national agenda and future directions in ECEC as "governments have at their disposal a rich resource of professional expertise in their various ministries and research universities" (OECD, 2001, p. 150).

Research is being conducted on some sections of the policy issues raised in these recent national and international reports on ECEC but will the research affect ECEC policy in Australia? Is a national research agenda necessary to maximize, coordinate, and focus Australian research efforts ?

CURRENT RESEARCH IN
EARLY CHILDHOOD CARE AND EDUCATION

Research in ECEC is an essential component in the development of programs, policies, systems, and theories about children and families. Research can document, assess, explore, investigate, examine, analyze, and contribute to future directions. This section will briefly review current research in early childhood education and care. Research publications, research scholarships and conferences to disseminate research findings will be described. Research areas will be identified, selected studies outlined, and ongoing issues discussed.

Growth in ECEC Research and Publication

Few early childhood academics held doctorates prior to 1990 although ECEC professionals contributed to innovative service provision and policy. The amalgamation of vocationally-oriented colleges into research-oriented universities in 1989 changed this with academic staff gaining higher degrees, participating in research activity, postgraduate teaching, and supervision of higher degree students. Teaching and research centers opened with senior staff appointed to facilitate development of research programs. Queensland was one of the first states to respond positively to this change and now most universities have viable early childhood research centers and research concentrations. Professorial chairs in early childhood education have been appointed to head university early childhood units and South Australia has a specifically designated Lillian de Lissa Chair of Early Childhood (Research), jointly funded by the University of South Australia and the Department of Early Childhood and Community Services with a major focus on applied research in ECEC. Specialized research training at honors, masters, and doctoral levels are available in most universities with early childhood degrees. Therefore, there has been an exponential growth in ECEC research and development.

Early Childhood Australia (formerly AECA) hosts national triennial conferences, which are attended by policymakers, academics, researchers, and practitioners, and publishes recent research in its widely-read refereed journal the *Australian Journal of Early Childhood* (AJEC). The journal publishes recent research from the annual Conference of Australian Research in Early Childhood Education (ARECE). The Department of Early Childhood Services in SA hosts international biennial ECEC conferences which have become the biggest in Australia with attendance from 20 countries in 2003. These research conferences provide excellent fora for discussion, networking, mentoring of new researchers and dissemination of research. Growth in conference attendance and the quality of evaluative studies and research papers attests to the vibrancy of ECEC internationally. Australian ECEC researchers also have access to international publication of their research and many international ECEC journals have Australians as associate editors or on their editorial boards. There is still an overreliance on overseas' research particularly from the United Kingdom and the United States and a "dearth of Australian research on young children" (Press & Hayes, 2000 p. 55). A clearinghouse would improve access to Australian research.

Most ECEC research studies in Australia are now applied studies and there has been a shift from use of quantitative methods to research designs using both qualitative and quantitative approaches. Since 1995 there has been an increase in collaborative research, with interdisciplinary teams combining to give multiple perspectives in ECEC research which makes for exciting and innovative research collaborations and outcomes.

Funding for Research

The federal government through the Australian Research Council (ARC) funds basic and applied research, but grants awarded are highly competitive with only a 20% success rate. From 1990-1999, only 16 projects related to young children and these were mostly grounded in traditional discipline areas such as psychology, mathematics, or science. Funding for ECEC research is more likely through joint research projects with industry partners through ARC-Linkage grants where the success rate is closer to 40%, and it is possible to focus on ECEC research issues (Press & Hayes, 2000). DETYA also funds research, awards DETYA research fellowships, and commissions evaluations and reviews particularly as these relate to schooling. At state level, the Office of Child Care in NSW, the SA Department of Education and Children's Services and WA Health Promotion Council commission research and award research grants as available funds permit. Private foundations and national early childhood scholarships (although competitive) are also sources of research funding. The Alice Creswick Scholarship is awarded annually to an outstanding early childhood educator for further study/research in Australia or overseas, and the Jean Denton, Margaret Trembath, and Lillian de Lissa Scholarships are awarded specifically for research in early childhood education and care in Australia. The federal Department of Family and Community Services (FACS) also commissions research in government priority areas and funds smaller community capacity-building projects in areas such as Indigenous childrearing in remote regions and strengthening families or community initiatives. The Australian Institute of Family Studies (AIFS) has, since its inception, contributed to research on family contexts, economic and social policy in relation to families, demographic trends, childcare, and child development, both through its recurrent budget and winning of competitive grants and commissions. The AIFS is the organization which could become a National Center for Research in Early Childhood Development as recommended by the National Senate Inquiry into Early Childhood Education in 1996 (Press & Hayes, 2000).

The consultation paper for a national agenda suggests that there is a need for "an Australian research strategy that includes evaluation of implementation and outcomes" (Commonwealth Task Force on Child Development, Health and Wellbeing, 2003, p. 8) and the federal government has nominated the Australian Research Alliance for Children and Youth (ARACY) to develop "a research agenda for early childhood which will support policy and action under the National Agenda" (p. 8). The question remains, will a national agenda become a reality and if so, when?

National Commissioned Research Studies

The federal government has recently commissioned two research studies of significance, both conducted under the auspices of the AIFS in Victoria. The first was the infant temperament study (1983-2000) which found that temperament is more genetic than environmental, but can be modified by parental behavior and stimulation exercises and activities (Prior, Sanson, Smart, & Oberklaid, 2000). The second is the largest study ever undertaken under the auspices of the Department of Family and Community Services (FACS). The federal government has allocated 9 years of funding for the first Longitudinal Study of Australian Children (LSAC) commencing in 2003. Data will be collected over 9 years from two cohorts every 2 years. The first cohort of 5.000 children (aged birth to 12 months) will be followed until they reach 6 or 7 years of age, and the second cohort will comprise 5,000 children aged 4 years in 2003. The LSAC participants will include children (at an appropriate age) together with their parents, caregivers, and teachers. Research questions include: discovering the impact of nonparental childcare on children's development over time; specific early experiences that encourage emerging literacy and numeracy; how socioeconomic factors contribute to child outcomes; what ECEC experiences impact positively on school outcomes for children; and how children's activity patterns relate to family attachment, fitness and social skills (Millward, 2003; Sayers, 2003). This project will provide a national perspective on Australia's children that will influence policy and practice across ECEC services. The first findings of the study released in November 2003 revealed that in the second cohort of 4,500 children in WA aged 4 years, 26% are not ready for school and 13% have been identified as being at risk (Nott, 2003). In this preliminary data it has been reported that the WA cohort "had lower averages than their Canadian counterparts across every category" (McCain & Mustard, 1999; Nott, 2003, p. 1).

Fleer (2002) suggested that Australia could learn from New Zealand, Canadian, and the U.K. longitudinal studies. Fleer reviewed research literature supporting ECEC and argued that communities should support early childhood education in the same way as they support free public primary and secondary education as "a public right not a privilege" (p. 1). The research question is not "Does early childhood education make a difference?" but "What are the factors (or internal variables) in the provision of ECEC which have lasting cognitive and social outcomes for children?" (p. 5) and what types of programs make the most difference? Then, Fleer suggests, a persuasive case can be made for parity of financial support with other sectors of education in Australia

Reconceptualization of Childhood and Sociocultural Factors

Reconceptualization of childhood and the sociocultural factors influencing ECEC have been explored by Grieshaber and Cannella (2001) and

Hughes and MacNaughton (2002) in attempts to "widen the arena of discourse(s) and action(s) available to early childhood educators," that is to look at power relationships, explore diversity, and reconceptualize "ways of knowing, listening to, being with and educating young children" (Grieshaber & Cannella, 2001, p. 4). Grieshaber pursues a feminist agenda in exploring the complexity, ambiguity, and uncertainty which early childhood educators face in their day-to-day responsibilities to children. Grieshaber and Cannella (2001) ask questions such as "how does one co-construct a new kind of research with children that reflects their perspectives?" (p. 19). This research perspective has been influential in Australia and the United States.

Hughes and MacNaughton (2002) have asked children about their play practices, identity, and sense of self in relation to popular culture and socialization practices and examined diversity and dissensus (the opposite of consensus) between early childhood staff and parents in formal and informal communication practices. Results from 20 ECEC staff in QIAS-accredited child care centers revealed significant discrepancies between staff and parent priorities and valuing of interactions. Parents regarded informal communication highly, whereas staff considered formal communication most relevant. The problem was how to give parents a "real voice" without feeling that this threatened staff's professional identity and expertise. MacNaughton (2003) urged researchers to consider children's voices as offering another perspective, but not the only one.

Over the past 7 years, Dockett and Perry (2003) have investigated perspectives, experiences, and expectations of all involved as children start school. Using a range of methodologies, including large-scale questionnaires and interviews with children, families, and educators, the project has developed a set of guidelines for effective transition to school programs which highlight the importance of relationships and communication in the transition process. These guidelines are being used by schools and systems to evaluate existing transition programs and develop new programs. A feature of the research has been the engagement of children as researchers. Strategies such as photo essays, drawings, and conversations about children's experiences as they start school, their expectations about school, and their perceptions of what happens around them, have informed the direction of research and the practical implications. The research aims to move away from a focus on the child as the center of transition and to consider contexts in which children live and ways in which these impact on transition experiences. Also relevant are family adjustments and those made by teachers as children start school. Petri-wskyj (2003) questions the change processes teachers go through to support the transition of a diverse group of socially marginalized and Indigenous children with little exposure to preschool prior to attending school. She asks how ready are teachers for these learners and how ready are schools for these learners? These research findings are influencing policy formulation at the local level to take account of children's rights and changing social, political, cultural perspectives.

Children from Birth to 3 Years in Care

A second group of research studies focuses on children under 3 years. Bowes et al. (2003) have a 3-year research project to investigate the effects of multiple and changeable child care arrangements on children from birth to 3 years. Results from the first year of the study (2003) indicate the NSW rural and urban parent sample (600) use multiple care arrangements through necessity not by choice. Future analysis will include parents' reasons for using multiple care and comparisons between rural/urban areas. Margetts' study (2003) found that children's experiences of multiple care arrangements varies with the complexity of the care, and complexity increases as children approach school age. Skouteris and Dissanayade (2003) looked at factors which facilitate the infant's well-being in child care. They report a dearth of literature on the transition of infants into child care. Pilot study findings are that infants placed into child care before 6 months of age settled faster, were happier in childcare, and were more likely to maintain their sleep routines than infants placed into care after 8 months. Preliminary data support the hypothesis, (based on attachment theory) that children under 8 months will have a more positive transition to child care than older infants and the success of this transition into child care has implications for parental well-being, in particular the success of the mother's return to the workplace. It is expected that the results of this study will have implications for policies and strategies that both government and nongovernment agencies put in place to meet "equal opportunities for women in the workplace" obligations.

Curricula for Under-Threes

Makin and Spedding (2003) worked with parents in an early literacy support program called SHELLS (Support at Home for Early Language and Literacies) and found that "closer the 'fit' between home and community literacy practices and school literacy practices, the more likely it is that literacy learning will be unproblematic" (2003, p. 47). Dolby (2003) uses the concept of "emotional availability" (p. 4) to draw attention to the important role care givers play in enabling young children to develop a sense of confidence and emotional maturity in their interactions. Diamond (2003) sought information from 40 middle-class mothers on their behaviors when their 2-year-olds do something dangerous. She found that children with low persistence were at more risk of accidental injury than children who had high persistence and that mothers sought to control the child's environment and to educate their child about the hazards. Control strategies were used with children who were irritable or had little language and educative strategies were used with older children who were active to encourage safe practices. Safety for toddlers should be part of child care curriculum. Rolfe, Nyland, and Morda (2002) looked at the nature of interactions in infant programs and how these contribute to the quality of care offered. From their research, they questioned whether regulations specify sufficient numbers of teachers to enhance infant/adult interaction in "socially-contrived child rearing settings" (p. 94) such as child care centers.

Everyday experiences of children may be taken for granted when early childhood professionals plan programs for young children in care. Broughton, Gahan, Henry, and McDonell (2003) research joint attentional sequences in the everyday experiences of young children. In a 4-year study with 12- to 54-month-old children, interactions between adult/child dyads engaged in four everyday activities (looking at books, playing with toys, changing clothing, and eating a snack) are videotaped. Parents and teachers also complete open-ended questionnaires about their feelings in undertaking activities with each child, and their perceptions of the child's feelings of engagement in shared activities. Results have confirmed shared everyday activities as significant contexts for young children's learning and development but have also demonstrated differences in the balance of power exercised by adults and children over time in maintaining joint attentional sequences, and have shown different parental approaches and interactions with boys and girls. Kowalski, Wyver, Masselos, and De Lacey (2004) looked at the influence of older peers on younger children's emerging symbolic play in child care centers. First-born toddlers exhibited higher levels of symbolic play in mixed age, free play sessions than later-born toddlers. Researchers have suggested that first-borns may be more experienced in symbolic play activity than later-born toddlers because of parental interaction and involvement in their play activities.

Winter (2003) evaluated the effectiveness of a new curriculum framework, the SA Curriculum, Standards and Accountability Framework (SACSA), specifically the section for children from birth to age 3. Winter found significant improvements in educators' practices and pedagogy, and that the process quality of young children's curriculum is improved by the use of a formal curriculum framework. Winter recommends that we reconceptualize care for very young children as enriching developmentally and socially and for the benefit of all children rather than care being seen as "a business that provides a safe place to leave children while families work or need respite" (Winter, 2003, p. xi).

Literacies in Early Childhood

The national government has been concerned with educational outcomes—in particular with standards in literacy and mathematics, so major longitudinal studies on children's emerging literacy development and applications of technology in ECEC have received government funding through Australian Research Council grants. Hill, Comber, Louden, Reid, and Rivalland's (2002) project *100 Children Turn 10* studied children's literacy development in the year prior to school to the fourth year of schooling. The longitudinal study took place in three states, SA, WA and Victoria, in school sites which were geographically and socioeconomically diverse. Most children made substantial growth in literacy. Two key findings were a broad range of performance by children at each site, those not achieving were children living in poverty. Tackling the problem of lower levels of literacy performance remains a major challenge for governments and educators (Hill et al., 2002, p. 5). However, early assessments of children did not always accurately predict future patterns. Gains in early reading development did not always persist in the face of negative life experiences which created difficulties for a child. "In many cases the language, social and textual practices of the home were similar to that of the school, creating a seamless connection between home and school values and attitudes" (p. 7) but "Some parents who were dealing with difficult life circumstances such as poverty and ill health mistrusted the school's diagnosis of children with learning difficulties or disabilities and feared teachers' judgements about poor parenting" (p. 7). The positive finding was that good teaching made a difference as did successful student/teacher social relations. Teachers' skills of observation, diagnosis, and responsive teaching made a difference, as did their "actual pedagogical and communicative repertoires" (p. 8). Successful teachers gave sustained attention to children's words, and analyzed what children were striving to do. This pedagogy "went beyond familiar routines and strategies" (p. 8).

Raban, Griffin, Coates, and Fleer (2002) investigated children's literacy in four states of Australia. The National Indigenous Literacy and Numeracy Strategy (NIELNS) is "to achieve English literacy and numeracy for indigenous students at levels comparable to those achieved by other Australians" (p. 74). A literacy profile was developed for use with children with seven descriptors relating to English print literacy. Profiles were taken of 385 children between the ages of 4.10 and 5.7 years. The findings were that the Indigenous children who were part of this preschool study appeared to be making comparable progress with their non-Indigenous peers prior to commencement at school. The researchers asked why then have Indigenous children fallen so far behind non-Indigenous children in literacy when tested in year 3 at school? Children speaking another language at home would be expected to take longer to master literacy in English. Researchers noted teacher's low expectations of Indigenous children and warned against teachers underestimating capacity by adhering to inappropriate views on child development. Raban et al. note that teachers need to be observant of children's developing literacy awareness, and that the discipline of interpreting culturally salient contexts into school-relevant, conceptual tools for understanding print literacy is crucial for later success (Raban et al., 2002, p. 84).

Hill, Yelland, and Mulhearn's (2003-2004) ARC-Linkage grant with the Department of Education and Children's Services in South Australia explores what children can do with literacy, numeracy, and information technologies (ICT) in homes and communities. The research is to determine where and how children use ICT, how their knowledge develops over time, and what they think of ICT. The framework draws on theoretical tools with a multiliteracy perspective (print literacy and other multimodal communications are labeled as literacies). The project targets primarily low-income communities and disadvantaged preschools and schools. Teachers as researchers visit homes in the community to gather data. Findings to date show that children use computers as machines for play and learning. The electronic literacies children are developing incorporate and extend print-based literacies (Hill, Yelland & Mulhearn, 2003). This research study will inform curriculum and professional development programs for teachers in the early years. In a university-school joint research project, Schiller and Tillett (2004) examined how children (aged 7) and their teacher acquired and developed their ICT skills and integrated digital images in the curriculum to change ways in which children were able to express their ideas. It also gave the teachers and support staff in the school the opportunities to become learners of ICT with the children. Children were able to present their views about "things that matter" in a medium adults and older children could relate to.

Child Health and Children with Additional Needs

The federal Department of Family and Community Services (FACS) funded a tri-state government group, the Warrki Jarrinjaku Aboriginal Child Rearing Steering Committee, for a project called *Working Together*

Everyone and Listening to study traditional child rearing and parenting practices and improve the well-being, health, and educational outcomes of young Aboriginal children living semitraditional lifestyles (Priest, 2002; Warrki Jarrinjaku Aboriginal Child Rearing & Associated Research Project Team, 2002). This steering committee is comprised solely of Aboriginal women living in the remote desert regions from the Northern Territory and Wirrimanu in Western Australia. Principles of the project reflect the view that Indigenous cultural knowledge is extremely valuable for the health and well-being of children and families (Priest, 2002). Their aim was to collate existing research material and information associated with indigenous child rearing, parenting, and learning. Priorities were to locate materials written or researched by Australian Indigenous people, which contained up-to-date information, focused on central desert communities, and were for children from birth to 5 years. The participatory methodology used was unique and the research will go back to desert communities to be shared, into curriculum to be used, and into national policy initiatives. Such research promotes listening and sharing in respectful ways between Indigenous and non-Indigenous communities.

Governments and health authorities are also concerned about increasing levels of obesity, diabetes, and physical inactivity in children. Commissioned by the South Australian government, a research study by MacDougall et al. (2004) elicited perceptions of 204 children (aged 4 to 12 years) about physical activity, play, sport, exercise, and fitness. The qualitative study combined focus groups, mapping, and photographic techniques to enable children to express ideas using these different techniques. Results indicated that the terms *physical activity* and *exercise* were seen as adult concepts which held little meaning for children. Children strongly identified with *play* as child-owned and saw *sport* as adult-controlled. The research shows that children challenge the views adults hold about them. Nossar (2003) has examined 7 years of data in SA on young children's health finding that obesity of 4-year-old children has increased in the last 5 years by more than 20%. To date, there is no explanation for this alarming phenomenon. Analysis of the data is ongoing.

Children who arrived in Australia as asylum seekers with their families are classified as illegal immigrants. They are held in detention centers with their families until their applications for residency can be processed. This takes years in some cases and the issue of children in detention has become a contentious community issue in Australia. Cologon's (2003) research found that "centres were considered to be inadequate for children and more detrimental than prison" (p. 26). Cologon's research also found numerous breaches of the Convention for the Rights of the Child (to which Australia is a signatory) in Australian detention centers. McInnes (2004) researched the impact of violence on mothers and children's needs during and after parental separation. She found that mothers who fled from violent relationships had continuing concerns about their children's behavior including withdrawal, anxiety, and aggression, and that access to professional help for their children was often inadequate. These recently emerging issues highlight polarities in the life experiences of some groups of children in Australian society.

Workforce Participation and Gender

Another research area looks at teacher characteristics, styles, and preservice preparation for the ECE profession. Russo and Feder (2001) in a preliminary study noted that despite the call for a balanced gender profile most males did not choose early childhood education as their first preference. Males in the program did not report institutional barriers but only 48% of female students considered that both males and females had equal chances of obtaining employment.

Sumsion, Lyons, and Quinn (2003) are currently undertaking the final phase of a project that is investigating the extent, impact, and possible implications of the gender imbalance within the children's services workforce in New South Wales. Funded by the New South Wales Department of Community Services, the study used a quantitative-qualitative design and involved participants from throughout the state. Quantitative data consisted of survey responses from preservice teachers (N = 112), staff in early childhood services (N = 107), and parents/caregivers of children enrolled in early childhood services (N = 140). Qualitative data were generated from telephone interviews with employers of early childhood educators and men employed in early childhood services, as well as focus group discussions with preservice teachers, early childhood educators, and parents/caregivers. The final phase of the study involved an ethnographic case study in a service in which two male early childhood educators were employed. In addition, children attending this service were asked about their perceptions about their male and female teachers. Preliminary analysis of the quantitative data has not detected stereotypical gender attitudes as barriers to increased male participation in the children's services workforce, a finding echoed in early findings emerging from the qualitative data. While this is an encouraging result in terms of recruitment of men, it suggests that the problem could shift to the retention of male staff, given the resilience of the sociocultural construct of the male breadwinner. There is also research into the less visible aspects of the workplace for those who work there. Briggs et al.'s (2003) research on the impact of violence, threat, and intimidation in the lives of professionals whose work involves child protection' exposes the complex web of responsibilities involved in the roles of ECEC professional work in child protection today and the necessity to keep child protection workers safe.

SUMMARY

Research in ECEC in Australia is plentiful but predominantly small scale and piecemeal. It is poorly supported in terms of overall funding compared with other sectors of education, and opportunities for large scale, sustained research are limited. Universities and other research groups/centers in ECEC are trying to establish research concentrations in particular areas but their viability depends on attracting funding. The priority has to be funded research projects and this comes mainly from short-term contract research. ARC grants support large projects in literacy, numeracy, technology, and science, but much needed research topics such as children in detention and child care in crisis are not funded partly because they are politically difficult. ARC-Linkage and industry grants have opened up the funding for new research areas but still do not tackle the really difficult questions. A research agenda is desperately needed to focus research efforts. A clearinghouse for publication would make research outcomes more accessible. A national center for ECEC research could be ideal but would it have the political independence that McDonald (2002) sees as necessary? Is Fleer's conclusion (2002) correct in that ECEC deserves to be publicly funded and on a parity with other education sectors but that research questions in ECEC need to change? The indication is that ECEC is a politically sensitive area and policy and research issues must be discussed and resolved at the national level so that there is a national agenda, a policy framework, and focus for future research in ECEC policy and practice.

REFERENCES

Australian Early Childhood Association. (1990). *Code of ethics*. Canberra, Australian Capital Territory, Australia: Author.

Australian Institute for Health and Welfare. (2001). *Australia's welfare 2001*. Canberra, Australian Capital Territory: Author.

Bernard van Leer Foundation. (1987). *Children at the margin.* The Hague, Netherlands: Author.

Bowes, J., Ungerer, J., Watson, J., Simpson, T., Harrison, L., Sanson, A., & Wise, S. (2003, January). *Parents' reports of use of and reasons for multiple and changeable childcare arrangements.* Paper presented at the 11th Annual Conference of Australian Research in Early Childhood, Monash University, Melbourne, Victoria, Australia.

Brennan, D. (1994). *The politics of Australian child care: Philanthropy to feminism and beyond.* Melbourne, Victoria, Australia: Cambridge University Press.

Brennan, D. (1998). *The politics of Australian child care: Philanthropy to feminism and beyond* (Rev. ed.). Melbourne, Victoria, Australia: Cambridge University Press.

Briggs, F., Broadhurst, D., & Hawkins, R. (2003). *Violence, threats and intimidation in the lives of professionals whose work involves child protection.* Report to the Australian Criminology Research Council. Canberra, Australian Capital Territory, Australia: Australian Criminology Research Council.

Broughton, B., Gahan, D., Henry, M., & McDonell, J. (2003). *Joint attentional sequences in the every day experiences of young children.* Unpublished paper, School of Early Childhood, Queensland Institute of Technology, Brisbane, Queensland.

Child Care Act 1972, 121 Commonwealth of Australia (1972).

Clyde, M. (2000). The development of kindergartens in Australia at the turn of the twentieth century: A response to social pressures and educational influences. In R. Wollons (Ed.), *Kindergarten and cultures: The global diffusion of an idea* (pp. 87-112). New Haven, CT: Yale University Press.

Clyde, M., Parmenter, G., Rodd, J., Rolfe, S., Tinworth, S., & Waniganayake, M. (1994). Childcare from the perspective of parents, caregivers and children: Australian research. *Advances in Early Education and Day Care, 6,* 189-234.

Cologon, K. (2003). Children in detention. *Journal of Australian Research in Early Childhood Education, 10*(1), 23-28.

Commonwealth of Australia. (1974). *Care and education of young children.* Report of the Australian Preschools Committee, November, 1973. Canberra, Australian Capital Territory, Australia: Australian Government Publishing Service.

Commonwealth Task Force on Child Development, Health and Wellbeing. (2003). Consultation paper: Towards the development of a national agenda for early childhood. Retrieved October 15, 2003, from http://www.facs.gov.au/internet/facsinternet.nsf/family/early_childhood.htm

Crawford, H. (2002, March). *Caring for Territory children from the 70's to the new millennium.* Darwin, Northern Territory, Australia: Northern Territory Department of Health and Community Services.

Creswick, P., Fasoli, L., & Hazard, H. (1999). Linking to learn: Developing links in the Northern Territory. *Every Child, 5*(2), 6-7.

Davey, C. M. (1960). *Children and their lawmakers: A social historical survey of the growth and development for 1836-1950 of South Australian laws relating to children.* Adelaide, South Australia, Australia: Griffin.

Denholm, M. (2003, October 30). Child care cap to go. *The Advertiser,* pp. 1-2.

Department of Education, Training and Employment. (2001). *South Australian Curriculum, Standards and Acccountability framework (SACSA).* Adelaide, South

Australia, Australia: Department of Education Training and Employment Publishing.

Diamond, A. (2003). *Toddlers and safety: Mothers' disciplinary strategies and their relationship to child characteristics*. Unpublished masters' thesis, Macquarie University.

Dockett, S., & Perry, B. (2003). Children's views and children's voices in starting school. *Australian Journal of Early Childhood, 28*(1), 12-17.

Dolby, R. (2003, August). On being emotionally available. *Gowrie RAP Reflections*, 4-6.

Dowd, C. (1983). *The Adelaide kindergarten teachers college: A history 1907-1974*. Adelaide, South Australia, Australia: South Australian College of Advanced Education.

Flannery, T. (Ed.). (2000). *Two classic tales of Australian exploration*. Melbourne, Victoria, Australia: Text.

Fleer, M. (2002). Early childhood education: A public right and not a privilege. *Australian Journal of Early Childhood, 27*(2), 1-7.

Grieshaber, S., & Cannella, G. S. (Eds.). (2001*). Embracing identities in early childhood education: Diversity and* possibilities. New York: Teachers College Press.

Griffiths, J. (2003). Child care staff angered at sell off plan. Retrieved August 20, 2003, from http://www.meu.org.au/counsellor/10/child_care.html

Harrison, R. (1985). *Sydney Kindergarten Teacher's College 1897-1981*. Sydney, New South Wales, Australia: Kindergarten Teachers College Graduates Association.

Hill, S., Comber, B., Louden, W., Reid, J., & Rivalland, J. (2002). *100 children turn 10: A longitudinal study of literacy development from the year prior to school to the first four years of school*. Canberra, Australian Capital Territory, Australia: Commonwealth Department of Education, Science and Training.

Hill, S., Yelland, N. J., & Mulhearn, G. (2002). *Children of the new millennium: Young children learning with ICT*. LERN Conference, Bejing, China.

Horin, A. (2003, October 4-5). When making money is child's play. *The Sydney Morning Herald*, p. 39.

Hughes, P., & MacNaughton, G. (2002). Preparing early childhood professionals to work with parents: The challenges of diversity and dissensus. *Australian Journal of Early Childhood, 28*(2), 14-20.

Jackman, C. (2003, August 9-10). Goward attacks baby leave half-truths. *The Weekend Australian*, p. 3.

Jeremy, J. (1996). *Making contact: The story of the Contact Project*. Sydney, NSW, Australia: Contact Incorporated.

Jones, H. (1975). The acceptable crusader: Lillian de Lissa and pre-school education in South Australia. In E. Mellor & S. Murray-Smith (Eds.), *Melbourne studies in education* (pp. 126-153). Melbourne, Victoria, Australia: Melbourne University Press.

Kelly, J. (1988*). Not merely minded: The Sydney Day Nursery & Nursery Schools Association 1905-1945*. Unpublished doctoral thesis, University of Sydney, New South Wales, Australia.

Ker, R. (2003, April 12). It's over and out to an era. *The Advertiser*, p. 3.

Kowalski, H., Wyver, S., Masselos, G., & De Lacey, P. (2004). Toddlers' emerging symbolic play: A first-born advantage. *Early Child Development and Care, 17*(4), 389-400.

MacDougall, C., Schiller, W., & Darbyshire, P. (2004). We have to live in the future: Children's perceptions of space and place. *Early Child Development and Care, 174*(4), 369-387.

MacNaughton, G. (1999). *Early childhood review: Curriculum issues in research and in action.* Discussion paper for consultation. Hobart, Tasmania, Australia: Department of Education Tasmania.

MacNaughton, G. (2003). Eclipsing voice in research with young children. *Australian Journal of Early Childhood, 28*(1), 36-42.

Makin, L., & Spedding, S. (2003). "Cause they trust their parents don't they?" Supporting literacy in the first three years of life. *Journal of Australian Research in Early Childhood Education, 10*(2), 39-48.

Margetts, K. (2003). Does adjustment at preschool predict adjustment in the first year of schooling? *Journal of Australian Research in Early Childhood Education, 10*(2), 13-25.

McCain, M., & Mustard, J. F. (1999). *Early years study: Reversing the real brain drain.* Final report to the government of Ontario, Toronto, Canada.

McDonald, P. (2002). Issues in childcare policy in Australia. *The Australian Economic Review, 35*(2), 197-203.

McInnes, E. (in press). The impact of violence on mothers' and children's needs during and after parental separation. *Early Child Development and Care.*

McLean, S. V., Piscitelli, B., Halliwell, G., & Ashby, G. (1992). Australian early childhood education. In G. Woodill, J. Bernhard, & L. Pochner (Eds.), *International Handbook of Early Childhood Education* (pp. 49-73). New York: Garland Press.

Mellor, E. J. (1990). *Stepping stones: The development of early childhood services in Australia.* Sydney, New South Wales, Australia: Harcourt Brace Jovanovich.

Millward, C. (2003, July). *Growing up in Australia: The Longitudinal Study of Australian Children (LSAC): What are we asking, who are we asking and how?* Paper presented at the Australasian Human Development Association Conference, Auckland, New Zealand.

Milroy, J. (1996). *The art of Sally Morgan.* Ringwood, Victoria, Australia: Viking Penguin.

Ministerial Council on Education, Employment, Training and Youth Affairs. (1998). *National report on schooling in Australia 1998.* Melbourne, Victoria, Australia: The Curriculum Corporation.

Ministerial Council on Education, Employment, Training and Youth Affairs. (2003). *Demand and supply of primary and secondary school teachers in Australia.* Retrieved October 20, 2003, from http://www.curriculum.edu.au/mceetya/public/demand.htm

National Childcare Accreditation Council. (1993). *Quality improvement and accreditation handbook: Putting children first.* Sydney, New South Wales, Australia: Author.

National Childcare Accreditation Council. (2001a). *Quality improvement and accreditation system. Source Book*. Canberra, Australian Capital Territory, Australia: Commonwealth of Australia.

National Childcare Accreditation Council. (2001b). Family day care quality assurance [Handbook]. Sydney, New South Wales, Australia: Author.

National Childcare Accreditation Council. (2003, September). *Putting Children First Newsletter, 7*, 1.

Nott, H. (2003, November 26). Many kids show developmental problems early: Study. *The Age*. Retrieved November 29, 2003, from http://www.theage.com.au/articles/2003/11/26/1069522657713.html

Nossar, V. (2003, October). *Obesity in young children: An emerging problem*. Paper presented at the Children's Week, de Lissa Oration, de Lissa Institute of Early Childhood and Family Studies, University of South Australia, Australia.

Organization for Economic Cooperation and Development. (2001*). Starting strong: Early childhood education and care*. Paris: Author.

Palmer, G., & Ebbeck, M. (1990). *On home ground: The Magill Aboriginal early childhood teacher education programme*. Adelaide, South Australia, Australia: Meranda Media and Associates.

Petriwskyj, A. (2003). Transitions: The early years teacher's role. Conference abstracts Australian *Research in Early Childhood Education* (p. 17). Frankston, Victoria, Australia: Monash University.

Press, P., & Hayes, A. (2000). *OECD thematic review of early childhood education and care policy. Australian background report for the Commonwealth government of Australia*. Canberra, Australian Capital Territory, Australia: Australian Government Printing Service.

Priest, K. (2002). *Working together (No more consultation please)*. Draft conference paper/case study. Cairns, Queensland, Australia.

Prior, M., Sanson, A., Smart, D., & Oberklaid, F. (2000). *Pathways from infancy to adolescence: Australian Temperament Project 1983-2000*. Melbourne, Australia: Australian Institute of Family Studies.

Raban, B. (2000). Just the beginning.... *DETYA Research Fellowship Report No. 1*, Canberra, Australian Capital Territory, Australia: Commonwealth of Australia.

Raban, B. (2003). Early childhood provision. *Directions in Education, 12*(3), 3.

Raban, B., Griffin, P., Coates, H., & Fleer, M. (2002). Profiling preschool literacy: Evidence of indigenous children's capabilities. *Journal of Research in Early Childhood Education, 9*(1), 74-85.

Reynolds, B. (2001). The history of R.I.C.E. 1976-2001. *25 years of the Remote and Isolated Children's Exercise Inc*. Canberra, Australian Capital Territory, Australia: Pirie Printers.

Rolfe, S., Nyland, B., & Morda, R. (2002). Quality in infant care: Observation on joint attention. *Journal of Australian Research in Early Childhood Education, 9*(1), 86-96.

Russo, S., & Feder, T. (2001). A preliminary investigation of barriers faced by male early childhood preservice teachers. *Early Child Development and Care, 170*, 57-75.

Saracho, O. N., & Spodek, B. (2003). Recent trends and innovations in the early childhood education curriculum. *Early Child Development and Care, 173*, 175-183.

Sayers, M. (2003, September). Growing up in Australia. *Putting Children First, 7*, 6-7.

Schiller, J., & Tillett, B. (2004). Using digital images with young children: Challenges of integration. *Early Child Development and Care, 174*(4), 401-414.

Schiller, W. E., & Lewis, G. F. (1996). Australian early childhood teacher education: Developments and concerns. *Journal of Early Childhood Teacher Education, 17*(3), 49-56.

Skouteris, H., & Dissanayade, C. (2003, May). Where does the end of maternity leave ... leave the baby? Investigating factors which facilitate the infant's well being in childcare. *Gowrie RAP Reflections, 11*, 7-8.

Spearritt, P. (1979). Child care and kindergartens in Australia 1890-1975. In P. Langford & P. Sebastian (Eds.), *Early childhood education and care in Australia* (pp. 10-38). Melbourne, Victoria, Australia: Australian International Press and Publications.

Stonehouse, A. (2002). NSW curriculum framework for children's services. The practice of relationships. *Essential provisions for children's services.* Sydney, New South Wales, Australia: NSW Department of Community Services.

Sumsion, J., Lyons, M., & Quinn, A. (2003). *An investigation of the extent, impact and possible implications of the gender imbalance within the children's services workforce in New South Wales, Australia.* Unpublished paper, Office of Child Care, New South Wales, Sydney, Australia.

Taylor, D. (2002). *Quality systems in Australian children's services.* Paper presented at the International Symposium on Accreditation of Early Childhood Education, Seoul, Korea.

Turney, C. (Ed.). (1975). *Sources of the history of Australian education.* Sydney, New South Wales, Australia: Angus and Robertson.

United Nations. (1989). *The Convention for the Rights of the Child.* New York: Author.

Vandell, D. L., & Wolfe, B. (2000). *Child care quality: Does it matter and does it need to be improved?* U.S. Department of Health and Human Services, Washington, DC. Retrieved October 17, 2003, from http://aspe.hhs.gov/hsp/ccquality00

Warrki Jarrinjaku Aboriginal Child Rearing & Associated Research Project Team. (2002). *Warrki Jarrinjaku Jintangkamanu Purananjaku Working together everyone and listening, Aboriginal child rearing and associated research: A review of the literature.* Canberra, Australian Capital Territory, Australia: Department of Family and Community Services.

Waters, J. (2000). *The Lady Gowrie Child Centre: The place, the people, the programs 1939-1999.* North Carlton, Victoria, Australia: Lady Gowrie Child Centre.

Westcott, K., Perry, B., Jones, K., & Dockett, S. (2003). Parents' transition to school. *Journal of Australian Research in Early Childhood Education, 10*, 26-38.

Winter, P. (2003). *Curriculum for babies and toddlers: An evaluation of the first phase (birth-age 3) of the South Australian Curriculum Standards and Accountability Framework in centre-based care.* Unpublished doctoral thesis, University of South Australia.

Wollons, R. (Ed.). (2000). *Kindergarten and cultures: The global diffusion of an idea.* New Haven, CT: Yale University Press.

Wooden, M. (2002). Childcare policy: An introduction and overview. *The Australian Economic Review, 35*(2), 173-179.

Yunupingu, G. (2002). *Legitimacy, governance and Aboriginal tradition.* Paper presented at the Indigenous governance conference, Canberra. Retrieved October 26, 2003, from http://www.reconciliationaustralia.org/textonly/info/publications/governance/speeches.html

CHAPTER 2

CONTEMPORARY EARLY CHILDHOOD EDUCATION AND RESEARCH IN CHINA

Jiaxiong Zhu and X. Christine Wang

Since the establishment of the first kindergarten in China in 1903, responsibility for young children's care and education has steadily been shifting from the home to early childhood facilities. In today's China, childcare and early education are readily available because the government encourages women to work outside the home. Particularly in urban areas, children as young as 1 or 2 years of age spend their whole day in nurseries and kindergartens while their parents work. According to the Chinese Ministry of Education (2002), 45% of children between the ages of 3 and 6, about 23 million, are being cared for and educated in 180,000 early childhood education facilities in the year of 2000. In addition, because of China's "one child" policy, these institutions are serving a major socialization function. As a result, formal early childhood education plays an important role in Chinese society as well as in children's development.

In China, education and care for children between the ages of 3 and 6 are primarily provided in kindergartens,[1] although there are some 1-year or half-year preprimary classrooms in elementary schools serving chil-

International Perspectives on Research in Early Childhood Education, 55–77
Copyright © 2005 by Information Age Publishing

dren the year prior to first grade. Informal early childhood programs such as family child care and mobile schools are also available in some areas of the country. Nurseries, on the other hand, serve children younger than age 3 and are not considered educational institutions or under the supervision of educational authorities. Consequently, this discussion of early childhood education in China will focus on kindergartens and not on nurseries. In this chapter, we provide a brief history of the development of early childhood education as well as a description of the current state of early childhood education in China. We then review and discuss research and policy issues.

A BRIEF HISTORY OF EARLY CHILDHOOD EDUCATION IN CHINA

In the past century, the evolution of early childhood education in China has gone through three major reforms: one in the 1920s and 1930s, one in the 1950s, and one that has been ongoing since the 1980s. Because these changes and reforms are closely aligned with the sociocultural changes that occurred during these periods, they reflect different cultural values.

The Child-Centered Curriculum Reform of the 1920s-1930s

The concept of a *kindergarten* was exported to China from Japan partially because of the latter's military victory over China in 1895. More importantly, the similarity between the Chinese and Japanese cultures, philosophies, and vocabularies made kindergarten fairly easy to transplant. Although Japan itself had borrowed the institution of kindergarten from the West, it transformed kindergarten culture and pedagogy to suit its own modernization in the 1860s (Bai, 2000).

As an imported concept and practice, kindergarten in China at first was heavily modeled after the Japanese version, including its content, methods, equipment, and toys. Then the May Fourth Movement of 1919 brought a significant shift in perspective, to an interest in the child development theories and educational philosophies of such Western educators as Frobel, Montessori, and especially Dewey with his progressive education theory. By the 1920s, the Chinese had achieved "the mature integration of modern theories and Chinese practice in preschool education" (Bail 2000, p. 160).

Influenced by Dewey's ideas, reformers of the kindergarten curriculum in the 1920s and 1930s emphasized a child-centered philosophy and practice. They advocated that the curriculum came directly from the children's lives and experiences and that it included children's natural activities. This era of curriculum reform also stressed teaching that was based on children's psychological development. For example, Heqin Chen (1925), an American-educated leader in early childhood education reform, pointed out that nature and society as a whole should be the core of a curriculum. He also proposed implementing "unit pedagogy" and adopted play as the method of education.

The Soviet Union Model of Curriculum Reform in the 1950s

After the People's Republic of China was established in 1949, the Maoist government set about rectifying, reorganizing, and reforming early childhood education in order to meet the needs of a communist society. Following the model of the Soviet Union's educational system, Chinese early childhood educators abandoned the child-centered philosophy and adopted teacher-centered theories and practices. Early childhood programs specified unified content and schedules, and required that teachers systematically teach the children different content subjects. At that time, the curriculum in kindergartens included physical education, language, science, drawing, handwork, music, and arithmetic. The scientific and logical character of each content subject was stressed. The curriculum also emphasized a teacher-centered pedagogy and advised that teachers instruct children in purposeful and planned activities.

China's kindergarten curriculum reform during this period was supported by psychological and educational theory developed in the Soviet Union. Despite the fact that the reform rejected existing theories and practice, the transition to subject-based education was smooth. This can be partially explained by the compatibility between traditional Chinese educational philosophy and a subject-based model of education, which emphasized learning outcomes, defined goals, and pedagogy, and could be performed systematically. In addition, the success of the reform was due to the centralized administration and planned economy in China, which allowed the government to utilize its limited resources to implement the new educational reform throughout the country rather efficiently. Due to scarce educational resources and an insufficient number of teachers, this type of curriculum offered some advantages in improving the quality of early childhood education.

However, during the Great Cultural Revolution (1966-1976), Chinese schools including kindergartens became a target for the revolutionaries because it was believed that education perpetuated traditional beliefs and values, and these needed to be destroyed. Many kindergartens were forced to shut down during this 10-year period of chaos. When the Great

Cultural Revolution finally ended in 1976, the government began to restore early childhood education following the model that had prevailed in the 1950s.

Early Childhood Curriculum Reform from the 1980s to Date

The two early childhood education reforms discussed so far were marked by adopting ideas and practices from the West and from the former Soviet Union, respectively. However, due to the societal and political changes that have been rapidly taking place in China for the past generation, it is difficult to ascertain the origin of the influence and the direction of the current curriculum reform.

In the early 1980s, China initiated efforts that were intended to transition the country to a market economy and open-door policy. These have greatly modified the traditional concepts of education. In the past 20 years different educational theories such as those of Dewey, Montessori, Bronfenbrenner, and Bruner, as well as those of Piaget and Vygotsky, have been introduced or reintroduced to China. These ideas have challenged the early childhood education system that existed for more than 30 years. The kindergarten curriculum reform began with spontaneous experiments in different parts of the country, gradually expanded from a single subject to the whole curriculum, progressed from city to village, and actively propelled kindergarten curriculum reform on a large scale (Zhu, 2002a).

The most influential mandate behind this reform was the issuance of the *Regulations on Work in Kindergartens* by the State Educational Committee in 1989. This publication reflects the doctrine that was adopted nationally for educational development: to be in tune with the political plans for the country's modernization, its future, and its place in the world. It not only stipulates the essential administrative requirements for kindergartens but also, in a special chapter, details ideological principles, goals, and requirements, for the kindergarten curriculum.

The document was immediately and widely disseminated throughout the country, and reform was implemented at all levels of administration and in all kindergartens. The new ideology of kindergarten education was based on these five assertions (Wang & Mao, 1996):

1.   The role of kindergarten education in promoting the development of young children is to be emphasized while its role in serving working mothers is to be deemphasized.
2.   Reasonable integration in organizing the curriculum contents in different domains is to be advocated in order to overcome the shortcomings of the traditional subject-based model.

3. The kindergarten child is to be viewed less as a passive recipient of knowledge and more as an active learner, while the teacher's role is to be changed from that of a deliverer of knowledge and skills to that of a facilitator and enhancer of children's activities, initiatives, and creativity.

4. The value of the child as an individual is to be gradually accepted, while the collective interest of the group is to remain a high priority. More attention than before is to be given to individual differences among children and to organizing activities in various forms, especially in small groups or individually instead of the whole class, as was done before.

5. A harmonious and democratic relationship is to be established between teacher and child.

The regulations adopted theories and practices from different cultures and presented progressive ideas and practices to early childhood educators in China. However, it has been difficult for practitioners to fully embrace this progressive ideology so long as powerful and deep-rooted cultural traditions run counter to modern scientific and democratic ideas (Wang & Mao, 1996). For example, the traditional values of obeying authorities and upholding unity are counterproductive to the goal of establishing a unique and democratic relationship between a teacher and each individual child. In addition, the lack of practical guidelines left many teachers not knowing how to implement the regulations. To solve these issues, the Ministry of Education issued the *Guidance for Kindergarten Education* (trial version) in 2001. The *Guidance* takes into consideration the gap between progressive ideas and reality and offers compromising solutions by stating specific requirements and content in different domains.

The reform movement is ongoing. The curriculum approaches are becoming more diverse and aligned with the increasingly open and diversified society. Different curricula such as the Project Approach, Reggio Emilia, and Montessori have been widely adopted and localized (Li & Li, 2003). As a result, many new curricula have been developed. For example, the Integrated Theme-Based Curriculum in Shanghai represents a localized progressive early childhood education approach (Zhu, 2002b).

A Hybrid of Traditional, Communist, and Western Culture

Based on the brief history of early childhood education in China, we see that three distinct cultural threads—traditional culture, communist culture, and Western culture—have mixed to profoundly shape Chinese people's lives as well as different aspects of Chinese early childhood education (Wang & Spodek, 2000). Thus, contemporary early childhood education in China can be seen as reflecting a hybrid of these three cultural threads.

The influence of this hybrid on early childhood education has been selective, dynamic, and changing. First, each of the three cultural threads has shaped different aspects of early childhood education. While the influence of the communist culture is evident in practical aspects of kindergarten education, such as organization, administration, and curricular goals and content, traditional culture has had a profound influence on the ideological and philosophical bases of kindergarten, including views of the young child, views of learning and development, and views of appropriate teacher-child relationships.

The pattern of influence has also changed over time. In the post-Mao era, Western culture has emerged as an important cultural source and has exerted an increasingly powerful influence. The progressive ideology toward children, educational values, and the curriculum has been a strong force in early childhood education reform in recent years. Meanwhile, the communist culture's control over early childhood education has been waning.

In addition, within each cultural thread, different aspects have been selectively emphasized and de-emphasized over the years. For example, since the 1980s, traditional culture has changed from emphasizing the absolute authority of parents and teachers to valuing mutual respect and understanding between children and parents and between parents and teachers. The communist culture's goal of fostering respect and affection for the Party has evolved to the cultivation of a sense of nationalism and national pride.

THE CURRENT STATE OF EARLY CHILDHOOD EDUCATION IN CHINA

As discussed above, contemporary early childhood education in China reflects the hybrid of three cultural threads: traditional, communist, and Western. In this section, we focus on specific aspects of early childhood education including different types of programs, the general state of kindergartens, administrative institutions, kindergarten budgets and finance issues, policy and legislation, as well as teacher education.

Three Types of Early Childhood Programs

In China, children are enrolled in elementary school at age 6. Prior to that, there are three types of early childhood programs serving children younger than age 6: nurseries, kindergarten, and preprimary classes.

Nurseries serve children between 2 months and 3 years of age. Because physical care and nurturing are the fundamental goals, the caregivers are trained as "nurses" rather than teachers. As stated earlier, nurseries are not considered educational institutions and they are not under the supervision of educational authorities.

Kindergartens as full-day programs serve children from age 3 to age 6. The children are generally grouped by age. Government regulations in 1981 recommended three groupings: junior (3-year-olds), middle (4-year-olds) and senior (5-year-olds) (Cleverley, 1985). In contrast to nurseries, education is the primary focus in kindergartens. Class size increases with age, ranging from 20 to 40 children. Each group typically has two teachers and a nurse. Some large and affluent centers also have one or more doctors on the staff to care for sick or injured children. They also provide other health-related services, such as performing health screenings, giving immunizations, and planning nutritious meals (Vaughan, 1993).

To meet the needs of parents who work special shifts, a small number of boarding kindergartens have been formed. These children stay in the boarding kindergarten 5 days a week and go home only on weekends or holidays. Usually boarding kindergartens have richer resources and higher quality teachers and staff than regular kindergartens do.

An alternative type of early childhood program is the preprimary class, which is actually part of an elementary school. It is typically a half-day program serving children the year prior to first grade. Comparable to kindergartens, these classes usually place greater emphasis on academics and use teaching methods similar to those in the Chinese elementary classrooms (Vaughan, 1993).

THE GENERAL STATE OF KINDERGARTENS

Kindergartens are sponsored by local educational authorities, the Women's Union, businesses, and communities. In 2000 there were 175,836 kindergartens with more than 1,144,000 staff members in China, including teachers, directors, and nurses (Chinese Ministry of Education, 2002). More than 22,440,000 children were enrolled. About 21% of the kindergartens were in urban areas; the rest were in counties, towns, and rural communities. The number of private kindergartens has been increasing in recent years.

Although a kindergarten class typically has two teachers and an aide, some, especially rural kindergartens, may have only one teacher per class with no aide. A class generally consists of 25 3- and 4-year-old children, or 30 4- and 5-year-old children, or 35 5- and 6-year-old children. However, in rural areas there usually are more children in any one class.

Table 2.1.   An Example of a Full-Day Kindergarten Schedule

Time span	Activity
7:30-8:00	Entrance, health checkup
8:00-9:00	Free play and morning exercises
9:00-9:20	Wash and snack
9:30-9:50	Learning activity
10:00-10:30	Outside activity
10:30-11:00	Learning activity or free play
11:00-12:00	Lunch
12:00-14:30	Walk/nap
14:30-15:00	Wash/snack
15:00-15:30	Learning activity
15:30	Free play and leaving

Class schedules vary from one kindergarten to another. The majority of kindergartens are full-day programs. The children are brought to the kindergarten early in the morning and after a health checkup they may engage in different activities such as morning exercises, play, games, and learning activities. An example of one kindergarten's timetable appears in Table 2.1. A few kindergartens are half-day programs. Approximately 5 to 10% of kindergartens are boarding kindergartens, to where children are brought on Monday morning and picked up on Friday afternoon.

Administrative Institutions of Early Childhood Education

The Ministry of Education is in charge of kindergartens, and the Ministry of Health supervises nurseries and their personnel. However, in some areas, nurseries are administered together with the kindergartens and in this situation come under the supervision of educational authorities.

A variety of sources operate kindergarten programs—the government, government-licensed private individuals, government-licensed neighborhood committees, and work units. Work units are government-operated comprehensive communities where workers and their families work and reside, such as those organized around a college or factory.

Policy and Legislation of Early Childhood Education

The Chinese government has increased its legislation efforts in early childhood care and education. In 1990, the government signed *The World Declaration on the Survival, Protection and Development of Children* and *The*

Implementation of the World Declaration Action Plan on the Survival, Protection and Development of Children at the World Heads Conference of Children's Problems. The Chinese Government also signed the United Nations' *Children's Rights Convention*. With the global goals proposed at the World Head conference in mind as well as its current social situation, China promulgated in 1992 *The Program Outline for Children's Development in the 1990's*. It was the first time the government had ever proposed a national action plan that focused on children. In 1996 the State Educational Committee issued *The Regulations for Kindergartens*, which, in emphasizing the whole development of children, accentuated the close relationship between the care and the education of children. It underscored the fact that the goal of early childhood education was to promote children's development.

Through the efforts of multiple levels of government and their relevant departments, the goals that had been set for the 1990s were mostly achieved by the end of the decade. It indicated great progress in early childhood education.

Recently another important piece of legislation was passed and is being implemented: *The Program Outline for Children's Development in the 21st Century*. Its stated goals for developing early childhood care and education are as follows: "in large- or medium-sized cities or in relatively developed areas, children under 3 years of age should receive 3 years of kindergarten education. In rural areas, enrollment in 1-year-long pre-primary classes should steadily increase." This program is built on the principles that children are the nation's priority, that provision must be made for children's survival and development, and that children have the right to be protected and to participate in proper learning activities. It is proposed that children's living conditions should be improved and that special support should be provided to those children who live in difficult situations. In other words, the objective of this legislation is to enhance the quality of children's lives and facilitate their healthy psychological development. Ultimately, the target is for children's health to reach the most advanced level of developed countries.

Budgets and Finance for Early Childhood Education

According to data from the Ministry of Education, the total budget for early childhood programs in China increased from 522 million RMB in 1991 to 2,912 million in 1996. The proportion of the budget for early childhood education to the total educational budget rose from 0.7% to 1.3% in that 5-year period. In 2000, on average, the government allocated 128 RMB to each child. This amount is still small compared to that of developed countries, but it is steadily increasing.

In 1989 the Ministry of Education issued the *Administrative Regulations for Kindergartens*. This act stipulates that different levels of government have the right to run nurseries, not only the state government. At the same time it encourages and supports enterprises and administrative departments, nonprofit organizations, village committees, and individuals that wish to handle or contribute to a kindergarten budget. These guidelines and policies have changed the venerable practice that all financial support for nurseries and kindergartens come from the state government. Now a new pattern has formed such that government, groups and individuals invest together and support early childhood education in China. Thus, funds earmarked for educational development are increasing annually.

Early Childhood Teacher Education

Before the 1980s, kindergarten teachers typically graduated from early childhood normal schools, from the early childhood program in normal schools, or from vocational high schools. These 3-year schools for training kindergarten teachers recruited students who had successfully completed junior high school.

Since the beginning of the 1980s, however, many early childhood programs in teachers' colleges or universities as well as the early childhood normal schools began to recruit students who had finished senior high school. These programs required between 2 and 4 years of additional study, and their graduates were placed into kindergartens.

In recent years, more effort has been put into improving the quality of early childhood teachers. Many 2-year programs in normal schools now offer advanced courses for which students can receive credits that can be applied toward college certification. Early childhood programs in many 4-year colleges and universities have been expanded or have become academic departments or institutes. Some programs have merged with local normal schools and established themselves as independent early childhood institutes.

The expansion of early childhood teacher training institutions provides opportunities for diverse and flexible teacher training programs. The preservice education component together with the student teaching component still constitutes the majority of teacher certification programs. Other programs might offer in-service training, distance education, a series of workshops for in-service teachers' professional development, and alternative teacher certification programs for noneducation majors.

These variations notwithstanding, the curriculum for early childhood teacher education generally includes the foundations of education, psychology, and child development; method courses in different subject areas, and a practicum with student teaching.

As a result, the quality of the average kindergarten teacher has greatly improved. According to statistics from 2000, there were a total of 946,448 kindergarten directors and teachers. Among them, 12% graduated from 2-year or 4-year colleges or universities, 45% from normal schools, and 16% from vocational schools, which are the equivalent of a 2-year college. The other 27% of kindergarten instructors graduated from either senior high schools (about 17%) or junior high schools (about 10%) (China Education and Research Network, http://www.edu.cn). According to the *Teachers Law* that was passed in 1993, certified kindergarten teachers must have at least a 2-year college education in early childhood education. In relatively developed areas, the requirements for teacher's qualifications are higher. For example, in Shanghai kindergarten teachers must have 4-year college degrees.

REVIEW OF
EARLY CHILDHOOD EDUCATION RELATED RESEARCH

Early Childhood Research Infrastructure in China

In order to review early childhood educational research, we present the research infrastructure in China first, including research funding, researcher training, research organizations, and information dissemination and exchange.

Research Funding

Funding mostly comes from the government. The National Educational Research Plan Committee (NERPC) is in charge of allocating central government research funding. Local governments also provide research funding. Certain affluent and more developed areas such as Beijing and Shanghai support large-scale projects like the Experimental Study of the Beijing Kindergarten Curriculum launched in 1998 (Shi, 2000) and the Integrated Theme-Based Curriculum Reform in Shanghai (Zhu, 2002b). In addition, sometimes an international funding agency such as UNICEF will support projects in rural and remote areas (e.g., Liang, 1993). Since the market-economy force came to the education sector, some private foundations and associations have also provided support for small-scale projects.

Researcher Training

Graduate training in early childhood education has been making great progress in recent years. Early childhood education programs have been expanded nationwide. Notably, the three leading early childhood education programs in Beijing Normal University, Eastern China Normal University, and Nanjing Normal University have all grown into academic departments or research institutes. In 1998 the first doctoral program in early childhood education was approved in Nanjing Normal University, and currently all three of these universities offer PhD degrees. The total number of current graduate students in both master's and doctoral programs in these three programs is about 200. All three but especially Eastern China Normal University have made efforts to send their students overseas in order to learn from other countries (Zhu, 2001). This type of exchange helps improve the quality of their own graduate programs.

Research Organizations

The leading research organization is the Chinese Early Childhood Educational Research Association (CECERA). Founded in 1979, it was originally named "The Young Children's Education Research Association." In 1986, it became a member of OMEP (Organization Mondiale pour l'Education Préscolaire) and has played an important role in helping the government make policy decisions concerning early childhood education. CECERA has five divisions focusing on different aspects of early childhood education: (1) institutional early childhood education, (2) family education and community outreach, (3) kindergarten personnel and management, (4) play, and (5) health and physical development. These divisions organize research forums on different topics every year. The association also facilitates research projects such as "Developing Suitable Early Childhood Education in China and Improving Young Children's Education" (Shi, 2000), and sponsors research journals.

Information Dissemination and Exchange

There are several channels in China for disseminating and exchanging early childhood research findings. The leading journal is the *Early Childhood Educational Research*, sponsored by CECERA, which publishes bimonthly and covers a wide range of research and practice issues. Other influential journals include *Young Children's Education* in Zhejiang, *Early Education* in Jiangsu, *Preschool Education* in Beijing, and *Shanghai Early Care and Education* in Shanghai.

Local governments, universities, or associations host national or regional conferences and occasionally an international conference focusing on early childhood development and education. However, there is no regular annual conference devoted to early childhood education.

As discussed above, the early childhood research infrastructure in China is in place. There are basic venues and means of support for early childhood research. However, there are some weaknesses to this infrastructure. First, most funding is provided for a few large-scale survey projects, which means there are insufficient funding resources for beginning researchers or for small-scale but in-depth studies. Second, vigorous evaluation of the quality of graduate programs is absent. Although the number of doctoral students is increasing, the dearth of quality control does not guarantee that graduates move into the workforce with the requisite training. Third, regularly scheduled research conferences are not available for educators to disseminate their latest research. Finally, not all of the journals have strenuous peer-review process. As a result, quality in published articles is not guaranteed. The majority of the articles found in these journals are viewpoints rather than empirical studies. This is partially because most research findings are published in books instead of in journals (H. Li, personal communication, November 3, 2003), yet the lengthy process involved in publishing a book constrains the dissemination among the research communities.

Major Research in the Past Two Decades

Although early childhood education in China has gone through a century-long course of development, early childhood research has a relatively short history as a consequence of the disruption engendered by the Cultural Revolution. In this section, we sum up some major research directions and projects in three periods beginning with the 1980s.

Early childhood research recovering: 1980-1985. During the Cultural Revolution, education in general and early childhood education in particular were destroyed. Consequently, the major task in this period was to reestablish early childhood education programs and teacher training programs. Research focused on collecting baseline data on young children's physical and psychological development. Two important survey studies were carried out. One examined the language development of young children between the ages of 3 and 6 (Shi, 1990), and the other one studied young children's physical development and education. Both projects were conducted by the Central Educational Research Institute. The survey results provided bases for later curriculum reform. Another project that examined young children's diet and nutrition in four selected cities (Hao, 1984) provided important information to help parents and educators improve children's health. Some small-scale projects included a survey study of children's observation skills and their creativity, and a study of children's personality and social skills.

A final noteworthy project in this period is the historical study titled "Early Childhood Education: Historical Lessons Since 1949" which in 1982 concluded the following: early childhood education must match the socioeconomic reality of China; educating children based on their age group is efficient; leadership is crucial; and early childhood research is needed to provide bases for education.

Steady progress in early childhood research: 1985-1990.   There were three research foci in this period. The first was a large-scale survey aimed at understanding young children's learning and development both inside and outside of school, identifying factors that facilitate or hinder children's learning and development, and providing bases for curriculum reform. The project sampled a total of 25,680 children in 88 cities, 70 small towns and 2,500 villages from 10 provinces. Data on the children's development as well as their educational environment at home and school were collected. This project was important in that it drew the public's attention to informal early childhood development, especially parenting practices. Based on the results of the survey, a follow-up study was conducted in six provinces in order to improve early children programs and provide support for parent involvement (Fang, 1997; Shi, 1991, 1997; Xiang & Liao, 1995).

The second direction was to focus on improving early childhood education in rural and remote areas. The early childhood program in Nanjing Normal University conducted a 3-year experiment to explore the efficiency of early childhood programs in rural areas. Their findings were published in a document titled "Curriculum for Pre-primary Class" (Nanjing Normal University, 1993). Other projects that explored the status of early childhood education in rural areas focused on utilizing the local resources to provide kindergarten-centered early care and education (e.g., Fang, 1997) or explored diverse channels and resources to provide at least 1-year education for young children (Tang, 1997).

The third category of projects was curriculum-related research. For example, Beijing Educational Research Institute and the local Early Childhood Normal School conducted a study on the effects of toys and playing material on children's cognitive development. Based on their results, suggestions for arranging toys and playing materials for different age groups in classrooms were provided to kindergartens and nurseries nationwide. Another project conducted by the Central Educational Research Institute explored young children's understanding and learning about nature and provided guidance for science education.

Rapid development in early childhood research: 1990–present.   Since the beginning of the 1990s, early childhood research has made great progress. The number of projects funded by NERPC has increased from zero in the early 1980s to nine in its current 5-year term. As summarized by Shi (2000), the research context in early childhood has extended from early childhood facilities to home, from cities to rural areas, and from child development to teacher education. The research foci have expanded to cover children's development and learning as a whole. The research methods have expanded from mainly survey studies to including experimental studies. Descriptions of the reported findings have changed from stressing a qualitative interpretation to expressing a combination of qualitative and quantitative results. Researchers are no longer limited to being college faculty or research scientists; some teachers also conduct research. There are more young researchers than ever before (p. 74).

A prominent direction in current research is the focus on local context and cultural background. More and more research projects rivet on how to improve early childhood care and education within the local contexts. The Integrated Theme-Based Curriculum Reform in Shanghai represents such an effort and has considerable influence at the national level. This new curriculum was built on these assumptions: (1) children's development as well as a sociocultural influence are the foundation for a curriculum; (2) it is crucial to balance child-initiated and teacher-initiated activities; (3) it is efficient to integrate content from different subject areas; (4) formative and process-oriented assessment provide an accurate evaluation of children's progress; and (5) the curriculum should be flexible and leave room for teachers to improvise as may be appropriate (Zhu, 2002b).

Some classroom teachers have become actively involved in research to solve problems and issues in their practice. For example, teachers at the October 1st Kindergarten in Tianjing compared their curriculum in their two programs (full-day and boarding programs) so as to improve their practice in both programs. Teachers explored a multicultural curriculum in Song QingLian Kindergarten in Shanghai.

RESEARCH AND POLICY ISSUES

Although great progress has been made in early childhood education in the past 2 decades, there are still many issues and problems facing educators, researchers, and policymakers in China. In the following section, we examine six important policy and research issues: the one-child policy and early childhood education, the formation of integrated birth-to-age 6 care and education, early childhood education in rural or remote areas, cultural changes and their effects on early childhood education, appropriation and localization of borrowed ideas and practices, and teacher education and curriculum reform.

The One-Child Policy and Early Childhood Education

To control its population growth, the government in 1979 enacted the one-child policy into law, which exerts severe social and economic penalties on couples who wish to have large families. In urban areas, where the one-child policy is strictly enforced, a second child may be denied medical and educational services, parents are likely to face a fine that is equivalent to 10 years' wages, and both husband and wife may even lose their jobs (Strom, Strom, & Xie, 1995). Enforcement is likely to be less strict in rural and remote areas where labors are important for agricultural activities, but nevertheless the one-child policy has effectively controlled population growth. According to the fifth national census conducted in 2000, the population growth rate was only 1.07% in the past decade.

The one-child policy is creating far-reaching cultural changes as it forces compliance with government mandates that are counter to traditional values (Freeman, 1998). A survey indicated that 75% of the urban couples would prefer to have two children rather than the state-mandated single child (Strom, Strom, & Xie, 1995). Many parents express their concerns that their only children are lonely and are missing out on valuable opportunities for social interaction (Deane, 1992; Tobin, Wu, & Davidson, 1989). These concerns were reflected in the "4-2-1 syndrome"—four doting grandparents, two overindulgent parents, all investing their hopes and ambitions on "an emerging generation of spoiled, lazy, selfish, self-centered and overweight children" (Deane, 1992, p. 216).

These issues create new challenges for early childhood educators. To counteract the spoiling effects of indulgent parents and grandparents has become an unwritten mission for kindergartens. Teachers often feel compelled to provide opportunities for children to learn how to get along with their peers. However, there is often not enough enforcement when children go home. The discrepancy between school and home makes the mission difficult.

The one-child policy has, however, also affected early childhood in a positive way. It has strengthened the emphasis on education for young children and the families' strong involvement and investment in their only child. Teachers report that parents are not only very interested in their child's school success, but also willing to challenge teachers if they feel their child has been treated unfairly or too harshly. Challenging teachers is a departure from the traditional teacher-parent relationship that values respect and trust for teachers and leads to more dynamic parent involvement. However, parenting and parent involvement has not received enough attention from early childhood researchers. In examining three leading early childhood journals—*Early Childhood Educational Research*, *Preschool Education*, and *Young Children's Education* in the past 3 years (2000-

2002)—we found that less than 5% of the published articles were devoted to parenting and parent involvement. *Preschool Education* was the only one that had set up a column called "Home and Kindergarten Working Together." The scarcity of research on parent involvement reflects the reality that early childhood educators mostly focus on classrooms instead of the broader social environment in which young children live.

Forming Integrated Birth-to-Age 6 Care and Education

In recent years, there has been an increasing effort to integrate nurseries and kindergartens and form continuous care and education for children from birth to age 6. Historically, nurseries and kindergartens are separated and overseen by the Ministry of Health and the Ministry of Education, respectively. Nurseries focus on health and care, and their personnel are trained as "nurses" instead of educators. With the increasing consensus on the importance of education for infants and toddlers, the educational administration is gradually taking over the responsibility of managing nurseries. The state advocates the establishment of a development index system to help parents and caregivers to "improve scientific care and education for young children" (Zhu, 2002a). More and more kindergartens have begun to enroll children as young as 2 or 3 years old. Some kindergartens even help nurseries to improve their educational services to young children and their families.

To achieve a unified care and education for children from birth to 6, the government established an ambitious goal for a system which is planned as a whole by government leaders, administered by state educational departments, and coordinated by other related departments; and which relies on the community and involves parents and various educational institutes. However, there are many barriers to these integration efforts. Two main issues are the separate administration and the lack of resources. The community, parents, and the administration at different levels will need to work together to achieve this goal. This integration effort, however, also provides new challenges for early childhood researchers. The long-time focus on kindergarten children from ages 3 to 6 results in a scarcity of studies of younger children's development and care. The early childhood community needs to take on the challenge and devote more resources and effort to exploring models for the successful care and education of children from birth to 3 years of age.

Early Childhood Education in Rural and Remote Areas

China has a vast territory, many minority groups, and a wide range of economic development levels. Historically, rural and remote areas have lagged behind in their educational resources and educational quality. Since the enactment of the market economy and open-door policy in the early 1980s, the gap between these areas and developed areas has been widening. While the cities and towns along the east coast are enjoying the rapid spread of modern conveniences, some areas in the west and southwest are still dealing with hunger. In recent years, the government has been pushing for a Western-style, forward-looking economic reform aiming to jump-start economic development in these areas.

Early childhood education in backward areas has also received great attention. Due to the limited resources in these areas, the state and local governments concentrate on establishing preprimary classes in local elementary schools. Built on the existing elementary education infrastructure, preprimary classes are set up to provide full-day or half-day early education program for children the year prior to first grade. This approach greatly expands much-needed early education in rural or remote areas. However, because the programs are put in elementary schools, the pedagogy and curriculum are often simply a lighter version of first grade. Although it helps prepare young children for elementary education, the practices of elementary education—long class sessions, rigid discipline requirements—are often risky for young children's development. These areas are in urgent need of teacher training, pedagogy, and curriculum that are tailored to preprimary classes. More research is needed to continue the curriculum reform research in rural areas that was initiated in the early 1990s and summarized above.

Recent Sociocultural Changes and Their Effects on Early Childhood Education

The rapid development in the economy and technology, as well as increasing integration into the world, have caused tremendous sociocultural changes in China. These changes demand that educational ideology match the future of modernization and globalization. In the process of changing its educational ideology, China faces many fundamental issues concerning early childhood education such as whether the curriculum should be driven by academic pursuit or based on children's development, whether the activities should be teacher-centered or student-centered, whether the curriculum should be organized based on subject areas or integrated knowledge from different domains, and whether teachers should focus on education outcomes or education process. Some of these issues are hardly unique to China. They have been an on-going debate in early childhood education in many nations. The most recent early childhood education reform in China also centered on these issues. Still, it will take years for Chinese researchers and teachers to find the proper solutions to these issues.

Another significant change is that the force of the market economy comes to play in early childhood education. In recent years, kindergarten's funding from local government has been shrinking, especially those affiliated to a work-unit that is tied to state-owned manufacturers. These kindergartens primarily serve the children of employees at the work units, and their budgets mostly come from the work units. However, many manufacturers are struggling with enormous budget difficulties or going out of business due to poor management and the shrinking of state subsidies. As a result, those kindergartens are thrown into the chaos of the market and have to rely on tuition to cover expenses. The transition from a service-oriented educational agency to a for-profit identity imposes great constraints on the quality of the kindergarten, producing such changes as larger class sizes and lower teacher-student ratios. To make matters worse, the lower birth control rate decreases the number of children eligible for kindergarten. According to statistics from the Ministry of Education, from 1996 to 2001 the total number of children in kindergartens decreased by 6.9 million. The decrease is even more acute in rural areas. Consequently, fierce competition for higher enrollment causes kindergartens to create many kinds of specialty classes (e.g., English, dancing, drawing) and offer rigid academic training classes to attract parents while ignoring a curriculum that would be appropriate for children. While some public and work-unit-affiliated kindergartens are shrinking or closing, more and more for-profit private kindergartens are emerging. Many private kindergartens charge high tuition and play the market economy to their advantage. There is a lack of legislation for supervising these private kindergartens. In addition, there is no unified certification and evaluation of private kindergartens. To overcome these problems, the central government and the local community need to work with researchers to control and improve the quality of kindergartens.

Appropriation and Localization of Borrowed Early Childhood Models

In recent years, many curriculum models and pedagogy have been introduced to China such as the Project Approach (Katz & Chard, 1999), the Montessori curriculum, Reggio Emilia, High/Scope, and the Whole Language Approach, to name just a few. Many kindergartens have tried to imitate these models, but many have failed. How to appropriate and localize borrowed ideas and practices to make them suitable to China is at the core of the curriculum reform debate (Li & Li, 2003).

Li's (2002) analysis of implanting the borrowed curriculum in Hong Kong also applies to such efforts in China. Li summarized six factors that limit the success of implanting these successful programs: the teacher-student ratio, the quality of the teacher, resources, parents' expectations, the educational system, and the sociocultural environment. Some of the above-mentioned successful programs, such as Project Approach and Reggio Emilia, require considerable educational resources to support the children's wide range of exploration and discovery. The need for a low teacher-student ratio and the limited resources in Chinese kindergartens impose constraints in implementing these programs. Many Chinese parents' high expectations and demands on academic achievement also challenge these student-centered and child development-based curricula. Finally, the values of unity, collectiveness, and a subject-based curriculum model that are traditional in Chinese culture run counter to these curricula that are built on a culture of individualism. It is important to look into the culturally embedded nature of these successful curricula (Hatano & Inagaki, 1998) and identify these cultural factors in the process of appropriating and localizing any borrowed curriculum.

Teachers' Education and the Curriculum Reform

It is acknowledged that teacher training is crucial to the success of curriculum reform. The current reform aims to modify curricula to be diversified and flexible to suit local and individual programs' needs. However, many directors and many teachers of kindergartens who are used to the traditional subject-based curriculum and teacher-centered pedagogy have great difficulties in implementing the new curriculum and pedagogies.

There are some fundamental problems in teacher training. First, students in early childhood education have relatively low academic credentials. Although new programs require 2-year or 4-year college degrees, many in-service teachers have only the equivalent of a secondary education. Low academic training hinder teachers' understanding and adopting of the new curriculum and pedagogies. Second, too much emphasis still tends to be placed on skills rather than on pedagogy in many early childhood teacher programs. Traditionally, students in early childhood normal schools spend most of their time improving or perfecting their art skills—drawing, singing, and dancing, which are deemed important characteristics for successful kindergarten teachers. Much less attention and less effort were put into pedagogy training. Although more and more programs are correcting this eschewed focus, the residual of the traditional view still affects teacher training. Third, there is too little classroom practice in teacher training, especially in 4-year university programs. For example, some universities require only 8 to 10 weeks of student teaching in their 4-year programs. A lack of experience in the classroom ill-prepares these future teachers. In addition, many faculty members in early childhood teacher programs do not have solid teaching experience in kindergarten. This greatly limits their ability to help their students to apply theories to their teaching practice. Finally, there is a severe lack of programs for training teachers for rural areas, which usually have a low quality of teacher to begin with due to low pay and a harsh environment. The lack of support and professional development only causes an already distressing situation to deteriorate. All of these problems need to be dealt with urgently in order to improve the quality of teachers and eventually to improve early childhood education in China.

In conclusion, early childhood education in China has gone through a century-long development process and has made great progress. It plays an important role in Chinese society and in children's development. Contemporary early childhood education is becoming diverse in its forms, funding sources, and educational approaches, and is aligning itself with the increasingly open and diversified society. It is clear that early childhood education in China is strongly influenced by sociocultural changes and conditions and reflects the hybrid of traditional, communist and Western cultures.

Regarding early childhood educational research, the infrastructure is in place; however, some weaknesses in professional organization, funding, conferences, and publications still constrain the development and dissemination of research. Some major studies in the last 2 decades have helped improve the quality of education for young children, especially in rural and remote areas. Despite this progress in early childhood education, there are still many issues to be solved, as we examined above. Some of these issues are unique to China, for example, the mandated one-child policy and its societal consequence and influences on children's development. Others are more common, such as the appropriation and localization of borrowed ideas and practices. As the world grows closer, China will continue learning from other countries while, at the same time, contributing its unique experience to the early childhood education community.

NOTE

1. The term *kindergarten* in China refers to full-day programs serving children from ages 3 to 6.

REFERENCES

Bai, L. (2000). The Chinese kindergarten movement, 1903-1927. In R. Wollons (Ed.), *Kindergartens and cultures: The global diffusion of an idea* (pp. 137-165). New Haven, CT: Yale University Press.

Chen, H. (1925). *Studies of young children's psychology* (in Chinese). Shanghai: Business Affair Press.

Chinese Ministry of Education. (2002). *National early childhood education bulletin (1990-2000)*. Retrieved January 15, 2004, from China Education and Research Network Web site: http://www.edu.cn/20020326/3023507.shtml

Cleverley, J. (1985). *The schooling of China*. Sydney, Australia: Allen & Unwin.

Deane, D. (1992, July 26). The little emperors. *Los Angeles Times Magazine*, pp. 17-22.

Fang, M. (1997). *Home and kindergarten work together to improve young children's education* (in Chinese). Beijing: Science Education Press.

Freeman, N. K. (1998). Look to the east to gain a new perspective: Understand cultural differences, appreciate cultural diversity. *Early Childhood Education Journal, 26*(2), 79-82.

Hao, X. (1984). *Preschooler's diet and nutrition* (in Chinese). Beijing: Educational Research Press.

Hatano, G., & Inagaki, K. (1998). Cultural contexts of schooling revisited: A review of The Learning Gap from a cultural psychology perspective. In S. G. Paris & H. M. Wellman (Eds.), *Global prospects for education: Development, culture, and schooling* (pp. 79-104). Washington, DC: American Psychological Association.

Katz, L. G., & Chard, S. C. (1999). *Engaging children's minds: The project approach* (2nd ed.). Stamford, CT: Ablex.

Li, H. (2002). Reforming the early childhood curriculum in Hong Kong (in Chinese). *Hong Kong Journal of Early Childhood, 1*(1), 44-49.

Li, H., & Li, P. (2003). *Lessons from implanting Reggio Emilia and Montessori curriculum in China* (in Chinese). *Early Childhood Education, 9*, 4-5.

Liang, Z. (Ed.). (1993). *Developing early childhood education in Chinese communities* (in Chinese). Beijing: Beijing Normal University Press.

Nanjing Normal University. (1993). *Curriculum for pre-primary classes* (in Chinese). Beijing: Educational Sciences Press.

Shi, H. (1990). *Preschool education reform and research* (in Chinese). Beijing: Educational Sciences Press.

Shi, H. (Ed.). (1991). *On the quality of early childhood program* (in Chinese). Beijing: Educational Sciences Press.

Shi, H. (Ed.). (1997). *To lay a foundation for young children's development* (in Chinese). Beijing: Educational Sciences Press.

Shi, H. (2000). *A brief 50-year history of early children in new China* (in Chinese). Beijing: Chinese Early Childhood Educational Research Association.

Strom, R. D., Strom, S. K., & Xie, Q. (1995). The small family in China. *International Journal of Early Childhood, 27*(2), 37-45.

Tang, S. (1997). *Developing multiple forms of early care and education to meet different needs* (in Chinese). Beijing: Popular Science.

Tobin, J., Wu, D., & Davidson, D. (1989). *Preschool in three cultures: Japan, China, and the United States*. New Haven, CT: Yale University Press.

Vaughan, J. (1993). *Early childhood education in China*. Retrieved January 15, 2004 from http://www.pbs.org/kcts/preciouschildren/earlyed/read_vaughan.html

Wang, J., & Mao, S. (1996). Culture and the kindergarten curriculum in the People's Repulic of China. *Early Child Development and Care, 123*, 143-156.

Wang, X. C., & Spodek, B. (2000, November). *Early childhood education in China: A hybrid of traditional, communist, and western culture*. Paper presented at the annual meeting of the National Association for the Education of Young Children, Atlanta, GA.

Xiang, Z., & Liao, Y. (1995). *Evaluation of early childhood programs in six provinces* (in Chinese). Beijing: Educational Research Press.

Zhu, J. (2001, June). *Introduction and reflection on staff training in Chin*. Paper presented at the International Conference on Teacher Education, Shanghai, China.

Zhu, J. (2002a, December). *Early childhood care and education in P. R. China*. Paper presented at 2002 KEDI-UNESCO Bangkok Joint Seminar and Study Tour on Early Childhood Care and Education. Seoul, Korea.

Zhu, J. (2002b, September). *Early childhood curriculum reform in Shanghai kindergartens: Case studies*. Keynote address at the OMEP/ICEC Asia Pacific Early Childhood Conference, Singapore.

CHAPTER 3

HOW FINLAND IS RESEARCHING EARLY CHILDHOOD EDUCATION

Mikko Ojala

AN ORIENTATION TO FINNISH EARLY CHILDHOOD EDUCATION

Compulsory education in Finland starts at age 7. Comprehensive school education (primary and lower secondary) takes 9 years (from age 7 to 16). After this, children can continue to upper secondary or vocational schools, which normally takes 3 years to complete. Higher education in Finland is provided by universities and polytechnics. Most degree programs in universities take 4-5 years to complete, at polytechnics 1 year less.

Early childhood education covers the years from birth to 6 years of age. During these years parents with young children receive both family support as well as extra-parental educational services in public day care either at day care centers (about 65%) or family day care homes (about 35%). Day care service is operating under social authorities. Quite recently (in 2000) all Finnish children received an opportunity to participate in a 1-year-long education at preschools provided either by social authorities at

International Perspectives on Research in Early Childhood Education, 79–117
Copyright © 2005 by Information Age Publishing
All rights of reproduction in any form reserved.

day care centers or by school authorities at elementary schools. At the moment more than 90% of all 6-year-old children take part in preschool education, most of them at day care centers.

Most of the educators working at day care centers are kindergarten teachers. Nowadays, all kindergarten teachers receive their training at universities in close collaboration with other teacher educators. The study program takes 3 years and results in a bachelor level diploma. The study program for primary school teachers is 1 year longer with master level examination.

The kindergarten teacher is usually works at a day care centre as a main educator responsible for her/his own group. The kindergarten teacher can even work with children under 3. However, most of the teachers will work with 3- to 6-year-old children. The average group size for children under 3 is 12-16 and for older children 20-21. Each kindergarten teacher has an assistant coworker in their group, who is responsible for care and daily routine activities. Because public day care service is offered in most cases as a full-time service, each child group has two kindergarten teachers daily. One is usually works from early morning until noon and the other from noon until 5 p.m. A typical day care center has about 60 children.

AIMS FOR THIS CHAPTER

This chapter has the following structure. First, I will briefly orientate readers to the terminology and context of Finnish early childhood education. After this the historical background and developmental trends are outlined. I describe the main ideas and key persons who have been responsible for developing the kindergarten movement in Finland from the middle of nineteenth century to the beginning of 1970s.

Following the historical description, I will more closely describe and analyze the current state of Finnish early childhood education. An important turning point for modern Finnish day care service has been the year 1973. In this year the government accepted the Act on Children's Day-Care. In 1980 the Finnish government accepted educational goals for day care. A more comprehensive description of pedagogical ideas and methods for day care centers, preschools (educating 6-year-old children), and core curriculum for comprehensive schools are also presented. Moreover, current teacher education for kindergarten teachers in Finland will briefly be described.

The main goal of this chapter is to analyze and describe research activities related to early childhood education. As an introduction, research strategies and policy issues are outlined. Thereafter, a more detailed analysis of research areas/themes is made. The following themes are discussed: cross-cultural comparison, leadership and expertise, children in connection with modern information and communication technology (ICT), language immersion, intervention of learning problems, historical research, and developmental activities for preschool education and transition to school.

Finally, I will evaluate and make conclusion about Finnish early childhood education and research activities by using national as well as cross-national perspectives.

HISTORICAL DEVELOPMENT OF EARLY CHILDHOOD EDUCATION

Early childhood education in Finland has had a long history (Ojala, 1985, 1989; Ojala & Kuikka, 1992). Even though the British infant school movement created by Robert Owen was reflected in Finland in the early and the middle of the 19th century, the historical roots of early childhood education are strongly based on Friedrich Froebel's ideas about the education of young children in kindergartens.

In the beginning, two roots can be recognized (Ojala, 1985, 1989, 1993a; Ojala & Kuikka, 1992). The founder of Finnish public education, Uno Cygnaeus, first became interested in Froebelian ideas for the education of young children. While developing ideas for organizing public education in Finland during the mid-nineteenth century he visited Germany. The Froebelian kindergartens that he saw there had such a strong influence on him that in 1863 he established the first crèche (for Cygnaeus under 4-year-olds) and kindergarten (for Cygnaeus 4 to 10 years of age) at the beginning of his time at the teacher training college in Finland located in Jyväskylä.

Cygneus wanted to integrate physical and mental education into the education for the children in the crèche. On the physical side, gross and fine motor activities associated with games and songs as well as using Froebelian gifts (play materials) were important. Educating the mind was spiritual in many ways, with the aim of distinguishing between children's right and wrong innate behaviors. In addition, Cygnaeus wanted to exercise the children's senses. Religious stories with pictures, concrete teaching, and the observation of natural events were used as educational methods with the goal of developing children's mental growth. Kindergarten, for 4- to 7-year-olds, was to be active. Educational activities were organized into groups of increasing difficulty and types of activities (active and quiet). The maximum period was 30 minutes for a single activity. Education for older children (8-10-year-olds) resembled school in many ways. Subjects taught were religion, grammar, writing, reading, mathematics, and voice.

After Cygnaeus' death (1888) his ideas about public education progressed and we have named him the father of Finnish comprehensive schools. However, his ideas about kindergarten being integrated into the public school did not come to fruition.

After Cygnaeus, two women, Hanna Rothman and Elisabeth Alander, had a powerful influence in developing the ideology and pedagogical practice for Finnish early childhood education; their impact can still be seen in many ways. Like Cygnaeus, Rothman and Alander had personal experience with Froebelian kindergartens in Germany during the late nineteenth century. In the establishment of the first Finnish kindergarten in Helsinki in 1888. Rothman's and Alander's pedagogical thought contained two crucial elements. On the one hand, they considered the social view of early childhood education to be important. According to this view, kindergartens should take special responsibility for working families and children living in poverty and poor economic and housing conditions. Based on this background they also saw the kindergarten and the Froebelian pedagogy as an important tool for preparing children and their families for school and society.

In their view of Finnish kindergartens, Rothman and Alander wanted to establish public kindergartens. Even though Cygnaeus and his female successors admired the Froebelian kindergartens, the Finnish pioneers created a unique educational ideology. In training female kindergarten teachers, the main idea for Rothman and Alander was to offer theoretical and practical skills for motherhood (Sillanpää, 1994). In contrast, Cygnaeus' thinking was more comprehensive and connected to public school education and curriculum. The two women considered the social political aspects of education to be very important. This view was not present in Cygnaeus' thought. When considering the religious education, the three early pioneers agreed that religion and spiritual education should be present and integrated into children's daily activities. Concerning the development and application of the Froebelian pedagogy, the two women were more active and achieved more than Cygnaeus.

These two female pioneers created an enduring pedagogical philosophy based on Froebelian influences for Finnish kindergartens (Hänninen & Valli, 1986; Ojala, 1993a). The central idea was to educate children toward an integrated unity of life. In this unity, nature, man, and the spiritual aspects of life (God) would be in harmony. In order to develop the whole personality of the child the pedagogical program was meant to activate the children's heart, reasoning and mental/spiritual life. In kindergarten the children learned and had concrete experience of the environment (e.g. home, kindergarten, market), nature (e.g. animals, birds, flowers, berries, fruits, plants, gardens, water, light, winter, spring) and work life (shoemaker, clocksmith, tailor, chimney cleaner). The main pedagogical methods were playing, learning, and working.

Kindergarten activities coincided with central themes that changed monthly (Hänninen & Valli, 1986; Ojala, 1993a). With the help of the central theme, the kindergarten teacher helped children to experience and understand how the thoughts and ideas that they learned were related to each other and how they could form a unity. The idea of central themes has continued to be an important pedagogical concern in day care centers and in the first 2 years of primary school. The development of the pedagogical methods used in kindergartens was important during the initial start of public kindergartens. A variety of pedagogical activities based on a central educational theme were used (Hänninen & Valli, 1986; Ojala, 1993a).

The following are some of those themes: free play, games, movement exercises, outdoor activities, many types of handicrafts, field trips, musical activities (music, playing, and singing), listening to stories and looking at pictures, and household activities (working in the garden and kitchen).

Daily activities in kindergartens were planned carefully according to a time schedule (Hänninen & Valli, 1986). A central part in the daily activity was a guided activity which lasted about 1 and a half hours. At the beginning of the guided activity the teacher would usually discuss previous learning experiences from the guided activities with the children. After that, the teacher would present and demonstrate a new learning task (e.g., block building with Froebel's gifts) allowing the children to practice the target activity. In addition to guided activities, the children had opportunities for free activities. The daily program also included whole group activities (usually singing and playing), a lunch time and times for short breaks (e.g., outdoor activities). The main content and schedule of the daily activities used in public kindergartens is in many ways present even today in Finnish day care centers.

The first kindergartens were built for children between the ages of 3 and 7. At the beginning of the nineteenth century, kindergartens began to organize separate activities for children under 3. Unlike kindergartens, crèches could not receive state aid until the enactment of the Act on Children's Day Care in 1973 (Ojala & Kuikka, 1992).

During the early decades of the 1900s, some important new aspects emerged in the Finnish kindergarten movement (Ojala, 1993a; Ojala & Kuikka, 1992). Special education and care for young children started in the 1920s, when hospitals began to arrange educational activities for young children based on those used in kindergartens. Since the beginning of the twentieth century kindergartens started to organize separate activities for children between the ages of 6 and 7 as a transition for children 1 year before the start of school. The kindergartens wanted to develop children's skills in language (speech and writing) and mathematics. In the1920s kindergartens started also to organize morning or afternoon activities for school-aged children (between the ages of 7 and 14).

In the early development of early childhood education we can also recognize services organized outside the kindergartens (see Hänninen & Valli, 1986; Ojala, 1993a). Public playgrounds (outdoor) began in the 1910s. This special service was planned for children, not younger than 4 year olds, operating 4 to 5 hours per day including a free meal. Activities included free and guided play, field trips, swimming, celebrations, and so forth. Another type of childhood service that started in the 1940s was the day club. This service was intended for children between the ages of 4 and 7 who were cared for at home. These part-time educational activities offered, three to five times each a week, lasted about 3 hours. The church (mainly Lutheran) has been an important provider of this type of service.

During the early decades of the twentieth century the kindergarten movement and the training of kindergarten teachers rose to have increasing social and pedagogical influence on Finnish educational policy (Ojala, 1989; Ojala & Kuikka, 1992). Most kindergartens were public and offered either half-day (4 to 6 hours) or full-day programs (7 to 8 hours) for children aged 3 to 7. The maximum number of children per group was 25. However, in connection with kindergarten activities for children under the age of 3, activities for school-aged children (7- to 14-year-olds) could be organized as well. In cities the usual enrollment in a kindergarten was from 75 to 100 children (with a minimum of 50 children). In the countryside and in sparsely populated areas the minimum might only be 15 children. Since the beginning of the twentieth century the costs of running both public and private kindergartens were subsidized by the state. The kindergartens were at first under the authority of school, but since 1924 they have been under the authority of social welfare. Presently most kindergartens, since 1973 called day care centers, are governed by social welfare authorities. However, based on local decision by the administrative organization they can also be placed under the educational authorities.

CURRENT STATE OF FINNISH EARLY CHILDHOOD EDUCATION AND ITS CONNECTION TO SCHOOL EDUCATION

Reorganizing Children's Day Care

A new period in Finnish early childhood education started in 1973 when the Act on Children's Day Care came into force (see Ojala, 1989, 1993a; Ministry of Social Affairs and Health, 2000). According to this act the local authorities are obligated to organize day care for children under school age. Day care is provided either in day care centers or in the form of family day care. Day care in Finland usually operates as a full-time educational and care service for working families. The need for full-time service is based on the fact that about 75% of women with small children are working outside the home, most employed full-time (Ojala, 1993b).

By the end of the twentieth century all Finnish parents of children under school age had the right to day care provided by the local authorities. If the child is under 3 years of age the parents have an unconditional right to municipal day care or to receive a child home care allowance in order to care for their children at home. Based on their choice, the parents can also receive a private child-care allowance in order to place their children in private care.

At the end of the twentieth century about 22% of children under 3 years of age and 54% of children 3-6 years old were in municipal day care (see Table 3.1). About 66% of these children were in municipal day care centers, and about 34% in family day care homes (see Figure 3.1). For all Finnish children up to the age of 6, about 50% percent were in municipal day care.

Educational Goals for Day Care

At the beginning, the children's day care act operated without any specification of educational aims. This situation changed in 1980 when the committee report on the planning of educational goals for children's day care was published (Komiteamietintö, 1980, p. 31). In 1983 these

Table 3.1.   Finnish Children in Muncipal Daycare in 1999

Type of Care	Percent (approximately)
Day care center	65
Family day care	35
Total	100
Under 3-year-old children	20
3- to 6-year-old children	80
Total	100
Full-time care	85
Part-time care	15
Total	100

Source: Ministry of Social Affairs and Health (2000).

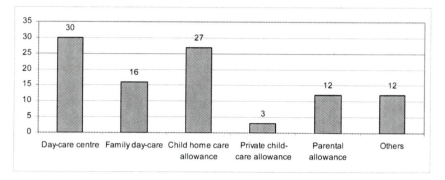

Figure 3.1.   Daycare in Finland for children under the age of 1 in 2000 presented in percentages (Source: Ministry of Social Affaires and Health, 2000).

educational goals were integrated into the children's day care act. According to these general educational goals, a children's day care should:

- Support the families of children in day care in their responsibility for educating children, and together with the family, promote the balanced development of the child's personality.
- Provide ongoing, safe and warm human relationships for children including activities supporting the children's total development and a favorable growth environment.
- Support the child's physical, social, and emotional development and the child's aesthetic, intellectual, ethical, and religious growth (while respecting the parents' convictions), according to the needs and age of the child and considering the general cultural tradition.
- Support the children's growth toward responsibility, peace, and concern for their environment.

Based on general goals, specific subgoals were defined for children's physical, social, emotional, intellectual, aesthetic, ethical, and maturation during their day care years (Ojala & Kuikka, 1992). The recommended pedagogical activities are basic care situations, games, small working tasks, crafts, small teaching periods, contact with the environment, celebrations, and excursions.

The priority of parents as primary educators for their children is emphasized as a basic educational philosophy at day care. In order to do this, education at day care has an obligation to plan and implement in line with child's upbringing at home.

Day Care Pedagogy

The Children's Day Care Act in 1973 and the educational goals for day care set in 1980 did not directly influence the practice. The Froebelian-oriented tradition that had developed in Finnish kindergartens was a dominant idea in day care centers during the 70s and 80s. An important pedagogical tool for integrating children's learning and experiences was based on the "old" idea of central themes. In 1975, when the Ministry of Social Affairs published the pedagogical booklet for day care, the idea of central themes was expressed by differentiating 12 central themes for autumn activities and 14 themes for spring (Iloiset toimintatuokiot, 1975). These thematic units had titles such as "Our daycare centre," "Autumn," "Traffic connections," "I—You—We," and "Children in other countries" and were presented with pedagogical explanations. The idea of organizing small adult-guided activities during the day was also present. Based on these recommendations, it was common for teachers to organize two to three small teaching periods in the context of the central theme each lasting 20-30 minutes during a day.

Because of increasing research and international influences, day care pedagogy has also developed and new ideas are emerging. Among other things, the dominant role of planned central themes with teacher-centred teaching periods was criticized (e.g. Lounassalo, 1977; Niiranen & Kinos, 2001). One criticism was that central themes did not focus enough on educational areas such as language, movement, art and music, or nature and environment. The criticism culminated in the conclusion that such pedagogical activities are solely based on adult-oriented thinking and knowledge.

As an illustration of how a typical Finnish day care center would organize activities for older children (3- to 6-year-olds), we can take one observational study from 1988. In this study Niikko found that about 60% (6 hours) of daily activities was connected to routine activities like eating, cleaning, resting, and playing outdoors (the latter was usually for two periods in a day). The amount of free play was about 25% (2½ hours). The proportion of guided activities with small teaching periods was about 10% (1 hour).

The pedagogical climate in the 1990s concerning early childhood education has moved toward child-centred pedagogy (e.g. Hytönen, 1992, 2002; Niiranen & Kinos, 2001). There has been a tendency to reduce pre-planned daily activities and to increase child-initiated activities. Such international influences as active learning, the Reggio Emilia movement and project learning have supported these changes (Ojala, 1993a). A new and still increasing focus has been on analyzing the connection between day care and the start of schooling in comprehensive schools (e.g. Brotherus, Hytönen, & Krokfors, 2002; Hytönen & Krokfors, 2002; Ojala 2002a; Ojala & Siekkinen, 1998). The topics for discussion have included self-evaluation, portfolio assessment (Kankaanranta, 1998), quality (Hujala-Huttunen & Tauriainen, 1995; Tauriainen, 2000), and evaluation with cross-cultural perspectives (e.g Hujala-Huttunen, 1996; Keskinen & Sato, 1997; Ojala, 2000). Some of these topics will be discussed in greater detail later.

Preschool Education for 6-Year-Old Children

To understand the educational context of Finnish early childhood education we need to understand the recent preschool reform (e.g. Early childhood education and care policy in Finland, 2000). Children start school at the age of 7 and spend 9 years in comprehensive schools (from the ages of 7-16). According to the legislation preschool education in Finland is instruction provided for 6-year-old children for the year before they start their compulsory education at school. Since the years 2001-2002, according to this government decision, all 6-year-old children must have had access to free-of-charge preschool instruction of 700 hours per year. The service can be organized either in day care centers or in connection with primary schools. After preschool hours the children have the right to use day care services if needed. However, this service is not usually free of charge. The local authorities are obligated to provide preschool education for children in Finnish, Swedish, Sami (spoken usually in Lapland), Romany (gipsy) or sign (for the deaf) languages based on the parents' decision. Authorities are also required to compensate for the travel expenses of transporting a child from home to the preschool setting.

An important pedagogical tool for the new Finnish preschool education for 6-year-old children is the core curriculum established in 2000 (Core Curriculum for Pre-school Education in Finland, 2000). The following general objectives are important in the core curriculum:

- to promote favorable growth, development, and learning opportunities for children;
- to support and monitor children's physical, psychological, social, cognitive, and emotional development and to prevent any difficulties that may arise;
- to strengthen a healthy sense of self-esteem with the aid of positive learning experiences and to provide opportunities for diverse interaction with other children and adults;

- to take into account the special needs of girls and boys;
- to guarantee equal opportunities for children to learn and to start school;
- to strengthen children's positive self-concept and their ability to learn skills;
- to learn the basic skills and knowledge of different areas of learning;
- to learn to understand the significance of a peer group in learning;
- to learn the joy and enthusiasm of learning and to face new learning challenges with courage and creativity;
- to learn how to reflect on what is right and wrong;
- to strengthen and develop children's linguistic and cultural identity and their ability to express themselves;
- to promote children's interest in nature and an idea of their own independence and responsibility for both nature and the man-made environment.

In implementing preschool education the core curriculum points out that knowledge cannot be directly transferred to children through teaching. Instead, children should themselves generate new ideas on the basis of their own previous knowledge and experience. More generally, the concept adopted into the learning process stresses the importance of a child-centred approach in which children should be active learners and adults are simply guides. To support the children's learning process and to guide children toward becoming conscious about their own learning process is important in everyday practice. Learning should also be based on playful and imaginative activities including drama, fairy tales, and stories. By using these types of activities, the preschool experience should also promote children's linguistic development.

An important pedagogical principle of the core curriculum is integration. Connected to this, it is important to recognize that the need for integrated teaching and learning has had a long tradition in Finnish early childhood education. As already described in the historical part of this chapter, the central theme was an important core element in the first kindergartens. It was an important curriculum tool when the school curriculum was implemented for Grades 1 and 2 in comprehensive schools at the beginning of the twenty-first century (Ojala, 2002a). According to the core curriculum, the integrated preschool education is to be based on themes related to the children's sphere of life in the community as well as to curriculum content which expands and analyzes the children's view of the world. The selection and specification of integrated themes should be negotiated with the children. Taking into account different branches of knowledge, the processing of experiences, interactions between adults and children, and a diverse use of working methods is important when working with themes.

Even as the importance of theme learning is recognized, the subjects for learning and teaching are also specified in the core curriculum. The core subjects are:

- Language and interaction;
- Mathematics;
- Ethics and philosophy;
- Environmental and natural studies;
- Health;
- Physical and motor development; and
- Art and culture.

The nature and procedures for assessment in preschool education are briefly documented in the core curriculum (Core Curriculum for Pre-school Education in Finland, 2000). There are two strategies. On the one hand, assessment is based on the achievement of the core subject objectives. On the other hand, the assessment should be based on the individual growth objectives set in the children's educational plans made for each child. Assessment is carried out on a continuous basis within the interaction and discussion between the teacher and the children in the regular learning processes. Important to assessment is that teachers promote the children's capability of self-assessment by supporting the development of the children's self-concepts and the analysis of their own learning. In general, more emphasis in assessment is toward the progress of growth and learning than the achievement of objectives.

There are still important elements to be recognized in the implementation of the new preschool curriculum (Core Curriculum for Pre-school Education in Finland, 2000). The importance of cooperation with parents is stressed in order to guarantee children's satisfaction, growth, and learning in the preschool year. A new suggestion is that the educational plan be made in cooperation with parents either on an individual or group basis. In this plan the factors essential to individual development such as the objectives for the child's growth and development and the assessment of the child's strengths and weaknesses are identified. Children in need of special support are then also identified in core curriculum. Other special preschool groups are children within extended compulsory education or those whose basic education has been decided to start 1 year later.

Based on the guidelines in the national core curriculum for preschools each preschool must prepare a detailed curriculum in order to organize provisions based on local circumstances and profiles.

Early Childhood Teacher Education

The education of early childhood teachers in Finland has had a long history. The first training course for kindergarten teachers was organized in Helsinki by Elisabeth Alander and Hanna Rothman in 1886 (Hänninen & Valli, 1986). In 1888 the length of training was changed from 1 year to 2. A longer period of college level training further developed in 1973 when experimental training started in connection with teacher training. At the beginning of the 1980s the training time was changed from 2 years to 3 both in colleges as well as in universities. In 1995 the college level of training ended and since then the kindergarten teacher training has been only available in universities. Nowadays the kindergarten teacher diploma is a bachelor level examination. More and more kindergarten teachers are continuing their studies toward the master level examination in educational science with an emphasis on early childhood education. In some universities most students will continue their studies for master level. An increasing number of researchers and kindergarten teachers interested in early childhood education are presently participating in doctoral studies.

Core Curriculum for Comprehensive Schools

After establishing the core curriculum for preschool education, the National Board of Education started to construct new curriculum aims and content for comprehensive schools. Today, the new core curriculum is in wide experimental use (*Perusopetuksen opetuskokeiluissa lukuvuonna 2003-2004 noudatettavat opetussuunnitelman perusteet vuosiluokille 3-9 ja peruso-petuksen opetussuunnitelman perusteet vuosiluokille* 1-2, 2002). From the view of early childhood education these two core curricula are important tools for connecting learning and teaching between preschool year (6-year-old children) and the first 2 years of comprehensive school (7-8-year-old children). The primary idea is to build a holistic and logical continuity between the preschool and the early school years called initial education. The continuity is based on a shared conception of learning. A demand for integrated teaching and continuity between curriculum subjects are important. The integration of the teaching in Grades 1 and 2 (7-8-year-old children) can happen by using units or themes which integrate several curriculum subjects. In order to help teachers in this task the core curriculum describes the following eight units in relation to objectives and content:

- To mature as a human
- Cultural identity and internationalism

- Skills in communication and the media
- Participatory citizenship
- Responsibility for the environment, well-being and ongoing development
- Safety and traffic
- People and technology

In the curriculum, the subjects during the first 2 years (7- to 8-year-old children) in comprehensive school are:

- Language (Mother tongue)
- Mathematics
- Knowledge of environment and nature
- Religion/ethics
- Music
- Art
- Craft
- Movement

From these subjects, the objectives for language and mathematics are expressed in more detail. The importance of these two subjects can be recognized in evaluation. The curriculum includes detailed criteria for evaluating what children have learned at the end of the second school year, but only in language and mathematics. Self-evaluation has an important role. The purpose of self-evaluation is to support children's growth in self-awareness and to develop study skills. In self-evaluation children are supposed to learn the following skills: to be conscious of goals, to learn skills in goal specification, to reflect on and control their own learning processes, to state goals for his/her working and cooperation with others, and to identify his/her own progress. Like in the preschool year (6-year-old children) the teachers are strongly encouraged to develop an individual learning plan for each student. In the school years (7- to 16-year-old children) this plan is more detailed and students take more responsibility in the development of the plan.

RESEARCH AND POLICY ISSUES RELATED TO EARLY CHILDHOOD EDUCATION

Before the Children's Day Care Act in 1973 research in early childhood education was only based on individual research interest (Husa & Kinos,

2001; Ojala, 1989, 1994). During this time not much research was done. A pedagogical orientation was present only in one dissertation in which the author analyzed how young children should be educated in connection with public education (Salo, 1939). The idea behind this chapter was to specify the pedagogical ideas for kindergartens and the early years in primary school as had been presented by Cynaeus, the Finnish father of comprehensive schools, in the early decades of the twentieth century. A few other studies were more sociological. In one study the social life in a kindergarten was analyzed (Päivänsalo, 1952) and in other (Helanko, 1958) theoretical aspects of play and socialization were studied.

A new orientation and more active period emerged in research when the Children's Day Care Act was established in 1973 (Ojala, 1994). Following some international examples like Bloom and Bronfenbrenner the possibilities of children's day care offering extra-parental education were seen as a new desired tool for stimulating children's development and learning before they enter school. Within this orientation also the interaction between family, preschool, and school was realized as crucial. Research policy was based on an enthusiastic day care ideology. The Ministry of Social Affairs also gave economic resources and support to researchers to develop the rapidly increasing day care service. The research approach was interventional. A common strategy was to compare samples of children cared for at home with children cared for in day care centers or preschool classes (e.g. Kiviluoto & Parkkinen, 1976; Ruoppila & Korkiakangas, 1995). Different types of day care services were included in studies such as family day care or day care services in sparsely populated areas (e.g. Ojala, Lius, & Pänttönen, 1981). According to Ojala (1994) the research paradigm used was based on stimulus-outcome connections without paying attention to mediated processes. An important impetus for the increase of research activity since the middle of the 1970s was the establishment of the first university professor in early childhood education at the University of Joensuu.

During the 1980s research in the field expanded. The central focus was to develop day care in the context of family and society. The research framework was associated with Bronfenbrenner's ecological model became increasingly popular. By using this model the interaction between home and day care was studied with the aim of activating parents' role in day care education (e.g. Huttunen, 1988). An interest in planning and implementing action studies can be noted (e.g., Huttunen, 1988; Niikko, 1988). A more society-oriented critical orientation within the research on day care can be recognized at the end of the 1980s (e.g. Lahikainen & Strandell, 1988). In this orientation, the organization and practices of the day care are analyzed in the contexts of childhood and societal development. Based on these influences in the 1990s, some experimentation was done in order to change some existing practices radically (e.g. Rusanen, 1995).

The social demand and obligations to develop children's day care along with increasing academic interest, forced a more comprehensive plan for research in early childhood education in Finland. This happened during the transition from the 1980s to the 1990s, and began when the Ministry of Social Affairs published a program for the development of research in children's day care and early childhood education in 1989 (*Varhaislapsuuden ja –kasvatuksen tutkimustoimikunnan mietintö*, 1989). For the reorganization of research, three major themes were presented:

- Childhood and the role of children in society;
- The activity and interaction of children; and
- Condition for children's individual development.

In 1992 the Finnish Academy, the major governmental organization for funding basic and applied research in universities, published a comprehensive program for research in early childhood education (*Lapsitutkimuksen tutkimusohjelma*, 1992). In this program early childhood education was viewed as closely linked to research on childhood and children with less emphasis on the pedagogical and educational aspects. This can be seen when looking at the four main research themes presented in the program:

- Childhood as a societal and cultural phenomena
- The everyday life of children
- Early childhood and interaction
- Quality of life of children

The influence of this research program has been powerful in Finland during the 1990s. Just after publishing the program, the Finnish Academy began funding 16 medium size research projects. The majority of which had either a psychological or medical orientation. The rest had sociological, sociopolitical (two projects), linguistic (two projects), or educational (two projects) orientations. In these educational projects, early reading and writing and the gender dilemma of children cared for in day care were studied. The small number of funded studies in education was a disappointment to researchers in early childhood education because psychological and medical research has had a leading position for quite a long time.

However, the amount and intensity of research in early childhood education during the 1990s has progressed in many ways. During this time all major universities have appointed professors with an orientation toward early childhood education. Among these professors, the major orientation has been either education science or psychology with an emphasis on developmental psychology (Husa & Kinos, 2001). At one university, the professor's orientation has a clear connection to sociology with an emphasis on childhood (University of Jyväskylä). The profile of the professors at another university is closely connected to the pedagogical aspect (curriculum and instruction) in early childhood education and beginning schooling (University of Helsinki).

During the 1990s research had a tendency to focus more on contextual and process variables with less emphasis on outcomes. An important aspect has also been that during recent years we can identity the training programs for researchers with an orientation in early childhood education. Some of these programs are shared among several universities. In order to coordinate their research activities and to organize doctoral studies with an early childhood education orientation, some major universities have established research centers (e.g., Universities in Helsinki, Jyväskylä, and Oulu). In other universities the aim is to find some elements for profiling the research.

CURRENT RESEARCH RELATED TO EARLY CHILDHOOD EDUCATION

Cross-Cultural Comparison

During the 1990s there has been an increasing interest among Finnish researchers in comparing early childhood education cross-culturally. By using a sociopsychological approach, the well-being of children in Estonia and Finland have been compared (e.g., Lahikainen et al., 1999; Lahikainen & Kraav, 2000, 2001). A special focus in these studies has been 5- to 6-year-old children's self-reported fears. In a more comprehensive study children's welfare has been compared in several cultures (Alanen & Mayall, 2001). A basic idea in this still ongoing macro-societal study is to analyze the resources for well-being and how subjective and objective welfare is constructed when children are seen as a specific generational group. A cross-cultural perspective has been present when studying the leadership of education centers in Finland, Australia, the United Kingdom, Russia, and the United States (Hujala & Puroila, 1998). The day care experiences of children and families have been compared among Finland, the United States, and Russia by Hujala-Huttunen (1996). Children's toy preferences have been compared between Finland and Estonia (Keskinen & Leppiman, 1997). In addition, Keskinen and Sato (1997) have studied the gender identity, satiability and constancy of 4-year-old children in Finland and Japan.

The most intensive cross-cultural comparison with focus on the early years of education has been conducted within the IEA (the International Association for the Evaluation of Educational Achievement) Preprimary Project (e.g. Ojala, 1993b, 1999, 2000, 2002b). In this follow-up study, the nature, quality, and effects of children's experiences was studied targeting children between 4 and 7 years old in Africa, Asia, Europe, and the United States. Among European countries a special interest has been taken in the comparison between Finland and Belgium (Siekkinen, 1999) as well as Finland and Ireland (Ojala, 2000, 2002b).When 4- to 5-year-old childern's daily activities were compared between Finnish day care centers and Belgian preschools the amount of activities connected to preacademics, art/music, and discussion were about two times higher in Belgium than in Finland. However, the amount of media-related activities (e.g., listening and watching television or video, looking at various picture books or pictures), helping activities (e.g., helping adults), and activities connected to personal care and sports were higher in Finnish settings.

Based on the context-process-development/learning approach several findings are available when comparing Irish preschools to Finnish day care centers. When studying teacher expectations for 4- to 5-year-old children's development and learning, Ojala (2000) found that two characteristics of Finnish early childhood education were the importance of social skills with peers and skills of self-sufficiency (see Table 3.2). In the observation of children's activities a special focus in Finland has been on child-initiated activities (Ojala, 2002b). One example of this is a rather high level of children's daily physical activities which develop cross- and fine motor skills. In addition, Finnish children are often able to participate in free activities (see Table 3.3). A characteristic of the social context of this environment was that children work much of the day in small groups (two to six children), alone, and with another child. The Finnish focus on certain areas of expectations and set activities can have some effect on developmental and learning outcomes in which a possible strength is in social skills.

Children Under 3

In recent years research targeted toward children under 3 has increased. An important focus in this research has been on children cared for in day care environments. To observe behavior, Lindahl has used video to collect different kind of data associated with small children (1-year-olds) cared for in toddler groups of day care centers primarily in

Table 3.2. Percentage of Teachers who Rated each Area of Development among the Three Most Important Ones (ranks in parentheses)

Country	N	Language Skills	Motor/ Physical Skills	Preaca- demic Skills	Self- assess- ment Skills	Self- expres- sion Skills	Self-suffi- ciency Skills	Social Skills with Adults	Social Skills with Peers
Finland	148	37 (3)	30 (4)	3 (8)	22 (7)	25 (6)	74 (2)	25 (5)	86 (1)
Ireland	113	61 (2)	16 (8)	34 (6)	32 (5)	37 (4)	42 (3)	21 (7)	76 (1)

Source: Ojala (2000).

Table 3.3. Child Activities in Finland and Ireland (%)

Country	n	Physical	Expressive	Preaca- demic	Personal/ social	Emotional	No Active Engagement	Others
Finland	113	30	15	5	19	2	18	11
Ireland	91	10	11	36	17	1	12	13

Source: Ojala (2002).

Sweden and later in Finland and Japan (e.g. Lindahl, 1995, 1998, 1999). In order to study the experience and learning of toddlers in their new preschool world, the researcher attempted to take the children's own perspective by observing the direction of children's awareness. The researcher uncovered that children must get or have an idea of a situation or of something they want to master, before they can act intentionally. Children's sudden insights were often occurring shortly after they had taken a break. More generally, new insights and understandings signified what the children have learned. In a recent research activity Lindahl (2002) has also analyzed the adult's competency in infant's groups based on the development program. As a result of this competency program the preschool teachers and their assistants developed their attention-giving skills and critically examined their colleagues' and their own actions in interaction with infants. The project participants also received new insights and understanding of the children's competency. This supported their desire and ability to stress the child's perspective in their work with children.

A new perspective in infant education has come when using laboratory conditions. Based on Vygotsky's ideas about the social origins of development and the development of communicative activity, the language acquisition of 9- to 34-month-old children has been studied (Helenius & Tolonen, 1999; Jakkula, 2002). This major study was conducted by observing longitudinally six mother-child pairs in a laboratory constructed in a day care context (Jakkula, 2002). Among the results the researcher revealed the adult's active role in the early stages of the object-giving development process. Children's words became associated with the giving of objects from 13 months but most commonly between 17 and 21 months. Very young (at 14-30 months) children's prelinguistic and linguistic skills have also been studied in order to predict children's further language development (Laakso, 1999). Laakso's findings indicated that individual variation on prelinguistic behaviors was related to individual variation in subsequent language skills. Children who showed early interest in shared reading and had advanced skills in intentional communication and symbolic play had more developed language skills compared with children having less advanced prelinguistic behaviors.

Based on the increasing research and attention given to education of small children (under 3 years of age) in day care the Finnish researchers have also produced several pedagogically oriented monographs in this area. One recent publication includes themes such as children's daily interaction, social conflict, play activities, and pedagogical support for language; music and movement development have been analyzed in the context of chaining and developing day care pedagogy (Helenius, Karila, Munter, Mäntynen, & Siren-Tiusanen, 2001).

Leadership and Expertise in Day Care

At the end of the1990s several researchers began to study how society regulates work in day care centers and what impact these regulations have on the leadership in day care centers (Hujala & Puroila, 1998; Nivala, 1999). By using ecological and sociological orientations the leadership was viewed as socially constructed, situational, and interpretative. By collecting data from self-reporting forms the researchers have analyzed the tasks of directors, preschool teachers, and day care nurses. One major finding has been that the leadership in the context of Finnish day care is searching for its own identity in the pressure between pedagogy and care-oriented interests. The study confirmed that the work of directors in day care has changed remarkably in Finland during the last 2 decades and is now multidimensional, including tasks connected to education, instruction, the basic care of children, cooperative work, educational self-updating, administrative and financial duties, preparations, and recreation/free time. The researchers (see Hujala & Puroila,, 1998) have also started to study the leadership in a cross-cultural context (Finland, Australia, Russia, the United Kingdom, and the United States).

In addition, focus has been on the nature of expertise in developing day care centers. By analyzing kindergarten teachers' developing expertise as a situational and cultural phenomenon, Karila (1997) was able to identity interactive elements of expertise. These were called (a) life history and I (personal dimension), (b) domain-specific knowledge, and (c) the working or learning environment. Recently a research-based monograph has been published in this field supporting day care centers in their multiprofessional tasks and learning processes at work (Karila & Nummenmaa, 2001).

Children with Information and Communication Technology

Finland is now known as a world-leading nation in developing and use of modern information and communication technology (ICT). Reaching this goal has not happened by accident. During the 1990s information technology has been a central issue in national plans for developing education and research. Higher institutes and schools have had their own programs for developing ICT-based activities. In this type of cultural context interest has been focused on the early years of education. At present time, Finland does not have a comprehensive national program for developing and supporting the use of ICT in children not yet of the school age. Instead, there have been a variety of research activities on this topic.

In most studies, the major interest has been on program development, which is often associated with in-service training for preschool teachers. One example is a study in which children's conceptual development, exploratory learning, and social interaction are examined in a pictorial computer stimulation environment in both day care centers as well as in schools (Kangassalo, 1997; Kangassalo & Kumpulainen, 2002). The computer program in this experimentation was science based.

Another example is the computer discovery project implemented in Finland and the United States at the end of the 1990s (e.g., Ojala & Siekkinen, 1997; Ojala, Siekkinen, & Wright, 1996). In this comprehensive project the goal has been to develop a technological curriculum for stimulating children's creativity and problem-solving skills in day care centers. Intensive cross-cultural in-service training and expert support was an important part of the project. The nature of the computer program was open-ended, allowing children to study different subjects in integrative and creative way. The results showed that both kindergarten teachers as well as 3- to 6-year-old children could learn to integrate computer activities into their daily educational activities with increasing interest and competency. The mean time used in the computer-based learning period was about 16 minutes. An interesting finding was that both boys and girls showed the same level of interest in computer-based learning and activities.

The adaptation of the computer programming language LOGO for 8-year-old Finnish pupils concerning problem-solving skills has been studied (Suomala, 1996). The results indicated that during problem solving passive pupils needed a lot of teacher support, independent students showed self-direction, and impulsive pupils demonstrated off-task behavior. In another study on 6-year-old children, the object has been to examine how dramatic play and a multimedia program can develop children's phonological awareness and emergent literacy (Suomala & Korhonen, 1999).

Among the pedagogically-oriented ICT studies one topic has been portfolio-based assessment. A special target in this theme has been the development of a digital portfolio to be used in day care centers and primary schools (Kankaanranta, 2002). In its development two related processes were combined: the evolution of capabilities in ICT and portfolio development. The teachers' ICT capabilities were analyzed in relation to access, motivation, and competence. It was discovered that sufficient access to computers as well as peripherals and information networks are important for digital portfolio development. Furthermore, teachers need to have a sound technological competence to be able to use ICT in their work. Enthusiasm and a need to experiment with new ICT applications were also found to be crucial.

Language Immersion

Even though a large majority of Finnish citizens speak Finnish as their mother tongue, Finland has Swedish speaking citizens (about 6%) who have the right to use Swedish, instead of Finnish, as their mother tongue. Based partly on this reality and partly on international influences from Southern Europe and Canada, during the 1990s a growing research interest in early language immersion in Finland appeared. In Finland most immersion programs in day care centers are based on early total immersion (Lauren, 1992). Their unique target has been to teach Swedish to Finnish speaking young children in preschool groups where Swedish is the dominant language. However, in early language immersion, any second language, like English, can be implemented. Some immersion programs can also adapt a part-time immersion model (e.g. 2 hours per week).

How to teach a second language to children in day care centers with the immersion approach has been an important aspect of development and research (e.g. Mård, 1995). The general approach has been to integrate language teaching into all activities in the entire preschool curriculum instead of using only well-planned formal teaching activities. In the immersion day care context, children can receive daily 1 hour and 45 minutes of formal teaching associated with guided activities (Mård, 1995). However, this is only about 43 % of the total time spent in the center. For developing total immersion, this means that the pedagogical focus should be even stronger on activities outside formal teaching periods including indoor and outdoor activities, free play, daily routines, lunch, and so forth. Very often the pedagogy in well-planned teaching periods is based on large-group activities guided by one teacher. However, in the light of preschool pedagogy more flexible and free activities in small groups are necessary for the purpose of language learning. When developing curriculum content and activities in immersion programs, using opportunities of combining different types of daily activities and teaching in a flexible and integrative way has been a major goal. In this way, daily routines (e.g. dressing, eating), stories, songs, music, drama, playing with words, working with teams, and more structured, teacher-directed activities can be used and integrated pedagogically in immersion programs.

When evaluating the impact of early immersion in the early stages of primary schools (e.g. Grandell, 1994) the general finding has been that learning a second language (usually Swedish) did not inhibit learning of the mother tongue (usually Finnish) as was often anticipated among linguistic experts. The only area which the immersion students did not learn as effectively as the control students was associated with the formal structures of the language (morphology and syntax). However, in relation to the creativity and fluency of communication, the immersion students were better in their language development compared to the control students. When studying the development of the written second language (Swedish) during the beginning of primary schools (Grades 1-4) Bergstöm (2002) found that students with poor written skills did not seem to have problems in creating cohesion in their texts. Thus, it seems that immersion can develop the ability in students with writing problems to communicate fluently in the second language without disturbing their orthographical difficulties in writing. This finding can open up a new possibility that immersion could be used as an effective tool for remedial instruction. More generally, several research findings showed the advantages of learning two languages during the early years of education. When Östern (1991) studied the development of linguistic awareness among children between ages 6 and 8, she found that bilingual children showed linguistic awareness in two languages and perhaps because of this were more linguistically aware than monolingual children.

Intervention of Learning Problems

Research on early intervention of learning problems has been quite intensive in Finland during the past 10 years. This issue is important because about 10-15% of young children have some kind of problem (Ahonen, 2001). Increasing attention has focused on a model in which learning problems in language, in attention (hyperactivity), and in behavior are seen as interacting elements (e.g., Ahonen, 2001).

Research has been especially intensive in the area in which the development of reading skills has been the central theme. When studying the problems in learning to read, the role of phonological awareness, verbal working memory, and rapid automatic naming are in many studies recognized as important predictors of reading skills (e.g., Hopolainen, Ahonen, Tolvanen, & Lyytinen, 2000; Lyytinen, Ahonen, Korhonen, Korkman, & Riita, 1995; Poskiparta, 2002; Poskiparta et al., 1999). In using remediation, the global training of phonological awareness has been important and new tools like computer-based remediation have been developed (Poskiparta, 2002).

One detailed example can be taken from a study by Poskiparta (2002). In this comprehensive study, the researcher identified 252 children with reading problems at the age of 6 (at the end of their preschool year). Remedial teaching on linguistic awareness with computer-assisted reading intervention was organized during the first 2 years of primary school (ages 7-8). The results showed that the half with weaker skills especially profited from the training given in the intervention. The researcher identified both children who resisted treatment and those who unexpectedly failed in reading. It was also found that by training in linguistic awareness, we can help children at risk to break the alphabetic code, but however, this help does not ensure reading fluency. The study also recognized a dramatic increase in motivational changes during the transition from the preschool to grade one. This happened only at the point when the children's task orientation collapsed under stressful performance situations.

A more pedagogical approach for phonological awareness is represented in a recent study implemented in preschools with 6-year-old children and their teachers (Mäkinen, 2002). In this action study the researcher developed pedagogical approaches for increasing children's phonological awareness with preschool teachers. In the training program, the children's ability to read and write was encouraged to develop from the stage of sensation (epiphonological) to the stage of manipulating the segments of words (metaphonological). In the epiphonological stage the child is able intuitively to pay attention for language and its use. When the child is in the metaphonological stage she/he can pay intentionally attention and control the language and its use. A premetaphonological subset of word segments was identified between these stages. This level of awareness was given special attention in the training of the children's abilities in syllable and phoneme analysis and synthesis. During the preschool year the researcher developed a method with teachers in which the focus was on actions, emotions, and thinking. The major pedagogical tools were thematic action play and the teaching of dialogue. The results showed improvement in attentiveness, and the method challenged their thinking, increased their interest, and gave more joy in the use of language.

There are also some studies about the development of writing skills. In a recent study (Mäki, 2002) the writing skills of primary school children were studied in Grades 1 to 3. The aim was to trace the preliminary skills of writing and to implement interventional procedures. The researcher found that girls outperformed boys in spelling and written compositions. It was possible to predict spelling skills with preschool measurements of phonological awareness and visual-motor skills. The boys, among the poor spellers, had a poorer noun vocabulary and earlier mastery of word inflections. Boys also showed difficulties both with oral and written composition. The intervention procedures included strategy instruction, procedural facilitation, and computer-assisted tutoring. It was found that the intervention produced gains in spelling accuracy, spelling revision, decoding accuracy, and knowledge about the writing process.

Recently, increasing attention has been given to development of new diagnostic tools for the early identification of problems and toward reading and writing skills used in the remediation of these problems. One promising tool is based on the computer program Audilex (Karma, 1998). This tool is associated with auditory and temporal factors. It assumes that difficulties in auditory structuring are causing basic problems in connecting auditory and visual signals. The computer-based diagnosis and remediation uses simple visual forms to be identified according to the temporal audivoice signals presented by the computer. The preliminary findings show that exercise and play with this program can open up a new opportunity for children to improve their reading skills before school age. This kind of effect is verified both by a reading test as well as by plastic neural changes (Kujala et al., 2001)

The History of Early Childhood Education

The value of history is recognized in Finnish research on early childhood education. The focus in most studies has been on macrohistory. in which the ideological, cultural, and political trends are analyzed. On the other hand, microhistorical studies focusing on certain persons, a subgroup in society, or phenomena, has not been as active.

By using critical theory, based on neo-Weberian and Bourdieaun framework, Kinos (1997) analyzed the development of professionalism among various professions (kindergarten teachers, social pedagogues, and nurses) in the day care field. The primary idea was to identify struggles both inside and outside the field. The document, based on historical data, covered the period between 1973 and 1992. The researcher showed that the internal struggle was based on the activity of the day care profession itself and the trade union. As a consequence of this, kindergarten teachers were barred from the teaching profession and social pedagogues from social work. The struggle between kindergarten teachers and nurses showed a similar kind of struggle and led to the developmental trend in which nurses lost important positions partly because of actions of the health care trade union.

Another example can be taken from a study in which the evolution of the children's day care system as an environment for early growth in the nineteeth and twentieth centuries was analyzed (Välimäki, 1998). The research material consisted of comprehensive historical documents and was analyzed by using content analysis, (the historical-narrative approach). Based on the analysis the researcher produced four different concepts of child care: (1) traditional, (2) educational-pedagogical, (3) societal, and (4) governmental. According to the traditional approach, the child care takes place in the family environment. This conception was dominant during preindustrial agricultural time, but is also connected with the use of family day care in modern time. Important grounds for educational-pedagogical perception of child care are kindergartens, infant schools, and the aim to raise the educational level of citizens. The societal conception is based on philanthropic ideas focusing on basic care and protection of children. This approach is still strong in the care ideology for youngest children cared for in toddler groups (children under 3 years). The governmental child care ideology is based on the ideology that the legislation and development of child care services must be under democratic control of the society. The modern public day care in Finland is strongly based on this conception

The cultural-historic theory of human development has also been under historic analysis. The focus has been on Vygotsky and the development of his theory (Veresov, 1998, 1999). In his historical and methodological analysis the researcher reconstructed the theoretical evolution of Vygotsky's views (Veresov, 1998). Two theoretical models of human consciousness were identified: (a) a reflexological model based on the thought in the years 1917-1924 and (b) a behavioristic-structural one based on the ideas in years 1925-1927. In the first period (1917-1924) consciousness was defined as a "reflex of reflexes" and as "inner space" between stimulus and reaction. In the later period (1925-1927) Vygotsky defined consciousness as an aspect of the structure of behavior. In this approach the response included both internal as well as external components.

There is also an historical analysis about ideas and trends in Finnish child-rearing and parenting. For this topic, Kemppainen (2001) has described and compared the memories and child-rearing beliefs of informants representing three consecutive generations. The study demonstrated that traditional ideas of child-rearing seem to have transformed from generation to generation without major changes. All three generations favored setting limits and rules as well as discipline. Working hard, however, as highly valued belief in Finnish society was not valued by the younger generation as highly as the older generation.

In addition to the studies reviewed above there have been several historical analyses about the Finnish kindergarten movement with its trends and its key persons (e.g. Hänninen & Valli, 1986; Ojala, 1984; Ojala & Kuikka, 1992; Salminen & Salminen, 1986).

Development of Preschool Education and the Transition to School

Perhaps the most intensive area recently research has been in analyzing and developing preschool education. In this area many different study topics have been presented.

One important topic has been the new preschool curriculum of 2000. Within this area the Research Centre for Early Childhood and Elementary Education (ECEE) at the university of Helsinki has started in 2001 to explore the organization and effectiveness of preschool education in the city of Helsinki. The research project is a follow-up study intending to follow children for 3 years. There are two integrated parts in the design of the project. In the quantitative part, the aims, pedagogy and evaluations of the population of the preschool teachers in Helsinki ($N = 554$) are examined through survey analyses. The effectiveness of preschool education and the transition from preschool to school are studied in samples of preschools. In the qualitative part of the project, the preschool education is examined in different contexts. Intensive case studies are carried out, for instance, in multicultural, cooperative (day care center/school), integrated (special education/general education) and heterogeneous (children from 1 to 6 together) preschool education groups. The Helsinki project will be extended to the University of Tallinn in Estonia. The first results show that teachers do realize the aims of preschool education with certain preferences (Hytönen, 2002; Hytönen & Krokfors, 2002). Aims related to altruism and the acceptance of differences, socialization, self-concept, and emotions were seen as among the most important. When the teachers evaluated at the end of the preschool year children's learning they found that areas related to health habits (including self-helping skills), language, mathematics, and psycho-motoric skills were among highest (Ojala, 2002c).

The development of preschool education within comprehensive schools has also been under study (Peltonen, 2002). In this study administrative authorities, parents, teachers, and children were interviewed for their opinions. The researcher found that administrators, parents, and teachers emphasized the teaching of manners while children, together with their parents, laid stress on the importance of play and emotional climate. The importance of playing outdoors and having a good environment was stressed. However, international relations and information technology were not seen as important.

There are also studies analyzing modern day care. In one recent study the practical work in day care centers was studied (Puroila, 2002). By using a frame analysis the researcher differentiated among five different frames. Within the educational frame the meaning of early childhood work was to support and promote learning. For the caring frame it was characteristic to view the work in early childhood from the context of the worker's private lives. Quite a new approach to studying care centers is a sociological approach focusing on childhood. By using this approach Lehtinen (2000) has analyzed children as actors in the day care center. Based on ethnographic observations, the researcher identified three mediated mechanisms for the acts done by children: negotiation, power, and resources for acting.

A new topic for research is the study of children's exclusion from social relationships during the early years of their education (Laine & Neitola, 2002). Based on the fact that an early dropout from social networks in day care centers is at risk for long-term exclusion, the researchers interviewed target children and collected data (interview and questionnaires) from day care personnel, and asked parents to rate their children's behavior in play situations. The results indicated that diverse peer problems were very common. Children with risk of exclusion had multiple problems in their peer relationships. Children with risk suffered both from internalized as well as externalized problems. They had a weaker self-concept, insufficient social skills, and more problems with peer interactions. Other children's reactions to risk children were negative. There were more problems with boys than girls and almost all bullies were boys.

An important issue in research has been quality. A quite popular instrument in quality analyses has been the ECERS (Early Childhood Environment Rating Scale by Harms & Clifford) or its modifications. Recently, new instruments are also used. One option has been the Leuven Involvement Scale for Young Children called LIS-YC (Laevers, 1994). Contrary to ECERS, in which the day care environment itself is the crucial factor for quality, the LIS-YC approach focuses on the degree of children's involvement as a crucial indicator of quality. However, when researching quality, the data is usually collected by using a variety of methods and instruments such as questionnaires, written documents, and interviews (see e.g., Tauriainen, 2001).

Based on a multiple use of instruments Tauriainen (2000) analyzed the staff's, parent's, and children's conceptions of quality in a day care center with integrated groups. The results showed that the common core of good quality was based on small group size, an emotionally warm atmosphere, and the enhancement of self-motivated behavior in children. Besides this, the results revealed that the stakeholder group perceived quality in their own way. The staff had a very general concept of quality which focused on adult-led activities, and the fluent running of care and daily routines. Parents looked to their children's individual needs and social interaction in the group. For children the important elements were joint power with adults and freedom to plan their activities. Family care has also been under quality analysis (Parrila, 2000). In this study quality was analyzed according to the views of family day care staff and parents using survey questions. In the results four different perspectives of quality were identified: (a) family day care providers's personality and professionality, (b) a functioning and functional family day care environment, (c) the goals of family day care, and (d) the impacts of family day care.

Play has long been an important pedagogical topic. Popular frameworks for researchers have been to analyze play according to the theories of Piaget and Vygotsky (e.g. Hännikäinen, 1995; Helenius, 1993; Mäntynen, 1997). A new approach to the study of play is a cultural-oriented approach. This approach attempts to analyze children's play culture related to societal change as Kalliala (1999) has done. In her analysis the researcher classified play according to the characteristics of (a) competition, (b) hazard, (c) imitation, and (d) dizziness (e.g., to shake for a moment or twirling round is creating an enjoyable feeling of dizziness). The results showed that the dependence of play on time and culture can be traced from the children's own play culture as well as from societal changes based on the changing roles of children and adults. Some gender differences were also found. The girls showed in their play an interest in human relationships as seen in play with Barbies and boys inspired often by action films associated with TV or video.

Recent research activity in preschool education has also encouraged researchers to publish research-based textbooks. These include topics such as pedagogical principles for preschool and early elementary education (Brotherus et al., 2002), new dimensions for preschool teaching and learning (Hakkarainen, 2000), research methodologies in early childhood education (Ruoppila et al., 1999), and theoretical approaches in early childhood education (Karila, Kinos, & Virtanen, 2001) .

CONCLUSIONS

The recent Finnish research in early childhood education has been particularly active during the last years of the past decade. All universities with their special areas of expertises are active in this national task. How can one explain this? One reason is no doubt the university-based teacher education in early childhood education. This educational solution is based on strong national agreement according to which childhood can be supported and developed in the best way by educators and teachers having scientific attitude and knowledge. One important aspect in this view is that modern childhood educators should work like researchers as much as possible. The condition in Finland for this task is favorable. We have a strong national consensus for offering to children the best possible public early childhood services. According to the educational policy, each child and family have an equal position, which is not dependent of their socioeconomic or educational background. Based on this, readiness to study and prevent risk factors during early childhood is becoming increasingly important.

Eventhough rapid growth and strong interest in early childhood research in Finland is a fact, some critical remarks for future research trends can be made. Due to the fact that Finland is a small and sparsely populated country, most of the studies are based on small samples and targeted to study local early childhood education. In the future we need to study early childhood education more comprehensively across the country. Within this enterprise we need nationwide samples and big cohorts to studded and follow up.

Another crucial research task is to study more carefully the scientific grounds of early childhood education. In this task we confront two demanding interrelated questions: (a) what is early childhood education and (b) how to study this phenomenon. Regarding the first question we try to find actual and relevant definition for early childhood education. A fruitful and perhaps most relevant framework for the definition is socio-cultural and value based. In this task analytical and meta-analytical research is important. The nature of the second question is more cross-cultural and global. By answering this question we can develop early childhood as a science. Science-based approach means many important things. On theory level the researcher must understand the role of relevant meta-theories as well as theories about children and their development, learning, and teaching. The methods for studying children in their educational env[...]d new elaborate methods need to be [...]s a science, we also need a more compreh[...]or research activities and results. Finally, [...]tion framework, which is both critical as [...]aspects are important in order to make p[...]ceptance for early childhood research a[...].

Our review [...]rly childhood education reflects on elem[...]l as pedagogical impor-tance. Since the[...]rtens in the nineteenth century there h[...]sus that Finnish society desires to offer t[...]service both to parents as well as children [...]s of the IEA Preprimary project that adu[...]w much stronger among Finnish parents [...]Finland. Associated with this, we have als[...]rent family policy is as a background for [...]rvices. Parents have real opportunities to [...]rvices. As expressed in a recent OECD (the Organization for Economic Cooperation and Develop-ment) country note, based on the evaluation of Finnish early childhood education and care policy that has been developed, we have had success in creating "an impressive system of early childhood education and care, a system which is underpinned by principles of universality, gender equity, and children's rights" (OECD Country Note, 2001, p. 44).

It is quite clear that the Finnish approach to early childhood education as a system is working, dynamic, and is able to reach high standards. Even though the initial viewpoints are clearly connected to adults and parents, researchers have started increasingly to study day care from the view point of children's needs. Research activities in which effective programs for early intervention, children as actors in modern society, and mechanisms in early exclusions and children at risk must be seen increasingly impor-tant.

It is also important, that activity in pedagogical studies is increasing. Traditionally, the role of play has been important in the Finnish context and this tradition is continuing with some new interests. The new stimuli have been the new preschool curriculum and the education of 6-year-old children before the start of school either in the daycare or school context. In this situation, Finnish researchers have had a unique opportunity to compare two quite different pedagogical models. The day care context offers access to observe activity-based and quite flexible pedagogical processes where the needs and well-being of children as well as parents are under focus. In this context the role of the kindergarten teacher is to support education at home and the children's individual development and learning. The school environment offers to the preschool pedagogy an environment in which the preparation for learning is usually more serious. In school context, for example, learning skills in mathematics but especially in language are seen to be important and evaluated more carefully.

The Finnish preschool options described are crucial from the point of recent international achievement studies made by the OECD. In a recent comparative OECD study, called PISA, Finnish 15-year-old-children ranked highest among 32 nations in reading and writing skills. In addition, our children's achievements were very high also in mathematics (4th place) and sciences (3rd place) at the end the primary school (Välijärvi & Linnankylä, 2002). When reflecting on these findings we are confronted by a paradox. In the Finnish educational context, school starts later (at the age of 7) than in almost any other country, and the early childhood strategy is strongly associated with the parents' needs and support instead of an early preparation of children for starting school. The recent PISA study raises many important questions. Can the Finnish approach in early childhood education be transformed to other countries? How much of the successful school learning can be explained by early childhood experiences? How important is the scientific-based teacher education in early childhood and its connections to school education? However, one answer is quite clear for answering these types of questions: we need more comprehensive and more carefully targeted comparative studies.

REFERENCES

Ahonen, T. (2001). Oppimisvaikeudet kehityspykologisena haasteena [Learning difficulties as challenge of developmental psychology]. *NMI-Bulletin, 11*(4), 33-36.

Alanen, L., & Mayall, B. (Eds.). (2001). *Conceptualizing child-adult relations.* London: RoutledgeFalmer.

Bergström, M. (2002). Individuell andraspråksinlärning hos språkbadselever med skrivsvårigheter [Individual differences in second-language learning of immersion pupils with writing difficulties]. *Acta Wasaensia, 106.*

Brotherus, A., Hytönen, J., & Krokfors, L. (2002). *Esi- ja alkuopetuksen pedagogiikka* [Pedagogy for preschool and early elementary education]. Helsinki, Finland: WSOY.

Core curriculum for pres-school education in Finland. (2000). Helsinki: National Borad of Education.

Early childhood education and care policy in Finland. (2000). *Publications of the Ministry of Social Affairs and Health, 2000(21).*

Grandell, C. (1994). Suomalaisten kielikylpyoppilaiden ensimmäisen kielen kehitys [The development of first language among Finnish immersion pulips]. In T. C. Lauren (Ed.), Kielikylpy: *Kahden kielen kautta monikielisyyteen* (pp. 101-110). Vaasan Yliopisto. Täydennyskoulutuskeskus.

Hakkarainen, P. (2000). *Kehittävä esiopetus ja oppiminen* [Developing preschool education and learning]. Jyväskylä, Finland: PS-Kustannus.

Hännikäinen, M. (1995). Nukesta vauvaksi ja lapsesta lääkäriksi: roolileikkiin siirtymisen tarkastelua piagetilaisesta ja kulttuurihistoriallisen toiminnan näkökulmasta [Transition to role play based on approaches of Piaget and cultural-historical theory]. *Jyväskylä Studies in Education, Psychology and Social Research, 115.*

Hänninen, S. -L., & Valli, S. (1986). *Suomen lastentarhatyön ja varhaiskasvatuksen historia* [The history of Finnish kindergarten movement and early childhood education]. Helsinki, Finland: Otava.

Helanko, R. (1958). Theoretical aspects of play and socialization. *Turun yliopiston julkaisusarja. Sarja B. Humanoria, 70.*

Helenius, A. (1993). *Leikin kehitys varhaislapsuudessa* (The development of play in early childhood). Helsinki: Kirjayhtymä.

Helenius, A., Karila, K., Munter, H., Mäntynen, P., & Siren-Tiusanen, H. (2001). *Pienet päivähoidossa* [Children under three in day-care]. Helsinki, Finland: WSOY.

Helenius, A., & Tolonen, K. (1999, September). The quality of proximal development. Individual differences between pre-language infants within the context of object manipulation in the company of adults. Paper presented at the ECER European Conference, Lahti.

Hopolainen, L., Ahonen, T., Tolvanen, A., & Lyytinen, H. (2000). Two alternative ways to model the relation between reading accuracy and phonological awareness at preschool age. *Scientific Studies of Reading, 4,* 77-100.

Hujala, E., & Puroila, A. -M. (1998). Towards understanding leadership in early childhood context. Cross-cultural perspectives. *Acta Universitatis Ouluensis,* E35.

Hujala-Huttunen, E. (1996). Day care in the USA, Russia and Finland: Views from parents, teachers and directors. *European Early Childhood Education Research Journal, 4,* 33-47.

Hujala-Huttunen, E., & Tauriainen, L. (1995). *Laadun arviointi varhaiskasvatuksessa* [Quality evaluation in early childhood education]. Oulun yliopisto. Kasvatustieteiden tiedekunta. Varhaiskasvatuskeskus.

Husa, S., & Kinos, J. (2001). Akateemisen varhaiskasvatuksen muotoutuminen [Formation of academic early childhood education). Suomen kasvatustieteellinen seura. *Kasvatusalan tutkimuksia, 4.* Turku: Pallosalama.

Huttunen, E. (1988). Lapsen käyttäytyminen ja kasvuympäristö. Osa I: perhe ja päivähoito kasvuympäristönä [Children's behaviour and growth environment. Part I: family and day care as growth environment]. Joensuun yliopisto. *Kasvatustieteeellisiä julkaisuja*, 2.

Hytönen, J. (1992). *Lapsikeskeinen kasvatus* [Child-centred education]. Helsinki, Finland: WSOY.

Hytönen, J. (2002, November). *Realization of the aims of preschool education in Helsinki*. Paper presented at the conference Paradoxes in Childhood: Reality and Perspectives, Tallinn Pedagogical University, Estonia.

Hytönen, J., & Krokfors, L (2002). Esiopetuksen toimintaympäristö, esiopetusta antava opettaja ja esiopetuksen tavoitteiden painottuminen toimintakaudella 2001-2002. Esiopetuksen toimivuus ja vaikuttavuus Helsingingin kupungissa vuosina 2002-2002. Tutkimusratortti I [Learning environments, preschool teachers and aims of education at the beginning of the legislative preschool education. The organization and effectiveness of preschool education in the city of Helsinki: Research Report 1]. *Helsingin kaupungin sosiaaliviraston tutkimukisa*, 1.

Iloiset toimintatuokiot [Happy action hours]. (1975). Helsinki, Finland: Sosiaalihallitus.

Jakkula, K. (2002). Esineiden antaminen. Kehityksen peili ja kieltä ennakoiva sosiaalinen merkki 9-34 kuukauden iässä [A mirror of development and a social sign anticipating language acquisition of 9-34 months old children). *Acta Universitatis Ouluensis*, E 52.

Kalliala, M. (1999). *Enkeliprinssi ja itsari liukumäessä. Leikkikulttuuri ja yhteiskunnan muutos* [Angelprincess and suicide on the playground slide. The culture of play and societal change). Helsinki, Finland: Gaudeamus.

Kangassalo, M. (1997). *The formation of children's conceptual models concerning a particular natural phenomenon using PICCO, a pictorial computer simulation*. Acta Universitatis Tamperensis, 559.

Kangassalo, M., & Kumpulainen, K. (2002). The dynamics of children's science learning and thinking in a social context of a multimedia environment. In H. Kangassalo & E. Kawaguchi (Eds.), *Proceedings of the 12th European-Japanese Conference on Information Modelling and Knowledge Bases*. Germany: Krippen, Swiss Saxony.

Kankaanranta, M. 1998. Towards digital bridges between educational cultures. Challenges for school based portfolio assessment. In H. Jokinen & J. Rushton (Eds.), *Changing contexts of school development – The challenges to evaluation and assessment. Report on the International SBD Seminar, April 21-26, 1997* (pp. 65-75). Jyväskylä, Finland: Institute for Educational Research.

Kankaaranta, M. (2002). Developing digital portfolios for childhood education. University of Jyväskylä. Institute for Educational Research. *Research Reports*, 11.

Karila, K. (1997). *Kehittyvä asiantuntijuus. Lapsirakkaasta aloittelijasta kasvatuksen asiantuntijaksi* [Kindergarten teacher's developing expertise. From student found of children to expert of education]. Helsinki, Finland: Edita.

Karila, K., & Nummenmaa, A. -R. (2001). *Matkalla moniammatillisuuteen. Kuvauskohteena päiväkoti* [Multiprofessionality in daycare centre]. Helsinki, Finland: WSOY.

Karila, K., Kinos, J., & Virtanen, J. (2001). *Varhaiskasvatuksen teoriasuuntauksia* [Theoretical approaches in early childhood education]. Jyväskylä, Finland: PS-Kustannus.

Karma, K. (1998) *Audilex. Tietokoneohjelma lukemis- ja kirjoittamishäiriön diagnosointiin ja kuntouttamiseen* [Audilex. A computer game and test to diagnose and train auditory/temporal matching]. Helsinki, Finland: Comp Aid.

Kemppainen, J. (2001). Kotikasvatus kolmessa sukupolvessa [Child-rearing in three generations]. *Jyväskylä Studies in Education, Psychology and Social Research,* 190.

Keskinen, S., & Leppiman, A. (1997). Finnish and Estonian children's toy preferences. The significance of play in children's early learning. Cross-cultural view and definitions. *Erasmus Early Years Network,* 69-67

Keskinen, S., & Sato, T. (1997, July). *Gender identity, stability, and constancy among Japanise and Finnish four years old children.* Paper presented at the 5th Fenno-Hungarian Conference on Developmental Psychology, Lahti, Finland.

Kinos, J. (1997). Päiväkoti ammattikuntien kamppailujen kenttänä [Daycare center as meeting point of struggles between professions]. *Annales Universitatis Turkuensis,* Ser. C, 133.

Kiviluoto, H., & Parkkinen, T. (1976). Varhaislapsuuden erilaisten hoitoympäristöjen vaikutus lapsen kehitykseen [The effect of different care environment in early childhood education on children's development]. *Turun yliopiston psykologian laitoksen julkaisuja,* 21.

Komiteamietintö (1980). *Päivähoidon kasvatustoimintakomitean mietintö* [Report of the Commission on the educational goals of day care]. Helsinki, Finland: Valtion painatuskeskus.

Kujala, T., Karma, K., Ceponiene, R. Belitz, S., Turkkila, P., Tervaniemi, M., & Näätänen, R. (2001). Plastic neural changes and reading improvement caused by audio-visual training in reading-impaired children. *Proceedings of the National Academy of Sciences, 98*(18), 10509-10514.

Laakso, M. -L. (1999). Prelinguistic skills and early interactional context as predictors of children's language development. *Jyväskylä Studies in Education, Psychology and Social Research,* 115.

Laevers, F. (Ed.). (1994). The Leuven Involvement Scale for Young Children (LIS-YC). Centre for Experimental Education. *Experimental Education Series,* 1.

Lahikainen, A. R., Kirmanen, T., & Kraav, I. (1999). Correspondence between parents' assessments and their 5-6-year-old children's self-reported fears in Estonia and in Finland. Haridus ja Kasvatusväärtused uhiskunnas. *Tartu Ülikooli pedagoogika osakonna väljaanne,* 9.

Lahikainen, A. R., & Kraav, I. (2000). Self report as a method for studying fears of young children. Haridus ja sotsiaalne tegelikkus. *Tartu Ülikooli pedagoogika osakonna väljaanne,* 10.

Lahikainen, A. R., & Kraav, I. (2001). Children's well-being in Finland and in Estonia. Kasvatus ja aated. Artikle kogumik. *Tartu Ülikooli pedagoogika osakonna väljaanne,* 11.

Lahikainen, R. -L. & Strandell,H. (1987). *Lapsen kasvuehdot Suomessa. Basun-projekti: tutkimus lapsuudesta, yhteiskunnasta ja kehityksestä Pohjoismaissa* [Children's growth conditions. Basun project: The study from childhood, society and development]. Helsinki, Finland: Painokaari.

Laine, K., & Neitola, M. (2002). Lasten syrjäytyminen päiväkodin vertaisryhmästä [Children's exclusion from peer group in kindergarten]. Suomen kasvatustieteellinen seura. *Kasvatusalan tutkimuksia*, 11. Turku: Pallosalama.

Lapsitutkimuksen tutkimusohjelma. (1992). Helsinki, Finland: Suomen Akatemia.

Lauren, K. (Ed.). (1992). En model för språk i daghem och skola [Language acquisition at kindergarten and school]. Vasa univeristet. *Fortbildningscentralen, Publ.* 2.

Lehtinen, A. -R. (2000). *Lasten kesken. Lapset toimijoina päiväkodissa* [Children as actors in daycare centre]. Jyväskylän yliopisto: SoPhi.

Lindahl, M. (1995). Inlärning och erfarande. Ettåringars möte med förskolans värld [Experinece and learning. On-year old children's encounter with the world of pre-school]. *Göteborg Studies in Educational Science*, 103.

Lindahl, M. [1998]. *Lärande småbarn* [Learning of young children]. Lund: Studentlitteratur.

Lindahl, M. (1999, August). *Learning and environment. One-year old Japanese children in day-care situations.* Paper presented at the 8th European Conference for Research on Learning and Instruction, Göteborg, Sweden.

Lindahl, M. (2002). Vårda-vegleda-lära. Effectstudie av ett interventiosprogram för pedagogers lärande i förskolemiljön [Care-support-learn]. *Göteborg Studies in Educational Science* 178.

Lounassalo, J. (1997). Keskusaihesuunnittelun arvointia [Evaluating the theme-based planning]. *Verso*, 2(1), 12-17.

Lyytinen, H., Ahonen, T., Korhonen, T., Korkman, M., & Riita, T. (1995). *Oppimisvaikeudet. Neuropsykologinen näkökulma* [Learning difficulties. Neuropsychological approach]. Porvoo, Finland: WSOY.

Mäki, H. (2002). Elements of spelling and composition. Studies on predicting and supporting writing skills in primary grades. *Annales Universitatis Turkuensis*, Ser. B, No. 255.

Mäkinen, M. (2002). Puheen palat ja sanan salat esiopetuksessa [Speech and words in preschool education]. *Acta Universitatis Tamperensis*, 902.

Mäntynen, P. (1997). Pikkulasten leikin edellytykset päiväkodissa [The play conditions of young children in day-care centre]. *Joensuun yliopiston kasvatustieteellisiä julkaisuja*, 37.

Mård, K. (1995). Immersion preschool as environment for early second language acquisition. In M. Buss & C. Lauren (Eds.) *Language immersion: Teaching and second language acquisition. Vaasan yliopiston julkaisuja*, 192, 141-151.

Niikko, A. (1988). Päiväkotihenkilöstön täydennyskoulutus ja päiväkotilasten sosiaaliset taidot [In-service training for day care personnel and children's socioemotional skills]. Joensuun yliopisto. *Kasvatustieteellisiä julkaisuja*, 7.

Niiranen, P., & Kinos, J. (2001). Suomalaisen lastentarha- ja päiväkotipedagogiikan jäljillä [Searching the Finnish pedagogy for kindergartens and day care centres]. In T. K. Karila, J. Kinos, & J. Virtanen *Varhaiskasvatuksen teoriasuuntauksia* (pp. 58-85). Jyväskylä, Finland: PS-Kustannus.

Nivala, V. (1999). Päiväkodin johtajuus [Leadership in daycare centre]. *Acta Universitatis Lapponiensis*, 25.

OECD Country Note. (2001). *Early childhood education and care policy in Finland.* Helsinki, Finland: Sosiaali- ja terveysministeriö.

Ojala, M. (1984). Friedrich Fröbel and the kindergarten movement in Finland. *Informationen zur Erziehungsund Bildungshistorischen Forschung.* Universität Hannover, Heft 25, 203-212.

Ojala, M. (1985, April). *A history of Finnish Daycare: Before and After 1973.* Paper presented at the 2nd meeting of the International Standing Working Group for the History of Early Childhood Education, Emboli, Italy.

Ojala, M. (1989). Early childhood training, care, and education in Finland. In P. P. Olmsted & D. P. Weikart (Eds.), *How nations serve young children: Profiles of childhood care and education in 14 countries* (pp. 87-118). Ypsilanti, MI: High/Scope Press.

Ojala. M. (1993a). *Varhaiskasvatuksen perusteita ja haasteita* [Grounds and challenges for early childhood education]. Helsinki, Finland: Kirjayhtymä.

Ojala, M. (1993b). IEA Preprimary Study in Finland 2. The use of early childhood settings in Finland. *Research Reports of the Faculty of Education*, No. 51. University of Joensuu.

Ojala, M. (1994). Lapsuuden ja varhaiskasvatuksen instituutti [The institue for childhood education]. *Ebeneser-säätiön julkaisu* 2.

Ojala, M. (1999). Teacher's and parents' predictions about each other's priorities for young children (Chapter VIII). In D. P. Weikart (Ed.), *What should young children learn? Teacher and parent views in 15 countries* (pp. 157-175). Ypsilanti, MI: High/Scope Press.

Ojala, M. (2000). Parent and teacher expectations for developing young children: A cross-cultural comparison between Ireland and Finland. *European Early Childhood Education Research Journal*, 8(2).

Ojala, M. (2002a). Esi- ja alkuopetus tutkimuksen ja kehittämisen polttopisteessä [Preschool and early elementary school education as focus on research and development]. *Didacta Varia* 2/2000. Helsingin yliopisto. Opettajankoulutuslaitos.

Ojala, M. (2002b). Examining cross- culturally the preschool education. T. J. Suortti & E. Heikkinen (Eds.), *Mieli, tiede ja teknologia.* Prof. Pertti Yli-Luoman juhlajulkaisu. Oulun Yliopisto. Kajaanin OKL:n julkaisuja. Sarja B: Opetusmonisteita ja selosteitta 17.

Ojala, M. (2002c, November). *Helsinki-Project. Follow-up study. The transition from preschool to school.* Paper presented at conference Paradoxes in Childhood: Reality and Perspectives. Tallinn Pedagogical University, Estonia.

Ojala, M., & Kuikka, M. T. (1992) . Early childhood education in Finland. In G. A. Woodill, J. Bernhard, & L. Prochner (Eds.) *International handbook of early childhood education* (pp. 193-203). New York: Garland.

Ojala, M., Lius. E., & Pänttönen, P. (1981). Perhepäivähoito osana päivähoitoa ja varhaiskasvatusta [Family day care as part of day care and early childhood education]. *Sosiaalihallituksen julkaisuja* 4.

Ojala, M., & Siekkinen, M. (1997). Tietotekniikan perusteista, sovelluksista ja haasteista alle kouluikäisen lasten opetuksessa ja oppimisessa [ICT for children under the school age). In T. E. Lehtinen (Ed.), *Verkkopedagogiikka* (pp. 143-157). Helsinki, Finland: Edita.

Ojala, M., & Siekkinen, M. (1998). Esi- ja alkuopetuksen kehittäminen: valtakunnallisen akvaarioprojektin esi- ja alkuopetuksen aiheverkon arviointia [Developing pre-school and early elementary school education). Joensuun yliopisto. *Kasvatustieteiden tiedekunnan selosteita*, 76.

Ojala, M., Siekkinen, M., & Wright, J. (1996). *Developing a multimedia vision of children's learning challenges from theory to everyday practice.* Paper presented at the Conference Matkalla tietoyhteiskuntaan. Interaktiivinen teknologia koulutuksessa, Hämeenlinna, Aulanko, Finland.

Päivänsalo, P. (1952). Yhteisöelämää lastentarhassa [Social life in the kindergarten]. *Hyvinkää: Suomen kasvatussosiologisen yhdistyksen julkaisuja*, 6.

Parrila, S. (2002). Perhpäivähoito osana suomalaista päivähoitojärjestelmää. Näkökulmia perhpäivähoidon laatuun ja sen kehittämiseen [Family daycare as part of the Finnish daycare system. Approaches to family daycare and its development]. *Acta Universitatis Ouluensis, E59.*

Peltonen, T. (2002). Pienten koulujen esiopetuksen kehittäminen-entisajan alakoulusta esikouluun [Developing of preschool education in small schools— From old times perimary school to preschool). *Acta Universitatis Ouluensis, E* 60.

Perusopetuksen opetuskokeiluissa lukuvuonna 2003-2004 noudatettavat opetussuunnitelman perusteet vuosiluokille 1-2 [Care curriculum for grades 1-2 in basic education]. (2002). Helsinki, Finland: Opetushallitus.

Poskiparta, E. (2002). Remediation of reading difficulties in grades 1 and 2. *Annales Universitatis Turkuensis*, Ser. B, 254.

Poskiparta, E., Niemi, P., & Vauras, M. (1999). Who benefits from training in linguistic awareness in the first grade, and what components show training effects. *Journal of Learning Disabilities, 32*(5), 437-447.

Puroila, A. -M. (2002). Kohtaamisia päiväkotiarjessa—kehitysanalyyttinen näkökulma varhaiskasvatustyöhön [Everyday encounters in daycare centres— A frame analysis of early childhood work]. *Acta Universitatis Ouluensis, E* 51.

Ruoppila, I., & Korkiakangas, M. (1975). Esikoulun, lastentarhan ja kodin vaikutus lasten kehitykseen, osa II: Vaikutuksia koskevat tulokset [Effects of preschool, kindergarten, and the home on children's development, part II: Results concerning the effects. University of Jyväskylä. *Publication of the Department of Psychology,* 17.

Ruoppila, I., Hujala, E., Karila, K., Kinos, J., Niiranen, P., & Ojala, M. (1999). *Varhaiskasvatuksen tutkimusmenetelmiä* [Research methods in early child education]. Jyväskylä, Finland: Atena.

Rusanen, E. (1995). *Ongelmalapset päivähoidossa. Tutkimus kasvatuskäytäntöjen kehittämisestä päiväkodissa ja perhepäivähoidossa* [Children with proplem in day care. The study from the development of practical skills in day care centre and family day care]. Helsinki, Finland: Suomen kuntaliitto.

Salminen, H., & Salminen, J. (1986). Lastentarhantoiminta osana lapsuuden historiaa. Friedrich Fröbelin lastentarha-aate ja sen leviäminen Suomeen [Friedrich Fröbel's kindergarten movement and how it came to Finland). *Mannerheimin Lastensuojeluliitto P 17.* Jyväskylä, Finland: Gummerus

Salo, A. (1939). *Pikkulasten kasvatus Uno Cygneauksen kansansivistysjärjestelmässä I.* [Educating young children in the public school system by Uno Cygneaus). Helsinki, Finland: Otava.

Siekkinen, M. (1999). Childcare arrangements and children's daily activities in Belgium and Finland. *Publications in Education, 48.*

Sillanpää, T. (1994). Lastentarhanopettajakoulutuksen synty ja kehittyminen Suomessa 1882-1912 suhteessa naisen asemassa tapahtuneisiin muutoksiin [The birth and development of kindergarten teacher education in Finland between 1892 and 1912 in relation to the situation of women and its changes). *Kasvatustieteen pro gradu–tutkielma.* Kasvatustieteen laitos. Helsingin yliopisto.

Suomala, J. (1996). Eight-year-old pupil's problem solving processes within a LOGO learning environment. *Scandinavian Journal of Educational Research, 40*(4), 291-309.

Suomala, J., & Korhonen, R. (1999, September). *Educational programmes as interventions and methods in learning processes of linguistic awareness.* Paper presented at the *ECCERA Conference*, Helsinki, Finland.

Tauriainen, L. (2000). Kohti yhteistä laatua. Henkilökunnan, vanhempien ja lasten laatukäsitykset päiväkodin integroidussa erityisryhmässä [Towards a common quality: Staff's, parents', and children's conceptions in an integration group at a daycare centr]e. Univeristy of Jyväskylä. *Jyväskylä Studies in Education, Psychology and Social Research, xxx.*

Välijärvi, J., & Linnankylä, P. (2002). *Tulevaisuuden osaajat. PISA 2000 Suomessa* [The future learners. PISA Study in Finland). Jyväskylä, Finland: Koulutuksen tutkimuskeskus.

Välimäki, A. -L. (1998). Päivittäin. Lasten päivä(hoito)järjestelyn muotoutuminen varhaiskasvun ympäristönä suomalaisessa yhteiskunnassa 1800- ja 1900-luvulla [The evolution of children's (day)-care system as an environment for early growth in Finnish society in the 19th and 20th centuries. *Acta Universitatis.Ouluensis*, E 30.

Varhaislapsuuden ja kasvatuksen tutkimustoimikunnan mietintö [Report of the commission on research and education in early childhood education]. (1989). Helsinki: Sosiaali- ja terveysministeriö. Komiteamietintö.

Veresov, N. (1998). Vygotsky before Vygotsky. The path to the cultural-historical theory of human consciousness (1917-1927). Historical and methodological analysis. *Acta Universitatis Ouluensis*, E 31.

Veresov, N. (1999). *Undiscovered Vygotsky. Etudes on the pre-history of cultural-historical psychology.* Frankfurt, Germany: Peter Lang.

Östern, A. -L. (1991). *Tvåspråkighet & lingvistisk medvetande* [Bilingualism and linguistic awareness]. Åbo (Turku): Åbo Akamemis Förlag.

CHAPTER 4

CONTEMPORARY PERSPECTIVES IN EARLY CHILDHOOD EDUCATION

The Case of Greece

Demetra Evangelou and Hara Cortessis-Dafermou

In Greece, research in education in general and in early childhood education in particular is at a nascent state. Through a complex interplay of
historical, social, and cultural antecedents, a new institutional structure is
emerging within which educational research is gaining appreciation. Perhaps this will bring about further development in research activity.
Research of early development and education can expand the intellectual
horizon by dispelling the obvious or revising commonsense approaches
that are often times both a curse and a blessing in countries with age-old
traditions connecting it to educational policy and decision making. In this
chapter we report on the current state of early childhood education
research in Greece and attempt to create a framework to understand and
anticipate future directions.

International Perspectives on Research in Early Childhood Education, 119–136

THE COUNTRY

Modern Greece achieved independence from the Ottoman Empire in the early 1800s. Since then, persistent efforts have been made to develop a modern state whose values are predicated on humanistic and socially constructive principles and ideas. Greece is a peninsular country at the southern tip of the Balkans surrounded by 13,676 kilometers of coastal line and reaching out to an archipelago of about 2,000 islands, a number of which have been continuously inhabited for the last 5,000 years. The Greek terrain consists primarily of mountainous ranges and its climate is mostly temperate.

The latest population estimate stands at 10,603,000, the majority of whom (67%) are between the ages of 15-64 years of age. The country's ethnic population is rather homogeneous, reported to be 98% Greek. In recent decades there is increasing sensitization and pressure, however, to acknowledge and appreciate the growing ethnic diversity of modern Greece. Over the last 10-15 years there has been an influx of immigrants mainly from neighboring Albania and from a number of former Eastern European countries. Immigration has increased diversity and raised awareness of diversity primarily on the part of teachers who must contend with issues of second language acquisition and student acculturation.

The recent immigration wave follows a familiar trend in Greek history. Greece has stood at the crossroads of many population movements over the millennia and yet has managed to assimilate and accommodate various groups of people. In response to these issues the government has, among other measures, created a number of intercultural schools as well as reception classes and courses to facilitate language learning and acculturation. The language of education is Modern Greek, a variant of Classical Greek, and the literacy rate stands at 97% for the total population.

Greece is a member of the European Union (EU) and the Eurozone (European monetary union), with a rather stable economy and relatively high per capita income (over $20,000/person). The majority of the active population is employed in the service sector (59%) with agriculture and shipping also important.

EDUCATION SYSTEM

The Greek educational system is a highly centralized hierarchical one that follows the basic organizational structure of the Greek government. At the top of the hierarchy is the Ministry of Education, followed by directorates and offices of education at the prefecture and county levels, which are followed by the school unit. Additionally, there are a number of professional councils that are organized into primary and secondary levels and deal with issues of hiring and firing and generally make recommendations for a number of employment-related issues within the system. The Ministry of Education is responsible for the legislation, the services, the financial support, the school program and the appointment of teachers at all levels. The majority of students, 96%, attend public schools, with the remaining 4% attending private schools (Stamelos, 2002)

Beginning with preprimary education, children 3½ to 5½ can, but are not required to attend kindergarten or *nipiagogio* (literally "a place in which to educate young children"). Compulsory education starts at the next level in primary school, *dimotiko scholeio*, (literally "public school") for children between the ages of 6 and 12 comprising six grades; this is followed by junior high school for students ages 12-15. The next level, the senior high school level for students 15-18 years of age is not compulsory. There are two types of senior high schools, *comprehensive* and *technical/ vocational* schools. An additional year of noncompulsory schooling is available to students graduating from vocational high schools in which they acquire training in various trades. A number of child care workers are graduates of these programs who are employed in the field primarily as classroom aides. Higher education is a two-tier system comprised of 18 National Universities and 14 Technological Educational Institutes (TEI). In nine of the National Universities there exist departments of Early Childhood Education which are responsible for the preparation of kindergarten teachers. Child care professionals are trained at the TEI or other postsecondary private schools.

HISTORY OF THE DEVELOPMENT OF
EARLY CHILDHOOD EDUCATION

Origins of Greek Kindergarten

The value of early childhood education in Greece has been recognized relatively recently. The history of the Greek kindergarten reflects changing values and increased awareness for the significance of the early years and its effects on the social fabric. Greece has always been the recipient of the enlightened efforts of a Diaspora, Greeks residing abroad which maintain close links to the Greek society and have aided efforts for modernization and development through the import and adaptations of ideas and which places value on social improvement and education (Mouzelis, 1978). The Diaspora produced enlightened individuals like Ekaterini Laskaridou (Charitos, 1996) the founder of the first kindergarten and the first child care center in Athens in the 1890s, who were instrumental in spearheading the initial private efforts for the establishment of the Greek kindergarten at the same time as women's education was emerging as a significant social expectation (Dimaras, 1974). Laskaridou, the daughter of a wealthy Greek merchant was born in 1842 in Vienna and moved to Greece in 1867 after the country gained its independence from the Ottoman Empire. In 1879 she left for Dresden where she studied the Froebelian method under the guidance of countess Bertha von Marenholtz-Bullow who had been Froebel's student.

In 1896, nearly 70 years after the establishment of the modern Greek state, the minister of Ecclesiastics and Public Education officially endorsed kindergarten in Greece. The original ministerial decree specified the conditions under which individuals of "demonstrated civic merit" and of "theoretical and practical ability in their roles as kindergarten teachers" were to engage in the education of children from 3 to 6 years of age (Dimaras, 1974, p. 7). "Kindergartens should aim at the physical and mental strengthening of children through the employment of games, exercises and the good teaching of elements necessary for children's continuation into elementary school, while maintaining intact the joy and tranquility of children's souls" read the official document (Dimaras, 1974). According to Charitos (1998), throughout the twentieth century the development of the Greek kindergarten remained a low national priority, poorly funded and institutionally stagnant, following an uneven path which reflected larger social changes while the majority of parents were not aware of its importance. In the beginning, kindergarten was conceived as an enrichment activity for middle class children. During the 1920s and 1930s it functioned as a compensatory mechanism for children of immigrants and refugees and was used as a vehicle for cultivating national and cultural identity. Things changed, and started improving significantly in the 1950s and 1960s when Greece was undergoing industrialization.

The Roots of Child Care Centers

Child care centers first opened in the early 1900s and they resembled, to a large extend, similar institutions in other countries. They were designed to provide day care services to working families. In the beginning these centers were mostly based on charity, operating like asylums, where the care aspects supersede educational ones, and were slowly expanded to serve the needs that resulted from the urbanization and industrialization of Greece in the 1930s. Most day care centers, like kindergartens, were created along the borders of Greece. The policy reflected the need for integration of the newly liberated parts of Greece which took place over a long period of nearly 100 years (1821-1912). The Greek state sought to establish the development of national identity "Hellinization" largely by imposing the modern Greek language on the various ethnic groups that were gradually incorporated into the modern Greek state. According to Papaprokopiou (2003) the charitable-asylum character legacy continued to define child care centers, as some of their stated goals of keeping the children clean, fed, and tranquil demonstrate. In recent times the absence of curriculum has been raised by many as a major concern. As a result, significant improvements are in the making in terms of training professionals and establishing curriculum guidelines.

GENERAL STATE OF
EARLY CHILDHOOD EDUCATION SERVICES

Greece is undergoing a long transition involving the transformation of institutions from traditional familism (Flaquer, 2002), where individuals are dependent on the family to provide the network of social welfare protections which are provided by the state in the case of modern postindustrialized forms of social organization. At the nucleus of this transformation there is tension generated from the conflicts which traditional societies experience as their accumulated wisdom makes them view change with great desire and equally great suspicion. Traditionally, Greeks have been wary of change demanded from outside. Yet, they embrace EU regulations concerning early childhood education services, and in the process discover rather conveniently that the changes better fit emerging needs. Such is the case, for example, with the recent expansion of kindergarten services from half day to full day; obviously a change that better fits modern day life and increased female employment. Professor Papaprokopiou (an expert in Greek child care) succinctly captures the spirit of these changes when saying "We are thankful for the European demands because for us they are more friend than foe" (personal communication, 2003).

Family Policy

In Greece maternity benefits include maternity grant, maternity allowance, and mandatory paid maternity leave of 17 weeks. While on leave women receive a cash benefit of 50% of their wages. Additional parental leaves are available for sick children and school visits. Female labor force participation is at 49%, lower than the European average of 52% but nonetheless family life changes taking place gradually over the recent decades are not matched by tradition-shaped self-perceptions. From the point of view of family policy, "familism" seems to be paid attention to in governmental policy (Koutrougalos, 1996). Greece has strong legislation protecting family and marriage, caring for large families, widows, and orphans of war as well as maternity protection, child protection and protection of the elderly. There is a national health care system available.

Child Care and Education

There exist two distinct national systems of publicly funded early childhood and education: Child care centers for children from birth to age 6 and kindergartens, which are free and universal for children 4 to 6 years. Approximately 60% of preschool age children attend some type of setting and 70% of 3½- to 6-year-olds are in kindergarten. By age 5, 99% of all children attend some preschool institutions (Olmstead & Montie, 2001). The Ministry of Social Welfare and the Ministry of the Interior share responsibility at the national level for early childhood care and the Ministry of Education has responsibility for Early Childhood Education.

Child Care Centers

Upgrading child care and education services is a work in progress. A large number of new centers are being constructed and a lot more are planned. Approximately 130 new centers are expected to be in operation countrywide by the year 2006 (Eurybase, 2003). The administration of approximately 60% of them (829 centers) has been transferred to local authorities in an attempt to decentralize and personalize the services by recognizing local communities' expert knowledge and sensitivity to the needs of families and children. This is a welcome change for many in the field. In addition, afterschool child care and other forms of alternative care are being planned and 220 new facilities are being constructed. These important steps are taken to address the issues of children being unattended for long periods of time (mostly "children of the traffic lights") by establishing programs to receive and care for these children initially. These are typically children of immigrant families struggling to survive by doing odd jobs, or begging at traffic lights in big cities (Houndoumadi, 2002).

Papaprokopiou (2003) points out several shortcomings of the national child care systems which are now slowly being addressed as a result of social pressures as well as demands to align Greek services with those of the more developed countries of the European Union. She argues, in particular, that a number of structural (such as teacher to child ratio) and contextual (such as appropriate curriculum) changes are in order for the system to move up to the next level which is that of qualitatively different services in line with modern scientific practices that are responsive to the needs of families. The current underway transfer of central control from the National Ministries to the local municipal authorities is heralded by many as a step in the right direction. They point to the example of the child care system of the municipality of Athens and to the high quality of its services as an example of how things can improve once local actors gain control and assume accountability.

Kindergarten

Both public and private kindergartens operate under the Ministry of Education. Most children attend for 2 years and classrooms are staffed by one or two teachers depending on the number of children. The recommended teacher to child ration is 1:14. The most important development of recent years is the expansion from half-day to full-day kindergarten. The stated goals of the full-day programs as delineated in the law 2525/ 1997 (Republic of Greece, Ministry of Education, 1997) are threefold: (a) To offer all children a well-rounded preparation for primary school; (b) To measure up to the state's responsibility for offering universal education as a vehicle for social equality; and (c) To provide a service to working parents. The first full-day programs started in 1998 and by 1999 350 kindergartens were already transformed. The government goal is for all kindergartens to become full-day programs.

In addition, a new national curriculum has recently been proposed (Republic of Greece, Ministry of Education, 2001). This new curriculum replaces the previous one which was also the first formal attempt at a national kindergarten curriculum (Evangelou, 1996). It takes an interdisciplinary approach to teaching in kindergarten. "The goal of the kindergarten, according to the 1566/1985 (Government Gazette No 1376, 1985), is to assist kindergartners in developing physically, emotionally, cognitively and socially within the context of the broader goals of the compulsory primary and secondary education" (p. 1623).

Since 1984, kindergarten teachers have trained at university departments of education, a fact which has contributed to elevating the status of early childhood education. These departments are responsible for establishing their own curricular and training guidelines for teacher education. No uniform set of guidelines exist outside the departments which remain the only places offering certification by virtue of the degree. The majority of their graduates are then employed by the State as kindergarten teachers.

RESEARCH AND POLICY ISSUES

In Greece, research in general and educational research in particular was off to a late start. As recently as the 1980s educational research was practically nonexistent. The small number of studies that were carried out were narrowly focused and conducted as individual efforts (Chatzidimos, 2000).

In this section we address the reasons for the underdevelopment of educational research and discuss recent changes.

Reasons for Underdevelopment

As the discussion about educational research is gaining ground, a number of experts identify various reasons for its underdevelopment. There is no tradition of systematic research. In Greece, educational studies and teacher training were only recently elevated to university status. Graduate studies in education were officially established in the last 5 years. There is a lack of coordinating agencies and no great financial investment and a very weak linkage between educational research and policy.

As research is a relatively novel activity, there is lack of tradition and appreciation that affects the development and use of educational research and the resulting knowledge (Flouris, 2000). Several research projects are rather duplicative. Sometimes similar projects are funded by different ministries and different groups of researchers seem to be working unaware of each other's efforts.

In addition, university departments of education in which secondary school teachers are trained operate on the basis of a transmission of knowledge model (Spodek, 1991) that is relevant to the content subject area. Little attention is devoted to how these various subjects ought to be taught. In other words, pedagogical content knowledge is not on the agenda. Pedagogy and teaching are not considered scientific subjects per se. The assumption is those that know something about the subject ought to know how to transmit this knowledge to others. Most kindergarten and primary school teachers were trained at 2-year training colleges with a clear vocational orientation through which they acquired practical teaching knowledge and skills. Their training was upgraded to university level in 1984.

Graduate studies in Greece were officially endorsed in the 1990s. Greek universities up to that time offered a single postgraduate degree, the doctorate, which was documenting an individual person's research efforts under the direction of a single professor. This type of supervision was scholastic in nature rather than elaborating substance (Kassotakis,

1998). The lack of graduate schools of education has had a negative impact in the training and education of qualified researchers within the educational community. This is anticipated to change as a number of graduate programs have been established within university departments of education.

The underdevelopment of educational research is certainly also related to the extremely low financial investment. In Greece in 1998, for example, a meager 0.5% of the gross domestic product was devoted to scientific research compared to the Organization for Economic Cooperation and Development average of 2.2% (Flouris, 2000). Kassotakis (2002a) also points to the absence of a national coordinating body that would assist in pooling resources, identifying needs, and disseminating information. So far, there has been no agency responsible for the establishment of a long-term research agenda (Flouris, 2000). Educational policy in Greece has not been based on research findings but rather on political vision. Frequent education policy changes and a very narrow planning window have been characteristic of educational matters in Greece. But even the very small number of educational research that is carried out in spite of the limitations of researcher training has often times been met with reluctance and inhibition about its scientific merit and validity (Kassotakis, 2002a).

Changes

In the 1980s a number of changes took place. The 2-year teacher training institutions were gradually replaced by university departments of education. Thus, pedagogy and the science of teaching were recognized as independent disciplines within the university and more importantly the need for the connection between educational research and practice emerged (Chatzidimos, 2000).

With the establishment of the university departments of education a number of positions were filled by scholars that had studied abroad and were trained in areas related to education. Since there was no university-level education specifically focused on early childhood education, the great majority of professors and researchers that sought out these new positions came from other disciplines and their focus on early childhood education developed more as a result of having accepted these new positions, than as previous career commitments in early childhood education.

Additional momentum was given by the passing in 1997 of a law that clearly delineates as part of the professorial responsibility the pursuit of research efforts in addition to the more traditional aspects of teaching. As a result, members of the Greek university community are now required to demonstrate evidence of research activity for promotion and tenure.

Government Guidelines

An important step in aiding the development of systematic research activities on a national scale is the establishment of social structures that can scientifically and financially support research aims. With globalization, small economies like the Greek one need to rethink and prioritize anew their budgetary structures by shifting resources from traditional defense and industry related aims to research areas with growth potential for which they can have inherent advantages. Greece is very well situated in that sense in that it enjoys a high standard of living, a highly educated population, and is securely positioned within the EU. The Greek General Secretariat of Research and Technology (GSRT, 2003) is one of these structures and in a recent document it has outlined a number of directives as part of strategic initiative undertaken by the Greek government in order to promote systematic research. The directives are the following:

1. Increase the demand for new knowledge and research results in the country.
2. Restructure the research system and the dissemination of knowledge.
3. Restructure the research system by further opening it to the global economy.
4. Develop the technological infrastructure to facilitate use of scientific and technological policy.
5. Establish thematic and departmental priority areas in scientific and technological policy.
6. Quantify aims/goals and establish systematic evaluation.

While these proclamations are steps in the right direction there is a lot of work to be done in reaching consensus and translating these aims into funded research activities. At this point, educational research and research in early childhood education appear to be a low priority as evident in the miniscule government budget devoted to them. On the other hand, the discussion has began and it is gaining momentum, and it would be difficult to turn the clock back now as a number of mechanisms are already in place such as the departments of higher education and the recently established Center for Educational Research (CER) (Kassotakis, 2002b).

Research Centers

The Pedagogical Institute (PI)

Since its inception it has been responsible for advising the government on educational policy, developing school textbooks (every Greek student at all levels receives free school texts every year) and designing national curricula. Included in its aims are the design and coordination of educational research.

Additionally, the PI acts as a facilitator of the process by examining requests for approval, granting entrance permissions to the schools, and by being a depository of research findings through its libraries.

The Center for Educational Research (KEE)

This is the first public institute of its kind in Greece. It was established in 1995 under the aegis of the Ministry of Education entrusted with the mission of coordinating research in education in Greece. It also publishes related documents as well as organizes meetings for the specific purpose of communication and dissemination of research findings. The center is connected to a number of international agencies and works in close collaboration with UNESCO and OECD (Kassotakis, 2002b).

University Departments

The establishment of departments of education as part of the university structure has resulted in the development of vital space for studying and researching educational issues. In the last 15 years their contributions are noteworthy. A number of dissertations have been carried out, a number of educational conferences are organized both annually on the national and international level, and a forum has been created for the discussion of research efforts occuring within Greece and abroad.

There are 19 departments of education in the National Universities, nine departments of primary education, nine of early childhood education and one special education department. In addition, there are four departments of philosophy, pedagogy, and psychology operating within the Schools of Philosophy. Since the official creation of postgraduate programs in 1992, a number of additional specializations have come about in the old teacher's schools that attempt to connect the teaching of subject with the pedagogical content knowledge of each area. For example, it is now possible to specialize in mathematics education or technology and education or teaching of Greek as a second language. In addition, students can pursue specializations that are interdisciplinary and some of the departments of education have been at the forefront of these initiatives.

REVIEW OF RESEARCH IN EARLY CHILDHOOD EDUCATION

In this next section we review some of the research that was conducted by the university departments of education, the PI and CER. Some of these studies are regularly carried out in the school setting. In these instances researchers have to apply for permission from the Pedagogical Institute to enter the schools for research purposes. The central data base of the Pedagogical Institute reveals the kind of studies for which there had been requests for school based research in all levels of education in the last 10 years. A second source for this type of research is the complete list of doctoral dissertations carried out in the education departments of all Greek universities. The third source originates in the research in the early years that funded by the European Union and carried out under the auspices of the CER.

Methodologically the majority of studies employ questionnaires. A few studies employ obtrusive and unobtrusive observations designs. Interviews are usually a very small sample, a fact that often may undermine the validity of the results. A small number of experimental studies are also reported.

University Departments

Professors of early childhood education often come to these departments from other disciplines and continue to pursue their old research interests. As a result, a significant number of their research publications reflect interests in older children or more general subject matter and only a small number of their work is focused on early childhood education issues. In Greece, graduate early childhood education students are quite often practicing teachers who secure release-time from the Ministry of Education in order to pursue graduate degrees. A review of educational research conducted in departments of early childhood education in the last 10 years reveals the following.

Doctoral Dissertations

Doctoral dissertations are a major category of educational research. During the last 10 years from 1992 to 2002 there have been 62 doctoral dissertations completed in the 19 university departments of early childhood education. Of the 62 doctoral dissertations, 24 (38%) deal with issues of early childhood education such as: "educational interventions for the development of geometric concepts in preschool children," "intervention for the function of poetic language in early childhood education," "teacher ideas about physic's concepts: an investigative study of their

knowledge and teaching of the physical science," "the receptive vocabulary of children 5½ to 6½." The remaining number of dissertations
address higher educational levels and investigate various other topics.
Some of the topics included are, for example, "self-perceptions of adolescents and their mothers' when there is a social needs person in the family," or "the birth of a painter in Macedonia: the case of George Paralis."

About 37% (23) of the dissertations have been carried out at the
department of Early Childhood Education at Aristotle University of Thes-
saloniki and about 17%, or 11 dissertations, have been completed at the
University of Athens, the two main national universities. To understand
these numbers one has to take into account the historical development of
these departments and the struggle to transform teacher education in
Greece in the last 2 decades. Aristotle University was the first to create a
department of early childhood education in 1984 under the enlightened
direction of Professor Christos Frangos, a pioneer of early childhood education in Greece. Frangos, whose career spans many decades, was educated in Greece and abroad and articulated a modern vision of early
childhood education and teacher training. He was instrumental in bringing together the scientific community and professional and trade
teacher's associations to capture the attention of the Ministry of Education in instituting very significant changes. Frangos (1983) mentored and
encouraged the efforts of many young scientists in the discipline and
delineated its scientific and social parameters.

The Pedagogical Institute Database

The Pedagogical Institute reviews research and grants entry to schools
for research purposes. When we examined the database of the Pedagogical Institute we found that they do not include only educational research.
So a large number of projects have school age children as participants
even though they do not always concern educational issues. Some are
focused specifically on the ideas and opinions of the students as for example in the case of a study titled: "investigating the parameters that contribute to the development of students' ideas about AIDS," or "the
religious organization of students as they graduate from primary education." Yet another strand of research projects is geared toward the effects
of a various agents on the psychological and behavioral development of
children and adolescents as for example in "the effects of repatriation on
adolescents" or "the effects of television on the behavior of children 4-12
years old." In addition, research permission requested for conducting
school-based research that concerns medical issues as in the example of
"tonsillectomy, adenoidectomy and appendectomy in children from the

Table 4.1.   Number of Studies by School Level

School Level	N	%
Kindergarten	33	4.22
Elementary	222	28.4
Junior high school	100	12.8
High school	130	16.6
Kindergarten elementary	30	3.80
Kindergarten, elementary and junior high school	1	0.12
Elementary and junior high school	35	4.50
Elementary, junior high school and +high school	33	4.20
Junior high school and high school	105	13.4
All levels	2	0.25
Other	90	11.5
Total	781	99.0

Source: Pedagogical Institute of Greece

Kilkis prefecture." Between 1992 and 2002 there were 781 such requests for research submitted to the PI. Of those, 126 were rejected and for the remaining number it is difficult to say which were actually completed.

The smallest number of studies in the PI database (about 8%) has children in the early years as participants. Following are some examples of the studies in this category: "An initial investigation for the appearance of dyslexia in early childhood," "The relationship between reading readiness and school success in the beginning of elementary school," "Loneliness and peer relationships in preschool." The number of studies increases in the elementary school (about 37%), while the majority of the studies (69%) involve students in the upper levels of secondary education. Regarding sponsorship of these studies, it appears that indeed a significant number are sponsored by seed university grants. These are small grants, around 50.000 euros, that each university can allocate from its budget and that are subject to internal reviews.

Center for Educational Research Studies

Finally, the last strand that we investigated refers to educational research sponsored by the Center for Educational Research (KEE) under the auspices and with cosponsored financial support from the European Union and the Greek Ministry of Education. In this program, a total of 48 studies were funded and were carried out by researchers in the university departments of education. Of those, there are 10 studies regarding educational policy and strategy with only one study evaluating the newly instituted full-day school programs. An additional 12 studies concern issues of curriculum evaluation and school effectiveness. Here, again, only one deals with early childhood education titled: "Evaluation of the Effects of Language Teaching in the Primary Grades." Another 14 studies deal with issues of the direction of the Greek educational system and the remaining 12 studies concern issues of teacher qualification and teacher education. Of those, only one focuses on the early years.

Educational Conferences

In recent years a number of educational conferences have taken place. They are organized by the university departments of education, by the Greek Educational Society and other professional bodies such as OMEP (Organization Mundiale pour l Education Prescolaire). These conferences provide a forum for Greek researchers in which to present their work and they are usually well attended. In reviewing the proceedings of three recent conferences we see that they cover a wide range of topics studied through a variety of methodological designs. Two main themes appear to dominate most research activity within the Greek context. First, there is an intense interest around issues of language within the school setting. The reasons for this preference are in our opinion the result of the long efforts on behalf of Greek intellectuals to approach language as a mechanism with the power to establish social equality. In the past different linguistic forms of Greek had been used to construct categories of people whose access to education has been limited. Historically, the field of education in Greece was seen by many as an extension of the linguistic departments and that origin is still evident in the research topics preferred by educational researchers today. The second research area that is receiving a lot of attention is that which studies the teaching methods of science and technology in the early years. Some of the other research topics include art education within which museum education seems to be an important component as well as an emphasis on the study of the expressive arts. Additional topics include teacher education issues as well as the development of children in the early years.

Research Journals

The signature of an active research community is often seen in the process of documentation established by the community to develop, promote, and disseminate knowledge.

Such efforts in Greece have been under way for a long time and there is now a small number of peer reviewed journals in the field. Additionally, as all Greek early childhood education professors and researchers are bilingual and sometimes trilingual they all have access to European journals some of which publish in a number of languages. Of the Greek journals the *Educational Review* is published biannually and out of the 15 studies published in 2002 three have an early childhood education focus.

CONCLUSIONS

Research in early childhood education in Greece is undergoing rapid growth characterized by a shift toward systematic and long-term efforts and a growing awareness of the importance of research as an instrument for policy. In this chapter we have reported on the current state of Greek early childhood education research and future directions. New graduate programs in university departments of early childhood education, the Pedagogical Institute and the recently established Center for Educational Research offer valuable information related to early childhood education research. Analysis of items found in their key databases reveals growth and a shifting focus in early childhood education research toward more systematic interdisciplinary type projects.

The broad context of early childhood education research in Greece includes transformations brought about by European Union initiatives in which university early childhood education departments have played a leading role. A new structure has emerged within which educational research appears to be connecting with policy and decision making.

Research provides a new venue for modernization in countries such as Greece where strong traditional structures often clash with transformations and changes perceived as imported from outside. The expansion of kindergarten services from half day to full day provides an example of a change that was instituted on the basis of research findings and gained widespread acceptance (addressing the needs of a society facing increased female employment). It appears that systematic research may offer a new opportunity for sustainable growth and balanced change in the educational system of Greece as it struggles to integrate with the global system while preserving those salient elements of an old and remarkably enduring legacy.

ACKNOWLEDGMENT

We would like to thank the following individuals for their invaluable assistance in gathering the information as well as for the enlightening discussions: Professors Anna Tsatsaronis, Haralambos Sakonidis, and

Athanasios Lainas; and the teachers and doctoral candidates, Georgia Sarigiannidou, Anna Klothou, and Georgios Manthos.

REFERENCES

Charitos, C. G., (1998). *The Greek kindergarten and its roots: Contributions to the history of early education* [in Greek]. Athens, Greece: Gutenberg.

Chatzidimos, D. (2002). Educational research in Greece: Current state, needs, trends. In A. Banou (Ed.), *Research in Greek education* [in Greek] (pp. 38-42). Athens, Greece: Center for Educational Research.

Dimaras, A. (Ed.). (1990). *The Reform that did not take place* [in Greek]. Athens, Greece: Hermes.

Evangelou, D. (1996). Culture and the Greek kindergarten curriculum. *Early Child Development and Care, 123*, 31-46.

Flouris, G. (2002). Educational research in Greece: Current state, needs, trends. In A. Banou (Ed.), *Research in Greek education* [in Greek] (pp. 30-32). Athens, Greece: Center for Educational Research.

Flaquer, L. (2002). *Is there a unique family policy model in Southern Europe?* [in Greek]. Athens, Greece: Gutenberg.

Frangos, C. (1983). *Fundamental pedagogical theses* [in Greek]. Athens, Greece: Gutenberg.

GSRT research and development: The priorities of the Ministry of Development. (2003). Retrieved March 19, 2003, from http://www.gsrt.gr/site.asp

Houdoumadi, A. (2002). *"... by a pool eating plums ..." Exploring the learning needs of children of Muslim families living in Metaxourghio.* Athens, Greece: Schedia.

Kassotakis, M. (1988). *Graduate education in Greece: Present and future* [in Greek]. Paper presented at the conference on Perspectives on Graduate Education in Europe, National and /Kapodistrian University of Athens.

Kassotakis, M. (2002a). Educational research in Greece. In A. Banou (Ed.), *Research in Greek education* [in Greek] (pp. 6-9). Athens, Greece: Center for Educational Research.

Kassotakis, M. (2002b). The necessity of educational research in Greece and the role of the center for educational research in the1997-2000 period. In A. Verevi (Ed.), The Work "Research" 1997-2000 [in Greek]. Athens: Center for Educational Research.

Koutrougalos, G. S. (1996). The south European welfare model: The Greek welfare state in search of an identity. *Journal of European Social Policy, 6*(1), 39-60.

Mouzelis, N. P. (1978). *Modern Greece: Facets of underdevelopment.* New York: Holmes and Meier.

Olmsted, P. P., & Montie, J. (Eds.). (2001). *Early childhood settings in 15 countries: What are their structural characteristics?* Ypsilanti, MI: High/Scope.

Papaprokopiou, A. (2003). Towards the development of a cooperative and collaborative in service training in early childhood education [in Greek]. Athens, Greece: Dardanos.

Republic of Greece, Ministry of Education. (1985). *Government Gazette*, No 1566

Republic of Greece, Ministry of Education. (1997). *Government Gazette*, No 2525
Republic of Greece, Ministry of Education. (2001). *Government Gazette*, No 1376
Stamelos, G. (Ed.). (2002). *The Greek educational system: Structure and quantitative data* [in Greek] Athens, Greece: Center for Educational Research.
Spodek, B. (1991). Early childhood curriculum and cultural definition of knowledge. In B. Spodek & O. N. Saracho (Eds.), *Issues in early childhood curriculum: Yearbook in early childhood education: Vol 2.* New York: Teachers College Press.
Summary sheets on education systems in Europe: Greece. (2000). Retrieved March 20, 2003, from http://www.eurydice.org/Eurybase/Application/print-all.asp

CHAPTER 5

RESEARCH AND POLICY ISSUES IN EARLY CHILDHOOD CARE AND EDUCATION IN JAPAN

Yoko Shirakawa and Sachiko Kitano

INTRODUCTION

People in Japan are taking an increasing interest in early childhood care and education. Its needs have appealed to public through media, financiers, businessmen, and politicians. However, the limitations of the research in early childhood care and education in Japan does not match the interest in practice. The current structural reforms in Japan are making matters worse. The number of university programs and research institutions in the field is decreasing. We seem to be on the edge of a difficult and complicated situation. We needed to make the problem clear and seek ways to improve early childhood care and education research in Japan. For this purpose, this chapter deals with the history, the current social status, and the reforms in early childhood care and education in Japan. Issues in policymaking and research will be the focus of our chapter.

International Perspectives on Research in Early Childhood Education, 137–160
Copyright © 2005 by Information Age Publishing
137

The first section introduces the historical development of early childhood care and education, presenting three different eras: the beginning of the Meiji Period (from 1886 until 1912), the Yochien reform from Froebelian orthodoxy to Japanese originals (around the turn of the twentieth century), and the period after WWII. The second section focuses on recent changes in society in general, and more particularly, on changes in family relationships and policymaking. As these changes cannot be examined in isolation, their interaction will be discussed. In the third section, the current state of early childhood care and education, such as programs and teachers are presented. The final section presents an overview of the present state of research and research related issues in early childhood care and education in Japan.

A BRIEF HISTORY OF EARLY CHILDHOOD EDUCATION IN JAPAN

Meiji Period

In 1872, the Meiji Government proclaimed the Education System Order, after examining the French administrative system and the educational methods used in the United States. In the Education System Order, pre-elementary level schooling was provided as a form of elementary education (Editing Committee of Dictionary of Japan Modern Educational History, 1972). It was to provide instruction for children under the age of 6. However, it never progressed beyond the planning stage. In 1875 the Ministry of Education of the Meiji Government sent three researchers to the state normal schools in the United States to study modern systems of childhood education and, as the result, to raise Japanese educational standards. One of the members, Shuji Izawa knew about Froebel Kindergarten Education before his visit to the United States, as he had read the kindergarten guide *The Child* (1872), an interpretation and translation of Baroness Marenholts's ideas by Matilda H. Kriege (Hashimoto, 1998). In 1871 the American Women's Education Center was founded in Japan by missionaries and there was a child care institution (kindergarten) as well.

Modern systematic preschool education started in Japan after the Meiji Government introduced Froebel's kindergarten. The government named the institution *Yochien*. In 1872, Tokyo Women's Normal School was founded. It established an affiliated Yochien in 1876. This Yochien and its training course became the model; graduates of the schools spread Yochien throughout Japan. Women's normal schools in local areas started to train Yochien teachers and also to create affiliate Yochiens. In 1898, there were more than one Yochien in 39 out of 47 prefectures (Ministry of Education, 1979).

During the last decade of the nineteenth century, the Ministry of Education created acts concerning Yochien education. In 1891, the requirement for becoming a Yochien teacher was first stated in a government ordinance. The very first act completely dedicated to Yochien was the *Yochien Hoiku no Setsubi Kitei* (the Regulations of Yochien Education and Equipment), which was enacted in 1899. At this time only 0.8% of 5-year-olds attended Yochien; this number rose to 4.4% in 1925. The highest percentage for 5-year-olds attending Yochien before the end of WWII, was 10.0% in 1941 (Ministry of Education, 1979).

Early childhood education research emerged from diverse contexts. One major stimulus came from the Japanese Government whose aim was to spread and standardize preschool education in Japan. The Meiji Government sent researchers abroad who translated books and gathered information on early childhood education.

Fujimaro Tanaka was one of the pioneers of early childhood education in Japan. He was both a researcher and an officer at the Ministry of Education. As a result of his efforts, he managed to found the first Yochien in 1876, mentioned earlier. He was greatly influenced by William T. Harris, the St. Louis School Superintendent. In fact, the Ministry of Education decided to have Harris's *American Journal of Education* translated rather than that of Henry Barnard's, in spite of its popularity and fame, in order to learn about school management (Hashimoto, 1998; Yukawa, 2001).

Yochien Reform: From Froebelian Orthodoxy to Japanese Originals

Around the turn of the twentieth century many countries saw different movements in early childhood education; the Yochien reform in Japan had its own particular features. The curriculum for training Yochien teachers gradually changed Yochien and free play was introduced.

The teaching staff of Tokyo Women's Normal School was the first to work on the adaptation of kindergarten education to Japan; they tried to promote their original ideas of the Yochien. In 1908, Goroku Nakamura and Minoru Wada of Tokyo Women's Normal School wrote *Yoji Kyoiku Ho* (*Early Childhood Education Method*), and they defined and started to use the words "Yudo Hoiku" ("*Yudo*" means to induce, conduct, or lead; and "*Hoiku*" means the early childhood care and education). They advised teachers to put emphasis on a child-centered education, rather than giving children direct teaching at an early stage of their life. Sozo Kurahashi, who is probably considered the most famous researcher of his time, shared their ideas and as a result helped to spread the expression of Yudo Hoiku and its definition. Effected by the New Education Movement (the

Progressive Education Movement), Kurahashi and others tried to reform Yochien education to be closely related to children's daily life, interests, and their own will. Kurahashi insisted on letting children play as they wanted in ways that reflected their personal experiences. He indicated the importance of the child-centered, play-based Yochien education with well-designed environment. He published the first original curriculum in early childhood education titled *Keitoteki Hoiku An no Jissai (Practice in Systematic Curriculum in Early Childhood Care and Education)* in 1935, with his colleagues from Tokyo Women's Normal School Yochien.

It was not only government-related institutions that helped to spread the idea of Yochien in Japan, but missionaries also founded Yochien and trained Yochien teachers. They also enriched research in Japan, translating the latest research findings and books from other countries. For example, Annie L. Howe, in Kobe, translated Froebel's *Mutter- und Kose-Lieder* (Froebel. Howe, Trans., 1895) into Japanese. Fujiko Takamori, another missionary, translated *A Conduct Curriculum for the Kindergarten and First Grade* (1923) by Patty Smith Hill (Hill. Takamori, Trans., 1936). Howe insisted on the reform of the curriculum for both the Yochien and its teacher training. Researchers like Kurahashi, Howe, and other pioneers maintained a continuous dialog with researchers in other countries and used their ideas and knowledge as to improve and propagate Japanese Yochien.

The Yochien reform was not limited to individual researchers, but spread quickly to educational associations. There were three large organizations founded during the Meiji Period and continued their activity until the Showa Period (from 1915). These were: (a) Froebel Kai (Froebel Association) organized in 1896 by the amalgamation of two organizations in Tokyo, (b) Keihanshin San Shi Rengo Hoiku Kai (Early Childhood Education Union in Kyoto, Osaka, and Kobe) organized in 1897, and (c) Japan Kindergarten Union organized in 1906 by Howe. It was not until 1936 that the first nationwide organization, Zen Nihon Hoiku Renmei (Japan Association for Early Childhood Care and Education) was founded; more than 2,000 people attended its first annual meeting in Osaka in 1937.

During the turn of the twentieth century, industrialization and urbanization had brought widespread needs for child care. In 1890, Mr. and Mrs. Akizawa founded the first day care center in Niigata, in the countryside of Japan. Some schools also established affiliated day care centers. These centers took care of younger children and let them play, sing, and study, so that older children could concentrate on studying. There are also records of child care centers which took care of children during the busy farming seasons in the countryside of Japan. Yochien for urban poor were also opened, such as, Zenrin Yochien in Kobe, Futaba Yochien in Tokyo, and Aizenbashi Yochien. The founder of Aizenbashi Yochien, Juji Ishii, who also opened one of the most well-known orphanages in Japan, was deeply affected by Thomas John Barnard. In 1909 the Department of the Interior started to subsidize child care institutions, but it was not until after World War II that the government named the child care welfare institution Hoikusho and began providing systematic child care services.

Early Childhood Educational Reforms after World War II

Soon after World War II, under the direction of the General Headquarters (GHQ) of the United States Army occupying forces, and as part of the reconstruction of Japanese society, a system of regulations for early childhood care and education was established. With the GHQ's advice, the Japanese cabinet established advisory committees/councils. The Education Renewal Committee/Education Renewal Council submitted its first proposal for a Fundamental Law of Education; and the Social Security Council submitted the proposal for a Child Welfare Law. In 1947, Yochien education was officially included as part of the regular school system, and day care centers were defined as welfare institutions and were given the name "*Hoikusho*."

Advisory committees were formed at the request of the cabinets and ministries. The reports they produced were based on research stimulated by the government. This became the protocol of the early childhood care and education research, which affects policymaking even today.

In 1948, the Ministry of Education established standards for educational guideline for Yochien, Hoikusho, and family (Hoiku Yoryo), which was revised in 1956 as Yochien Kyoiku Yoryo (Yochien Education Guideline). The revision was in response to criticism on the lack of smooth transition from Yochien to elementary school, especially in the field of academic expectations and achievements. The next revision, in 1964, was motivated by the objections to the high expectations for academic achievements.

The Ministry of Health and Welfare established enforcement regulations (Hoikusho Hoiku Shishin) in 1965.

CHANGES IN SOCIETY, FAMILY, AND EARLY CHILDHOOD EDUCATION

Changing Society and Family

After 10 years of postwar rehabilitation, Japan plunged into a period of high economic growth which continued until the early 1970s. At that time, Japan became one of the most highly industrialized countries in the

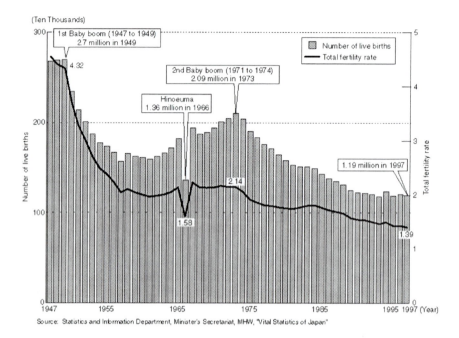

Figure 5.1.   The change in the number of births and fertility rate.s

world. In the late 1980s, Japan enjoyed a "bubble economy," which soon collapsed; since then the Japanese economy has slowed down. Japanese people are beginning to search for a new lifestyle that will suit the postindustrial society, such as a welfare society that is "slow and tender." As Figure 5.1 shows, the number of births has decreased since 1973. The first baby boomers are now entering their 50s as Japan becomes an aging society. The average Japanese life span was 67.75 (female), 63.60 (male) in 1955, 78.76 (female), 73.35 (male) in 1980, and about 84.93 (female), 78.07 (male) in 2001.

The changes in the society (fewer children, more elderly people, and low economic growth) affected the lives of children and their parents. In a society with more children and where most people lived in poverty, children studied in a crowded classroom, competing with others to achieve academics goal. Children more or less grew up vigorously. In the outdoor open space, children got together and formed multiaged playgroups where they developed social skills. Today, in contrast, fewer children are being taken care of by more adults. Despite the economical recession, people spend more money on children. In the 1990s it is said, "A child has six pockets, two parents' pockets and four grandparents' pockets." As the result of being brought up in material affluence, children are losing a lust for life. Childhood educators have suggested that parents be more concerned about the spiritual education of children. Furthermore, with less concern for the educational functions (strengths) of home and community, society faces serious problems with childhood education, such as bullying, absenteeism at school, class disruption, and vicious crimes committed by 12- to 14-year-olds. Because of this, the Ministry of Education issued a white paper in 1994 setting forth government's educational policies: "New direction in School Education: Fostering Strength for Life."

In the field of early childhood education, the Yochien Education Guideline (1989), which was revised after 25 years, introduced the fundamental principle of Yochien education as education through children's free-play in an educational environment. At first, under the new guideline, many Yochien teachers pointed out that some children did not know how to play voluntarily, because they were used to a whole class activity based on teacher's instructions.

The changing society also impacted parents of young children. As a result of longevity, a young couple becomes parents at a comparatively early stage of life. After their children grew up and left the family, the parents would still have about 20 more years of life. The longevity has changed especially for woman. More women could now become mothers and still have time to achieve their own self-realization. They are beginning to establish their own life-long careers in society. Thus, the number of working mother is wholly increasing.

However, many mothers whose youngest child is under the age of 3 do not work outside the home. In 1995, 24% of mothers of children 0-2 years old, including single parents, are working; in 2000 this was 27.3%. According to the same survey (Ministry of Health, Labour, and Welfare, 2000); by the time the youngest child reached the age of 6, the number of working mothers exceeded the number of nonworking mothers. Almost 70% of the families with children under age 3 are rearing their infants without using day care facilities. Generally these families are nuclear families, with mother taking care of the young children and father working away from home for long hours. In a society with few children, these nuclear families are now the minority and are isolated from other families in the community. During the past decade, many problems related to child rearing, such as the anxieties of mothers that sometimes causes child abuse or attempted double suicides among these families. In the spring of 1999, the Ministry of Health and Welfare started a campaign of father involvement in child rearing. However, it did not receive a positive response, because fathers, especially young company workers, felt they were too busy to take care of their child at home.

Current Policy Issues in Early Childhood Care and Education in Japan

When the Japanese economy was growing, preschool education expanded and not only its quantity but also its quality became more and more controversial. In 1971, the Central Council for Education submitted a report on Basic Measures for the Comprehensive Expansion and Improvement of Future School Education (46 Report). One of the important issues treated in the report was the quality of public education. This report discussed each stage of development and introduced the idea of developing an appropriate curriculum for each stage. The need to improve Yochien education and special education was also argued for. This report made it clear that high quality early childhood education can contribute to young children's early learning, and affects future social and academic outcomes. Responding to the 46 Report, the Program for the Promotion of Kindergarten Education was formulated in 1971 and the Law Concerning Support for Private School Promotion enhanced opening private Yochien with public funds.

The issues of an individualized, internationalized, and information-oriented society have created a turning point in Japanese education. The National Council of Education Reform was inaugurated in 1984 and submitted its recommendations, which include keywords such as respect for the individual, enforcement of a lifelong learning system, adjustment to internationalization, and coping with information in society. In this context, the Yochien Kyoiku Yoryo was revised in 1989, focusing on the individual child and the developmental appropriateness of education for the individual. Child-centered, play-based approaches were widely accepted and used in preschool education in Japan.

In 1996 the 15th session of the Central Council for Education submitted its first report concerning the model for Japanese education in the perspective of the twenty-first century. The keywords of the report were "Yutori" (which means more time to improve individual children's ability). To achieve this, a compulsory 5-day school week system was started; and a focus on "Ikiru Chikara" (which means the competence, strength, or ability to live in a complex world). As a result of the first report, Yochien Kyoiku Yoryo (Yochien Education Guidelines), the National Curriculum Standards for Yochien was enforced from 2000, with some revisions. In 2000, the National Commission on Educational Reform was established and reported and made some recommendations. On the basis of these, the Ministry of Education, Culture, Sports, Science and Technology (MEXT) developed the Education Reform Plan for the 21st Century in 2001.

The Japanese government began to consider the decline in the fertility rate as a national crisis. Not only the Ministry of Education but also other ministries began to reform, and many of the measures have affected early childhood education and care.

The Ministry of Health, Labour and Welfare awards "Special grants for measures against the declining birth rate" (a total of 200 billion yen was budgeted for 1999) to support the local governments to improve the actual conditions of their local communities. The Angel Plan (1994-1999) and the New Angel Plan (1999-2004) are concrete plans to implement measures to stop the declining birth rate. These plans were unique because many ministries signed the agreement and the whole government supports these plans by introducing measures in various sectors. Under the plan, the Ministry of Health, Labour and Welfare started to promote services for infants, the integration of early childhood special education, extended hours for child care services (more than 11 hours a day), holiday child care services, temporary child care services, and community service (such as counseling services for parents about raising children).

The Child Welfare Law was revised in 1997, 2001, and 2002. Before the amendment of the Child Welfare Law in 1997, parents were not able to select Hoikusho that they wanted to have their children attend. Parents were restricted in sending their children to Hoikusho. For example, if both parents had to work, they had to send their children to the Hoikusho in their own district. Now, children are able to attend the Hoikusho of their parents' choice, for example near their parents' work place, according to the agreement between each Hoikusho and the family. Since the amendments of the Child Welfare Law in 2001, Hoikusho teachers must get a license registration number from the government and become nationally certificated (since 2002). The amendment to the Child Welfare Law reflects the current reform in the social security system in Japan. The previous top-down system has changed to a contract-based service system. Evaluation is now done by a third party, and institutions are required to release more information to the public.

The problem of child abuse has become a serious social issue and the Child Abuse Prevention Law was enacted in 2000. Under the law, pre-school teachers are seen as one of the professionals who can most likely detect abuse and save children.

In 2000, there were 52,035 children who applied to attend Hoikusho but could not because of the lack of capacity. Then, the Koizumi government started the No Children on Waiting List Project and started the project to allow 150,000 more children attend the Hoikusho by 2004.

Current needs for preschool care and education can be summarized as follows; (a) more alternative services in early childhood education and care; such as extended hours, are needed to answer local and cultural appropriateness and sensitivity to particular families' needs, (b) both Yochien and Hoikusho teachers have to take the roles of a social worker, a counselor, and a family supporter and also promote parental involvement, and (c) the integration of Yochien and Hoikusho is needed to accomplish integrated administrative responsibility for day care and educational services to provide a universal framework of registration and inspection.

The Current State of and Suggested Reforms in Early Childhood Education and Care

Since the end of World War ll, there have been two major early childhood programs; Yochien and Hoikusho (see Table 5.1). Yochien provides noncompulsory education through free play and group activities, while Hoikusho provides care and education for infants and children in multiaged groups.

According to estimates by the Ministry of Education, Science and Culture in 2000, 33.1% of all 5-year-olds in Japan are enrolled in Hoikusho and 61.1% are enrolled in Yochien, that is 94.2% of 5-year-olds in Japan were enrolled in early childhood programs before they enter elementary school. Table 5.2 shows the percentage of enrolled infants and children both in Yochien and Hoikusho by age group.

Whether a child is enrolled in Yochien or Hoikusho depends on the local government, city, town, or village, where the family lives. Generally, a large city like Kobe in Hyogo prefecture provides sufficient public Yochien and private Yochien, but a small city like Sumoto in Awaji Island or a town in the countryside of Hyogo prefecture may not have a municipal Yochien but only Hoikusho. Thus, some prefectures provide more Yochien than Hoikusho, and some other prefectures provide more Hoikusho than Yochien. For example, in Nagano prefecture, 70.2% of 5-year-olds go on to elementary school from Hoikusho and 26.8% of 5-year-olds from Yochien, whereas in Hyogo prefecture, 23.1% of 5-year-olds go on to elementary school from Hoikusho and 71.3% of 5-year-olds from Yochien. This difference does not always come from women's work forces in the prefectures. Rather the difference arises from interface arrangement problems between preschools and elementary schools in each prefecture.

Public versus Private Yochien, Public verus Private Hoikusho

There are public and private Yochien as well as public and private Hoikusho. Local governments, those are cities, towns, or villages, sponsor public institutions. Private institutions were usually established by Chris-

**Table 5.1.   Two Major Early Childhood Programs,
Hoikusho and Yochien**

	Hoikusho	*Yochien*
Jurisdiction	Ministry of Health, Welfare and Labor	Ministry of Education, Culture, Sports, Science and Technology
Law/Act	The Child Welfare Law/ Enforcement Regulations	The School Law/Enforcement Regulations
Purpose	To take care and educate a child whose family needs an extensional service with considerable reasons	To educate a child, and to enhance the child's physical and mental development
Age	From birth to 6-year-old	From 3- to 6-year-old
Types of Sectors (sponsorship/ governed by)	Public (Municipal office) Private (Social welfare foundation/Prefectural office)	Public (Municipal office) Private (School foundation/Prefectural office)
Session (period of services)	The head has the right to make decisions according to the families' needs. About 8 hours per day About 300 days per year	The principal has the right to make decisions according to climate around the kindergarten and children's developmental needs. About 4 hours a day More than 39 weeks a year
Curriculum guideline	Guideline of care and education in Hoikusho	The Yochien education guideline
Curriculum contents	From birth to 3-year-old: health, play, language From 4-year-old: health, human relations, environment, language, expression	Health, human relations, environment, language, and expression

**Table 5.2.   The Number and the Percentage of
Enrolled Children by Age Group (%)**

Age Group	*Hoikusho*	*Yochien*
0 year old	40,075 (3.42)	
1 year old	171,163 (14.68)	
2 year old	251,851 (21.13)	
3 year old	361,897 (30.44)	398,626 (33.72)
4 year old	433,240 (36.56)	657,316 (55.07)
5 year old	429,943 (35.71)	713,154 (59.95)
6 year old	215,739 (17.86)	

Hoikusho's age group is surveyed on October 1, 2000. Yochien's age group is surveyed on May 1, 2002 (Ministry Health, Labor and Welfare, 2002; Population by age group is an estimate from MHLW, 2002).

**Table 5.3.   The Number of Hoikusyo and Yochien and the
Number of Enrolled Children and Infants**

	Total	*National*	*Public*	*Private*
Hoikusyo	22,211	0	12,719	9,492
(Enrolled children)	(1,934,272)	0	(1,010,381)	(923,891)
Yochien	14,279	49	5,820	8,410
(enrolled children)	(1,769,096)	(6,804)	(363,281)	(1,399,011)

Hoikusho's number is surveyed on March 1, 2001. Yochien's number is surveyed on May 1,
2002 (Ministry Health, Labor and Welfare, 2002).

tian churches, Buddhist temples, or private individuals and are now run
by social welfare foundations (Hoikusho) or school foundations (Yochien).
The number of Hoikusho and Yochien and the number of children
enrolled is presented in Table 5.3.

Almost four times as many children are enrolled in private Yochien as
are enrolled in public Yochien. Private Yochien is usually larger, have
more classes, and provide classes for 3-year-olds. Tuition and an enrollment fee for a private Yochien costs almost 3.7 times as much as for a
public Yochien. Although prefecture governments and the national government subsidize the private Yochien, the expenses—including teachers'
salary—at private Yochien is paid from children's tuition and fees,
whereas local government pays teacher's salary and other expenses at
public Yochien. Thus, kindergarten education in Japan is dependent on
private sectors. Slightly more children are enrolled in public Hoikusho
than in private Hoikusho. The national government, and prefectural and
municipal governments subsidize private Hoikusho as well as public
Hoikusho. Each government subsidizes, respectively, one half, one fourth
and one fourth of the balance of one child's costs and the child's fee. In
addition to these private and public Hoikusho, there are a number of
unauthorized Hoikusho that do not meet the minimum criteria set by the
Ministry of Social Welfare and Labor and are not subsided by either
national or local governments. As a result, a fee for these unauthorized
Hoikusho is very high.

Diversifying Early Childhood Education and Care Programs

The national government is advancing privatization in child welfare
undertakings. The government has eased controls over child welfare facilities such as Hoikusho on one hand. The government has also withdrawn
subsidies from the Hoikusho system. In consequence, a variety of early

childhood education and care programs have appeared, responding to the multiple needs for childcare and education by parents. These programs include unauthorized childcare centers, baby hotels, baby homes, preschools, and child classroom. Some of these programs offer poor environments for children and poor education and care. Some other programs, those are inappropriate for young children, are offering academic drills using worksheet or flash cards.

Professionals in Early Childhood Education and Care

All Yochien teachers in Japan must hold a valid teaching certificate. In the open teacher preparation system, a graduate of any university or junior college can obtain teacher certificate after she/he satisfies the requirements established by the Teacher Certification Law (1949). Table 5.4 shows the requirements for granting teaching certificate by the Law, Article 5.

In 1999 the Ministry of Education revised the Teacher Certification Law. More requirements in professional study in teaching were added, because the educational policymakers realized that to raise teachers' professional quality, an understanding of children, child development, and children's lives in families and communities is more important than professional knowledge about subject matter areas. It also added new subjects, understanding children and counseling with parents.

Table 5.4.   The Requirements for Granting Teaching Certificates for Elementary School and Yochienn; TCL, Article 5

Type of School	Type of Certificate	Basic Academic Qualification	Professional Study in Subject Area (A)	Professional Study in Teaching (B)	(A) or (B)
Elementary school	special certificate	masters degree	8	41	34
	type 1 certificate	bachelor's degree	8	41	10
	type 2 certificate	2-yr junior college	4	31	2
Yochien	special certificate	masters degree	6	35	34
	type 1 certificate	bachelor's degree	6	35	10
	type 2 certificate	2-yr junior college	4	27	

Note 1: Professional study in subject area includes music, art & craft, physical education, Japanese, mathematics, life study, and so on.

Note 2: Professional study in teaching includes early childhood development, history and philosophy of ECE, policy and administration of EC and elementary education, teaching methods in five content areas, understanding childhood, student practice and so on.

According to the 2001 survey by the Ministry of Education, among all Yochien teachers in Japan, 82.9% had 2-year junior college diplomas and 14.4% had 4-year degrees. The corresponding figure for elementary school teachers was 15.2 % and 82.5% respectively. Furthermore, 0.9% of kindergarten teachers and 2.0% of elementary school teachers had master's degree. In 1998, the Central Teacher Preparation and Education Council issued a draft report to the Ministry of Education. The draft proposed to develop professional qualifications for teachers in the compulsory education sectors, by making use of master degree courses at graduate schools for teachers' in-service training and raising the percentage of teachers with the special teaching certificate to 25% by the year 2010. However, financial deficiencies in municipalities make it difficult for them to send public school teachers to graduate schools of teachers colleges or to faculties of education at universities.

There are two ways to obtain a teaching certificate for Hoikusho teachers. One is to complete the program in a training school or in the course of a 2- or 4-year college or university, that has been approved by the Minister of Health, Welfare and Labor. The other is to pass a national examination for Hoikusho-teacher. Recently, the courses for Hoikusho-teachers are increasing, and the number of Hoikusho-teachers who get their certificate by passing the national examination is decreasing.

The curriculum of the courses for Hoikusho-teacher is defined by the Regulation for Enforcement of the Child Welfare Law. It requires such courses as social welfare, seminar in social work practice, child welfare, early childhood education, early childhood care, education, child development, educational psychology, child health, child nutrition, child mental health, family support, contents of early childhood education, infant care and education, early childhood special education, and contents of infant care. According to the Ministry of Health and Welfare (2001), 40 four-year universities or colleges, mostly women's colleges, (2,971 students admission in all), 217 two-year junior colleges (22,845 students admission), 60 special training schools (4,790 students admission) and 16 other miscellaneous schools (790 students) provided the courses for the Hoikusho teacher certificate in 2000.

A person who has completed a 2-year junior college or junior of 4-year college or university program can apply for the national examination for Hoikusho teacher. An examinee must pass eight subjects: social welfare, child welfare, child psychology and mental health, child health, child nutrition, early childhood education, general education and care, and child care practice.

The Conditions of Early Childhood Teachers

There is a wide gap between the conditions of public Yochien teachers and those of private Yochien teachers. According to the 2001 survey by the Ministry of Education, 13.2% of private Yochien teachers and 17.8% of public Yochien teachers had bachelor's degrees, while 83.8% of private Yochien teachers and 80.7% of public Yochien teachers had 2-year junior college diplomas in 2000.

The years of teaching experience also differs between private Yochien and public Yochien teachers. Generally the experience of teachers at private kindergartens is very short. According to the same survey by the Ministry of Education (2001), 54% of private Yochien teachers have less than 5 years' teaching experience, and 75% have less than 10 years' experience. The experience of public Yochien teachers is 19% within 5 years and 32% within 10 years. The average years of teaching for private Yochien teachers was 8.4 years, while the average teaching years of public Yochien teachers was 18.1 years.

The salary scale of public kindergarten teacher is based on the national scale for education and government employees determined by the National Personnel Authority. However, the starting step of the scale for Yochien teachers is lower than that for elementary and secondary school-teachers. It also varies among municipalities. It is a major financial problem that municipal government must fund all the personnel costs in public Yochien, whereas salaries of teachers in compulsory schools are half funded by national subsidies and the other half by prefectural funds.

Each private Yochien has its own salary scale. The survey (2001) shows the average basic salary that was paid for a public Yochien teacher in September 2001 was 338,200 yen, and that for a private kindergarten teacher was 199,200 yen. On the other hand, the average basic salary for a public elementary school teacher in September 2001 was 389,200 yen. These figures show that private kindergarten teachers' salary is extremely low.

One of the biggest differences between Hoikusho and Yochien staffing structure and equipment is that Hoikusho requires cooking equipment and cooking staff. Hoikusho staffs, including cooking staff, in public Hoikusho are all government employee. The salary scale of a Hoikusho teacher is based on Government Employee Salary Scale. The scale is rescheduled on April 1 of every year. Local governments sum up personnel costs on the base of this standard scale.

Of the total costs for taking care of a child in public Hoikusho as well as in authorized private Hoikusho, about one half is funded by parent's fees. The other half of the total costs are split one half by national expenditure, one fourth by prefecture, and the last one fourth is funded by municipality. Parents' fee varies according to the family's income tax.

As the number of the working mothers who take care of children under the age 6 is increasing, the role of Hoikusho in Japan is now very important. Hoikusho teachers take care of and educate children from birth to age 6 while their parents are working out of the home. The work is hard as well as professional. Although the social status of public Hoikusho teachers as government employees went up gradually, a number of Hoikusho teachers at private unauthorized Hoikusho are doing this hard and professional work under poor conditions. They have less opportunity to attend training programs that local governments implement.

Unsolved Problem: Unifying of Yochien and Hoikusho

Since the late 1990s, representatives both from the Ministry of Education, Science and Culture and the Ministry of Welfare and Labor have discussed the relationships between Yochien and Hoikusho. The negotiation, however, made no progress to unify the two systems, Yochien and Hoikusho. The Ministry of Education just managed to propose that Yochien should keep close connections with Hoikusho. Some Diet members who have connections with the Ministry of Welfare and Labor organized the meeting to declare against unifying Yochien and Hoikusho. (2003)

Regardless of these central governments' intentions, small local government, such as Yashiro-town in Hyogo prefecture have established unified early childhood education and care institutions. At present, several other local governments are following in this direction. For a local government with a declining child population, it is financially difficult to maintain both public Yochien and public Hoikusho. Some cities and towns have closed public Yochien and created Hoikusho in their place. A local government officer explained that it is because a Hoikusho could get about 10 times as much national subsidy as a Yochien could get.

The trend is influenced by political and economical situations. The reformation of early childhood education programs needs to be, first of all, for the sake of young children and parents. Children from birth to about 8 years old need both education and care. Some parents need long-hour child care; other parents may want to take care of their child in their home. Shirakawa (2004) figured out the relationship of education and care for young children.

The younger the child is, the more care she/he needs, such as nutrition, sleeping, toilet, and attachment. The older the child becomes, the more education she/he needs. Children above 3 in both Yochien and Hoikusho are to learn in the five content areas: health, human relations, environments, languages and expression.

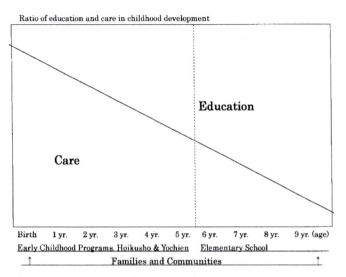

Figure 5.1.   Ratio of education and care in childhood development (Shirakawa 2004).

CURRENT ISSUES IN RESEARCH ON
EARLY CHILDHOOD CARE AND EDUCATION

Early Childhood Education Researchers at Universities and Colleges

The preparation of kindergarten teachers at 4-year national universities started in 1966 and the last time such a course at a national university was approved was in 1978. In 2000, there were 50 national universities, two universities established by local governments and 50 private 4-year colleges that offered training courses for kindergarten teacher preparation either in departments of education or in departments of literature. University and college teachers teaching these courses have researched in the field of early childhood education. Most of these college or university teachers had qualification in education, educational psychology, music education, art education, and physical education and shifted their interest of research to the field of early childhood education. An early childhood education group was organized in Japan Association of Universities of Education (which was established in 1949) and they issued a yearly research review titled *Research on Early Childhood Education*. Early childhood education researchers at universities and colleges have usually been members of one of the following research organizations: Kyoiku Gakkai (the Japan Society for the Study of Education), Kyoiku Shinri Gakkai (the

Japan Society for the Educational Psychology), or other research organizations. Some research presentations and two or three sessions are offered at the annual conferences of many other professional organizations in the field of education, for example, Nihon Kyoiku Gakkai (the Japan Society for the Study of Education), or Nihon Kyoiku Shinri Gakkai.

Although universities and research institutions have helped to improve the field, recent reductions of departments of education (especially those of teacher training colleges) have worsened the situation. Teacher training courses for early childhood education have been reorganized and amalgamated with those for elementary school education. Even in the case of the courses that survived, their quota has been decreasing. The numbers of teaching staff in early childhood education is also decreasing. Although several series of complete works on early childhood education were published in the 1970s and 1980s, there have not been many publications recently. The field is now facing a serious crisis.

Professional Organizations in Early Childhood Care and Education

Professional organizations have also taken part in the improvement of the field of early childhood education. The biggest organization, Nihon Hoiku Gakkai (the Japan Society of Research on Early Childhood Care and Education) was founded in 1948. Sozo Kurahashi, Professor of Ochanomizu Women's University, was its first president.

There were only 69 members when Nihon Hoiku Gakkai was founded in 1948. However the number rose to more than 1,000 after 1962 and now there are more than 3,600 members. It has published annual reports and invited papers from 1962, and started to publish submitted manuscripts in 1980. All manuscripts and papers were on special issues until 1986. In the first 10 years, the contents of the annual reports included: (1) the reports of each annual conference; (2) list of books in early childhood education; (3) current changes in the field of early childhood education; and (4) papers on special issues. Because of financial reasons, it changed its style and contents, which mainly meant publishing more manuscripts. The title and the character of the annual report changed in 1992. It became a research journal and was renamed as *Hoiku Gaku Kenkyu (Research on Early Childhood Care and Education in Japan)*. The contents of the journal are: (1) papers on special issues; (2) research papers in any field of early childhood education; and (3) the current state of early childhood education in Japan. From 1995, it started to publish the journal twice a year.

Nihon Nyuyoji Kyoiku Gakkai (the Japanese Society for the Education of Young Children) was founded in 1991. Its current membership is about 600. From 1991 to 2002, it published 11 annual journals and 83 papers that had been submitted.

Association culture can be said to be immature in Japan, and Japanese professional organizations have had little effect on public policy, and even less on early childhood education practices. The associations have a limited number of members in Japan.

Areas of Research in Early Childhood Care and Education

Nihon Hoiku Gakkai (the Japan Society of Research on Early Childhood Care and Education) published special issues on the following topics in the last 10 years:

- The Kindergarten and Nursery Education in the Community (1993),
- The Mutual Support between the Family and the Institution to Improve the High Quality Early Childhood Education (1994),
- The Child Development and Contents in Early Childhood Care and Education (1995),
- Practical Research to Improve the High Quality Early Childhood Education (1996),
- Preschool Daily Life and Safety Education (1997),
- Musical Performance and Expression in Early Childhood Care and Education (1998),
- Multicultural Education for Young Children (1999),
- Development of Child and Human Relations (2000),
- Specialty and Professionalism of Early Childhood Practitioner and its Teacher Training (2001),
- Family Education in Early Childhood (2002),
- Play and Learning in Early Childhood (2003).

In 1997, *Early Childhood Care and Education in Japan* was published to cerebrate the 50th anniversary of the society. Shiro Moriue analyzed the articles presented at the annual conferences from the very first in 1948 until the 49th in 1996, in chapter 17 (pp. 332-342) of this book. Based on his charts on pages 333 and 334, most research articles—about one quarter—dealt with the contents of early childhood care and education. The second biggest group of research articles reported findings on child development, educational environment and culture, family and community, special education, and teachers.

In the journal of Nihon Nyuyoji Kyoiku Gakkai (the Japanese Society for the Education of Young Children), there were 83 papers published during these 11 years. Forty percent of them were on child development, 27% on curriculum and contents, 12% on history and theory, 6% on reviews of early childhood education abroad, and 6% on teacher education. The rest of the papers reported research result on other topics, such as peace education, special education, and multicultural education.

Current Government-Oriented Research Topics in Early Childhood Care and Education

Advisory committees have been working very actively on research and their reports have been strongly reflected in administration and policy-making.

Advisory committees and councils, such as the National Council of Education Reform, the Central Council for Education, and the National Commission on Educational Reform were formed by people selected by the government.

Current outcomes of the report spread the recognition that matters of academic achievement are closely associated with mental health, and school education has to address both at the same time. "*Kokoro no Kyoiku*" (moral education) is one of the keywords of the current reform by the MEXT, which include teaching children self-confidence, ambition, and joy of self-fulfillment. From that standpoint, moral education has been promoted at every stage of educational activities. In 2001, the "*kokoro no note*" (the notebook for moral education) was distributed to all students of elementary and lower secondary schools. In view of the importance of infancy as a period of basic character building and awakening of morals, the importance of Yochien education has been certified through the MEXT, as the Collection of Case Studies on Cultivating the Awakening of Morals in Yochien Children was given to all Yochien as a reference for teachers in guiding children.

Other issues in recent educational reforms are enforcing community-wide support for school education; creating life-long learning society; and improving of the quality of teachers.

The success of school education depends considerably on the quality and ability of teachers who have direct contact with children. As the quality and ability of teachers are formed through university education, recruitment and in-service training, there are needs for relevant measures to be systematically implemented to improve them.

The ministry just started to introduce the in-service training for pre-school teachers. In 2002, the Research Committee on Improvement of High Quality Preschool Teachers under the MEXT created a report titled *Yochien Kyoin no Shishitsu Kojo ni tuite: Mizukara Manabu Yochien Kyoin no Tameni* (Promoting High Quality Preschool Teachers: For the Self-learning Preschool Teachers). The report mentioned that current professional needs for preschool teachers are; (a) professional knowledge and skills to understand children and synthesize them with practice, (b) professional knowledge and skills to plan and to practice them appropriately in various educational situations, (c) professional knowledge and skills to collaborate with the community and the families, (d) professional knowledge and skills to collaborate with elementary school teachers and Hoikusho teachers, and (e) wide understanding and consideration of human rights.

Methodologies in Early Childhood Education Research in Japan

Psychological quantitative research, such as the research on child development, child learning, and impact of early childhood care and education on children's later development, provides a lot of research evidence on early childhood development and learning. Measuring effects of early childhood institutions, quantitative researches revealed that high quality early childhood care and education can contribute to young children's early learning and future social and academic outcomes.

As early childhood educators work with very different children from very different cultural and family contexts, it seems very hard to systematize the practice. Maybe that is the reason why more and more qualitative approaches, such as case studies, ethnography, participant observations have spread in Japan, just like in other counties. T. Muto, Y. Yamada, T. Aso, H. Minami and T. Sato started to publish professional research series titled Qualitative Research on Child Development in 2002.

Torimitsu, Kitano, Yamauchi, Nakatsubo, and Koyama (1999) examined fundamental issues regarding the methodologies used to analyze early childhood education practice in Japan, focusing Makoto Tsumori, the ex-president of Japan OMEP (Organisation Mondiale pour l'Éducation Préscolaire: World Organization for Early Childhood Education), ex-president of Nihon Hoiku Gakkai (the Japan Association of Early Childhood Care and Education). Tsumori started his career as a positivistic psychologist, using quantitative inquiry, such as statistical research methods. However he modified his research methods to incorporate interpretive research and other qualitative inquiry. He has established his own interpretive and subjective research method with sympathy, re-realization, and reconsideration. His method is widely accepted in early childhood care and education in Japan.

Conclusion

Early childhood education policy and research in Japan have strongly been affected by the government from the very beginning of their existence. The Froebel Kindergarten was introduced through the United States with the strong initiative of the Meiji Government. Though the education system of Yochien was a new and imported system, people started to change it gradually to meet the requirements of Japanese culture. After WWII, the government again took big initiative in the reconstruction of Japanese society under the direction of the GHQ. However, current rapid changes in society require more reforms in the field of early childhood care and education in Japan. In order to reflect and meet diverse and complex needs for our field, more bottom-up research is needed to carry out the researches rather than only top-down research oriented by the government. Grassroots research that can reflect practical needs and change the practice is much desirable.

Research that promotes high quality early childhood care and education just started to bloom in Japan. New professional organizations in the field (with a few hundred memberships) have recently been established. In addition, dissertations and PhD theses on early childhood care and education have been completed.

Though, the early childhood care and education field research started to improve, the practical situation to improve is getting more and more difficult. The numbers of departments of education, of students, of teaching staff, and of researchers majoring in early childhood care and education are decreasing. There is an urgent need to establish a solid foundation of early childhood care and education in Japan.

The problem of unifying two separate early childhood care and education institutions, which are the Yochien and Hoikusho systems, is not yet solved. In order to develop an integrated early childhood care and education system, early childhood care and education researchers, practitioners, and parents need to cooperate in building developmentally and educationally appropriate practices for children and their parents. The actual political situation and forces in economy do have an influence on reforms of early childhood care and education. What the two systems should do immediately is to adopt positive features of both systems: The Hoikusho needs to put more stress on education and the Yochien needs to give more consideration to child care.

REFERENCES

Central Council for Teacher Preparation and Education. (1998.) *Shushi-katei wo sekkyokutekini riyo shita Kyouin-yosei no arikata ni tuite* [A proposal on teacher preparation and education making use of master courses of teacher's college or educational university.]

Editing Committee of Dictionary of Japan Modern Educational History. (1972). *Nihon Kindai Kyouikushi Jiten* [Dictionary of Japan Modern Educational History] Heibonsha.

Froebel, F. (1895). *Haha no Yugi oyobi Ikuji Ka (Mutter- und Kose-Lieder)* (A. Howe, Trans.) Shoei Yochien.

Hashimoto, M. (1998) *Meijishoki ni okeru America Kyoiku Jyoho Jyuyo no Kenkyu (Research on Acceptance of American Educational Information in Early Meiji)*. Kazamashobo.

Hill, P. S. (1936). *Yochien oyobi Teigakunen no Koui Katei* [A conduct curriculum for the kindergarten and first grade] (F. Takamori, Trans). F. Ra Lambuth Jogakuin.

Kitano, S. (2003). Cultural contexts and current issues in the preparation of preschool teachers in Japan. *International Journal of Human Academic, 2*.

Ministry of Education. (1979). *Yochien 100 Nen Shi* [Yochien Education: A History of the Hundred Years.] Hikarinokuni.

Ministry of Education, Culture, Sports, Science, and Technology. (1998). *Yochien Kyoiku Yoryo* [National curriculum standards for Yochien]. Tokyo. Author. Available at http://www.mext.go.jp/

Ministry of Education, Culture, Sports, Science, and Technology. (1999). *Kyoiku Shokuin Menkyo Ho.* [Teacher Certification Law]. Tokyo. Author. Available at http://www.mext.go.jp/

Ministry of Education, Culture, Sports, Science, and Technology. (2001). *Report on statistical survey of schoolteachers.*

Ministry of Education, Culture, Sports, Science, and Technology (2002). *Report on fundamental survey of schools*. Available at http://www.mext.go.jp/

Ministry of Education, Culture, Sports, Science, and Technology. (2002). *Yochien Kyoin no Shishitsu Kojyo ni tsuite: Mizukara Manabu Yochien Kyoin no tameni* [Promoting high quality preschool teachers: for the self-learning preschool teachers]. Author. Available at http://www.mext.go.jp/

Ministry of Health, Labour and Welfare. (2000). *Kokumin seikatu kiso chosa* [Fundamental survey on the national life].

Ministry of Health, Labour and Welfare. (2001). *Vital Statistics of Japan*.

Ministry of Health, Labour and Welfare. (2002). *Jinko dotai chosa* [Trends in population]

Ministry of Health, Labour and Welfare (2002). *The survey of social welfare institutions*. Available at http://www.mhlw.go.jp/.

Moriue, S. (1997). Issues in early childhood care and educational research. In Japan Society of Research on Early Childhood Care and Education (Ed.), *Early childhood care and education in Japan* (pp. 332-342). Sekaibunkasha

Nakamura, G., & Wada, M. (1908) *Yoji Kyoiku Ho* (Early Childhood Education Method). Froebel Kai (Froebel Association).

Niyon Nyuyoji Kyouiku Gakkai (The Japanese Society for the Education of Young Children). (Ed.) (1992-2002) *Nyuyoji Kyoikugaku Kenkyu* [The Japanese Journal for the Education of Young Children] Vols. 1-11.

Shirakawa, Y. (1996). Culture and the Japanese kindergarten curriculum: A Historical View. *Early Child Development and Care, 123*.

Shirakawa, Y. (2002). Early Childhood Education in Japan in the Twenty-First Century. In L. K. S. Chan & E. J. Mellor (Eds.), *International developments in early childhood services*. New York: Peter Lang .

Shirakawa, Y., Kitano, S., & Okuyama, T. (2004). *Nyuyoji Kyouiku Hoiku* [Early childhood education and care; co-educare]. Yukikaku.

Tokyo Women's Normal School's Yochien. (1935). *Keitoteki Hoiku An no Jissai* [Practice in systematic curriculum in early childhood care and education]. Japan Yochien Association.

Torimitsu, M., Kitano, S., Yamauchi, N., Nakatsubo, F., & Koyama, Y. (1999). Methodologies used to analyze early childhood care and education: A study on the evolving research methods of Makoto Tsumori. *The Annual Research on Early Childhood, 21*, 1-8.

Yukawa, K. (2001). *Nihon Yochien Seiritu Shi no Kenkyu* [Research on the Establishment of Yochien in Japan]. Kazamashobo.

Zenkoku Hoiku Kyogikai. (2003). *Hoiku nenpo* 2003 [Annual report on Hoiku]. Zenshakyo.

CHAPTER 6

EARLY CHILDHOOD EDUCATION AND CARE IN KOREA

Current State and Research

Unhai Rhee, Won Young Rhee, and Young-Ja Lee

HISTORY OF THE DEVELOPMENT OF EARLY CHILDHOOD EDUCATION

Education for young children under 6 in Korea is divided mainly into two systems, kindergartens and child-care centers. Parents have the freedom to choose between these two systems until their children reach the compulsory schooling age, which is 6. This section presents the history of the two channels for early childhood education in Korea: the kindergarten and the child-care center.

The History of the Development of Kindergarten

The starting point of kindergarten education in Korea was the Ewha Kindergarten attached to the Ewha Hakdang (Ewha Secondary School), established in 1914 by an American missionary, Charlotte Brownlee (S. K.

International Perspectives on Research in Early Childhood Education, 161–189
Copyright © 2005 by Information Age Publishing
All rights of reproduction in any form reserved.

Lee, 1987). Ms. Brownlee earned her kindergarten teacher certificate from Cincinnati Kindergarten Training School. In 1918, Edna Van Fleet, who also graduated from Cincinnati Kindergarten Training School and later received a BA and MA from Columbia University, was dispatched to Ewha Kindergarten when Brownlee took sabbatical leave. In 1916, Chung-Ang Kindergarten, associated with Chung-Ang University, was established by Heedo Park, who was one of the 33 signatories of the 3-1 Independence Declaration from Japan (March 1, 1919). The first principal of both Ewha and Chung-Ang Kindergarten was Ms. Lulu E. Frey, who was the principal of Ewha Secondary School. Ms. Brownlee also supervised Chung-Ang Kindergarten at the beginning.

Ewha and Chung-Ang kindergartens were the forerunners of Korean early childhood education. The early kindergartens followed the ideas of Friedrich Froebel and John Dewey. Following John Dewey's progressive views on education, Ewha Kindergarten emphasized free play as well as play-centered and experience-based education. According to the regulations for kindergarten in 1922 (S. K. Lee, 1987), kindergarten was for children aged 3 to 7. The curriculum in those days was composed of movement, singing, telling and showing, and basic daily skills.

In 1915, Brownlee opened Ewha Kindergarten Teacher Training Center to educate high school graduates as kindergarten teachers. This was the first early childhood teacher education program in Korea. Brownlee translated and published classic works by Froebel such as *The Education of Man* and *Mother Play and Songs*. In 1932, *Conduct Curriculum for the Kindergarten and First Grade* by Patty Smith Hill was translated into Korean and was used as a text. In 1922, Chung-Ang Kindergarten Teacher Training Center was established. Ewha Kindergarten Teacher Training Center became the Education Department (Early childhood education major within the department) of Ewha Womans University in October, 1945 and Chung-Ang Kindergarten Teacher Training Center grew into a 4-year university in 1948.

During the 1930s and 1940s, when Korea was under Japanese rule, national leaders and educators tried to increase the number of kindergartens in the hope that this would help spread Christianity and maintain the Korean language and spirit. Following the emancipation from Japan in 1945, the number of kindergartens first decreased and then gradually increased during the next 2 decades. With the increase in the number of kindergartens, the Ministry of Education enacted the Education Act in 1949. Under article 81 of the Education Act kindergarten was described as a preschool system. When this Education Act was revised in 1991 kindergarten became responsible for educating children aged 3 to 5 (Ministry of Education, 1998).

Up to the 1970s most mothers with young children in Korea stayed home to take care of their children. Mothers did not feel it was necessary or right to send children to an expensive private kindergarten when they could educate them by themselves at home. The traditional Korean extended family consisting of three generations living together also hindered the expansion of kindergarten (G. L. Lee, 1997).

During the late 1970s the Ministry of Education and the Korean Institute for Research on Behavioral Sciences (KIRBS) conducted comprehensive research to provide a master plan for the revitalization of early childhood education with UNICEF funds (Rhee, Park, Lee, & Cho, 1999). In 1981, when the government enacted the Early Childhood Education Promotion Act, the foundation of education for young children was consolidated and the number of kindergartens increased rapidly. The expansion of kindergartens was also due to several other factors, such as the rapid growth of industry, changes in family structure, equal education and employment opportunities for women, the low birth rate, the public recognition of the importance of early childhood education, and extensive government involvement in the provision of educational services for young children. On January 29, 2004 the Early Childhood Education Act was enacted and kindergarten became legally recognized as a branch of the school system, along with primary, middle, and high schools.

Table 6.1 shows that the number of kindergartens has expanded dramatically since 1980. There was only one public kindergarten until the early 1970s. However, four public kindergartens were established in Seoul in 1976 and since then with the enactment of the Early Childhood Education Promotion Act, the number of public kindergartens has increased drastically. Public kindergartens are established mainly to provide education for children in remote rural areas and for low-income families. The government pays the salaries of the teachers in public kindergartens so that low-income parents only have to pay minimum fees for educational materials.

In the 1970s, the percentage of children attending kindergarten was less than 3%. In 1992, the entrance age for kindergarten was lowered to 3 years. The percentage of 5-year-old children attending kindergarten reached 44.6% in 2002 (Ministry of Education and Human Resources Development, 2002).

Despite many years of history, Korean kindergartens did not have national kindergarten curriculum guidelines until 1969 when the Ministry of Education set up the first kindergarten curriculum. The curriculum for Korean kindergarten has been revised five times by early childhood curriculum specialists, in 1979, 1982, 1987, 1993, and 1998.

Graduates with kindergarten teacher certificates authorized by the Ministry of Education and Human Resources Development are appointed

Table 6.1. Growth in the Number of Kindergartens, Kindergarten Teachers, and Kindergarten Children

Year	Number of Kindergartens			Number of Kindergarten Teachers			Number of Kindergarten Children		
	Public	Private	Total	Public	Private	Total	Public	Private	Total
1914		1	1		3	3		36	36
1920		10	10		18	18		671	671
1930		206	206		365	365		8,343	8,343
1940		358	358		684	684		20,024	20,024
1945	3	141	144	8	365	373	324	8,945	9,269
1950		159	159		474	474		6,779	6,779
1960		297	297		1,150	1,150		15,795	15,795
1970	1	483	484	3	1,657	1,660	80	22,191	22,271
1975		611	611		2,153	2,153		32,032	32,032
1980	69	832	901	80	3,259	3,339	2,324	64,109	66,433
1990	4,604	3,783	8,341	4,736	13,775	18,511	127,144	287,388	414,532
2000	4,176	4,318	8,494	6,145	21,867	28,012	122,208	423,055	545,263
2001	4,209	4,120	8,329	6,217	22,224	28,460	122,425	422,727	545,152
2002	4,219	4,089	8,308	6,243	23,278	29,521	119,632	430,518	550,150

Sources: 1914-1940: S. K. Lee (1987) and Seoul Metropolitan Office of Education (1981); 1945-1995: Ministry of Education (1955) and Korean Educational Development Institute (1997); 1970-2002: Ministry of Education and Human Resources Development, Republic of Korea and Korean Educational Development Institute (2000, 2002).

as kindergarten teachers. They are graduates from the junior colleges or 4-year universities majoring in early childhood education and related areas including child studies, child-welfare, and child-care and education. The number of junior colleges and 4-year universities with departments of early childhood education increased during the 1980s. In 1997, 84 junior colleges and 37 4-year universities offered early childhood education programs and produced 11,222 graduates who received kindergarten teacher certificates (Ministry of Education and Human Resources Development, 1997).

The History of the Development of Child-Care Centers

The history of child-care centers in Korea can be divided into four periods (Rhee et al., 1999). The first period is between 1921 and 1960;

the second period between 1961 and 1980; and the third period between 1981 and 1990; the fourth period from 1991 to the present.

The very first day-care center was founded in 1921 and two more nurseries were established in 1923, including a child-care center opened by Taiwha Christian Social Work Institute. There were only 11 child-care centers in 1939, serving 435 children. Child-care centers at that time had philanthropic purposes.

From 1961, the government started to regulate child-care centers. During the 1960s, the government's economic plan resulted in the growth of the numbers of working mothers with young children. Under the Child Welfare Act enacted in 1961, many child-care centers for working couples and for young children from low-income families were established and governed by the Ministry of Health and Social Affairs (H. I. Kim, 1997).

In 1981, the government enacted the Early Childhood Education Promotion Act, which contained a comprehensive plan for the promotion of early childhood education. Various types of child-care centers were integrated into the "Saemaul nursery." Saemaul nurseries received support from the Ministry of Home Affairs. However, the Ministry of Education supervised the educational programs and the Ministry of Health and Welfare was in charge of the health and nutrition of children in child-care centers. The number of Saemaul nurseries increased to 419 in 1990. However, most of the Saemaul nurseries ran only on a half-day or extended-day basis and offered programs for children aged from 3 to 5. Facilities for infants and toddlers under 3 years old were limited. Some private corporations such as Samsung established child-care centers for the children of low-income families and working mothers. Samsung Welfare Foundation started its child-care project in 1989 (Samsung Welfare Foundation, 1995) and had established 34 child-care centers serving 3,900 children by 2003.

In 1991, the government enacted the Infant Care Act and invested about a billion dollars over the next 7 years to establish and manage child-care centers, the so-called *Orinijip* (meaning "young children's house" in Korean) (Rhee et. al, 1999). The purpose of establishing child-care centers is to take care of infants and children who cannot be cared for by their guardians due to work, illness, and the like (Article 1, Clause 1 and 2 of the Article 2 of the Infant Care Act). In 1997 there were about 12,000 child-care centers serving about 300,000 children up to the age of 6. The Ministry of Health and Welfare and the family welfare departments or social welfare departments of cities or counties are in charge of the child-care centers, and child-care centers follow the childcare curriculum rules set by the Ministry of Health and Welfare. Table 6.2 shows the growth in the number of child-care centers, child-care teachers, and children in child-care centers.

Table 2. Growth in the Number of Child-Care Centers, Child-Care Teachers, and Children in Child-Care Centers

	Number of Child-Care Centers					Number of Children					Number of Teachers
Year	Public	Private	Employer Support	Family Care Home	Total	Public	Private	Employer Support	Family Care Home	Total	Total
1921	1				1						
1939	3	8			11					435	
1960					24					1,130	
1970					377					29,906	
1980					619					42,794	
1985					2,403					197,423	5,585
1990	360	39	20	1,500	1,919	25,000	1,500	1,500	20,000	48,000	7,432
1995	1,029	4,125	87	3,844	9,085	78,831	170,412	2,388	42,116	293,747	
2000	1,295	11,304	204	6,473	19,276	99,666	510,567	7,807	67,960	686,000	64,104
2001	1,306	11,794	196	6,801	20,097	102,118	546,946	7,881	77,247	734,192	
2002	1,329	13,644	236	8,933	24,142	103,351	597,971	8,730	90,939	800,991	

Sources: 1939-1980: From Korean Association of Child-Care Centers (1980); 1980-1985: Ministry of Education, Republic of Korea (1986); 1990-2001: Ministry of Gender Equality, Republic of Korea (2001); 1995–2001: H. J. Yu, (2002).

As described earlier, the first child-care center for young children in Korea opened in 1921. However, child-care centers concerned with both care and education for young children started to be established after 1991, with the enactment of the Infant Care Act. The Ministry of Health and Welfare has been actively involved in the care and education of young children in Korea since then. The Infant Care Act was revised and passed by congress on January 28, 2004 and went into force January 30, 2005. On March 2, 2004 the Revised National Government Organization Act was passed by congress and the Ministry of Gender Equality was given responsibility for child-care centers.

CURRENT STATE OF EARLY CHILDHOOD EDUCATION

Similarities and differences between kindergarten and child-care centers in the provision, funding and administration of early childhood education, curriculum, and teacher qualification will be explained here. The main similarities are the increasing number of children, the use of the same curriculum for children aged from 3 to 5 and the increasing financial support from the government. The differences are in the areas of supervision, with different ministries in charge of each program, the applicable laws, the age of the children served by each program, and teacher education.

Provision, Funding, and Administration of Early Childhood Education

Children who reach the age of 6 before March 1st, the beginning of the school year, are admitted to primary school at that time. All children aged 6 except those with special problems receive a notification of admission to a primary school located in their residential area. Since 1996 the Educational Basic Law allows some 5-year-old children to start earlier or to delay entering primary school according to their academic readiness.

Information regarding kindergartens and child-care centers is summarized in Table 6.3. Kindergartens are under the supervision of the Ministry of Education and Human Resources Development and aim to provide education to children aged from 3 to 5, whereas child-care centers, which are under the jurisdiction of the Ministry of Gender Equality since June 12, 2004, aim to provide care for children aged from birth to 6 years old whose mothers are working. Before this change, child-care centers had been under the supervision of the Ministry of Health and Welfare. In order to coordinate the services for families and child-care centers for

**Table 6.3.   Main Characteristics of
Kindergartens and Child-Care Centers**

	Kindergartens	*Child-Care Centers*
Jurisdiction	Ministry of Education and Human Resources Development	Ministry of Gender Equality
Law	Early Childhood Education Act	Infant Care Act
Target age	3- to 5-year-olds	Birth to 6-year-olds
Teacher certificate	Kindergarten teacher certificate	Child-care teacher certificate
Hours of operation	Half-day (3 or 4 hours) Extended-day (6 hours) Whole-day (8 hours)	12 hours
Funding source	Public: Ministry of Education and Human Resources Development Private: Mainly parents	Public: Ministry of Gender Equality Private: Mainly parents, with some contribution from the Ministry of Gender Equality

working women, the Korean government changed the Government Organization Act by transferring the child-care service from the Ministry of
Health and Welfare to the Ministry of Gender Equality whose main
responsibility is promoting women's rights. According to the Educational
Basic Law, which governs kindergartens, primary schools and secondary
schools, all children aged from 3 to 5 can attend kindergarten. However,
less than one third of young children aged from 3 to 5 are actually attending kindergarten because of the insufficient number of kindergartens.

Kindergarten has three different schedules of operating hours. Traditionally kindergartens in Korea run a half-day program for 3 hours from 9
a.m. to noon. The daily routine of a half-day program consists of free
choice play, circle time, snack, storytelling, outside play, physical education, singing, and so forth. From the 1980s, kindergartens extended the
morning program to 2 or 3 p.m. and started to offer lunch. The rapid
increase of women in the workforce since 1995 stimulated many private
kindergartens to have a whole-day program. The whole-day program provides lunch, rest hours, an afternoon snack, a free-play period and some
educational activities in the afternoon. Child-care centers usually open 12
hours a day as planned for working mothers. A few child-care centers
open 24 hours a day for mothers who work a night shift.

The Ministry of Education and Human Resources Development funds
public kindergarten teachers' salaries and a small portion of management
expenses but does not provide financial funding in either of these areas
for private kindergarten. However, since September 1999 the Ministry of
Education and Human Resources Development has given about $80

monthly to lower-income families who have 5-year-olds attending kindergarten, including private kindergartens, and is planning to give more financial support to 3- and 4-year-olds from lower-income families. On January 8, 2004, the Korean Parliament passed the Early Childhood Education Act. This law allows the Ministry of Education and Human Resources Development to obtain more funds from the government. After the Early Childhood Education Act was passed, the Ministry of Education and Human Resources Development was given a budget of $6.5 million for the 3- and 4- year-old kindergarten children from lower income families for the first time. The Ministry of Health and Welfare used to provide financial assistance monthly to lower-income families who send 5-year-olds to child-care centers and has supported some 3- and 4-year-olds from lower-income families since 1997. Altogether, in 2003, the Korean government covered about 20% of all 5-year-old children in Korea through kindergarten and child-care center. The Korean government plans to provide all families who have 5-year-olds with tuition assistance by 2008.

Table 6.4 shows the enrollment in kindergartens and child-care centers. According to the statistics compiled by the Ministry of Education and Human Resources Development for the year 2003, only 45.1% of 5-year-olds, 26.8% of 4-year-olds, and 12% of 3-year-olds attend kindergarten. There are several reasons for the rather low percentage of kindergarten enrollment. First, there are not enough kindergartens to serve all young children in some areas. Second, some working parents prefer child-care

Table 6.4.   The Enrollment in Kindergartens and Child-Care Centers (2003)

Age	Total	Kindergartens		Child-Care Centers	
		N	%	N	%
Under 1	566,388			9,312	1.6
Under 2	598,585			45,939	7.7
Under 3	617,346			122,293	19.8
Total	1,782,319			177,554	10.0
3 years old	624,032	74,635	12.0	192,526	30.8
4 years old	642,011	172,376	26.8	198,638	31.0
5 years old	671,651	303,139	45.1	158,030	23.6
Total	1,937,694	550,150	28.4	549,194	28.34

Sources: Korea National Statistical Office, Republic of Korea (2003); Ministry of Education and Human Resources Development, Republic of Korea (2003); Ministry of Gender Equality, Republic of Korea (2003).

centers near their homes. Third, parents with a strong desire to give their young ones academic training in various subjects send their children to private institutes instead of kindergartens or child-care centers (Lee, Chang, Chung, & Hong, 2001).

Child-care centers are required by law to accept young children from birth to 6 years old, whose parents are working. As shown in Table 6.4, 23.6% of 5-year-olds, 31% of 4-year-olds, and 30.8% of 3-year-olds are enrolled in child-care centers. More 5-year-olds are attending kindergartens while twice as many 3-year-olds are attending child-care centers. About 19.8% of 2-year-olds, 7.7% of 1-year-olds and only 1.6% of infants under 12 months receive child-care services. Working women who have children under the age of 3 are pushing the Korean government strongly to build and support new child-care centers.

Very few child-care centers run after-school programs for primary school children from age 6 to 12. Only 1.14% of children in that age group are taken care of in after-school programs.

Curriculum and Quality Assurance

The Ministry of Education and Human Resources Development revises the national curriculum for kindergarten periodically. The national curriculum which sets a minimum quality standard for kindergarten education throughout the nation is also applied to the children aged 3 to 5 in child-care centers. Child-care teachers develop their own curriculum content for young children under three.

National Curriculum

Kindergartens for children aged 3 to 5 follow the national curriculum offered by the Ministry of Education and Human Resources Development, as well as guidelines formulated by local education authorities to meet the needs of children and parents in their region. The national curriculum provides general curriculum guidelines, teaching-learning activities, teaching methods, and methods of assessment. The national curriculum, which kindergartens are using at the present time, was revised for the sixth time in 1998 and aims to promote the overall development of young children. The specific aims of the national kindergarten curriculum are:

- to promote the healthy development of minds and bodies
- to help children acquire good basic living habits and adopt a cooperative attitude toward others

- to enable children to express their own thoughts and feelings in creative ways
- to promote proper language competency
- to help children learn to think for themselves when they are faced with problems in daily life.

The content of the national curriculum for kindergarten consists of five areas: physical health, social relationships, expression, language, and inquiry. Each area is provided with developmentally appropriate content. The contents of each area are divided into two categories, category I and category II, according to the level of difficulty. The content of category I is easier to perform and is suitable for 3-year-olds and some 4-year-olds. The content of category II is more advanced, and is mostly for 4-year-olds and some 5-year-olds.

The educational contents of category I and II are described sequentially according to the developmental level and young children's experiences. Teachers are required to choose the educational contents that are appropriate to their own children's developmental level and interests.

The national curriculum for kindergarten recommends teaching methods that are appropriate for young children's developmental characteristics. First, teachers have to plan activities for young children that can integrate the contents of the five areas with the young children's interests. All the educational contents chosen should be introduced through activities and play. Second, teachers can introduce the contents of category II, which are more advanced than category I, to younger children if the children can manage them.

The kindergarten classroom should be divided into different interest areas and sufficient educational materials should be provided in each area. For active learning, real objects that allow direct experience should be used whenever possible. The method of grouping children varies depending on the type of activity in both kindergarten and child-care centers. For example, at free choice playtime children have their own individual time or are grouped in pairs or small groups spontaneously. Teachers give help during this time if they think that a child or a group of children needs assistance based on their observation. Circle time, story telling time, and time for games are scheduled in a large group.

Daily routines should be balanced, with active and quiet activities, indoor and outdoor, individualized and large-group, and child-initiated and teacher-initiated activities. The national curriculum emphasizes daily educational activities that can promote various types of interactions between child and teacher, child and child, and child and materials. Teachers should adopt positive and supportive language and attitudes when interacting with children and should ask many open-ended questions in order to stimulate curiosity, to provide motivation to explore, and to improve creative thinking.

Evaluation should focus on children's health, basic living habits, emotional security, social adaptation, creative expression, and the ability to communicate, and explore. The national curriculum recommends that teachers apply various methods of evaluation, such as observation, anecdotal records, analysis of children's work, and interviews. The evaluator must have an understanding of the characteristics of the child's development level. The results of the evaluation should be written in descriptive form, and they should be utilized to promote young children's growth as a whole, to raise the effectiveness of curriculum planning, and to help parents understand their children.

Quality Assurance

The Department of Early Childhood Education in the Ministry of Education and Human Resources Development makes policies for kindergarten education. In addition, 35 city and provincial local education authorities, with a total of 180 regional educational sections, supervise kindergartens in their region periodically as well as carrying out the policies of the Ministry.

Each authority at the city, provincial, and regional level has one or two supervisors who specialize in early childhood education. Korea has 215 supervisors nationwide responsible for the quality of education in kindergarten. These officials visit and observe public and private kindergartens regularly to see whether or not they maintain programs developmentally appropriate for young children.

Even though there is no evaluation system for child-care centers at the government level at the present time, the Ministry of Gender Equality revised the Infant Care Act on January 8, 2004, in order to prepare for a system of accreditation of child-care centers. The accreditation system will be implemented in 2005. At the present time some directors of child-care centers organize self-supervision circles in their region. Some local Departments of Family Affairs inspect child-care centers whenever necessary.

Teacher Provision

Information regarding qualifications for kindergarten teachers and child-care teachers is given below and summarized in Table 6.5. Teachers with a kindergarten teacher certificate can work as child-care center teachers, but not vice versa. Since 1991 many child-care teachers have been trained in 1-year child-care teacher training centers.

Table 6.5.   Qualifications for Kindergarten Teachers and Child-Care Teachers

	Kindergarten	Child-Care Center
Level II	• Graduates from the Dept. of Early Childhood Education of 4-yr-Universities or 2-/3-yr-Colleges	• Completion of a 1-year training course
Level I	• Level II kindergarten teacher certificate • 3 yrs experience in kindergarten • In-service education by Ministry of Education and Human Resources Development	• Level II kindergarten teacher certificate • Level II child-care teacher certificate • 3 yrs experience in child-care center • In- service education by Ministry of Gender Equality
Vice-director	• Level I kindergarten teacher certificate • 3 yrs experience in kindergarten • In-service education by Ministry of Education and Human Resources Development	
Director	• Vice-director's certificate • 3 yrs experience in kindergarten • In-service education.	• Level I certificate • 5 yrs experience in child-care center

Qualification for Kindergarten Teachers

The Ministry of Education and Human Resources Development requires kindergarten teachers to have a college or university education. After graduating from the department of early childhood education at a 2- or 3-year junior college or a 4-year university, the graduates can obtain a level II kindergarten-teacher certificate (beginner's certificate) automatically. According to the statistics for 2002 there are 94 junior colleges and 53 4-year universities that have departments authorized to award the kindergarten-teacher certificate. In 2002 alone, 4,019 kindergarten teachers received degrees from 4-year universities and 9,750 graduated from 2-year junior colleges.

From 2003 the early childhood education departments of 2-year colleges have been able to offer 3-year programs. Already 82 out of 94 colleges decided to offer 3-year programs. The purpose of this policy is to enhance the quality of kindergarten teachers.

As shown in Table 6.5 the kindergarten teacher qualification and requirements set by the Ministry of Education and Human Resources

Development have four levels, level II kindergarten teacher, level I kindergarten teacher, vice-director, and director.

In order to qualify for a level II kindergarten teacher certificate, one should graduate from a department of early childhood education of a 2-/3-year junior college or university after completing courses including practicum in a kindergarten. To be a level I teacher one should have a level II kindergarten teacher certificate, 3 years' experience in a kindergarten, and in-service education offered by the Ministry of Education and Human Resources Development. A teacher with a level I kindergarten teacher certificate, 3 years' experience in a kindergarten and in-service education offered by the Ministry of Education and Human Resources Development can become a vice-director.

The requirements for the kindergarten director certificate are a vice-director certificate, 3 years' experience in a kindergarten and in-service education by the Ministry of Education and Human Resources Development.

Qualifications for Child-Care Teachers

There are three levels for child-care teachers: level II child-care teacher, level I child-care teacher, and director.

To become a level II child-care teacher one must complete a 1-year training course, after finishing high school. In Korea there are 84 centers for child-care teacher training and more than 30,000 child-care teachers are trained every year. The annual surplus of new child-care teachers results in low salaries and low status for child-care teachers. To become a level I child-care teacher, one should have a level II child-care teacher certificate, 3 years' experience at a child-care center and in-service education offered by the Ministry of Health and Welfare. The requirements for director are a level I child-care teacher certificate and 5 years' experience in a child-care center.

Holders of the level II kindergarten teacher certificate can become level I child-care teachers if they do a practicum at a child-care center while they are in college or university. About 48% of the total of 47,152 child-care center teachers are kindergarten teacher certificate holders, according to the statistics for 2003 compiled by the Ministry of Health and Welfare, whose responsibility was transferred to the Ministry of Gender Equality from June 12, 2004.

Number of Kindergarten Teachers and Child-Care Teachers

As shown in Table 6.6, the total number of kindergarten teachers is 30,205. Of these, 6,357 are public kindergarten teachers and 23,848 are private kindergarten teachers. Even though the number of private kindergartens and public kindergartens is similar, there are nearly four times

**Table 6.6.   Number of Kindergarten Teachers and
Child-Care Teachers (2003)**

	Number of Kindergartens	Number of Kindergarten Teachers	Number of Child-Care Centers	Number of Child-Care Teachers
Public	4,284	6,357	1,329	7,218
Private	4,008	23,848	22,813	50,205
Total	8,292	30,205	24,142	57,403

Sources: Ministry of Education and Human Resources Development, Republic of Korea
(2003); Ministry of Health and Welfare (2003).

as many private kindergarten teachers as public kindergarten teachers.
This is because there are many private kindergartens that have more
classrooms than public kindergartens. It is also due to the fact that most
of the public kindergartens are located in rural areas, while most of the
private kindergartens are located in big cities.

The number of child-care teachers altogether is 57,403. It is noticeable
that the number of kindergartens has remained about the same since
1995, but the number of child-care centers is increasing drastically
because of the rapid growth in the number of working women and as a
result of government policy for the expansion of child-care centers.

Staff to Children Ratios

The Elementary-Secondary Education Law that lays down guidelines
for kindergartens sets the upper limit for one teacher at 40 children. This
means that teacher may teach up to 40 children at once but nowadays the
number of children per teacher is in many cases less than 30. Some private kindergarten directors manage to have only 20 children to one
teacher because parents prefer smaller classes. Some local education
authorities require the kindergartens in their region to have a smaller
number of children per teacher.

The government recommends smaller class sizes in general, but for the
exceptional areas such as newly developed apartment complex areas
where the number of kindergartens cannot keep up with the increase in
the number of children, kindergartens may have 40 children in a class.

The local education authorities decide the proper number of children
per class in their region. For example, the director of the Board of Education of Seoul decided that for 4- and 5-year-old children the limit is 30
per class, for 3-year-olds 20 per class. Where kindergartens cannot organize classes with children of the same age the authority allows them to
have a mixed group of up to twenty-five 3-, 4-, and 5-year-olds in one
classroom. Some local education authorities set the limit at up to 35.

The Infant Care Act enacted by the Ministry of Health and Welfare in 1991 limits the number of children per child-care teacher. For children under 2 the ratio is five children per child-care teacher. The ratio is seven for 2-year-olds, and 20 for children over 3. Besides the regular classroom child-care teachers there are one or two more adults to provide extra help, which raises the ratio of staff to children.

CURRENT RESEARCH IN
EARLY CHILDHOOD EDUCATION AND CARE

Research in early childhood education and care is essential not only for developing appropriate programs for young children, but also for developing policies. Although early childhood education in Korea has a 90-year history, research publications were not regularly documented until the late 1970s.

This section provides a brief review of current research related to early childhood education and care, in terms of (1) quantitative increase in research publications, (2) major types of research and research methods, (3) areas of research, and (4) research and policy issues.

Growth in the Number of Research Publications

Research activities in the field of early childhood care and education have been fostered by the establishment of two professional organizations, the Korean Society for Early Childhood Education (KSECE) in 1975 and the Korean Association of Child Studies (KACS) in 1979; these associations both sponsored professional journals. During the 1980s, fewer than 20 research articles on early childhood education were published per year. The number of articles has increased rapidly since 1990, and more than 100 articles per year have appeared since 1996. The number of published research articles in the period 1996-2001 was 10 times greater than in the period 1986-1990.

Such a quantitative growth in research was possible partly due to the increased number of professionals in the areas related to early childhood education and care. In addition, more professional journals began to be published, such as *The Korea Journal of Child Care and Education* in 1994, *Journal of Future Early Childhood Education* in 1995, and *Journal of the Korean Association for Open Early Childhood Education* in 1996. The total number of research papers published by these five professional journals in 2001 was about 250 (Heo, 2002).

Table 6.7.   Number of Articles from Five Journals in Korea

Journals	1976-1980 N (%)	1981-1985 N (%)	1986-1990 N (%)	1991-1995 N (%)	1996-2001 N (%)	Total N (%)
Korean Journal of Early Childhood Education	11 (0.7)	20 (1.4)	35 (2.4)	72 (5.0)	206 (14.2)	344 (23.7)
Korean Journal of Child Studies	7 (0.5)	37 (2.5)	56 (3.9)	118 (8.0)	314 (21.5)	532 (36.4)
Korean Journal of Child Care and Education	0 (0)	0 (0)	0 (0)	34 (2.3)	272 (18.6)	306 (20.9)
Journal of Future Early Childhood Education[1]	0 (0)	0 (0)	0 (0)	9 (0.6)	115 (7.8)	124 (8.5)
Journal of Korean Association for Open Early Childhood Education	0 (0)	0 (0)	0 (0)	0 (0)	154 (10.5)	154 (10.5)
Total	18 (1.2)	57 (4.0)	91 (6.3)	233 (15.9)	1,061 (72.6)	1,460 (100.0)

Table 6.7 shows the number of articles published by the five journals in various time periods. About 60% of the total research papers published since 1976 were from two leading Korean journals published by the Korean Society for Early Childhood Education and the Korean Association of Child Studies. The Korean Society for Early Childhood Education has been publishing six volumes per year from 2004 and the Korean Association of Child Studies has been publishing six volumes per year since 2002.

Another source of research products in the field of early childhood education and related areas is the master's theses and doctoral dissertations submitted to universities in Korea. A similar trend is evident in the quantitative growth in the number of theses since 1980. For instance, of the total 2,926 theses that Hwang (1998) reviewed, only 5% were written during the 1970s, whereas 41% were written during the 1980s, and 54% from 1990 to 1997. Hwang explained that such a growth in the number of theses was mainly due to the increase in the number of departments of early childhood education and related areas such as child studies in graduate schools as well as graduate schools of education.

Such a rapid increase in research publications could be attributed to the recent social context of Korea. The field of early childhood education and care has experienced a tremendous growth in recent years. As described in the history section, the Early Childhood Education Promotion Act (1981) and the Infant Care Act (1991) increased public awareness of the importance of early childhood care and education. The growth of professional groups and the pressure on university professors to publish may also have stimulated them to be more active in research. Yet another factor in this trend is the increase in the number of employed mothers with children, and their demands for quality care as well as for appropriate practices in early childhood education.

Types of Research and Research Methods

As research publications have multiplied, other changes have followed, especially in types of research and research methods. Research by a single author has gradually decreased, and studies by two or more authors have increased over time (Rhee & Shin, 2000). This means that cooperative work by researchers is more prevalent today than in the 1980s.

In terms of the type of research, empirical research has dominated and increased over time, while the number of analytic reviews of literature has decreased (Choi, 1994; Rhee & Shin, 2000). The majority of analytic reviews were in the area of curriculum. Among the different research types, correlational studies comprised about 31%, followed by experimental studies and surveys, constituting about 15% each (Rhee & Shin, 2000). It was also noted that correlational studies have become more diversified, and data analysis techniques such as multiple regression, path analysis, and LISREL have been used recently.

The quantitative approach is also predominant in master's and doctoral theses (Hwang, 1998). However, more surveys and experimental studies were found to come from theses than from professional journal papers. Hwang also indicated that most experimental studies have used simple pre-post design or experimental-control group comparisons.

Despite the continuing dominance of quantitative research studies, research papers using qualitative approaches have increased steadily since the early 1990s, and comprised almost 10% of published papers in recent years (Rhee & Shin, 2000). This is encouraging because qualitative research, which is researcher-involved, subjective and gives a rich description of early educational phenomena, can present data from a different perspective (Yeom, 2001).

The participants in studies were mostly preschool and primary school children, followed by parents and teachers. Infants, toddlers, and children with special needs constituted 3% or less of the subjects studied. This may stem from difficulties in obtaining access to and working with infants, toddlers and special needs children. The sample size was less than 100 in most studies, while samples between 100 and 200 were the next largest group. The sampling method was not reported by many studies (Choi,

1994). Other shortcomings in research methods were also noted. For instance, the reliability of the research instruments was neither examined nor reported in many theses. Moreover, studies reported since 1990 relied heavily on instruments developed in foreign countries, and the translated version was applied without any testing to examine its validity (Hwang, 1998). In addition, the majority of the research in child development applied a cross-sectional approach, and more longitudinal studies are needed to fully describe life-span development.

Areas of Research

The major areas of research found in journal articles and theses are child development, early childhood curriculum, and parents and family. These three areas constituted 70% to 80% of the research work in early childhood care and education, although there are some differences in methods of categorizing the research topics into different areas. Master's and doctoral theses seem to emphasize the curriculum area more, especially in recent studies (KSECE, 1995).

Research on child development was exclusively focused on cognitive and socioemotional development, with some attention paid to language development. Research on cognitive development seems to be decreasing from the peak it reached during the 1980s and early 1990s. However, research on socioemotional and language development has increased and expanded somewhat recently. Research topics in the area of socioemotional development included social competence, emotion, attachment, self-concept, peer relations, and moral development, while emergent literacy and story comprehension were popular topics in language development research.

Research on curriculum includes a variety of topics, such as goals and philosophy of early education, different subject areas, teaching and learning methods, program development and effectiveness, and educational materials and media. Teaching and learning methods was the most frequently studied area, indicating that issues relating to how to teach young children have continued to be important. Also, this reflects the preference for the process model of curriculum rather than the objective model in early childhood education (Y. O. Kim, 1993). Among the subject areas, language and music/movement were frequently studied, especially in theses. Research on instructional media and computers began to appear more frequently between the late 1980s and early 1990s (KSECE, 1995).

Research on the history of early childhood education and early education practice until the early 1980s focused in many cases on Western history and scholars, such as Froebel, Dewey, and Montessori. However, there has been a noticeable change in this trend since the mid 1980s. More attention has been paid to the history of Korean kindergarten and Korean traditional plays. Examples include a study on the history of the early development of Korean kindergarten (S. K. Lee, 1987), and research to identify Korean traditional games relevant to early childhood classrooms (E. W. Lee, 1990).

Research on parents and family was mostly focused on parent-child relationships, parental roles, and parent education. Research articles on parent-child relationships have mainly dealt with parents' child-rearing attitudes or practices in relation to child development. They have supported the view that parental warmth-acceptance is generally related to children's social development. Studies on parent education have been pursued only occasionally (A. S. Lee, 1986), with topics such as surveys on parent education, the development of parent training programs, and the effects of parent participation.

Research on teacher education has also not been found frequently, although a slight increase was noted recently. Studies included factors affecting teacher education such as teacher characteristics and institutional variables, relationships between teacher behavior and student outcomes, and teacher beliefs or thinking processes (Ko, 2000). Ideally teacher variables need to be incorporated in teaching strategy research, so that the effects of a method can be more completely explained. However, teaching methods and teacher quality were in fact studied separately.

The development of research in the area of young children's well-being and child-care has been prominent since 1990. The research topics on child care include the history of child-care services, the quality of day care, the effects of day care, the current state and evaluation of day care centers, and day care policies. As a result of the increased interest in child welfare, the Korean Association of Child Welfare was formed. It published the first volume of its journal in 1993. Research articles cover future trends in child welfare, the adoption of children by Korean families, child abuse, children in divorced families, neglected families, and so on. This is encouraging, but further studies are needed on infants and toddler care, the long-term effects of day care on children combined with day care quality, and the well-being of children in the family context.

A relatively small proportion of research efforts have been devoted to children with special needs, and to educational policies. Children with special needs are disadvantaged due to their physical or mental disabilities. Early childhood educators need to include these children in the mainstream rather than separate them and place them in special education, in order to provide education that is appropriate to all children. Research on educational policies is urgently needed in order to provide necessary information and to guide the future direction of early child-hood care and education.

It is worth describing two examples of research publications that were initiated by professional associations and conducted as a cooperative project. One is the *Comprehensive Report of Early Childhood Education* by the Korean Society for Early Childhood Education (1995), and the other is the *Child Development Report 2001* by the Korean Association of Child Studies (2002). The first publication is a comprehensive collection of information on early childhood education and care, curriculum, teacher education, laws and regulations, administration, finances, and research trends in theses and journal articles. It provides a good source for basic data on early childhood education and care in Korea up to 1994. This project was carried out by a large number of professionals in early educa-tion, and the Korean Society for Early Childhood Education published the second report in 2003.

The Child Development Report 2001 by the Korean Association of Child Studies is a different kind of publication. This is not a source book, but a report of empirical research based on a national survey of questionnaires completed by 15,315 families. The questionnaires were developed for five age groups (0-1, 1-2, 3-5, 6-12, 12-16 years old), and deal with children's prenatal, physical, cognitive, and socioemotional development, family life and home environment, parent-child relations, and early education. Mothers completed the questionnaires for their children aged from birth to 12 years old, while middle and high school students (aged 12-16) com-pleted theirs by themselves.

The results showed that 44% of 4-year-olds and 76% of 5-year-olds could read books, and 69% of 5-year-olds could count up to 100. Mothers reported that the majority of infants did not have separation anxiety. About 90% of primary and secondary school children owned computers, and about 70% of secondary school children used the Internet for 2 hours or more per day. Most of the parents were positive toward early education, and more than half of them expected their children to graduate from 4-year colleges. This research may be the first nationwide survey by a pro-fessional group with descriptive data on child development and family context, although there are some limitations in the data reported by mothers.

Research and Policy Issues in Early Childhood Education

The major issues and problems to be solved in this field are mainly concerned with maintaining and developing high-quality early childhood education. As we have discussed, research in the field of policymaking is rare. However, some of the research issues are connected with policy issues. We will discuss research issues and policy issues below.

Research Issues

The early childhood education professionals claim that to improve the quality of early childhood education, the major tasks to be carried out are the development and implementation of the curriculum for quality care and education (Moon; 2001). Some strongly recommend the development of a range of different programs that allow parents to select programs for their children depending on the needs of the children and family (Cho, 1999; Seo, 2002).

Moon (2001) claims that the program in child-care centers should be different in that it should be oriented toward care. What parents want most from the child-care services is care rather than education (Kim, 2001). However, others claim that we cannot separate care from education from a child's point of view. For children, both care and education should be included in child-care programs, with different aspects of care and education being stressed according to children's age level (G. H. Yu, 2001). The level of expectations with regard to curriculum and facilities is different even for children of the same age and even though kindergarten and child-care centers are located in the same area, since the departments that guide and supervise the educational contents and teaching methods for kindergarten and child-care centers under the same conditions are different. In particular, the programs for infants and toddlers should be different from the programs for children aged 3 to 5. There are no comparative studies on the different aspects of care and education and the proportion of care needed according to the children's ages.

The localization of the national curriculum is strongly recommended. However, this localization is now carried out in only a very limited way (Jeon, 1998). In order to provide more effective education for young children, the localization of the national kindergarten curriculum should be expanded.

It is necessary to evaluate programs in order to monitor and improve their quality. Early childhood education professionals recommend evaluating programs by using accreditation standards and then using the evaluation as a standard for funding, as well as a criterion of program quality and a guide to self-supervision (Rhee & Lee, 1996; Yang, 2000). Yang (2000) suggests that representatives of appropriate agencies evaluate all kindergarten and child-care centers every 3 years. Accreditation standards should cover facilities and equipment, curriculum, nutrition, health and safety, administration and management, and support systems (Kwon,

Lee, & Harms 1999; Lim, Jo, & Hwang, 1066; Rhee & Lee, 1996; Rhee, Song, Shin, & Choi, 2002; Yang, 2000). However, accreditation standards are not applied to kindergartens and child-care centers yet.

It has been found that smaller class sizes and high teacher-child ratios lead to an improvement both in children's behavior and in their cognitive performance since teachers can interact more frequently and in ways more appropriate to the children's needs under such conditions (H. J. Kim, 1992; Lee & Kim, 1995). Early childhood education professionals insist that we should adopt enrollment limits of 15 children per classroom for 3-year-olds (Lee & Kim, 1995) and 20 children for 4- and 5-year-olds (H. J. Kim, 1992). From 2002, the number of children per classroom in elementary school was reduced to a maximum of 35 (Seoul Metropolitan Office of Education, 2001). The Bureau of Early Childhood Education in the Ministry of Education and Human Resources Development has suggested reducing the number of children for a kindergarten class of 5-year-olds to 30, although the Elementary-Secondary Education Law currently sets the limit at 40 children per teacher. The issue has been presented and discussed, but not taken up as a research project at a kindergarten due to financial considerations; hence, it should be taken up as a research project by some national educational institution. Furthermore, we need research on group size and adult to child ratio for infants and toddler groups since there has been no study related to this issue yet.

Two teachers per classroom are recommended for the reason that when there are two teachers in one classroom, they show more tolerance, approval, physical contact, helpfulness and person-to-person communicative behaviors (H. J. Kim, 1992). But in reality it is difficult to have two regular teachers in every classroom because of the budgetary limitations. Therefore, it is necessary to find some other solutions such as having parents or student teachers as helpers. It seems critical for child-care centers to have two adults for classes of children under 3 years old. For the children under 3 years old in child-care centers two or three teachers should form a team and do team teaching in one room. We need hard data to convince the decision makers responsible for early childhood policy related to this issue. When the appropriate class size and teacher to child ratio for Korean children are presented, the case should be fully supported by research data.

Policy Issues

There are at least three main policy issues currently under discussion in Korea: the expansion of public education for young children, the enactment of the Early Childhood Education Act, and the improvement of teacher quality and teachers' working conditions.

Since 1949, article 81 of the Education Law made it clear that elementary school, middle school, high school, and university form a system of basic educational levels (6 years / 3 years / 3 years / 4 years), while kindergarten was not included in these basic levels. The first Educational Reform Committee decided to include kindergarten in the system of basic educational levels in September 1994. However, when the second Educational Reform Committee discussed the inclusion of kindergarten as a school system, they rejected the plan since only 45% of 5-year-olds were enrolled in kindergarten (Second Educational Reform Committee, 1997). However, the committee decided to increase the number of kindergartens and provide financial support for 5-year-olds. It is generally acknowledged that not only to reduce the burden of educational expenses on parents but also to improve early childhood education at the national level, it is necessary to bring early childhood education into the public system. It is also proposed that in order to create equal opportunity in early childhood education, there should be financial support for the private kindergartens and child-care centers. At least 1 year of free education before elementary school should be guaranteed whether young children are in public or private kindergartens or child-care centers (Ban, 1997). As kindergarten became one of the basic-education levels with the enactment of the Early Childhood Education Act in 2004, all the 5-year-olds in both public and private kindergartens and child-care centers will receive financial support from the government from 2008. In the budget of the Ministry of Education and Human Resources Development, the allotment for early childhood education is under 1.24% (Na et al., 1996). It is necessary to increase the budget for early childhood education to back up the financial support for public and private kindergartens and full-day kindergarten programs.

The issue of public education for young children is closely related to the second issue. Under the current Elementary-Secondary Educational Law and Infant Care Act, the contents of education and care in kindergarten and child-care centers are prescribed as almost identical and are not conceptually specific enough to be distinguished from each other.

As described in the previous section, the administrative systems for 3- to 5-year olds are overlapping. The Ministry of Education and Human Resources Development is in charge of kindergarten education for 3- to 5-year-olds and the Ministry of Gender Equality is in charge of child-care centers for children from birth to the age of 6. Kindergarten operates half-day, extended-day, and full-day programs, and the percentage of children in extended-day and full-day programs is over 70% (Meyers & Gomick, 2000). Early childhood educators believe this is a waste of time, energy, and resources. They recognize that kindergarten and child-care centers share common tasks of educating and caring for young children. Therefore, there should be a unified system for kindergarten and child-care at least for children aged from 3 to 5.

The third issue is the improvement of teacher education and teachers' working conditions. To improve the quality of early childhood education it is necessary to improve the quality of teachers. Producing a high-quality teacher requires training of at least 2 or 3 years in colleges, where the curriculum for early childhood teacher education should include courses for the teaching profession and early childhood education subjects covering the program for children aged from birth to 5. It is recommended that the same teacher-education policy should be applied to all early childhood teachers whether they work in kindergarten or child-care centers (G. L. Lee, 1997). The period of college training in early childhood education should gradually be extended from 2 years to 3.

Early childhood education professionals strongly insist that the policy of appointing people with only 1 year's training to child-care teacher training centers should be abandoned. Regular in-service training for early childhood teachers is also recommended in terms of the teachers' experience and the on-site evaluation.

Teachers with training in early childhood education are paid less than their colleagues who have specialized in other areas of education. The basic salaries of teachers in early childhood education are important for the improvement of teacher quality. Teachers' salaries should be based on the training and qualifications of the teacher, whether they are working in kindergarten or child-care centers. Public kindergartens have certification standards for teachers and salary schedules that guarantee pay increments for extra training and experience. However, private kindergartens tend to pay teachers less due to their limited financial resources. The base salary for teachers in child-care centers is lower than the base salary for kindergarten teachers.

Considering the importance of the responsibilities of kindergarten and child-care center teachers, these teachers should have a similar social status to other professionals. In addition, teachers' working hours should be arranged in such a way that they include time to plan curricular activities, prepare materials and arrange the environment, especially for those teachers assigned to all-day programs.

In this section, major research trends and research and policy issues in early childhood education in Korea have been discussed. It is evident that further research is necessary to provide answers to many questions raised in connection with the improvement of quality in early childhood education and policy related issues. We need well-documented research on localization of the national curriculum, hard data on the most effective class size and teacher-child ratio in the Korean context, comparative studies of children and teachers in the two types of educational institutions, and studies on the long-term effects of different types of child-care. These will help in formulating recommendations to policymakers regarding the future direction of early childhood education in Korea.

REFERENCE

Ban, U. K. (1997). *Fundamental direction of early childhood education reform propulsion.* Paper presented at the annual conference of the Korean Society for Early Childhood Education, Seoul, Korea.

Cho, K. J. (1999). *A task and developmental direction of administration and finance of early childhood education.* Paper presented at the annual conference of the Korean Society for Early Childhood Education, Seoul, Korea.

Choi, M. S. (1994). A review of research methodology in early childhood education: Based on *Journal of Early Childhood Education* articles. *Korean Journal of Early Childhood Education, 14*(1), 199-220 (in Korean).

Heo, W. J. (2002). *The trend analysis of research papers on early childhood education.* Unpublished master's thesis, Pusan National University, Pusan, Korea (in Korean).

Hwang, H. I. (1998). A study on the analysis of research methods used in the thesis of early childhood education area. *Journal of Early Childhood Education, 8,* 111-135 (in Korean).

Jeon, S. Y. (1998). *A study on the localization of the national kindergarten curriculum.* Unpublished doctoral dissertation, Chung-Ang University, Seoul, Korea (in Korean).

Kim, H. I. (1997). *Comparison of educational policies for infants and babies.* Unpublished master's thesis, Ewha Womans University, Seoul, Korea (in Korea).

Kim, H. J. (1992). *A study of teacher's/child's behavior according to variation in class size and the number of teacher.* Unpublished doctoral dissertation, Ewha Womans University, Seoul, Korea (in Korean).

Kim, Y. O. (1993). Research trend in early childhood education and future tasks. *Korean Association of Education Newsletter, 29*(3), 12-14 (in Korean).

Ko, S. M. (2000). *The analysis of trend in early childhood teacher education based on theses.* Unpublished master's thesis, Ewha Womans University, Seoul, Korea (in Korean).

Korean Association of Child-Care Centers. (1980). *Information on child-care centers.* Mimeograph.

Korean Association of Child Studies. (2002). *Child development report 2001.* Seoul, Korea: Hansol Education (in Korean).

Korean Educational Development Institute. (1997). *Educational indicators in Korea.* Seoul, Korea: Author.

Korea National Statistical Office, Republic of Korea. (2003). *Statistical yearbook.* Seoul, Korea: Author.

Korean Society for Early Childhood Education. (1995). *Comprehensive report of early childhood education*. Seoul, Korea: How Press (in Korean).

Kwon, Y. R., Lee, Y. J., & Harms, T. (1999). The development of assessment scale of educational environment for kindergarten and lower grade level of elementary school. *The Journal of Educational Research, 37*(3), 341-364 (in Korean).

Lee, A. S. (1986). *An analysis of theses in the field early childhood education (1982-1985)*. Unpublished master's thesis, Ewha Womans University, Seoul, Korea (in Korean).

Lee, E. W. (1990). *The application of Korean traditional group games to early childhood education*. Unpublished doctoral dissertation, Yonsei University, Seoul, Korea (in Korean).

Lee, G. L. (1997). The characteristics of early childhood education in Korea. *International Journal of Early Childhood, 26*(2), 44-50.

Lee, K. S., Chang, Y. H., Chung, M. R., & Hong, Y. H. (2001). *Project for the reformation of early childhood education for raising creative and well-balanced children*. Policy Project for Early Childhood Education 2001-24, The Ministry of Education and Human Resources Development, Republic of Korea (in Korean).

Lee, S. K. (1987). *History of modern kindergartens in Korea*. Seoul, Korea: Ewha Womans University Press (in Korean).

Lee, Y. J., & Kim, H. S. (1995). Teacher/child social behavior and language patterns by class size in a classroom of three-year-olds. *Korean Journal of Early Childhood Education, 15*(1), 79-100 (in Korean).

Lim, J. T., Jo, H. S., & Hwang, H. I. (1996). The development of a diagnostic assessment scale for early childhood programs in child-care centers. *Sung Kok Collection of Studies, 27(4)*, 401-500 (in Korean).

Meyers, M. K., & Gomick, J. C. (2000). *Early childhood education and care (ECEC): Cross national variation in service organization and financing*. Paper prepared for A consultative meeting on international developments in early childhood education and care: An activity of Columbia Institute for Child and Family Policy.

Ministry of Education, Republic of Korea. (1955). *Statistics of educational institutions*. Seoul, Korea: Author.

Ministry of Education, Republic of Korea. (1986). *Early childhood education sources*, 12. Seoul, Korea: Author.

Ministry of Education, Republic of Korea. (1998). *Kindergarten curriculum*. Seoul, Korea: Author.

Ministry of Education and Human Resources Development, Republic of Korea. (1977). *Handbook of educational statistics*. Seoul, Korea: Author.

Ministry of Education and Human Resources Development, Republic of Korea and Korean Educational Development Institute. (2001). *Statistical yearbook of education*. Seoul, Korea: Author.

Ministry of Education and Human Resources Development, Republic of Korea. (2002). *2002 statistics on kindergarten*. Seoul, Korea: Author.

Ministry of Education and Human Resources Development, Republic of Korea. (2003). *2003 Statistics on kindergarten*. Seoul, Korea: Author.

Ministry of Education and Human Resources Development, Republic of Korea and Korean Educational Development Institute. (2000, 2001). *Handbook of educational statistics*. Seoul, Korea: Korean Educational Development Institute.

Ministry of Gender Equality, Republic of Korea. (2001). Yearbook of health and welfare statistics. Seoul, Korea: Author.

Ministry of Gender Equality, Republic of Korea. (2003). 2003 Statistics on child-care centers. Seoul, Korea: Author.

Ministry of Health and Welfare, Republic of Korea. (2001). *Yearbook of health and welfare statistics (the 47th edition)*. Seoul, Korea: Author.

Ministry of Health and Welfare, Republic of Korea. (2002). *Yearbook of health and welfare statistics (the 48th edition)*. Seoul, Korea: Author.

Ministry of Health and Welfare. (2003). *2003 statistics of child-care centers*. Seoul, Korea: Author

Moon, S. H. (2001). *Qualification condition of child-care professionals in infant-child care centers*. Paper presented at the autumn conference of the Korea Association of Child Care and Education, Seoul, Korea.

Na, J., Cheon, S., & Jang, M. (1966). *A study on the policy development of the public education for kindergarten* (CR 96-19). Seoul, Korea: Korean Educational Development Institute.

Rhee, U., & Lee, K. S. (1996). *An assessment scale for early childhood education programs: Guidelines for teachers*. Seoul, , Korea: Chang-Ji Co. (in Korean).

Rhee, U., Park, E., Lee, J., & Cho, E. (1999). *Education and care of young children in Korea*. Paper presented at the meeting of OMEP regional conference.

Rhee, U., & Shin, Y. (2000). Trends in early childhood care and educational research in Korea. *International Journal of Early Childhood Education, 5*, 111-121.

Rhee, U., Song, H. R., Shin, H. Y., & Choi, H. Y. (2002). The development of assessment scales for day care programs. *Korean Journal of Child Studies, 23*(4), 199-214 (in Korean).

Samsung Welfare Foundation. (1995). *The Samsung Welfare Foundation: Working for a better society for all*. Seoul, Korea: Author (in Korean).

Second Educational Reform Committee. (1997). *Fourth educational reform report to the president of the Republic of Korea*. Mimeograph.

Seo, M. H. (2002). *Problems of infant-child care policy and its improvement plan*. Paper presented at the 2002 autumn conference of the Korean Association of Child Studies, Seoul, Korea.

Seoul Metropolitan Office of Education. (1981). *The history of Seoul education*. Seoul, Korea: Author (in Korean).

Seoul Metropolitan Office of Education. (2001). *Statistical yearbook of Seoul education*. Seoul, Korea: Author. (in Korean).

Yang, O. S. (2000). Accreditation standards and procedures for institutions of early childhood education and care. *Korean Journal of Child Studies, 21*(4), 177-196 (in Korean).

Yeom, J. S. (2001). Alternative research approaches in early childhood education: Topics and methods. *Korean Journal of Early Childhood Education, 21*(2), 185-204 (in Korean).

Yu, G. H. (2001). *Discussion on the qualification condition of child care professionals in infant and child-care centers presented by Sun Hwa Moon.* Discussion paper presented at the 2001 autumn conference of Korea Association of Child Care and Education, Seoul, Korea.

Yu, H. J. (2002). *New child-care policy: Dream-tree plan.* Paper presented at the meeting of Korean Women Development Institute, Seoul, Korea.

CHAPTER 7

A GLOBAL PERSPECTIVE ON EARLY CHILDHOOD EDUCATION

Characteristic Traits and Research in Norway

Ole Fredrik Lillemyr

THE DEVELOPMENT OF
EARLY CHILDHOOD EDUCATION IN NORWAY

In Norway the history of early childhood education and care institutions (ECECs) originated from two sources: the children's asylums and the kindergartens inspired by Friedrich Froebel. In Europe the asylums were established somewhat earlier than the kindergartens. In England and Germany the first asylums developed in the latter part of the 1700s, whereas the first kindergarten was established in Germany in 1837. The children's asylums were philanthropic institutions aimed at providing care for children from poor families. Most often these institutions provided a safe place to stay for children while their parents were out working. In Norway the very first early childhood education and care institution, a children's asylum, was established in the city of Trondheim in 1837. It was

International Perspectives on Research in Early Childhood Education, 191–232

financed by private benefactors in addition to receiving money from the king. The asylums established in Trondheim still exist today as day care centers.

The first Froebel-inspired kindergarten in Norway was also established in Trondheim in 1870. In a few years several Froebel-kindergartens were started in the largest cities in the country. Still, in Norway as in other European countries, the first ECECs were established far later than the first primary schools. Inspired by Friedrich Schiller, Froebel outlined that man is most human when playing, taking this as a point of departure for content and methods, a fact treasured even today (Levy, 1997). The asylums, taking in children from age 2 to school age, had at first a very large number of children. Up to 200 or more, supervised by a single adult woman called the asylum mother was not unusual. In addition to the asylums, there were crèches for children below 3 years of age. Both asylums and crèches were social ventures, often taking care of children from labor families.

Ideas from Germany, England, France, and Italy were influencing the Scandinavian countries. The kindergartens emphasized learning and development and were often better equipped and had fewer children enrolled in them than the asylums. In the middle of the 1800s, children stayed in the asylum or kindergarten for as much as 12 hours a day. In addition to a religious and moral focus and learning through play, children were taught some reading, writing, and mathematics. Songs and physical education were included as well. But especially the asylums were basically social institutions providing care for children from disadvantaged environment (Sletvold, 1983; Søbstad, 2000). From this we can infer the emergence of the Norwegian early childhood education and care institutions have two roots: a social root and an educational root. This indicates the intention of the institutions to meet societal needs as well as to prepare for compulsory school. In the late 1800s children from poor families were cared for in the asylums, whereas children from well to do families went to kindergartens. Around 1900 there were fewer asylums and crèches and more of what was called people-kindergartens. The first public kindergarten was established in Oslo in 1920. This was an important event as all child care institutions till then had been financed through private funds and gifts, and run by idealism. Because of scarce economical resources and attitudes that it was best for children to stay at home with the mother, the development of Norwegian child care institutions was not easy. Advocates met many hurdles, not least from policymakers and educational authorities. Several women's organizations were central in advocating the importance of care and educational support for preschool children, in particular immediately after World War II. Since 1953 the ECECs were regulated as a part of the Child Welfare Act. In the 1960s the state as well as municipal authorities increased their involvement in developing and financing early childhood education institutions, which were called the Norwegian kindergarten (children 0 to 6 in age). This resulted in many more children gaining access to the institutions, although in 1970 the coverage (or access rate) was still as low as 2.8% of the children below the age of 7. Around 10 years later the coverage was 21%. In 1990 it was 37%. In 1997, the age of school admission was lowered to age 6, a fact that influenced the coverage rate (Tønnessen, 1995). The first act specially developed for early childhood education and care institutions came into force in 1975—The 1975 Act on Kindergartens. After some years of implementation this act became the responsibility of the Ministry of Children and Family Affairs. The act maintained that a qualified preschool teacher should be responsible for education in the kindergarten or day care institution.

In the 1800s Norway did not have training for the women working in these institutions. Most of those who were trained received their education in Germany. The first institution providing training in early childhood education in the Nordic countries was established in Finland in 1892. The first training of preschool teachers in Norway was established in Oslo as late as 1935; the second was established in Trondheim in 1947. Today there are 20 university colleges in Norway that offer training in early childhood education and care (preschool teacher training); 18 state colleges and two private colleges. The key for the asylum and kindergarten ideas to be spread in Norway was the establishment of preschool teacher training throughout the country. A revision of the 1975 Act on Kindergartens resulted in the 1995 Act on Child Care Institutions. In 1985 the access rate was 28%; in 1997 the rate was 51% for children under 6 (school start age lowered to 6). Today the coverage rate is estimated close to 70% (defined as full coverage). The ECECs in Norway today intend to provide children with care as well as stimulate their learning and development.

The first primary schools in Norway, called the common school, came in 1739, as the act for the common school passed the Parliament the same year. Main subjects were religion (Christianity), reading, and arithmetic. From the start, school was obligatory to all children that could take advantage of the teaching. These day schools aimed to providing parent support for the education of their children. The main idea for the Norwegian school, then and now, is *the principle of one school for all*. This means that all children, in some way or another, go together in all grades, or at least that all students should be given equal opportunities as far as possible. But of course the realization of the principle has changed with societal conditions. According to the latest reform, Reform 97, the principle is formulated as follows: "the obligatory school shall provide equitable and suitably adapted education for everyone in a coordinated system of schooling based on the same curriculum" (see Ministry of Education, Research and Church Affairs, 1996). Generally, all students shall follow the same direction of schooling and learn the same subjects. Other important principles in the Norwegian school have been and are: the principle of the active student, and the principle of adapted learning. The subject syllabuses constitute a common binding basis for the teaching. From a 7 years of schooling in the first part of the 1900s, the compulsory school extended to 9 years of schooling in 1971. After a long and hard debate, school entrance age was lowered to 6 years and school extended to a 10 years in 1997. Most important according to Reform 97, is that 6-year-olds are included in primary school. Furthermore, the parental and adoption benefits (a paid leave of absence because of birth or adoption) removed the need of care for most children up to 1 year old. Today mothers can decide to have 80% salary in a year's time during their leave. It is common now that fathers take up to 2 or 3 months of this mother's leave. For the development of the ECECs and increase of access rate, these parental benefits mean a lot.

THE CURRENT STATE OF
EARLY CHILDHOOD EDUCATION IN NORWAY

Today there are different solutions for child care in Norway, meaning children up to age 5. The ECECs of today provide for children ages 0-5 years, because of the lowering of the school entrance age. For the first time in history, since 1996, a National Framework Plan has been in force, including guidelines for all child-care institutions. There are no subjects suggested, but five broad themes are outlined for all ECECs to work with during the year, such as "language, text, and communication," and so forth (Ministry of Children and Family Affairs, 1995, 1996; Organization for Economic Cooperation and Development, 1998). The form of operation of an ECEC varies, as do the types of ECECs. There are, in addition, different kinds of ordinary ECECs, for example family day care (mostly set up in ordinary homes) and outdoor ECECs (based mainly on outdoor activities the year around). It is also possible to organize a primary school and an ECEC as a unit. Children do not have a legal right to a place in an ECEC, but today it is close to full coverage (access rate of 70%), meaning that all who wish to have a place can have it. If they do not use a day care, parents with 1- and 2-year-olds can instead receive a cash benefit according to the Cash Benefit Act; which allow parents to have more time with their children.

From the year children turn 6 years they start in elementary school Grade 1, or in what is called the comprehensive school, understood as the school for children from 6 through 15. In some districts children go to elementary (primary) schools at first (age 6-12), and then move to a lower secondary school for students aged 13-15. In other districts children go to a full comprehensive school from the beginning, sometimes called "a 1-10 grade school." It is called a comprehensive school because the overall objective is to include the largest possible proportion of the population. It is thought that this yields a high general educational standard, and thus improves the quality of life of the whole population. This is based on the basic principle of Norwegian educational policy that all children and young people have an equal right to education and training irrespective of domicile, sex, social or cultural background, and physical ability. All public education is free.

In the new Curriculum Guidelines of 1997 for the school, stronger emphasis is put on common subject matter as well as on the requirement to adapt to local cultural conditions and individual students. This means obtaining a balance between the social and cultural objectives of the school *and* the objectives of learning and intellectual development. Actually Reform 97 has been termed a child reform, a family reform, and a culture reform, in addition to being a school reform. Not least important, *play* was included *as an integral element* of the school curriculum, which has to be seen as a rather unique trait internationally. No other country's curriculum guidelines as far as I know, emphasize play as an integral element as strong as this. The inclusion of play can also be seen as a new perspective on school motivation, as play also intends to motivate children toward a personal investment in learning (Lillemyr, 2002). Another important characteristic is the method of working with themes and projects across different subjects throughout the school years. The school is seen in three stages: the initial stage (primary school) Grades1-4; the intermediate stage (middle school) Grades 5-7 and the lower secondary stage (junior high school) Grade 8-10. In the initial stage the education shall be grounded on the traditions from both early childhood education and the tradition from the school, to merge into a new primary school tradition. The first year is based on the preschool methods with play and age- and subject-mixed activities. In Norway it can be argued that early childhood education encompass ages 0 through 9, thus including both the ECECs and the initial stage in school. In the 1990s, national reforms dominated the educational picture in Norway, as it has done so for the last two or three decades and at all levels from early childhood education and care and up to university level.

A DESCRIPTION OF RESEARCH AND POLICY ISSUES

The most relevant research and policy issues in Norway through this relatively short history can be characterized as follows:

- Preschool policy, the need for and development of preschools (ECECs)
- The quality of ECECs, "preschool and day care research"
- Preschool teachers and assistants in ECECs: education and professional role
- Children's play and activities in ECECs (content)
- Learning and everyday life perspectives in ECECs
- Special education perspectives in ECECs
- Research on the transition from ECEC to primary school
- Research in primary school (the first four grades of comprehensive school)

Below I present a selection of the most relevant studies and discussion, in particular from recent years.

Preschool Policy, the Need for and Development of Preschools

What is early childhood education in Norway? Influences from other countries in Europe, especially England and Germany, on Norwegian early childhood education has been strong from the beginning. This has not changed much, although a stronger independent position in this concern has been taken over the last few years. The influences from other Nordic countries and the United States on Norwegian early childhood education have also been important. Leira (1992) has shown that the care for children in Norway developed somewhat later than in Denmark and Sweden. She claims that this is fundamentally related to women's increased opportunities to work outside the home. In her opinion the development of enough ECECs therefore must be seen as a fundamental factor in women's participation in production in our society. Even if there has for some years been some ambivalence about women's occupational activity in Norway, a child development policy can hardly be set up today unless the development of ECECs is included.

An extensive program providing full coverage of ECECs was started by the Ministry of Child and Family Affairs (1995-1997). However, Reform 97 for comprehensive school (school entry lowered to age 6) improved the situation substantially for all children where parents desired an ECEC placement for their child. So did the extension of the parental and adoption benefits to provide income compensation for a whole year. For that reason children in ECECs today are aged 1 to 5. In some municipalities there is still limited access rate for children below 3 years. The aim is to eliminate this in a couple of years. The full coverage definition as 70% access rate has been upgraded to "for all children that want an ECEC placement."

But does early childhood education in Norway really have a tradition of its own? The question has been asked for years in Norway as in other countries. The question was also asked in accordance with the latest reforms for the school and for the day care institutions. Why? Because Reform 97 for the comprehensive school suggested that "the best from" two traditions should be taken as a platform for developing a new primary school education. The two traditions were: early childhood education and primary school education. Policymakers as well as professors and researchers in teacher training meant to meld these two traditions to improve the school's education, that is: early childhood education was meant to renew the school educationally (Brusling, 1996). In some people's opinion early childhood education and care in Norway have been and represents today a tradition. Further, it can be argued that it is established as a distinct global model of its own. This global model has certain fundamental values, even if it is applied in other areas of work as well (Lillemyr, Fagerli, & Søbstad, 2001).

The Quality of ECECs: Preschool and Day Care Research

One of the main challenges for preschools and day care centres in the 1980s was to adapt adequately to the local culture. The Local Society—Preschool Project was carried out from 1977 to 1979, to illustrate how preschools and day care institutions adapted their programs to characteristics in the local culture around the institution, in cooperation with parent's ideas (Balke, Berg, & Fagerli, 1979). Later, in 1981 The 4 to 9 Project started with the ambition to integrate the educational program of 4- to 6-year-olds in ECEC and the program of 7- to 9-year-olds in primary school. In this concern play was seen as an important educational method in preschool and school (Rese, Røtnes, Svendsen, & Vedeler, 1986). It has also been found that preschool children as well as school children have developed a relatively clear self-concept, at least by the age of 5 to 6. Therefore, self-concept has to be considered a main source of intrinsic motivation among preschool children, as well as among school children (Lauvland, 1987; Lillemyr, 1989; Strømsnes, 1990). Further it has been argued that development of self-concept cannot be explained and under-stood without relating it to the socialization process and the cultural con-texts. This was found to have consequences for the educational work in ECECs (Hyrve & Lillemyr, 1987). In these studies raising the quality of the ECEC was a main focus.

An important move toward raising quality was also the Framework Plan for Day Care Institutions, acting from 1996 (Ministry of Children and Family Affairs, 1996). For the first time Norway had a framework plan or national guidelines for all ECECs in the country. Reference to the frame-work plan (FP 96) was included in The Child Care Institutions in Norway Act. According to FP 96 all ECECs should teach the children *basic compe-tence* (heavily focused on social and communicative competence), and aim at developing the ECEC as an organization functionally according to con-ditions and needs in society. Further, all ECECs have to cover the follow-ing five main themes during the year:

- society, religion and ethics
- aesthetics
- language, text and communication
- nature, technology and environment
- physical activities and health

The implementation of FP 96 in all municipalities in Norway has taken some time, but seems to be fully established today. It plays an active role in the development of the day care institutions (cf. Lillemyr & Søbstad, 1993).

Röthle (1996) highlights the importance of working with themes in day care institutions. Studying two different institutions she finds that the staff's arrangement of theme work has to be closely tied to children's cre-ativity and involvement. In one of the two ECECs themes work was of great importance for the everyday activities, and social interactions as well as for play situations. All worked with the same theme in different con-texts over a long time. After a while it turned out to be a common point of reference for all the children. In the other ECEC theme it was different. Here the theme work did not mean as much in other situations and con-texts. Different age groups were occupied with different themes at the same time. Here the theme activities did not strengthen the common interests among children in the ECEC, as it did in the other ECEC. It was found that the interest for the theme as such was more persistent in the first ECEC than in the other. In analyzing these data Röthle finds the con-cept of meaning, for the child as well as for the staff members, to be cru-cial. In other studies the focus have been quality in ECEC assistants' work

Here too, involvement and genuine interest in children's life and development is seen as fundamental (Haugen, 1996).

Still it has been asked if Norway really has established a well-organized ECEC research. However, the situation is not necessarily better in other countries. In Norway, it can be argued that one source of ECEC research have been the graduate dissertations at the two university colleges providing a masters program in early childhood education (Johansson, 2002; Søbstad, 2002a). A program of ECEC research was just announced by the Norwegian Research Council (Nilsen, 2002). This research program generated from the addressing of the quality question in a white paper to the Parliament (Norwegian Parliament, no 27, 1999-2000), where quality in the ECEC was the focus. A main objective was to raise the quality of preschools and day care centres in Norway. Quality has of course many aspects. One of them is well-being among the children, a perspective not focused on too often. However, Næs and Mordal (1997) addressed this question in a study using observations of children under 5 and interviews of 5-year-olds in eight ECECs from different locations in the country. A main intention was to get to know what a good ECEC is from a children's point of view. Feeling safe, friendship, being together with others, and participating in decisions were fundamental to their feelings of well-being. It was concluded that children's well-being is high, and the youngest children seemed to have the highest sense of well-being. They found aspects of the inner life of the ECEC to be more influential than structural aspects. The educational competence of the staff seemed important. The level of well-being seemed to increase when the staff listened to the children and gave them opportunities of choice in some situations.

Gulbrandsen (2002) describes the extent to which Norwegian day care centers (ECECs) have initiated quality improvement strategies based on the quality in ECEC program identified by the Ministry of Child and Family Affairs in 2001. According to the program all ECECs should establish instruments and systems for maintaining and developing further day care quality by the end of 2003. The project carried out as a survey in 576 day care centers (10%) in Norway documented that quality improvement efforts are well underway in most centers, in particular in the largest centers. Moreover, great stability among day care center staff was found, especially high stability was found at small centers. In general, in 58% of the day care centers no employee had left during the last year. Only 7% of the employees were men. An important goal of the quality effort is to raise the percentage of men to 20%. User surveys are becoming a common practice. Most centers were found to have an acceptable level of routines written for information to parents, new children, and new employees. Observation was most often applied for recording children's well-being and progress. It was found that children can still be brought further into the process of planning and evaluation. The head masters of the centers were found to have a positive attitude toward the quality effort program as such.

A more recent study on this quality focus has been The Norwegian Preschool Quality Project, supported by a grant from The Ministry of Child and Family Affairs. It started in 2001 in five municipalities and continued for 2 years. In the first report Søbstad (2002b) is "hunting" for good quality in Norwegian ECECs. The project attempted to describe, develop, evaluate, and document quality in Norwegian day care centers. Selected ECECs from five different municipalities in mid Norway (one in a city) participated in the studies. Each ECEC was free to take its own point of departure aiming at raising quality along their own plan, guided by advisors from a college early childhood education teacher training program. In addition there was a professor directing the research studies. It turned out that the staffs in the participating ECECs were primarily concerned about social interaction, play, and evaluation as well as documentation of their work. The developmental projects focusing different selected aspects of ECEC quality were directed by local project leaders.

Certain presuppositions were found to be characteristic of the Norwegian ECEC quality compared to ECEC in other countries: more out-door activities, fathers more visible in the ECEC, less weight on language and intellectual activities, more emphasis on play and social interaction, and more interaction with the local society. These were hypotheses to be examined. Data were collected from children, parents, ECEC staffs, and methods applied were observation, interviews and questionnaires. To evaluate quality, different scales have been developed and several attempts presented as definitions of quality (Organization for Economic Cooperation and Development, 2001; Sheridan, 2001). In these studies neither of the scales was actually applied, but some of the definitions were taken as point of departure (Borge, 1995). The results indicated that parents most frequently identified as important for their children: Gets to play with other kids (97%), learn to relate to others (81%), have fun with other kids and adults (79%). Taken all together the data found that the following traits characterized the ECECs examined:

- An environment with positive social interactions, happiness and humor
- Play is important and emphasized
- Deemphasizing school preparing activities
- A stimulating out-door environment nearby
- Frequent tours to forests, fiords, etc.

- Frequent contact and cooperation with parents
- A listening (responsive) staff

A great similarity between the ECECs was found. However, as Søbstad (2002b) underlines, for the quality work to be meaningful to the ECEC, continually evaluations have to be made. Furthermore, questions concerning quality have to be set up at all levels in the municipality, in the region, and in the whole nation.

In Norway ECECs that express Sami[1] language and culture as their foundation get a special financial support to cover extra expenditures. Special kinds of Sami arrangements, handicrafts and tools, use of Sami artists, as well as producing books often cost extra. Eikeland and Krogh (1999) interviewing head masters at Sami ECECs and evaluating their year plans found that the financial support was employed in a flexible way and well adapted to local needs. A special focus was directing language and identity and the staff competencies in Sami language. It was concluded that further competency building among staff is needed, as some areas seem to have problems getting qualified personal to the ECECs. Here the Sámi allaskuvla (The Sami College of teacher training at Kautokeino) is providing important contributions.

Preschool Teachers and Assistants in ECECs: Education and Professional Roles

For many years authors have been writing books of great importance for the education of preschool teachers; many of them covering main fields of early childhood education. More specifically areas like educational psychology, didactics, and occupational socialization have been of basic interest (Askland, 1997; Bruun, 1967; Evenshaug & Hallen, 1984; Gunnestad, 1993; Lillemyr & Søbstad, 1993). In recent years areas like the aesthetics, child culture, and administration and the collaboration between parents and ECEC have been highlighted (Gotvassli, 1990; Holthe, 1998; Moen, 2000; Paulsen, 1994; Selmer-Olsen, 1990). A focus on infant age has also been reflected (Smith & Ulvund, 1991). Later approaches including children's educational environment and didactics and working methods across different subjects have been favored (Eik, 1999; Hiim & Hippe, 1998; Skaalvik & Kvello, 1998).

Løkken (1992) examined the different roles among the staff in day care institutions: the leader, preschool teachers, and assistants. Questionnaires and interviews were used and analyses showed that expectation from children as well as expectations from each other indicated a clear adult was wanted, with a professional competence, varied knowledge, a good lap to sit on and a warm heart. In practice this means she is able to change between closeness and distance. This demands knowledge in acting, as well as in reflection of acting and detached reflection. In all three roles working close to children according to their needs, and a good coopera-tion between all personal, is expected. Though, the responsibility of the various roles will differ. The study documented a lot of silent knowledge going on in the the the ECECs.

Aanderaa (1997) examined the ECEC staff's ability to change and develop their competence. From questionnaires and interviews it was found that most staff members had positive attitudes to change and inno-vation, although a few warned against being too consumer oriented. This provides a challenge for the owners of ECECs, she claims. For changes in an ECEC to be meaningful and results in new developments according to needs in families and society, the motivation and involvement among staff members will be crucial. For this reason some consider knowledge of self-concept development and sense of competence to be a necessity for all staff, including preschool teachers (Lillemyr & Søbstad, 1993, p. 211).

Bratterud, Granrusten, and Lillemyr (2000) examined in a national study what seem to attract and motivate men and women respectively, for beginning the teacher training in early childhood education. In 1998/1999 there were about 7-8% men in the training programs throughout the country. A questionnaire was developed, focusing on motivation, involvement, well-being, and working effort. It was found that students choose preschool teacher training because they like working with chil-dren, it is an interesting job and a secure job. For those who have experi-ences from working with children, this seemed important for their choice. In general, students were highly motivated for the training and later work as a preschool teacher; not least important most students considered the training to be meaningful. They also had a high sense of well-being. The relatively high number of male students dropping out of training during the first 3 months was found to be a serious problem. More women than men were strongly motivated at the start of training. However, signifi-cantly more male students than female students were high in occupational self-concept. As much as 73% of male students see themselves as highly competent in the occupation (63% female students). The motivation pro-file of the two sexes was found to be quite different. Male students showed a clear drop in motivation the second year of training, with an increase again in the third year. Female students had a small increase in motivation from first to second year, and a small decrease to the third year. For both sexes it seemed important to be able to apply their leisure activity inter-ests at job. However, even if motivation and sense of well-being were high among most students, both men and women evaluated their work effort to be rather low, particularly male students. Most students considered their working effort to be low or average.

Søndenå (2002) studied how students, advisors, and professors at the college view the concept of reflection in accordance with their early childhood education teacher training. From a phenomenological point of view she examines how the traditional pedagogy in ECECs can be extended by the students. She found professors often apply reflection as a tool in their reproducing of the traditional preschool teacher. This was found among most students as well. She discloses that the communication in the guidance conversation is used more to guide the students in a desired direction than to reflect on experiences in a way that can extend beyond the dominating picture of a preschool teacher.

Kvistad (1997) studied 14 preschool teachers' experiences and cognitive as well as phenomenological perspectives, participating as advisors in a teacher training program of early childhood education. Results indicated that these preschool teachers/advisors needed several guidance strategies in promoting their development. Visualizing their professional role as advisor in terms of "master" was important in the development of their professional identity. Most of them emphasized the meaningfulness of being an advisor, not least because they often act alone as a preschool teacher. Considering guidance as a dialectic process[2] caused the advisor as well as the student to experience being an integral part of the reflection process between theory and practice. This was interpreted as indication of an increased consciousness of their tacit knowledge. Others too claim that in teacher training programs theory as well as practice aim at suppressing adaptation and promoting formation in the process of occupational socialization, providing students with self reflection and development towards the role as a preschool teacher (Malmo, 1986; Lillemyr & Malmo, 1989). Malmo (1986) observed how preschool teachers in ECEC experience the interactions with children, staff, and parents in the formation of their occupational role as a preschool teacher. She found that they often tended to take active responsibility in the dialectic processes with children and parents, just to stimulate the dynamic processes, to get movement into the relations.

Another aspect of quality and professionalism in ECEC concerns the head master. The leader needs to be an educational leader more than merely an administrative leader. In a way the leader also participates and leads the process of culture-shaping in the ECEC. It is important that the leader makes visible a model of thinking and reflection regarding the values and the educational practice the ECEC would like to be known by (Hjort, 1996; Mørreaunet, 1997). Partly this commensurate with Edgar Schein's (1983) emphasizing the value of the human resource in the development of an organization. Sataøen (2002) evaluated five college programs in the teacher training of early childhood education, applying self-evaluations. They nearly all found a lack correspondence between the curriculum guidelines of the teacher training in early childhood education and the Framework Plan for the ECEC, and between the curriculum guidelines of the teacher training in early childhood education and other teacher training programs. Most students had a positive attitude toward the training. To some degree they all find the integration between theory and practice should be better. The general conclusion was that a more integrated and professionally oriented program is needed. In the new primary school according to Reform 97, the two educational traditions, the primary school tradition and the preschool tradition, should integrate into a new educational tradition for grades one to four. In a study Riksaasen (1998) found that the two traditions aim at quite different perspectives of teaching and learning. In the cooperation between the two kinds of teachers she expects the school tradition to become the "winner" in this merge of traditions, first of all because the school traditionally is a stronger tradition.

Children's Play and Social Activities in ECECs (content)

Recently many Norwegian authors have written about the importance of play in early childhood education, presenting the most relevant theories for describing and understanding children's play (Åm, 1984, 1989; Buaas, 2002; Kibsgaard, 1999; Lillemyr, 1990, 1999a, 2001b; Vedeler, 1987, 1999). More recent studies have been published shedding light on the issue of children's play: what are the antecedents, how does play relate to culture, how can play influence language development, and adults organize play, and so forth (Bae, 1994; Halsnes, 1989; Hoven, 1987; Nilsen, 1988). Vedeler (1997a) found documentation of children's language being affected positively if they had experiences of role play in stead of other kinds of group play. Children in the age of 5 and 6 that had experienced role play developed a significantly more advanced language, used more complex expressions, and presented more complete sentences. In later years authors have argued for the relevance of play in primary school, as Reform 97 does (Lillemyr, 1999b; Trageton, 1994, 1997). Play is a complex phenomenon, though, as some have discussed and emphasized (Sutton-Smith, 1997; Steinsholt, 1998).

Lamer (1997) focused on the importance of social competence for all children. In an applied research project she developed a method of promoting children's self-concept and social competence. She found that essential aspects of social competence are: empathy and role-taking, prosocial behavior, self control, self assertion, and lastly play, joy, and humor.

She views this as a framework for ECEC staffs to promote social competence in practice, based on a broad or holistic concept of learning. Others see group processes or social interactions as especially important when children in preschools and schools develop social abilities (Stensaasen & Sletta, 1996). Social abilities and social competence as means to promote learning in school are focused in other countries too (Dockett & Fleer, 1999; Wasserman, 1990).

Søbstad (1990, 1995) examined how play and humor could take place in children's communicative activities in ECECs and found the parathelic[3] state typical for children's way of behaving in play and humor. He stated humor is important for the person's development of self-concept, and considers a playful attitude an antecedent for humor. In his studies he examined humor among preschool children and found their humor to be influenced by their environment. He documented lingual humor, incongruent and absurd humor, aggressive humor, tabu humor, and societal humor. He claimed the parathelic state to be a common trait typical for creative activities, humor, and play. In this respect to be able to see oneself in relation to others seems to be fundamental. In all cases a "here and now" state or "flow," is characteristic (Csikszentmihalyi, 1985). When children generate humor Søbstad claims, the following traits can be seen: a signal, transformations, some kind of liberation, certain feelings for the context, and interest and autonomy. He considers humor intrinsically motivated and challenges ECEC staffs to be aware of the positive value of humor for children's development.

Later others like Løkken (1996) argues for focusing on children's play, to get to know more about children's development and everyday life in preschools or day care centers. While playing, children aged 1 or 2 years clearly communicate with each other. Not always orally, but often by applying their body. The communication is often deep between two or more children. In her opinion freedom, spontaneity, and happiness are characteristics of play. The spontaneity often conveys into different kinds of creative activities. These are facts that were observed in groups of young children (Løkken 1989). It can be clearly seen that even such young children can have pleasure and satisfaction of each others company. Later, in a more thorough study of toddlers, Løkken attempted to find the social style of the toddler. In analyzing toddler studies carried out by researchers, she found that they disclosed bodily or physical play to be the richest play in terms of variation and social aspects. This made it natural to draw on the theory of Merleau-Ponty (Løkken, 2000a, 2000b). In her own study she found the characteristic toddler's social style to be based on bodily communication. The toddler's way of being in social play can be seen as a struggle to understand itself and others in the world. She attempted to make visible how toddlers are social persons and sees this as useful in the work of preschool teachers. More and more authors are referring to the importance of considering humor, play, aesthetics, and creativity as member of the same family of concepts (Søbstad, 1999). In all these aspects the communication process is of primarily concern (Skodvin, 1998).

Learning and Everyday Life Perspectives in ECECs

In an ethnographic study Nilsen (2000) attempted to understand the socialization process among children in ECECs from a perspective of adaptation versus resistance. In a multidimensional perspective she finds a conflict line between the child and the adult in various situations in an ECEC. Children's strategy of adaptation and their strategy of resistance becomes a natural part of the socialization process. Methods were participant observation and video tape recording of children and interviewing staff. In the analyses of the interactions child—adult collected, she finds that a conflict—power perspective often arises. Adaptation seems to be tied to the power aspect of the socialization process, whereas resistance underlines children as acting subjects and active operators in relation to the adult generation regarding the socialization process in early childhood education institutions. Based on the fact that a main aim for the socialization process is to promote children as active, independent individuals in their growth into society, the aspect of resistance seems crucial.

Eide and Winger (1996, 2002) have studied institutionalized childhood as mastery or shortcoming in day care centers or schools. They focus on the development of identity during children's lives in educational institutions. They find the strong focus on children as participants and actors to be characteristic for our society, also reflected in the new curriculum guidelines of the school. Children's participation has important consequences for their self-concept and identity development. However, to meet this challenge of children's participation it is necessary for the institutions to organize their programs with choice between alternatives as well as having a share in determinations. A broad perspective on learning is needed as well as a well-functioning relation between child and educator.

Another aspect of the life in ECEC concerns the children's role in planning and evaluation processes among staff members. Kristoffersen (1995) examined how ECECs have routines to ensure children a share in determinations. Based on interviews of staff and children she focused on what kinds of information children can provide that will be important in staff members' planning and evaluations. Play was chosen as a point of departure for the analyses. Results indicated that staff members often know, see and do what they think is best for the children, also in play. She found that to look at children as important informants in cases that concern themselves, seems yet a little immature in most day care centers. Schram (1991) examined life in ECECs by focusing how children justify their actions of care for others. Children 5 to 7 years in two ECECs were interviewed in response to stories about morality. Justifications concerning hypothetic and real stories were compared. Results indicated that the answer "don't know" was more frequent in hypothetic stories than with real stories, which supports Piaget's theory. It was found that children most often apply empathic and practical justifications for what they actually had done, girls in particular. Boys more often than girls used justifications of principle, even if both genders applied empathic and practical justifications most often. It was concluded that applying real stories is preferable to applying hypothetic stories when examining prosocial activities among children.

A few studies have focused on parents' roles in early childhood institutions. Bø (2002) studied differences between mothers and fathers in bringing and picking up situations. Interviews with mothers, fathers and staff indicated that mothers use more time in the bringing situation. Sometimes this is experienced as unfortunate by the staff. They seem to prefer fathers' more short and uncomplicated bringing activities. Most parents in this study found the ECEC was open and accepting in bringing and picking up situations. More of the mothers had reflections and beliefs about how to avoid complex and unfortunate situations for the child. Grythe (2000) applied a questionnaire with fathers of children in ECECs asking how they look at their own effort in the parent- institution cooperation and how they explain their own participation in the cooperation. A selection of 78 fathers in two different ECECs participated. Results indicated that fathers only participated about a third of the parent-institution cooperation (bringing-picking up, meetings, parent conversations, etc.); mothers participated about two thirds. Based on the situation where most fathers and mothers are both working, this is not exactly sexual equality. One reason for this, Grythe claims, lies in the organization of the ECEC. The meeting times need to be better adapted to fathers, and a more active effort from the ECEC can help. Fathers tended to value their effort in the parent cooperation activities somewhat higher than reality indicated. When expectations were higher than their effort, they tended to refer to interfering factors around them. They still did not feel they had to participate more. In general almost all fathers thought it was important for them to participate in this work, and most of them wanted to participate as much as the mothers if possible. How fathers take out their right to paid leave of absence in connection with child births is important here. It is possible for fathers to take out 4 weeks or even more of the 1 year leave of absence for the mother. It has been found that most fathers do not feel forced to take such a leave. They take the leave of absence period because they want to. For this reason it can be concluded that in Norway the opportunity for fathers to stay at home with their child a few weeks after the birth must be considered successful (Brandth & Øverli, 1998).

Special Education Perspectives in ECECs

In Norwegian ECECs handicapped children have priority at application. This has been so according to the Act of ECEC since 1975. But this of course implies that children in need of special care and support have to be integrated in the day care institution. On this background a definition of malfunctionality had to be presented (Vedeler, 1982). Not least important in this sense is of course the language development of the children (Bleken, 1987). The change of laws in day care institutions and schools implying integration was active in Norway from 1976. After years with this priority and increased access, the objective of an ECEC for all children has become the overall undertaking. In Norway as in many countries the most frequent kind of malfunctionality is social emotional difficulties (Sjøvik, 2002). Tøssebro (2000) has been following the process of growing up in Norway with a malfunction. Using a questionnaire and follow-up interviews it was found that children 3 to 5 years in need of special support and care do get into the ECECs. While going to an ECEC these children live at home. In fact these children more often than other children go to an ECEC. A total of 31 families with children in need of special support were interviewed. For more than 50% of these the parents had no problems with the program at the ECEC. A few felt they were nearly forced to receive a placement in an ECEC, others experienced they had to fight to get it. For some parents the decision to allow their child to attend the ECEC, first have to be taken. However, it is in accordance with the official policy that children in need of special support and care should go to ordinary ECECs (Tøssebro & Lundby, 2002). Ytterhus (2002), as Tøssebro and Lundby finds ECECs to be extraordinary open to diversity and offer relatively good conditions for children with special needs. These children are often nicely included in the social environment at the ECEC. Ytterhus finds the ECECs to be rather unique as integrated institutions, first of all because there is a manifold of children living there.

Another group of children with special needs are immigrant children. Kibsgaard (1992) studied the reciprocity in interactions between 16 bilingual children in seven different ECECs in Norway, representing two different cultures: the Latin-American and the Norwegian. Observations and interviews of the Latin-American and the Norwegian children in play were carried out, with a focus on their preferred play mates. A clear documentation of lingual communication was found to be essential to the interactions. The Latin-American children were significantly less often chosen as play mates by Norwegian children, than the other way around. Indications were found that establishment of close intercultural friendship must be based upon a relatively fluent Norwegian communication. Because of this some immigrant children seem to have problems of being accepted in play with Norwegian children. This of course will influence the self-concept of the child and suppress a healthy development of identity. Children being denied access into play situations often reacted with anger. However, the Latin-American children were more eager to play with some of their own sex than playing with some of their own ethnicity. As Smilansky (1990) and others have pointed out, it is extremely important to help these children participate in social role play, so they also later can be included in role play situations. In ECECs with immigrant children a mother language teacher is fundamental.

In general it has been found that parents of minority groups seem to be satisfied with the ECEC, although cultural diversities and critical comments come through in a few projects. For instance Somalian, Turkish and Pakistanian parents did not consider ECECs necessary for children below 4 to 5 years. The argued it was better for children in these ages to stay at home. But independent of ethnicity, parents in this survey expressed that they were very satisfied, rather satisfied or satisfied with their ECEC. A few said they were not feeling safe for their children in outdoor activities. Most of them asserted staff at the ECEC was creative and competent in their professional role (Djuve & Pettersen, 1998).

Sand and Skoug (2002) studied cultural integration in ECECs and pointed to the fact that learning language must be considered basic, in particular to immigrant and minority children. A questionnaire was sent to head masters at ECECs and year-plans of eight ECECs were examined. They found Framework Plan for Day Care Institutions clearly referred to the importance of Sami children's language and culture, but not as clear in relating to culture and language of the immigrant children. Just one of the eight ECECs had intentions of integration formulated in their year-plan. The conclusion was that children from cultural minorities are marginalized, or in many cases invisible. Others have found that oftentimes Norwegian ECECs does not apply the special kind of knowledge children and parents from a cultural minority represent as a resource for the institution as such (Østbye, 2001). In an evaluation of programs of ECECs in Oslo where immigrant children are in dominance, the lack of stimulation from children with Norwegian ethnicity was found to be a great weakness (Sand & Skoug, 2002).

Research on the Transition ECEC—Primary School

Research and development in this field were important issues to pre-schools and day care institutions as well as for schools. In Norway educational development and research on the transition from preschool to school has been going on extensively the last 40 years. Between endeavors a rather strong debate went on: at what age should children start school, and what kind of educational program was best for the 6 year olds? For years the age of school start in Norway had been seven. In the 90s all 6-year olds that wanted to could have an educational program. An important project initiated by the politicians, "The Educational program for 6-year-olds project", was carried out in 1986 through 1990. For the first time a framework plan was developed and recommended for all 6 year old programs (Lillemyr, 1988). Haug (1991) when evaluating the project found teachers who received students from the program were in average more secure, more used to the school, and practically more competent, compared to students not having such a program. Later he pointed to a severe degree of adults directing activities in the school's activity program (classroom and after school activities), even if there was a tendency of less directing in after school activities (Haug, 1996). Recently Haug (2000) argued that, in terms of educational policy, there were primarily ideological reasons for the so-called "6 year reform" in Norway, not primarily new challenges for the school. Still, it was a fact that what actually started as a 6 year reform, ended as Reform 97, a reform of the whole comprehensive school. Haug shows that most people in the country agreed to the need for an educational program for 6-year-olds, but they did not reach consensus on what terms it should be done. There was also disagreement as to in what kind of institution the programs should be developed: day care institutions or primary schools. However, many agreed that the content in such programs should include the best from both educational traditions. On this background Trageton (1992) developed what he called "workshop education" for the program of 6 year olds as well as for students in the first grades of the primary school. Workshop education was primarily based upon developmental theories (Piaget, Erikson, etc.) and children's play.

In an attempt to focus "the competent child" Eide and Winger's (1996) point of departure was a global perspective on learning as well as a holistic perspective on the child. They interviewed a sample of 10 children when they were 6 years old and again when they were 8, and found that the 8-year-olds were well adapted to routines and rules in school and did not seem to mind the less degree of freedom in play and learning they had achieved, compared to what they had in the program for 6-year-olds. Routines and calmness provided children with general view and security, even if it also inhibited motivation and interest in learning. However, at both age levels children seemed to register a clear difference between play and learning. The researchers claim that practicing a broad (global) perspective on learning depends on the application of varied methods where children can actively co-decide and perform. They concluded that learning through play depends on external frames regarding time and space and on teachers view on the value of play as such. Eide og Winger consider active participation of competent students as a necessity in an updated (modern) learning and socialization process. They emphasize that first of all it is a question of how to understand children, knowledge, and learning. Interpretations of the relation between teacher and student and the school environment are of great importance. The perspective of active, competent students in learning is taken continually by researchers, most recently by Nordahl (2002).

On this background teachers need qualifications in taking the perspective of the child and creating positive relations. Bae (1992) from the theory of Schibbye (1988) argues that the interaction between the adult and the child in order to provide children with memorable interrelation experiences is of foremost importance, not least for preschool children soon to start school. The building of relations is fundamental to the development of the child's self-esteem, and therefore for the child's experience of self and others, which is basic to the learning process. For years Bae has done research to examine how relations are expressed in day care institutions. She conceives mediated learning and role expectations to be important, in addition to how adult dependence and definition power are expressed in real situations. Bae claims that it is of fundamental importance that the adult *express approval* to the child, and acts showing approval. Analyzing what the adult and the child both contribute to the interaction, she illustrates how our communication to children conveys attitudes and values that in the next run affects the development of the child, and then the child's view of self and others. She concludes that these are aspects of substantial value to the teachers as mediators of culture, for instance concerning children's play. How should the teacher act as far as play among children is concerned? Is it legitimate for the teacher to interact with children's play? (see Lillemyr, 2003).

The field of self-concept and motivation was the background for a field experiment study focusing students' school motivation, carried out in 1991-1993 in two different counties (Seljelid, 1994). The study documented what is often seen in practice that student motivation decreases substantially with increasing age. Being a research and development project the study encompassed nearly 1,500 students from first to eight' grade, and data collected through interviews, questionnaires and observations. Systematic means of motivation of students were carried out in one county but not in the other (Engen, 1994). It was found that most children in lower grades looked forward to go to school, although a few even in first grade were not happy to go to school. In classrooms with increasing motivation during the project period, high engagement by the teacher and student concurrency, were typical. At all grade levels it was concluded that the high motivation classrooms were characterized by emphasis on students' concurrency, teacher involvement, and parents interested in student participation. The undertakings in one county did have an affect on student motivation. Zachrisen (2000) in "The When play is ready for school project" examined how play as a way of working can be integrated in primary school teaching. Relating to Reform 97 and the Curriculum Guidelines 97, it has been advocated that play in school must address both learning through play and the value of play as such. Zachrisen found that teachers consider play a source of social learning, an activity strengthening children's self esteem and a motivating factor. In general, teachers were less concerned about play and professional learning, not least because of a traditional view on play and learning. In her opinion introducing play in the curriculum guidelines means it is considered a central method within subjects as well. The teachers in her study showed little concern for play in the promotion of learning in subjects. She found most teachers lack training in identifying that learning actually take place in children's play. She argues that teachers' and parents' attitudes towards play in school should be further examined.

Liv Vedeler, through a series of studies, documented the relation between role play and children's development of language to be important to their development and learning. She found 6-year-olds phonetic syntax was better developed through role play than with other kinds of play (Vedeler, 1997a). Furthermore, Vedeler (1997b) in a study focusing the quality of programs of learning activities in a group of 6- and 7-year students in need of special support in school, interviewed teachers and head masters at 10 schools. Her analyses showed that head masters emphasizing the preschool tradition also valued play in relation to learning. She concluded that social objectives and a positive self-concept are central antecedents for stimulating learning. However, she found that teachers lacked competence in the application of play in the curriculum. In this concern she is pointing to the need of developing a new "primary school code" founded on the preschool tradition as well as on the school tradition (Vedeler, 1997b, 1999). In relation to Vedeler's research, Hærås (1998) examined organizational as well as educational factors of relevance in the learning among school starters with special needs. She wanted to study the application of play in a didactic view from a practice-theory perspective (Handal & Lauvås, 1983). As Vedeler, she found that teachers seemed little concerned with theory in their understanding of the concept of play, except differentiating between free play and directed play. The teachers considered play in terms of developmental psychology, evaluating the play as important to the 6-year-olds' learning and development, but did not comment on what qualities in the play that promotes cognitive, lingual and social development. How much play was actually employed in the program varied a lot.

A qualitative research study carried out in Norway in 1995-98, recognized students' competencies and self worth at the start of school as crucial, and argued that 6-year-olds have essential knowledge and are quite able in many things (Lillemyr et al., 1998). The main research question directed was how to develop a common platform for a new education with the oldest children in day care and the youngest children in primary school (5- to 9-year-olds). Close to 500 students in six schools and six day care institutions participated and data from observations, interviews and questionnaires were collected from students, teachers, head masters and parents. A framework theory combined goal theory and self-determination theory (Deci & Ryan, 1991; Maehr & Midgley, 1996), and resulted in four guiding principles: promote sense of competence (cognitive and social), support autonomy, provide structure and feedback in objectives and expectations, and teachers should involve with students. The results disclosed that some children among 6- and 7-year-olds (17%) worried about starting school. Social sense of competence decreased at the age of school start, then increasing again. A significant drop in intrinsic motivation from 5 to 7 years was found and students' strong interest in play persisted through the first four years of school, in particular free play. Interestingly, students' interests in free learning (characterized by students' choices of what and how) decreased strongly from 5 to 9 years, indicating that students did not expect much of this kind of learning in school. In many classrooms preschool teachers and primary school teachers were found to cooperate well. More than anything the results indicated the need of supporting children's self-concept during these years, in particular for school-starters. Further, the results support what several other studies have indicated, that it is critical during the transition period to emphasize social and affective aspects in the classroom (Broström, 1996, 1999; Eide & Winger, 1996; Ladd, Buhs, & Seid, 2000; Patrick & Townsend, 1995). It was concluded that the concept of school learning now has to change towards a broader and more holistic kind of concept to be in accordance with the intentions of the reform (Lillemyr, 2001a; Lillemyr et al., 1998). The results seemed to document the close relation that exists between self-concept, intrinsic motivation and the development of interests in learning. This compare to what other researchers in Norway have found with older students (Skaalvik, 1997).

Interview and curriculum development studies carried out in Oslo, included five classrooms at five schools, focusing on 6-year-olds in first grade (Germeten, 1999). In these studies the research question examined was first of all: How are 6-year olds managing first grade in the new comprehensive school? Analyses of interviews, observations and curriculum plans, disclosed that first graders seem to meet quite different educational programs, in terms of content as well as organization. In most cases a preschool teacher and a primary school teacher collaborated in the same classroom; and many teachers thought the combination of the two traditions would turn out for the best. The two kinds of teachers seemed to complement each others competencies in search of a new primary school pedagogy. More time outside the classroom, but also more time with quiet sitting down activities inside than expected, was observed. Most teachers found the school reform quite necessary. In general first grade teachers were more positive to the school reform, than eight grade teachers. Surprisingly, a strong agreement on how to understand play in school was documented, meaning learning through play as well as play as a value of it own. In some schools an early childhood education perspective was taken, in others an ordinary school tradition predominated. It was concluded that neither institution nor professional tradition alone settled the direction of the educational program for the 6 year olds. She finds that the content and philosophy of the program in the new first grade have to find its own direction, concepts and frames. The old frames and concepts are not adequate any more (op. cit.: 151). Germeten (2002) later elaborated on these perspectives into a discourse frame of analysis based on Michel Foucault (1972) asking what the limitations for teaching the first grades in school are. To sum up, it is of great importance to see that school reforms as well as research are necessary and useful to future school change and educational development in practice. To sum up, it has turned out that school reforms as well as research is necessary to future school change and educational development.

Research in Primary School: The First Grades of Comprehensive School

After Reform 97 starting in 1997, a study was carried out getting information about parent's emphasis on motivation when their child attends Grade 1 (6-year-olds). Rødstøl (1999) based upon the theories of Deci and Ryan (1991) and Nicholls (1984), applying a questionnaire with 207 parents, found that twice as many of the mothers as compared to fathers answered the questionnaire. Most of the parents noted that stimulating children's intrinsic motivation is fundamental at this stage. However, more mothers than fathers found it important to support intrinsic motivation in relation to schoolwork. This result confirms the result of Grolnick and Ryan (1989) in the United States.

Reform 97 guaranteed that all students in Grade 1 to 4 should have an after school program if they so desired. So far few studies have focused after school programs (in Norwegian abbreviated SFO), although a few have been completed. Øksnes (2001) asked the question "In what way is after school programs to become important aspects in directing children's leisure?" In her study of relevant literature and official documents, she discusses critically how today's society mixes children's leisure arena and school arena. She is sceptic to the tendency to direct children's play during their after school programs, this is getting even more complex as the official documents often stands out as compromises between different political standpoints. She concludes that the concept of freedom has to be discussed more seriously, a fact that will have consequences for the SFO activities in Norwegian schools. One of these consequences is that staff in SFO needs professional competence. Recently a national research study focused on after school programs in Grades 1 to 4 was carried out by Kvello and Wendelborg (2002), applying questionnaires and interviews. They directed questions like: How are the quality of after school programs? What activities are emphasized and how is the cooperation between the actors involved? It was found that sense of well-being in ECEC seem to predict sense of well-being later, in school and in SFO. Further, SFO adapts reasonably well to students' antecedents, needs, and interests. The good SFOs were characterized by stability in staff, experienced staff persons, and where the leader of SFO was joining the group of leaders in school. They found that the SFOs meet the demands of constituting an arena with adult care, and collaborate well with parents. However, the staff seemed to have rigid thoughts about play, and the school's headmaster knew little about "leasure pedagogy." On the other hand, SFOs did not meet the demands of a close cooperation with local cultural activities, a social educational profile, a preventive function, and organized cooperation between parents and school. Their recommendations were:

- establish a closer , formalized cooperation between school and SFO, to provide students with a holistic environment in total
- SFOs should have the same proportion of educated persons as the ECECs
- A mix of different backgrounds and educations is recommended among staff

- The leader of SFO should meet in the school's leader group
- More staff in relation to students

They found that a majority of the SFO staffs have a rigid view on what learning is all about. A challenging question was what would be the target arena for SFO to compare to?

One of the main issues in the debate regarding primary school education in relation to Reform 97 and the new Curriculum Guidelines of 1997 is targeting children's play. When play is included as an integral element in the early school years, how should it influence the teaching? In particular, how should play influence the program of learning to read, write and calculate? Furthermore, what aspects of play should be included in school? More or less this has to be an ongoing and never ending discussion. Still, when the 6-year-olds for the first time attended primary school in 1997, it was a concordant voice among politicians and researchers alike that a new education should develop from a platform of the best from two traditions: the preschool education and the school's education. In the beginning years this merge of two traditions of course had to be ennobled and take some time. The reason for this first of all is that preschool teachers and school teachers had not earlier been working together. From 1997 preschool teachers with a year of specialization could teach in first through fourth grade in cooperation with primary school teachers. It was stated as a principle that when it is 18 or more students in first grade, there should be two teachers present. This opened for a preschool teacher and a school teacher working together, developing a new pedagogy based upon the best from the two traditions. Many city schools and several of the municipal schools chose to apply such a solution. In other schools and municipalities they did not. In the schools the class teacher of first, second or third grade could either be a preschool teacher or a primary school teacher. These facts one has to bear in mind when considering the research presented below.

Several studies have focused aspects of the new school in terms of children's play. Other studies have focused on the important aspects of learning how to read, write and calculate. Tangen (1998) carried out a case study focused on play in primary school in the first two grades, applying observations as main method. He found that more than 30% of the time per day was used for free play inside or outdoor, but only 2/3 of this was actually play in the correct sense of the word. Of the play time just a small part was used for role play. A lot more time was applied for constructive play, particularly in second grade. The teacher did not participate much in role play, but spent some time in constructive play. In general, a strong tendency of increased teacher directedness in play activities was found from first grad to second grade. It was documented clear positive attitudes towards play and learning in school. It turned out that the teachers had not thought much of the learning effect of children's play experiences. Tangen concludes that if the Curriculum Guidelines are to be taken seriously, the socio-dramatic play has to get more time in school, even if it is challenging the teacher.

Another case study in three classrooms was carried out by Hannsen (1999). The form and content of play and the methodical application of play in first grade classrooms was examined by observations. The teacher was taken as the important premise giver, for play activities as well as for learning activities. She found examples of teacher contributions to children's play. She documented changes in teachers' attitudes towards play in the classroom, in terms of the learning through play aspect as well as the value of play as such aspect. Like Tangen, she found an essential amount of time in class dedicated to play. Play as such, learning through play, and a playful approach to subject matter, all occurred in the classroom, even if the differences of the three kinds of play were not so clear. She found that this kind of priority in play obviously made students active in their learning. However, the teachers differed regarding to what extent they see play as important for learning the syllabuses. But both educational traditions were represented in the classrooms.

In a case study with observations and interviews Henningsen (1999) studied first grade students from a child perspective. The results indicated that children define play relatively narrow and seem to confine play to certain areas. In this study too some children were found to worry about going to school. First of all they worried about having friends at school or not, since the children valued friendship highly. Observations showed that the organization and managing of play in the classroom had great influence on promoting play among children and thereby strengthening their self-concept. In another study Aspaas (1999) was examining how first grade teachers looked at play from a curriculum development perspective. The twelve teachers from six schools were 4 primary school teachers and 8 preschool teachers all working in first grade. All teachers agreed that the early childhood education tradition was useful in teaching 6-year-olds. Still, they all considered their specific teacher background relevant for the work. Both types of teacher favored an integration of the two traditions. Moreover, they both considered play in teaching important, both as a method of learning and as a value of its own. However, they found it easier to use play in connection with learning than as a value of its own. It was found that attitudes towards the application of play in school vary. Because of results from national and international research on teaching in relation to children's play in school, it has been advocated that a new teacher role have to develop. First of all this is caused by the changing of the concepts of play and learning in school. In this concern the influence of early childhood education is obvious (Lillemyr, 2003).

Norway has for some time participated in follow-up studies arranged by the International Association for the Evaluation of Educational Achievement (IEA). In Norway, Høien, Lundberg, and Tønnessen (1994) have been leading these investigations. Relatively great variation in reading skills have been found among students in general, and gender differences in favor of girls seem to increase. Recently there has been presented important studies on student's reading skills among 2 and 3 grade students (Engen, Solheim, & Tønnessen, 2001; Oftedal & Dahle, 2002). Unfortunately, an increase of weak readers has been found comparing data from 1994 and 2000. The screening tests developed in 1994 are informative to the class teacher to organize for support of the 20% weakest readers. It was found in a new study done in 2001 that the results of teachers with long experience and post graduate education was better than with young teachers without postgraduate education. Furthermore, it was found that primary school teachers had better results regarding means than preschool teachers. From this some are implying that preschool teachers need more training in methods of introductory reading, others think this could be caused by all the factors influencing when a reform is started. Engen and Solheim accentuate that the screening tests does not measure the size of the problems weak readers have or how good the best readers are. (Reform 97 was fully implemented in 2000.) Austad (1999) is arguing that several factors of social and environmental type have to be considered carefully in terms of providing good readers in school. Most important among them are aspects of social background, interests and meaningfulness. He underlines the excellent work done in many day care centers regarding stimulation of phonological consciousness. This arguing contradicts the research interpretation of others, mentioned above. Most likely the lack of reading abilities of many students results from a combination of factors.

Recently students' self-concept and social competence and their relevance for the learning environment of students have been strongly emphasized in research. It is found that teachers that support autonomy and contribute to students' sense of safety and confidence and stimulate their self-concept and interests, and who are themselves involved in student's everyday life, have less behavior difficulties in class. Further, their students participate more in class and achieve better. This is important to realize as it has been shown indications that students and teachers often seem to live in two different worlds in school (Backe-Hansen, 1998; Ogden, 1998; Nordahl, 2000). This seem to commensurate with results mentioned above from studies in the lower grades (Ladd, Buhs, & Seid, 2000; Lillemyr et al., 1998). The discussion of reading abilities and achievement in basic skills in the first years of school therefore has to be viewed in perspective of a holistic definition of school learning and a broad perspective of students' learning environment (Covington, 1998). More or less the final question discussed here leads to the phenomenon of motivation, and how to get students interested and active in their own learning, promoting a personal investment in learning by the students (Maehr & Midgley, 1996).

CONCLUSIONS BASED ON CURRENT RESEARCH

In Norway children's time in ECECs is considered important to their learning and development in school. The early childhood education tradition, first of all as practiced in ECECs, has recently become important as one of the two main ingredients of the new primary school education. This can be seen as a unique trait in Norway, but still corresponds with the new picture of early childhood education outlined by others (Klugman, 1990; Wood & Attfield, 1996). Obviously, this has upgraded the early childhood education tradition in Norway. On background of the last reforms in ECEC and school, it has been pointed out that the transition period is fundamental to the child's development. Recent research has focused the transition period in perspective of motivation and learning, not least in relation to play. The child's experiences in this period need to be examined thoroughly from different angles and with various informants. Research from the perspective of the child has often been lacking. Research indicates that the collaboration between ECECs and school is basic to provide a common educational platform, and for ensuring the integration between the early childhood education tradition and the primary school tradition.

Furthermore, a new concept of school learning is needed. In Norway it is argued a consequence of play in the curriculum is the need of a broad, holistic concept of school learning. The new Curriculum Guidelines of 1997 are recommending a broad perspective on learning, as in other countries as well (Covington, 1998; Schoenfeld, 1999). Schoenfeld asks for a theory of learning explaining how people develop increased understanding and capacity in all areas, like the school yard, at home and in the after-school club. I am sure the rich arena of children's play is not meant to be left out in this concern. Unfortunately, research documents that students see learning in school in a rather narrow way. Presumably, the students do not expect learning in a broad sense, with elaboration, experimentation and creativity, to be going on in school. Unfortunately, this stands out in clear opposition to the intentions of Reform 97 in Norway. In school practice, an important question to ask will be: How is it possible to include in the educational program varied forms of play and learning? Perhaps this means to deal with learning in a Deweyian way, taking up once again principles like "learning by doing" and "reflective thinking." These were some of the reasons why over the years I have come to understand learning in school as follows (Lillemyr, 2001b, 2004):

1. Learning is internal processes caused by training or experience, providing increased capacity to comprehend, experience, feel, reflect and act.
2. Learning includes acquisition of knowledge and skills, as well as application, experimentation and creativity.
3. Learning comprises individual processes, and social competence and sociocultural aspects.
4. Learning affects personality, and vice versa, because learning affects the whole child.
5. Learning changes the child's competence, and hence its sense of competence.

These components are aiming at a broad understanding of learning of an active and involved student, as outlined in the Curriculum Guidelines of 1997 as well as in the Framework Plan 1996 (Ministry of Children and Family Affairs, 1996; Curriculum Guidelines, 1997). So what challenges are there to be seen for the ECEC reform and Reform 97 to be successful? Obviously, the two reforms do have a potential of providing new perspectives on care, involvement (motivation) and learning, first of all because of their inclusions of aspects like play, creativity, experimentation and wondering. However, to achieve this, certain challenges in the institutions have to be met, foremost among which are:

- Make children feel contented in the first year, based upon their social sense of competence
- ECEC and school and parents have to support children's autonomy, to make them feel competent and to develop a positive, realistic self-concept
- Develop children's interests for free as well as structured play and their interests for free as well as structured learning; that is: provide varied forms of play and learning
- Provide children with choices to promote alternative solutions to tasks and challenges, to increase their self-confidence in activities, so they can take responsibility for their learning

In order for the reforms to be successful, parents, ECEC- and school-leaders and teachers will have to take responsibility for developing an educational environment of high quality, based on satisfying physical and economical resources. It is critical in this concern that children can increasingly collaborate in important decisions already from preschool on.

NOTES

1. The Sami people constitute the largest national minority in Norway. The Sami people have their own language and culture and long traditions of working with reindeers. From 1997 they have their Sami Curriculum Guidelines for the comprehensive school.
2. A dialectic process develops through contradictions and is a process where two parts or two perspectives reciprocally influence each other's development.
3. Apter (1982) uses the concept parathelic condition to mean a situation characterized by a here-and-now attitude where one wants to enjoy the moment as much as possible, for example as in play. Compare Csikszentmihalyi's (1985) concept of "flow." In a thelic situation, however, the individual is goal-oriented and acts to achieve certain goals.

REFERENCES

Aanderaa, B. (1997). Si at vi har hele dagen! En kartlegging av barnehageansattes endringskompetanse [Say we've got all day! A mapping of day care centre personal's competence for change], (Sluttrapport) [Final report]. Oslo, Norway: Ministry of Children and Family Affairs.

Åm, E. (1984). Lek i barnehagen – de voksnes rolle [Play in day care institutions—The adult's role]. Oslo, Norway: Universitetsforlaget.

Åm, E. (1989). På jakt etter barneperspektivet [Hunting for the perspective of the child]. Oslo, Norway Universitetsforlaget.

Askland, L. (1997). På veg mot førskulelæraryrket [To the preschool teacher profession]. Oslo, Norway: Universitetsforlaget.

Aspaas, I. (1999). Lek eller alvor? En studie av læreres oppfatning av lek i første klasse "Play or serious?" A study of teachers' attitudes towards play in first grade]. Unpublished doctoral dissertation, Oslo College, Norway.

Austad, I. (1999). Lesing og lesevansker. Norsklæreren [The teacher of Norwegian], 4, 5-10.

Backe-Hansen, E., & Ogden, T. (Eds.) (1998). 10-åringer i Norden. Kompetanse, risiko og oppvekstmiljø [Ten-year-olds in the Nordic countries. Competence, risk and the educational environment]. Copenhagen: Nordic Council of Ministries.

Bae, B. (1992). Relasjon som vågestykke – læring om seg selv og andre [Relation as a daring deed—learning about self and others]. In B. Bae & J. -E. Waastad (Eds.), *Erkjennelse og anerkjennelse* [Aknowledgement and recognition]. Oslo, Norway: Universitetsforlaget.

Bae, B. (1994). "Hei Løve! Er du farlig eller grei?" Om lekende samspill ["Hello, Lion! Are you dangerous or OK?" About play interactions] *Norsk Pedagogisk Tidsskrift*, 5.

Balke, E., Berg, B., & Fagerli, O. (1979). *Barnehage – Heim – Lokalsamfunn.* [Pre-school—home—local community] *Nærmiljø-barnehage-prosjektet* [The local community-preschool project] hefte no 10. Oslo, Norway: Ministry of Consumer and Administration Affairs

Bleken, U. (1987). *Språkstimulering i barnehagen for barn I alderen 3-7 år* [The stimulation of language development in day care centres for children 3-7 years] Oslo, Norway: The Academy of Early Childhood education (now Oslo University College)

Borge, A. I. H. (1995). *Kvalitet i barnehagen. – en kunnskapsoversikt* [Quality in day care centres: an overview of knowledge.] Oslo, Norway: Statens institutt for folkehelse.

Brandth, B., & Øverli, B. (1998). *Omsorgspermisjon med "kjærlig tvang." En kartlegging av fedrekvoten* (Child birth leave of absence "cordially forced." A mapping of the farthers quota). Trondheim, Norway: ALLFORSK, Norwegian University of Science and Technology.

Bratterud, Å., Granrusten, P. -T., & Lillemyr, O. F. (2000). *Hva er så spesielt med menn? En kartlegging av menns og kvinners motivasjon for førskolelærerutdanningen* [What is special about men? A mapping of men's as opposed to women's motivation for applying to teacher training in early childhood education]. Trondheim, Norway: Queen Maud's College Publications. (Research report)

Broström, S. (1996). Frame Play with 6 Year Old Children. *European Early Childhood Education Research Journal*, 3(2).

Broström, S. (1999). Changes in early childhood education in Denmark: The appearance of literacy in early childhood education. In Brougère & R. Sylvie (Eds.), *Culture, Childhood and Preschool Education.* Paris: Université Paris-Nord & INRP.

Brusling, C. (1996). Finns det en egen förskolepedagogik? [Is there something called early childhood education?]. *Norsk Pedagogisk tidsskrift*, 3-4.

Bruun, U. -B. (1967). *Förskolålderns psykologi* [Preschool age psychology] Göteborg, Norway: Akademiförlaget.

Buaas, E. H. (2002). *Med himmelen som tak. Uterommet som arena for skapende aktiviteter i barnehage og skole* [With heaven as ceiling The outdoor room as arena for creative activities in day care institutions and school] Oslo, Norway: Universitetsforlaget.

Bø, I. (2002). Mors og fars foreldreskap når barnehagen er med i bildet [Mothers and fathers parenthood when day care institutions are in focus.] *Nordisk Pedagogik*, 22(1), 1-13

Covington, M. V. (1998). *The will to learn. A guide for motivating young people.* Cambridge, England: Cambridge University Press.

Csikszentmihalyi, M. (1985). Emergent motivation and the evolution of the self. In D. A. Kleiber & M. L. Maehr (Eds.), *Motivation and adulthood* (Vol, 14, pp. 93-120).

Curriculum Guidelines of 1997. (In Norwegian: Læreplanverket for den 10-årige grunnskolen.) See the following brochures in English: Core Curriculum - for primary, secondary and adult education. 1993, Oslo, Norway: Ministry of Education, Research and Church Affairs.

Deci, E. L., & Ryan, R. M. (1991). A motivational approach to self: Integration in personality. In I. R. Dienstbier (Ed.), *Nebraska symposium on Motivation: Perspectives on motivation* (Vol. 38, pp. 237-288). Lincoln: University of Nebraska Press.

Djuve, A. B., & Pettersen, H. C. (1998). *Må de være ute om vinteren? Oppfatninger om barnehager i fem etniske grupper i Oslo* [Do they have to be outside in winter time? Perceptions of day care centres in five ethnic groups in Oslo]. Oslo, Norway: FAFO

Dockett, S., & Fleer, M. (1999). Play and pedagogy in early childhood: Bending the rules. Marrickville, New South Wales, Australia: Harcourt Brace.

Eide, B., & Winger, N. (1996). *Kompetente barn og kvalifiserte pedagoger i den nye småskolen* [Competent children and qualified teachers in the new primary school]. Oslo, Norway: Cappelen Academic Publications.

Eide, B., & Winger, N. (2002). *Fra barns synsvinkel. Om barn som deltakere og informanter: Teoretiske perspektiver og metodiske utfordringer* [From children's perspective, children as participants and informants: Theoretical and methodical challenges]. Oslo, Norway: Cappelen Akademisk Forlag.

Eik, L. T. (Ed.) (1999). *Storyline. Tverrfaglig tilnærming til aktiv læring* [Storyline: A cross-subject approach to active learning] Oslo, Norway: Tano Aschehoug.

Eikeland, S., & Krogh, U. (1999). *Samiske barnehager. Evaluering av det særskilte tilskuddet* (Sami Day care centers: Evaluations of the special kind of support]) Oslo, Norway: NIBR-notat 17/99 (NIBR= Norwegian institute of city and regional research).

Engen, T. O. (1994). Problemstillinger og metode. Et oversyn over utviklings- og forskningsprosjektet "Med iver og lyst" [Research problems and method An overview of the research and development project "With interest and involvement"). In T. Seljelid (Ed.), *Med iver og lyst. Beskrivelse og vurdering av et prosjekt om motivasjon i skolen* [With eager and lust description and evaluation of a project on motivation in school]. Hamar, Norway: Kapére Forlag.

Engen, L., Solheim, R. G., & Tønnessen, F. E. (2001). *Leseferdighet i 3. klasse våren 2001* [Reading skills in 3. grade spring 2001]. Stavanger, Norway: Senter for leseforsking.

Evenshaug, O., & Hallen, D. (1984). *Barne- og ungdomspsykologi* (Child and youth psychology). Oslo, Norway: Gyldendal.

Foucault, M. (1972). *The Archaeology of Knowledge*. London: Routledge.

Germeten, S. (1999). Evaluering av Reform 97 "På vei mot ny grunnskole i Oslo". [The Evaluation of Reform 97: "Heading towards a new obligatory education in Oslo"].) Report I: Results from a questionnaire fall 1998. Oslo, Norway: Oslo College Publications.

Germeten, S. (2002). *Grenser for undervisning? Frihet og kontroll i 6-åringenes klasserom* [Are there limitations for teaching? Freedom and control in 6 year olds classrooms]. Stockholm: Dissertation for dr. degree at Stockholm Institute of Education.

Gotvassli, K. -Å. (1990). *Ledelse I barnehagen* [Management in day care centers] Oslo, Norway: Tano AS.

Grolnick, W., & Ryan, R. W. (1989) Parent styles associated with children's self-regulation and competence in school. *Journal of Educational Psychology,* 81, 143-154.

Grythe, J. (2000). *Fedrene har ordet! - om fedres syn på egen deltakelse i foreldresamarbeidet i barnehagen* [Fathers speak! Fathers' evaluations of their participation in cooperative activities in day care centres].

Gulbrandsen, L. (2002). Kvalitetssatsing i norske barnehager: statusrapport midtveis [Emphasizing quality in Norwegian day care centres]. Temahefte no. 2/02. Oslo, Norway: Norsk institutt for forskning om oppvekst, velferd og aldring.

Gunnestad, A. (1993). *Didaktikk for førskolelærere. En innføring* [Didactic for pre-school teachers. An introduction] (2nd ed.). Oslo, Norway: Tano AS

Halsnes, A. Ø. (1989). *Når vaksne og barn samhandlar i uteleiken. En studie av kommunikasjon mellom voksne og barn i barnehagens utemiljø* [When adults and children interact: A study of communication between adults and children in the outdoor environment at a day care center]. Unpublished dissertation, Queen Maud's College/University of Trondheim, Norway.

Handal, G., & Lauvås, P. (1983). *På egne vilkår. En strategi for veiledning med lærere* [On your own terms A strategy of guidance with teachers] Oslo, Norway: J.W. Cappelens forlag.

Hanssen, T. (1999). "Me ska' vel leka i dag o'?" Lekens vilkår i 1. klasse i grunnskolen ["We're gonna' play to day too, aren't we?" Play conditions in the first grade]. Unpublished dissertation, Queen Maud's College/Norwegian University of Science and Technology, Trondheim, Norway.

Haug, P. (1991). Institusjon, tradisjon og profesjon: Sluttrapport frå vurderinga av "Forsøk med pedagogisk tilbod til 6-åringar" [Institution, tradition and profession: Final report from the evaluation of "Try-outs of educational programs for 6 year olds"]. Volda, Norway: Møreforsking.

Haug, P. (1996). Barnehage på skule. Evaluering av kjernetilbod og skulefritidsordning for 6-åringar. (Day care centre at school Evaluation of school and after school programmes for 6 year olds) Rapport nr 43 Trondheim: Norsk Senter for Barneforskning.

Haug, P. (2000). When to start school? The case of Norway. *Nordic Educational Research, 20*(1), 30-45.

Haugen, S. (1996). *Kvalitet i familiebarnehagetilbod for små barn* [Quality in ECE, family version for small children]. Unpublished graduate dissertation, Norwegian University of Science and Technology/Queen Maud's College, Trondheim, Norway.

Henningsen, G. (1999). *La lek være lek! En undersøkelse om lek i 1. klasse fra et barneperspektiv* [Let play be play! An examination of play from a child's perspective]. Oslo, Norway: Oslo University College

Hærås, B. (1998). *Bruk av lek i tilpasset opplæring for 6-åringer i skolen* [Employing play in adaptive teaching for 6 year olds in school]. Unpublished graduate dissertation, The University of Oslo, Norway.

Hiim, H., & Hippe, E. (1998). *Læring gjennom opplevelse, forståelse og handling. En studiebok i didaktikk* [Learning through experiencing, understanding and acting: A study book of didactics]. Oslo, Norway: Universitetsforlaget.

Hjort, K. J. (1996). *Førskolelærerens forståelse av pedagogisk lederskap* [Preschool teachers' understanding of educational leadership]. Unpublished graduate dissertation, Queen Maud's College/Norwegian University of Science and Technology, Trondheim, Norway.

Holthe, V. G. (1998). *Profesjonalisering av oppdragelsen. Muligheter og utfordringer for foreldre og pedagoger* [Professionalism of education: Possibilities and challenges for parents and educators]. Oslo, Norway: Tano Aschehoug.

Hoven, G. (1987). Lek som spesialpedagogisk metode [Play as a method of special education]. Unpublished graduate dissertation, Queen Maud's College/Norwegian University of Science and Technology, Trondheim, Norway.

Hyrve, G., & Lillemyr, O. F. (1987). Barns selvoppfatning i lys av sosialisering og kulturformidling [Children's self-concept in perspective of socialization and culture communication]. *Tidsskriftet BARN*, 1.

Høien, T., Lundberg, I., & Tønnessen, F. E. (1994). *Kor godt les norske barn?* [How is the reading skills of Norwegian children?] Stavanger: Senter for leseforsking.

Johansson, J. -E. (2002). Vi mangler et miljø [In lack of an environment] I artikkelen Stemmer fra norsk barnehageforskning [In the article Voices from Norwegian Day care centre research]. *Barnehagefolk*, 2.

Kibsgaard, S. (1992). Ei bru til vennskap. Gjensidighet i samspill mellom barn fra to kulturer [A bridge to friendship: Reciprocity in interactions between children from two different cultures].

Kibsgaard, S. (1999) Lek som livskvalitet [Play as the quality of life]. In S. Kibsgaard & A. Wostryck (Eds.), *Mens leken er god*. Oslo, Norway: Tano Aschehoug. Trondheim: Graduate dissertation at Queen Maud's College/Norwegian University of Science and Technology.

Klugman, E. (1990). Early childhood moves into the public schools: Mix or meld. In E. Klugman & S. Smilansky (Eds.), *Children's play and learning: perspectives and policy implications*. New York: Teacher's College, Columbia University.

Kristoffersen, A. E. (1995). *Barnas rolle i personalets planleggings- og vurderingsarbeid. "Mein du æ ska syns de henne e arti?"* [Children's role in the staff's planning and evaluation. "Do you really mean I should think this is funny?"], Unpublished graduate dissertation, Queen Maud's College/Norwegian University of Science and Technology, Trondheim, Norway.

Kvello, Ø., & Wendelborg, C. (2002). *Nasjonal evaluering av skolefritidsordningen. Belyst i et helhetlig perspektiv på barns oppvekstmiljø* [National evaluations of after school programs analysed in a holistic perspective of children's educational environment]. Steinkjer, Norway: North Trøndelag Research Institute.

Kvistad, K. J. (1997). *En lærer sjøl vet du! Øvingslæreres erfaringer og opplevelser* [One is learning by oneself, you know! Preschool teachers as advisor in teacher training: their experiences in terms of knowledge and feelings]. Unpublished graduate dissertation, Queen Maud's College/Norwegian University of Science and Technology, Trondheim, Norway.

Ladd, G. W., Buhs, E., & Seid, M. (2000). Children's initial sentiments about kindergarten: Is school liking an antecedent of early classroom participation and achievement? *Merill-Palmer Quarterly, 46*(2), 255-279.

Lamer, K. (1997). *Du og jeg og vi to! Om å fremme barns sosiale kompetanse* Teoriboka. ["You and me, the two of us!" About promoting children's social competence Book of theory]. Oslo, Norway: Universitetsforlaget.

Lauvland, A. (1987). *Motivasjon hos 6-åringen. En feltstudie i barnehagen* [Motivation among 6-year-olds: A field study in day care centres]. Unpublished graduate dissertation, Queen Maud's College/University of Trondheim, Norway.

Leira, A. (1992). *Welfare states and working mothers. The Scandinavian experience.* Cambridge, England: Cambridge University Press.

Levy, J. (1997). Play: The highest form of human expression. In C. Carpenter (Ed.), *Childhood in Canada: Cultural images and contemporary issues.* Waterloo, Ontario, Canada: Wilfried Laurier University Press.

Lillemyr, O. F. (1988). *Rammeplan for forsøk med pedagogisk tilbud til 6-åringer* [Framework plan for try-outs with an educational program for 6-year-olds]. Oslo, Norway: Ministry of Children and Family Affairs and Ministry of Education and Church Affairs.

Lillemyr, O. F. (1989). Selvoppfatning hos barn i alderen 5-6 år [Self-concept among children 5-6 years of age]. In L. Heyerdahl-Larsen (Ed.), *Hva skal vi gjøre med 6-åringene?* Oslo, Norway: Praxis Forlag.

Lillemyr, O. F. (1990). *Leik på alvor* [Play seriously]. Oslo, Norway: Tano AS

Lillemyr, O. F. (1999a). *Lek - opplevelse - læring, i barnehage og skole* [Play - Experience - Learning, in preschool and school] Oslo, Norway: Tano Aschehoug.

Lillemyr, O. F. (1999b). Hvorfor er barns lek så viktig ved overgangen barnehage - skole? [Why is children's play important in the preschool-school transition?]. In S. Kibsgaard & A. Wostryck (Eds.), *Mens leken er god.* Oslo, Norway: Tano Aschehoug.

Lillemyr, O. F. (2001a). Play and learning in school A motivational approach. In D. M. McInerney & S. VanEtten (Eds.), *Research on sociocultural influences on motivation and learning.* Greewich, CT: Information Age.

Lillemyr, O. F. (2001b). *Lek på alvor* [Play seriously] (2nd ed.). Oslo, Norway: Universitetsforlaget.

Lillemyr, O. F. (2002). "Reform 97" in Norway: A new perspective on motivation and learning? *Nordic Educational Research, 1*(22), 38-52.

Lillemyr, O. F. (2003). Play in school—The teacher's role: Reforms and recent research. In O. N. Saracho & B. Spodek (Eds.), *Contemporary perspectives on play in early childhood education.* Greenwich, CT: Information Age.

Lillemyr, O. F. (2004). *Lek—opplevelse—læring, i barnehage og skole* [Play—experience—learning, in preschool and school]. Oslo, Norway: Universitetsforlaget.

Lillemyr, O. F., Bergstrøm, S., Eggen, A., Skevik, S., Støp, K., & Voll, A. L. S. (1998). *Overgangen barnehage - småskole. Et forsknings- og utviklingsprosjekt i Nord-Trøndelag* [The preschool - school transition. A research and development project in North Trøndelag]. Report to Ministry of Education, Research and Church Affaires. Steinkjer: North Trøndelag Research Institute.

Lillemyr, O. F., Fagerli, O., & Søbstad, F. (2001). *A global perspective on early child-hood care and education: A proposed model.* Paris: UNESCO (Monograph 17/2001).

Lillemyr, O. F., & Malmo, B. (1989). *Førskolelærerens yrkesidentitet: Hvilken form for yrkeskompetanse skal danne grunnlag?* (Preschool teachers' occupational iden-tity: What kind of occupational competence makes the basis?]. *Norsk pedago-gisk tidsskrift*, 3/89.

Lillemyr, O. F., & Søbstad, F. (1993). *Didaktisk tenkning i barnehagen* [Didactic thinking in day care institutions]. Oslo, Norway: Tano AS.

Løkken, G. (1989). *ATTI! Om flirekonserter og små barns gruppeglede I barnehagen* [Funny! On glee concerts and toddlers' grouip glee in day care institutions]. Unpublished graduate dissertation, Queen Maud's College/University of Trondheim, Norway.

Løkken, G. (1992). *Yrkesrollene i barnehagen* [The occupational roles in day care centres]. Trondheim: Queen Maud's College Publications. (Research report)

Løkken, G. (1996). *Når små barn møtes* [When young children meet]. Oslo, Norway: Cappelen Akademisk Forlag.

Løkken, G. (2000a). Using Merleau-Pontyan phenomenology to understand the toddler: Toddler interactions in child day-care. *Nordic Educational Research, 1,* 13-23.

Løkken, G. (2000b). Tracing the social style of toddler peers. *Scandinavian Journal of Educational Research, 44*(2), 163-176.

Maehr, M. L., & Midgley, C. (1996). *Transforming school cultures.* In M. Csikszentmi-halyi (Ed.), *Lives in context.* Boulder, CO: Westview Press.

Malmo, B. (1986) *Å arbeide i barnehagen* [To work in day care institutions]. Unpub-lished graduate dissertation, Oslo University College, Norway.

Ministry of Children and Family Affairs. (1995). Lov om barnehagen av 5. mai 1995. (Act no 19 of May 5, 1995 on Day Care Institutions.) Oslo, Norway: Author.

Ministry of Children and Family Affairs. (1996). *Framework plan for day care institu-tions: A brief presentation* (English ed.). Oslo, Norway: Author.

Ministry of Education, Research and Church Affairs. (1996). *Reform 97: The Com-pulsary School Reform.* Oslo, Norway: Author

Moen, K. H. (2000). *Styring og samarbeid i barnehagesektoren* [Administration and collaboration in the field of early childhood education]. Oslo, Norway: Uni-versitetsforlaget.

Mørreaunet, S. (1997). *Fra tråsnella te' vya. Styreren som personalmessig og faglig leder* [From thread spools to perspectives: The head master in day care institutions as personal and professional leader]. Unpublished graduate dissertation, Queen Maud's College/Norwegian University of Science and Technology, Trondheim, Norway.

Nicholls, J. G. (1984). Conceptions of ability and achievement motivation In R. Ames & C. Ames (Eds.), *Research on motivation in education: Student motivation* (pp. 39-73). San Francisco: Academic Press.

Nilsen, R. D. (1988). *Rollelek i et kulturperspektiv* [Role play in a cultural perspec-tive]. Unpublished graduate dissertation, Queen Maud's College/Norwegian University of Science and Technology, Trondheim, Norway.

Nilsen, R. D. (2000). *Livet i barnehagen. En etnografisk studie av sosialiseringsprosessen* [Life in day care centres An ethnographic study of the process of socialization]. Unpublished graduate dissertation, Norwegian University of Science and Technology, Trondheim, Norway.

Nilsen, R. D. (2002). *Barnehager - en del av velferdsprogrammet* [Day care centres, a part of the well fare program) *I artikkelen Stemmer fra norsk barnehageforskning* [In the article Voices from Norwegian Day care center research]. *Barnehagefolk, 2.*

Nordahl, T. (2000). *En skole – to verdener. Et teoretisk og empirisk arbeid om problematferd og mistilpasning i et elev- og lærerperspektiv* [One school—two worlds: A theoretical and empirical work on problem behavior and mal-adaptation in a student and teacher perspective]. Oslo, Norway: Norsk institutt for forskning om oppvekst, velferd og aldring.

Nordahl, T. (2002). *Eleven som aktør. Fokus på elevens læring og handlinger i skolen.* [The active student. Focus on students' learning and acting in school.] Oslo, Norway: Universitetsforlaget.

Norwegian Parliament, white paper no. 27 (1999-2000). *Barnehage til beste for barn og foreldre* [Day care centers for the best of children and parents]. Oslo, Norway: Ministry of Children and Family Affairs.

Næs, T., & Mordal, T. L. (1997). *Barns trivsel I barnhagen* [Children's well-being in day care centers] [SIFO-report no. 13]. Oslo, Norway: Statens institutt for forbruksforskning.

Organization for Economic Cooperation and Development. (1998). *Thematic review of early childhood education and care policy. Background report from Norway.* Oslo, Norway: Ministry of Children and Family Affaires.

Organization for Economic Cooperation and Development. (2001). *Starting strong early childhood education and care.* Paris: Author.

Ogden, T. (1998). *Elevatferd og læringsmiljø. Læreres erfaringer med og syn på elevatferd og læringsmiljø i grunnskolen* [Student behavior and learning environment: Teachers experiences with and perspective on student behavior and learning environment in comprehensive school]. Oslo, Norway: Ministry of Education, Research and Church Affairs.

Oftedal. M. P., & Dahle, A. E. (2002). *Lese- og skriveopplæring: Kartlegging og vurdering av leseferdighet i 2. klasse* [Teaching introductory reading and writing: Mapping and evaluation of reading skills in 2. grade]. Stavanger, Norway: Rapport fra Senter for leseforsking.

Øksnes, M. (2001). *Pedagogisering av barns fritid. På hvilken måte blir SFO et viktig ledd i styring av barns fritid* [Educationalization of children's leisure. In what way is after school programmes (in Norway abbreviated SFO) to become important aspects in directing children's leisure?]. Unpublished graduate dissertation, Queen Maud's College/Norwegian University of Science and Technology, Trondheim, Norway.

Østbye, I. (2001). *Om sosialisering i en norsk kommunal barnehage - en studie av barn med ulik kulturell bakgrunn* [Socialization in a Norwegian public day care center—A study of children with different cultural background]. Unpublished graduate dissertation, University of Oslo, Norway.

Patrick, H., & Townsend, M. A. R. (1995, April). *The influence of perceived social competence on school beginners' emergent academic intrinsic motivation.* Paper presented at the annual meeting of American Educational Research Association, April, San Francisco, CA.

Paulsen, B. (1994). *Det skjønne. Estetisk virksomhet i barnehagen* [The beautiful. Aesthetic activity in day care institutions]. Oslo, Norway: Ad Notam Gyldendal.

Rese, M., Røtnes, K., Svendsen, A., & Vedeler, L. (1986). *Lek – en viktig pedagogisk metode i barnehage og skole* [Play—an important educational method in day care centers and school]. Oslo, Norway: Pagina Forlag.

Riksaasen, R. (1998). *Visible and invisible pedagogies in teacher education: A comparison of Norwegian primary and pre-school teacher education.* Unpublished doctoral dissertation, Norwegian University of Science and Technology, Trondheim, Oslo, Norway.

Rødstøl, C. (1999). *Foreldres vektlegging av motivasjon når barnet går i 1. klasse* [Parent's emphasis on motivation when their child attend first grade]. Unpublished graduate dissertation, Queen Maud's College/Norwegian University of Science and Technology, Trondheim, Norway.

Röthle, M. (1996). *Eg skal laga meir, allikevel. Perspektiver på temaarbeid i barnehage* [I am still going to make some more. Perspectives on theme-working in day care centers]. Unpublished graduate dissertation, Queen Maud's College/Norwegian University of Science and Technology, Trondheim, Norway.

Sand, S., & Skoug, T. (2002). *Integrering - et sprik mellom intensjon og realitet? Evaluering av prosjekt med gratis korttidsplass i barnehage for alle femåringer i bydel Gamle Oslo* [Integration—A difference between intention and reality? Evaluation of a project with free short-time-placement in a day care institution for 5-year-olds in Old Oslo]. (Report no 1) Elverum, Norway: University College of Hedmark.

Sataøen, S. O. (2002). *Evaluering av førskulelærerutdanningea ved fem norske institusjonar: Rapport frå en ekstern komité* [Evaluations of the teacher training in early childhood education Report from an external committee]. Oslo, Norway: Norgesnettrådets rapporter.

Schein, E. (1983). *Organisasjonspsykologi* [Organizational psychology]. Oslo, Norway: Tano AS.

Schibbye, A. -L. L. (1988). *Familien. Tvang og mulighet: om samspill og behandling* [The family Force and possibility: Interaction and treatment]. Oslo, Norway: Universitetsforlaget.

Schram, M. (1991). "Så dæm slepp og gjørra alt sjøl!" En metodisk sammenligning av faktiske og hypotetiske prososiale begrunnelser ["So they don't have to do everything themselves!" A methodical comparison of factual and hypothetic pro-social justifications]. Unpublished graduate dissertation, Queen Maud's College/Norwegian University of Science and Technology, Trondheim, Norway.

Seljelid, T. (Ed.). (1994). *Med iver og lyst. Beskrivelse og vurdering av et prosjekt om motivasjon i skolen* [With interest and involvement: Description and evaluation of a project on motivation in school]. Hamar, Norway: Kapére Forlag.

Selmer-Olsen, I. (1990). *Barn imellom – og de voksne. En bok om barns egen kultur* [Between children—and the Adults: A book on child culture]. Oslo, Norway: Gyldendal.

Sheridan, S. (2001). Pedagogical quality in preschool: An issue of perspectives. *Göteborg Studies in Educational Sciences, 160.*

Schoenfeld, A. H. (1999). Looking toward the 21st century: Challenges of educational theory and practice. *Educational Researcher, 28*(7), 4-14.

Sjøvik, P. (Ed.). (2002). *En barnehage for alle. Spesialpedagogikk i førskolelærerutdanningen* [A day care centre for all: Special education in preschool teacher training]. Oslo, Norway: Universitetsforlaget.

Skodvin, A. (1998). *Kommunikasjon og kognisjon: Piagets og Vygotskijs syn på voksen-barn-kommunikasjonen i forhold til førskolebarns kognisjon: en teoretisk drøfting og empirisk konkretisering* [Communication and cognition: Piaget's and Vygotskij's perspective on adult-child-communication related to preschool children's cognition: A theoretical discussion and an empirical concretization]. Unpublished doctoral dissertaion, University of Oslo, Norway.

Skaalvik, E. M. (1997). Issues in research on self-concept. In M. L. Maehr & P. R. Pintrich (Eds.), *Advances in motivation and achievement, Vol. 10.* Greenwich, CT: JAI Press.

Skaalvik, E. M., & Kvello, Ø. (Eds.). (1998). *Barn og miljø. Om barns oppvekstvilkår i det senmoderne samfunnet* [Children and environment: Children's educational conditions in the postmodern society]. Oslo, Norway: Tano Aschehoug.

Sletvold, S. (1983). Fra børneasyl til barnehage [From children's asylums to kindergarten) I *Festskrift for Astrid Vatne* (In the memorial publication of Astrid Vatne) Trondheim, Norway: Queen Maud's College Publications.

Smilansky, S. (1990). Sociodramatic play: Its Relevance to behavior and achievement in school. In E. Klugman & S. Smilansky (Eds.), *Children's play and learning: Perspectives and policy implications.* New York: Teachers' College Press.

Smith, L., & Ulvund, S. E. (1991). *Spedbarnalderen* [The infant age]. Oslo, Norway: Universitetsforlaget.

Steinsholt, K. (1998). *Lett som en lek!* (Easy as play). Trondheim, Norway: Tapir.

Stensaasen, S., & Sletta, O. (1996). *Gruppeprosesser. Læring og samarbeid i grupper* [Group processes: Learning and collaboration in groups]. Oslo, Norway: Universitetsforlaget.

Strømsnes, M. (1990). *Selvforståelse og kompetanseopplevelse – to sentrale variabler relatert til indre motivasjon* [Self-determination and sense of competence: Two basic variables to intrinsic motivation]. Unpublished graduate dissertation, University of Oslo, Norway.

Sutton-Smith, B. (1997). *The ambiguity of play.* Cambridge, MA: Harvard University Press.

Søbstad, F. (1990). *Førskolebarn og humor* [Pre-school children and humour]. Unpublished doctoral dissertaion, University of Trondheim, Norway.

Søbstad, F. (1995). *Humor i pedagogisk arbeid* [Humour in educational work]. Oslo, Norway: Tano AS.

Søbstad, F. (1999). Humor i lekfamilien [Humor in the play family.) In S. Kibsgaard & A. Wostryck (Eds.), *Mens leken er god* [While the play is good]. Oslo, Norway: Tano Aschehoug.

Søbstad, F. (2000). *Førskolepedagogikk i barnehagen* [Early childhood education in day care centres]. In O. Fagerli, O. F. Lillemyr, & F. Søbstad (Eds.), *Hva er førskolepedagogikk?* [What is early childhood education?]. Kristiansand, Norway: Nordic Academic Press.

Søbstad, F. (2002a). DMMH - et knutepunkt (Queen Maud's College - a junction) I artikkelen Stemmer fra norsk barnehageforskning (In the article Voices from Norwegian Day care centre research). *Barnehagefolk, 2.*

Søbstad, F. (2002b). Jaktstart på kjennetegn ved den gode barnehagen. Første rapport fra prosjektet "Den norske barnehagekvaliteten" [Starting hunting for characteristics of the good day care center: First report of the project "The Norwegian day care center quality"]. *The Queen Maud's College Publications, 2/ 02.*

Søndenå, K. (2002). *Tradisjon og transcendens: En fenomenologisk studie av refleksjon i norsk førskolelærerutdanning* [Tradition and transcendence: A phenomenological study of reflection in Norwegian teacher training of early childhood education]. Doctoral dissertation Göteborg: Göteborg studies in educational sciences no 175.

Tangen, D. (1998). *"Jeg lærer meg å leke med kunnskapen på en måte." Lek i småskolen - et studium av barns lek i to småskoleklasser* [I am learning to play with knowledge in a way. Play in primary school—A study of children's play in first and second grade classrooms]. Unpublished graduate dissertation, Oslo University College.

Trageton, A. (1992). *Verkstadpedagogikk 6-10 år* [Workshop education 6-10 years]. Stord, Norway: Stord University College Press.

Trageton, A. (1994) Workshop Pedagogy—From concrete to abstract. *Reading Teacher, 47,* 350-351

Trageton, A. (1997). *Leik i småskolen* [Play in primary school]. Bergen: Fagbokforlaget.

Tønnessen, L. K. B. (1995) *Norsk utdanningshistorie. En innføring* [Norwegian History of Education An introduction]. Oslo, Norway: University Press.

Tøssebro, J., & Lundeby, H. (2002). Å vokse opp med en funksjonshemming – de første årene [To live with a mal-function—The first years]. Oslo, Norway: Gyldendal.

Vedeler, L. (1982). *Integrering i barnehagen* [Integration in day care centers]. Oslo, Norway: Universitetsforlaget.

Vedeler, L. (1987). *Barns kommunikasjon i rollelek* [Communication of children in role play]. Oslo, Norway: Universitetsforlaget.

Vedeler, L. (1997a). Dramatic play: A format for "literate" language? *British Journal of Educational Psychology, 67,* 153-167.

Vedeler, L. (1997b). *Tilpasset opplæring i skolestarten sett i organisasjonskulturelt og pedagogisk-psykologisk perspektiv* [Adaptive teaching at the school start in an organizational and educational-psychological perspective]. Oslo, Norway: Report from University of Oslo, Institute of special education.

Vedeler, L. (1999). *Pedagogisk bruk av lek* [Educational application of play]. Oslo, Norway: Universitetsforlaget.

Wasserman, S. (1990). *Serious players in the primary classroom: Empowering children through active learning experience.* New York: Teachers' College Press.

Wood, E., & Attfield, J. (1996). *Play, learning and the early childhood curriculum.* London: Paul Chapman.

Ytterhus, B. (2002). *Sosialt samvær mellom barn – inklusjon og eksklusjon i barnehagen* [Social company between children—Inclusion and exclusion in day care centers]. Oslo, Norway: Abstrakt Forlag.

Zachrisen, B. (2000). Når leken blir skolemoden [When play is becoming ready for school]. Hamar, Norway: *University College of Hedmark Publications.*

CHAPTER 8

EARLY CHILDHOOD
EDUCATION IN POLAND

Barbara Murawska

INTRODUCTION

The time after 1945 was difficult in Poland, not only for education. State policy was mainly aimed at subordinating society to the interests of a communist state, and this was also seen in the organization and programs of education for young children. The building of a totalitarian state assumed the creating of such a family model in which state institutions had a significant influence on the bringing up children. The curriculum in those institutions followed the communist ideology.

The end of the 1980s brought the beginning of systemic changes. Political changes made significant reforms of education in Poland possible. Private kindergartens and schools, as well as the ones established by parents' associations appeared alongside the state schools. Those educational institutions had independent curricula.

Educational decentralization also brought some changes in the state school system. A uniform curriculum was abandoned and many curricula based on the assumptions of a programme minimum worked out by the Ministry of Education were introduced.

International Perspectives on Research in Early Childhood Education, 233–257
Copyright © 2005 by Information Age Publishing

The main aim of preschool programs was the preparation of a young child for school learning and providing equal of chances for children from country and poor or disfavoured families.

At the same time early school education (the period of the first three years of an elementary school) is focused on teaching children with the basic skills like reading, writing and basic maths.

The term elementary education is defined in Poland in the same way as in the other European countries, as educating and bringing up children between 3 and 9 years old. The basis for that stage of education is a structure of educational institutions in Poland. It comprises two levels of school organization: the preschool-level children between 3 and 7 years old; the first three years of the elementary school education, called early education—children between 7 and 9 years old.

Caring and bringing up tasks are mainly carried out by kindergartens and—in the oldest group of children—more important schooling tasks, too. At that stage at school, teaching and educational issues are predominant, while caring has assumed lesser significance.

For a few years now there has been a discussion on including in the topic of care of 0-3-year-olds into the stage of elementary education. More and more often—while discussing the education policy in Poland—there are same proposals for that stage of development to be covered by the legal regulations issued by the Ministry of Education. This idea is present in considerations concerning equal educational opportunities. Up to now, however children of the ages in question have only been able to be under the supervision of care institutions. Despite the efforts of many people dealing with the education of young children in Poland, the traditional institutional structure and the associated way of thinking predominate and are reflected in many acts of law.

Child care for 0-3 year-olds is still an area governed by regulations of the Ministry of Health and Social Welfare, not the Ministry of Education and Sport.

The description of early childhood education contained in this article is in two parts: preschool education and early school education. It starts at the beginning of the 1960s, as at that time the legal acts emphasizing the significance of this stage of education first appeared.

PRESCHOOL EDUCATION

History

An important document in the post-war history of preschool care was the Educational Development Act (Ustawa o rozwoju oswiaty i wychowania) of 1961 (Wilgocka-Okon, 1993), which emphasized that preschool care is the first stage of the school system, taking place in kindergartens. That act also reduced the age at which children could go to kindergarten from 4 to 3, and defined the aim of preschool education as the all-round development of children and preparing them to start a primary school. That general aim is still quoted in all documents regulating work with children aged 3 to 7. More detailed objectives were described in the program of preschool education from 1963, which emphasized health care and developing fitness and physical abilities in young children. A turning point in ways of thinking about preschool education was the 1973 curriculum, which introduced the notion of "school maturity"—a degree of intellectual, social and emotional development necessary to enable a child to succeed at school (Program, 1973). The main aim of kindergarten was therefore to create conditions in which such development might be achieved. The so defined aim led in 1977 to the introduction of general preschool education for six-year-olds. Groups of six-year-olds in kindergartens and the so-called "year zero" in schools were established and given a special curriculum for six-year olds designed by the Institute of School Curricula. For the first time in the history of Polish preschool education organized instruction in reading was introduced at this stage. The curriculum became notorious for the idea of separating reading from writing, the latter being left until year 1 of primary school. It also included a more general, but socially important aim: equalizing the level at which children enter school. Under the former socialist regime, a curriculum noticing social differences and the need for equalizing opportunities was something new in that it revealed the state's problems with education. That curriculum was in use in the preschool education of six-year olds until the mid-1980s. At that time the first signs of political change became apparent also in education. The first organizational changes in kindergartens and the emergence of independent preschools run by the Educational Society (Spoleczne Towarzystwo Oswiatowe) and other non-governmental organizations led to a loosening of the central government's grip on education and the emergence of various preschool syllabuses. The organizational and program changes continued throughout the 1980s and 1990s gradually, but consistently and systematically.

The Act of 1991 (Ustawa 1991), which started the gradual transfer of responsibility for and the financing of kindergartens from central to local government, also marked the beginning of a decline in the impact of preschool education. It soon turned out that local governments (gminas) had no funds for kindergartens; parents were required to cover a substantial part of the costs. The general difficult economic situation in the country further led to many kindergartens being closed, especially in rural areas.

Despite many protests by people aware of the consequent dangers to the development of education, the proportion of children attending kindergarten in Poland is alarmingly small in comparison with other European countries (Euridice 2002). Only 51% of children aged between 3 and 6 go to kindergarten, which makes Poland one of the last countries in Europe in that respect (Branska 2002).

The educational reform introduced in 1999 (Ustawa 1999) did not explicitly deal with preschool education in Poland, but this Act has opened discussion about that period in child's education.

Current Preschool Reforms

The project of educational reform published in 1998 (Reforma 1998) did not propose or discuss any changes in preschool education. This provoked protests from those who appreciate the importance of that period for the child's educational achievements. It was especially alarming, as the number of kindergartens had already fallen significantly. The proposal of reform of the child care system, which emerged in the Ministry at that time, also addressed problems concerning children in the 0-7 age group (Kostynowicz, Kuklinska 2003). It was based on the assumption that the main aim of education should be to facilitate a child's development in accordance with his or her individual needs. This should be done through support by the family, which in this period of a child's life has the basic responsibility for his or her development and upbringing. It was emphasized that such support should include a variety of elements: health care, education, psychological and legal assistance. Unfortunately, that project, which attempted to include all aspects of a young child's development, was never implemented. The spirit of its ideas appeared again in the national curriculum for preschool education (Podstawa 2000), a document issued in 2000—nearly a year after the reforms were launched. The national curriculum states that the main aim of preschool education is to facilitate a child's all-round development in accordance with his or her individual needs and potential. It identifies four spheres of educational influence on a child: one regards getting to know oneself and the world, the second—acquiring skills through activity, the third—developing social competences, the fourth—building a system of values. The document is sufficiently open to give teachers plenty of scope to choose and create syllabuses of preschool education. As a result, scores of such syllabuses came into being, about 40 of them recommended by the Ministry. This did not, however, result in improving the quality of work in kindergartens; it forced teachers to choose syllabuses without providing them with tools to make informed choices, recognizing the best syllabus for each particular group of children. In this situation, the choice of syllabus was often determined by economic factors and by the publishers' marketing efforts.

The problem of kindergartens and preschool education became the subject of particularly intensive debate at that time for two reasons. Firstly, the time of preparation for accession to the EU encouraged comparisons between Poland's education and other European countries. The 1999 UNESCO report shows that we have one of the smallest proportions of children in preschool education in Europe. In countries such as France, Belgium, Norway, Italy between 80 and 100% of children at kindergarten age go to kindergarten. Moreover, in nearly all European countries, including former-Communist ones, that proportion is on the rise. In Poland it has been declining for many years (Kaminska 2003).

Secondly, the results of monitoring the state of education in Poland in the first year of reform by the Institute of Public Affairs with the support form the Ministry of Education show that the change in the structure of the school system—creating *Gimnazjum* or junior high school (a second stage of compulsory education after six-year primary school for children aged 14–16) has not lived up to expectations of equalizing educational opportunities (Konarzewski 2001). Experts declared unanimously that the time to equalize educational opportunities was in a kindergarten. Thus the problem of preschool education emerged in the public debate in the context of social inequalities, which resulted first in a report on the state of preschool education and then in suggestions for improvement.

The decision to make kindergartens the responsibility of local government resulted in 30% of them closing down in the years 1990–1999. The proportion was higher in rural areas (38%), lower in cities (22%). As a result, the number of children attending kindergarten fell by 14% in cities and by as much as 24% in rural areas (Blumsztajn 2002). Due to demographic factors the percentage of children attending kindergarten in cities has actually increased; in the countryside the trend is downward. In urban areas 56.3% of children aged 3 to 6 attended kindergarten in 1990; by 1999 that number had risen to 63.9%. In rural areas the corresponding numbers are 36.6% and 35.2% respectively. It must, however, be added that these figures give a distorted picture, because they include six-year olds, 99.7% of whom are in preschool education (data for 2001/2002, Education 2002). If we look at the 3 to 5-year-old-group separately, the proportion of children in kindergarten is 15.7% in rural areas and 49.3% in cities. Figure 8.1 shows the distribution of kindergarten attendance.

The analysis of the presented figures shows all too clearly that kindergarten attendance in the countryside is dramatically low. This situation is largely due to economic factors, but also to parents' ignorance of the educational role of kindergarten. Parents still tend to perceive kindergarten simply as a day care center. Appreciation of its impact on children's devel-

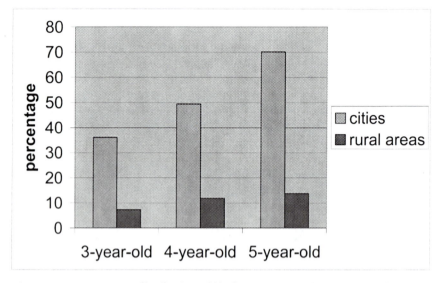

Figure 8.1.   Percentage distribution of kindergarten attendance in Poland.

opment depends on education and professional status. This problem concerns not only parents, but also local representatives and civil servants responsible for the education in a given *gmina* (borough or community). They are often more willing to finance primary and junior high schools than to seek funds for preschool education for children who may remain at home in the care of their parents, who are either farmers or unemployed. It is this way of thinking that has led to such low kindergarten attendance in the country and such huge differences between rural and urban areas (Blumsztajn, 2002).

An obvious conclusion for the Ministry and for many non-governmental organizations interested in education was the need to take particular care of preschool education. As a result, a draft law was initiated lowering the age for compulsory primary education (Poland is one of the few countries in Europe where compulsory education begins at the age of 7). In November 2002 the government accepted a draft amendment of the law on education, proposing not exactly lowering the school age, but introducing one years' compulsory preschool preparation for six-year-olds (Kostynowicz, Kuklinska, 2003). It would take place either in kindergartens or in preschool groups in schools, and would be in force from September 1, 2003. By March 2003 the proposed amendment had not passed through the Parliament; it is unlikely that it would enter into force from September 1, 2004. The responsibility for its implementation will fall on local governments, who will be obliged to provide enough kindergartens or preschool groups in schools for all six-year-olds to be able to attend. If an educational institution is further than 3 kilometers from a child's home, the local government has to arrange free transportation accompanied by a teacher present.

Many activities led by institutions concerned with education bore fruit in the form of numerous projects aimed at improving the situation of children from rural areas and giving them equal educational opportunities. In 2002 the Society for the Development of Educational Initiatives (Towarzystwo Rozwijania Inicjatyw Oswiatowych) in collaboration with the Central In-Service Teacher Training Center (Centralny Osrodek Doskonalenia Nauczycieli) initiated the project *Male Przedszkole* ("Little Kindergarten," Sutkowska, 2000). The main idea of the project was to adapt unused school buildings (where village schools had closed down) for kindergartens and to create one-group village kindergartens with mixed age groups. Educational authorities did not definitely support this project, but they did offer grants for educational initiatives over two years, which made it possible to conduct research and partially implement model solutions.

A year earlier, in 1999, the Polish Foundation for Children and Teenagers (Polska Fundacja Dzieci i Mlodziezy) launched the program *Tam, gdzie nie ma przedszkola (Where there is no kindergarten)*, aimed at making preschool education more widely available in rural areas. Since January 2002, 23 preschool centers have been operating in 8 rural *gminas* (communities) (Grzelak, 2003; Ńotys, 2003). They are attended by 300 children, looked after by 35 teachers trained by the Foundation's Training Center. Despite many legal, economic, organizational and social obstacles, those centers are functioning and their work has had observable effects, such as parents' involvement in the work and new energy in the communities.

Drawing on those experiences the Polish Foundation for Children and Teenagers, commissioned by the Ministry of Education, developed in November 2002 a concept for equalizing educational opportunities for young children (Ogrodzinska 2002). Their report presents the current state of preschool education and a plan for extending such education to 3-6-year-olds from rural areas throughout the country. The plan refers to Portugal's experience 17 years ago, when it addressed the same problem; the steps taken there proved effective and decidedly improved the state of education in that country (Eurybase 2001). The Polish project involves setting up preschool centers in villages that have no kindergarten. Such centers are places where teachers organize 3-4 hours of activities for children aged 3 to 6 several times a week with the help of parents and the support of local organizations and inhabitants. The project proposes a new form of work by teachers, never before practiced in Poland: they are to be *mobile teachers*, not attached to one center, but working in several villages of the same *gmina* on different days of the week. The centers might be located in different places, depending on each *gmina's* resources. It might be a community center, the building of the local library, a primary school, the building of a school that was shut down. There are no plans to run centers in parents' houses, as in Portugal. The plan proposes general organizational ideas, assuming that specific solutions will depend on each community's needs and resources. The project is complete; it includes ideas for teacher training and methods of evaluation of the preschool centers, in order to ensure a high standard of the education received by the children.

It is not yet clear whether the state will support the centers through legislation establishing this form of preschool education nationwide as a standard option, alongside kindergartens and preschool groups at schools. It is certainly a valuable idea; so far the only feasible attempt at solving the problem of preschool education in rural areas.

EARLY PRIMARY EDUCATION

History

Early primary education underwent many transformations in Poland. In the 1960s and 1970 it was called introductory teaching, then the name early primary education came into use. Since the launching of the reform in 1999 it has been known as integrated education (Ustawa 1999).

After the adoption of the 1961 Law on the Education System (Ustawa 1961), early primary education consisted of four years, from the age of 7 up to 10. One national curriculum was in use in the whole country, relying on subject teaching and traditional methods. The 1977 amendment of the education law significantly changed the status of early primary education and introduced a new curriculum (Ustawa 1977). The time of early education was shortened to three years, for children aged 7 to 9, modern curriculum was introduced, especially in mathematics. That curriculum was considered too difficult by teachers and parents and in subsequent years underwent many changes, losing much of its educational value (Program 1979).

The late 1980s saw a weakening of the central government's control over education. The Ministry allowed independent schools to be established by associations or individuals. The 1991 Law on the education system was a next step towards decentralization (Ustawa 1991). The same law that handed over kindergartens to local authorities did the same with primary schools. Now the condition of schools in an area depends on the

wealth of the community and the managerial skills of the local government. There were schools whose financial situation improved, and others,
who were doing very badly. The latter were usually small village schools,
which cost the most to run. The new law gave head teachers considerable
latitude, also with regard to curricula. In that area a certain attempt at
regulation was made by publishing the document *Minimum national curriculum (Minimum programowe)*, which described the basic amount of knowledge that any primary syllabus should contain. (Minimum 1992). The
Minimum was a reaction to the ever increasing number of individually
designed syllabuses created by teachers. The *Minimum* also included early
primary education and in that point in did not differ much from the uniform national curriculum from 1977. The 1990s were a time of openness
to innovation and experiments in early primary teaching, accepted by the
educational authorities as "designer syllabuses". It was then that integrated teaching, new methods, new course books and workbooks (reading, mathematics, science) appeared in many schools. Many teachers,
being used to uniformity, felt a bit lost among that diversity.

Current Primary Education Reforms

Another important moment for early primary education was the educational reform of 1999 (Ustawa 1999). As I have mentioned earlier, the
authors of the reform were not concerned with young children of the 3-6
age group, but they had a lot to say about work with students aged between
7 and 9. The directive introduced integrated education (unified curriculum) as a requirement in years 1 to 3 of primary school. The integrated
education has not been defined satisfactorily; it is clear that there is in
opposite to devoted to subjects: mats, science, Polish language and others.
It's an appeal to alternative education in the first half of the twentieth century. In this system the knowledge connected with subject is unified. The
main aim of education in that period was defined as supporting the student's harmonious, all-round development. A national curriculum for that
stage was published (Podstawa, 1999). That document lists the detailed
aims of school: it is expected to equip the students with skills which will
serve them as learning tools: reading, writing, arithmetic; social skills—
making contact with peers and with adults, including people of other races
and nationalities. The curriculum also sets the subject matter that is to
provide a basis for the realization of those aims. Such a curriculum gives
the authors of syllabuses almost unlimited liberty. All teachers and all people interesting in education may creates syllabus. The resulting situation
was similar to the situation in preschool education: about 100 integrated
education syllabuses obtained the Ministry's recommendation. In such cir-

cumstances it is virtually impossible for a teacher to make an informed choice; economic factors and the marketing skills of the publishers of syllabuses and related course books have become a major influence.

The most important educational problem of that time was connected with the transition form traditional to integrated teaching. Most theoretical discussions in that period were devoted to the interpretation of the concept of integration in teaching (Zytko 2002, Klus-Stanska 2001). Most teachers emphasized that syllabuses need to be so structured as to give greatest prominence to the themes that provide the basis for integration. In such a situation the individual approach is often forgotten, and the classes are attractive and instructive, but mostly for children for whom school is not the only place where they are educated.

Another serious problem was evaluation. The directive regulating the implementation of the reform instructed teachers to use descriptive evaluation in integrated teaching (Rozporzadzenie, 19 April 1999). Before 1999, evaluation in the form of grades was in general use. The change of thinking about evaluation was very difficult for teachers, students and parents. Some parents felt they lacked the means to compare their children's performance with that of others, students did not feel motivated to study, teachers felt helpless, deprived of an instrument affording direct influence on students. The debate on the right way to evaluate children's performance in years 1 to 3 continues. Teachers and education experts are trying to find the most efficient form of descriptive evaluation, which will be informative, motivating, and will not require an unreasonable amount of work from the teacher.

TEACHER TRAINING

In order to accomplish the goals of educational reform in Poland it is vital to make the teacher a true authority. The authors of the reform have taken steps to activate teachers as a group. They tried to create a system that would motivate teachers to work better, restore the prestige of the teaching profession (also in financial terms) and create conditions for positive selection to the profession. In order to reach those goals, changes are being implemented regarding teacher training and in-service training, professional advancement and teachers' remuneration.

The basic forms of teacher training have remained the same. As before, there are two paths preparing for the teaching profession. One is to complete university studies in a chosen subject plus a course in pedagogy, or an M.A. course in early education (preparation for work with small children). The other is to complete a college of education and receive a BEd diploma. The latter path may be supplemented with an MA course.

Considerable changes have been introduced in the procedures of professional advancement. Attaining higher professional ranks now requires ongoing development. Many in-service training courses for teachers are being run by institutions of higher education and by local government agencies. In the first two years of the reform many of those courses were financed by the Ministry of Education through grants. Courses aimed at supplementing qualifications are also in great demand; those are mostly run by universities as post-graduate courses. The reform obliges the teachers whose qualifications are, in the light of new regulations, incomplete, to supplement those qualifications by the year 2006. This decision has caused much agitation among teachers, as it appeared that according to new regulations many of them had "lost" their qualifications, and their professional position is endangered.

The law on educational reform increased the number of teachers' professional ranks to four: "trainee teacher," "contract teacher," "appointed teacher," and "certified teacher."

A teacher who enters the profession is a trainee teacher. After 9 months, and on fulfilling the requirements of a qualifying board, the head of the school promotes him or her to the next rank—contract teacher. In the training period the teacher is supposed to follow his or her own professional development plan. A trainee teacher and a contract teacher both do that under the direction of a supervisor—a teacher of a higher rank appointed by the head of the school. The supervisor's role is to provide help in solving professional problems.

For higher ranks the training period is longer; for the ranks of appointed teacher and certified teacher it lasts 2 years and 9 months.

After the training period, to attain the rank of appointed teacher, one must pass an exam before a board consisting of the head of the school, representatives of the local educational authority and three experts from a list compiled by the Minister of Education. The local authority then promotes the teacher to Appointed Teacher.

Promotion to the rank of certified teacher, after the required training period, is the result of approval from a qualifying body consisting of representatives of the local educational authority and three experts appointed by the minister of education.

A certified teacher who has at least 20 years of experience in the profession, including at least 10 years as a certified teacher, and considerable achievements, may be awarded the honorary title of Professor of Education by the Minister of Education.

The introduction of the promotion procedures described above has inspired teachers to take up in-service training. It has also resulted in many creative initiatives, livening up everyday work with students. However, there is also a down side. Decisions regarding promotion made by the qualifying committees are mostly based on paper evidence of professional activity. Teachers often try to accumulate as many certificates of attendance at courses as possible. There is a danger that the hunt for evidence of professional development may be carried on at the cost of real work at school. This problem will have to be solved in the years to come.

A REVIEW OF RESEARCH ON ELEMENTARY EDUCATION

The review is the result of analysis of the contents of educational journals published in Poland as well as collected works that have appeared on the book market in the last 10 years. The research projects on young children in Poland over that time have been interesting but few in number. One can not find here well-defined and overlapping research domains.

The only analysis, which is worth quoting because of its homogenous character, is the research on factors in the development of preschool education children. The research was run by Early Education Group at the Institute of Educational Studies in the years 1991-1997. Between 1991 and 1995 research was conducted within the framework of the international project entitled: Quality of Life Study coordinated by the High Scope Educational Foundation and IEA (International Association for the Evaluation of Educational Achievement). Fifteen countries participated in the project.

Other research projects are more often of a smaller scale and are not long-term in nature. The most frequently analyzed field is the child's language and reading learning. A second group of projects is that on social functioning; a third concerns changes in the education system. The ones that are described present evaluation and educational inequalities. Another piece of research worth describing is the project resulting from cooperation between academic circles and local educational circles.

Factors in the Development of Preschool Education Children

The main aim of this research was to recognize a child's varied experiences and to look for links between those experiences, the child's milieu and his or her development (Karwowska-Struczyk 2000). The study was part of an international research program and results was publication in many report (Bielen, Zegadlo-Malkowska 1998, Karwowska-Struczyk 1993, 1998, 1999, 2000). In order to explain certain problems, the authors of the research, Malgorzata Karwowska-Struczyk, introduced the notion of "ecological niche" for the physical and social conditions of the child's environment and the relations between the developing child and his or her immediate milieu. The research was long-term; in the years 1991-1996 a group of 4-year old children in kindergarten was studied; during the second stage, the same children were studied at the age of 7, as primary school pupils. The data about the children, their development, and the environments in which they live were gathered in a variety of ways: surveys, tests and observation. The analysis was multi-dimensional. It yielded information regarding the functioning of a child's developmental niches, the work of a kindergarten teacher, the activities in which children engage, the knowledge possessed by four- and seven-year-olds. This made it possible to look for links between the features of "ecological niches" and a child's development, and to analyze a more complicated model: process-person-context. Apart from providing the detailed findings in the areas mentioned above, the research has changed our way of thinking about children's development. It has shown that the impact of the environment on that development is not uniform. A child's development is the result of a transaction between his or her individual traits and the changing features of his or her developmental niches.

The Development of a Child's Language

Another interesting area of research is children's language. Barbara Bokus has conducted several observations of narration by preschool age children (Bokus 2000). The assumptions of the study and the interpretation make use of the concepts of the line of narration and field of narration, developed by the author. A line of narration presents a series of changes in reality over time, arranged by the narrator. Narrative fields provide the space for narration; their content is the various situations of characters in the field as described by the narrator. Those characters are participants of the main character's life situation.

The studies were carried out in the years 1996-1998 in 17 kindergartens in Warsaw with children aged from 3 to 7. The children narrated to their peers the adventures of two boys, the heroes of two picture books. The listener did not have access to the illustrations. The research project consisted of three studies. Each of them focused on mental states ascribed to characters in the narration field. The researcher had posed the question if and in what way preschool narrators make references to intellectual activity by the characters in the narration field. The studies showed that that the child narrators make references to cognitive activity by the subjects in the field and line of narration. Data were collected regarding creating by children stories in a dual scenery—the scenery of action and the scenery of consciousness. The research showed that the children's stories do not merely reproduce the visual material the narrator is looking at. An in-depth analysis of the collected data by the researcher provides a basis for developing methods of building up a young child's language.

The way 8 to 10-year-olds function with regard to language was studied by Ewa Filipiak (Filipiak 1996). The research took place in 1995 and involved a group of 120 early primary students from schools in a large city. The purpose of the study was to diagnose the level and features of the children's linguistic activity, both spoken and written, in two aspects: productivity and creativity. An analysis of the results led the author to interesting conclusions. The children's activity in the sphere of spoken language suggests problems in the learning process and threats to development resulting from inhibiting and deprecating verbal expression. A crisis in the second year of education is to some extent a natural consequence of the process by which a structure of links between spoken and written language is established. New experiences and new challenges connected with learning the skill of communicating through writing, directed at creating the awareness of the structure of the written sentences should, in the author's opinion, aim at realizing and mastering linguistic operation and knowledge in both spheres of language. The intensification of didactic expectations in the sphere of written language with a simultaneous lack of challenges and stimulation in the spoken language, observed in early primary education, needs to be modified; it needs a different approach to the process of developing language skills. The indicators of children's narrative skills in the first years of education are: priority given to free expression in the first year, a technical approach to linguistic education in the second, and technical development of language skills plus a growing sense and development of communicative competence in the third. Empirical indicators of linguistic activity with regard to productivity and creativity show that the child makes use of the multi-faceted and multi-functional system of a language in an individual and subjective way. The children's verbal messages were created along two semantic paths: metaphorically—one unit of language is associated with another, or metonymically—through adjacency. In conclusion Filipiak emphasized the presence of unexploited areas of children's linguistic activity at all levels of early education, which is the result of the inefficient process of teaching linguistic skills in Polish schools.

A similar conclusion was reached by Malgorzata Zytko as a result of an opinion poll among teachers on the linguistic education of children aged between 6 and 9 (Zytko 1999). The survey was carried out in 1998, based on a group of 302 early primary teachers, who were a diverse group with regard to the place of residence and seniority at work. A questionnaire was used which consisted of 53 statements about children's linguistic education. The respondents were asked to express their attitude to the statements on a four-point scale. The analysis of the responses made it possible to distinguish four types of views on linguistic education: linguistic formalism, with the teacher as a guard of correctness; spontaneity in linguistic development, with the teacher supporting the child's linguistic independence; didactic pessimism, with the teacher as critic of the effectiveness of linguistic education; linguistic communication, with the teacher as facilitator in contacts with others.

It turned out that the followers of the first view—linguistic formalism—are the most numerous. In that approach the teacher, as a monopolist of linguistic knowledge, carefully sets and organizes linguistic tasks for the children, taking care that they do not make mistakes. The student becomes a recipient of rules and principles regulating the use of language, and should try to imitate the teacher as a model, and patiently do exercises. He or she is not expected to show self-reliance in using language. The system of teaching language to young children might be improved, according to the author, if the system of teacher training was reformed. What is needed is not only a change in curricula and raising the linguistic awareness of early primary teachers, but also overcoming the stereotype of the decisive importance of formal, theoretical knowledge about language in the education of young children.

Teaching Reading

The next area of interest is teaching reading. Ewa Arciszewska approached the problem of the effectiveness of the methods used to teach reading skills to preschool children (Arciszewska 2000). In the first stage of her research she identified and described those methods used, and then attempted to determine their effectiveness. Eighteen groups of children from three regions were studied. The groups were chosen based on the methods used to teach them reading: either innovative or standard, as determined by a survey among teachers. Diagnostic tests were administered in seven "standard" groups, where the teacher uses traditional, analytical-synthetic and phonetic methods in teaching reading skills (those groups comprised 161 children), three groups described as "extended", where standard methods were supplemented with some innovations, or where the teacher used innovative methods in other fields than reading (73 children), and eight alternative groups, which worked using non-standard methods (192 children). The author found that the effective use of both standard and alternative models depends on the knowledge, skills and motivation of the teacher. Inappropriate application of any method may deform the mechanisms and instruments a child needs to build up new knowledge. A wise teacher's flexibility—the readiness to modify planned activities according to the situation and the students' needs, applying the principle minimize the presentation of ready-made knowledge and examples of problem-solving strategies; provoke, as often as possible, situations in which a child can discover or construct knowledge by himself/herself is enough to effectively develop reading skills in most children. It is necessary to be reconciled to the fact that despite the teacher's and students' efforts, some children will always read better, others worse, and others will learn it later. The main advantage of innovation and alternative methods is that they make it easier to apply that principle and do not limit the teacher or the child. There is therefore a case for moving away from the traditional model of teaching reading. The attachment to the routines of the standard model, such as instructions, excludes flexibility, limits the age at which a child is expected to read and therefore shortens the possible time for training and makes more intensive practice necessary. The value of being able to read is not clear to the child, or is made clear too late, so he or she does not understand the purpose of the exercises. These and other conclusions drawn by the author demonstrate that using uniform methods to teach reading is the least effective way.

The problem of teaching reading in year 1 was investigated by Barbara Murawska in 1999 (Murawska, 2003). The aim of the project was to diagnose the school-type skills of children starting their school education in order for the teacher to be able to adjust the syllabus to what they already know and can do. A total of 36 first-year classes and 5 classes of six-year-olds form 15 primary schools in a big city were studied. The skills of 770 first-year students and 86 six-year-olds were diagnosed. The analysis of the findings allowed the formulation of valuable recommendations for educational policy. Firstly, between the ages of 6 and 7 a very rapid progress in reading, writing and arithmetic skills is observed. It is certainly due to preschool education, but it probably also has developmental reasons. This openness to education suggests that six-year-olds might be subject to compulsory education and benefit from it. Secondly, the children's skills in the studied areas were much higher than could be expected at the start of primary school in accordance with the curricula. This shows that the curricula currently in force are only effective when working with a small groups of children—those whose reading, writing and arithmetic skills are poor. Those children—and they constitute more than a half of all—who can read, write and perform simple calculations when starting primary school are not learning so much as they may. At the same time children who have none of these skills are doomed to failure at school. Thirdly, there are enormous differences in school-type skills between children entering primary schools. School education can only be effective if it is individualized—not in isolated cases, but as a rule. Curricula taking such individualization into account should provide a starting point.

Social and Moral Development

Conflicts among preschool children are among a teacher's most important problems. Malgorzata Cywinska has attempted a description of conflict situations, focusing on the motives of the conflicts, behavior during a conflict and ways of exiting conflicts. (Cywilska, 1996). The main research methods were observation and interview. Sixty-five children aged 5 and 6 from one urban kindergarten were studied. The analysis of the gathered information allowed the author to classify conflicts between children. The most common type are rivalry conflicts, where the motive is the will to possess something. Conflicts of norms have also been noted: their motive was the demand for set and accepted rules in games to be strictly observed. The third type are conflicts related to the sense of identity, where a child wants to defend his or her rights or position. Conflicts among children, the author stresses, are aggressive in character; she observed physical and verbal violence. Aggressive behavior in conflict situations is related to children's contact with their parents: the more negative the parents' emotional attitude to the child, the more prone he or she is to violent behavior. The most difficult moment of a conflict is the exit phase. The most common forms of behavior are complaining to a teacher or withdrawing. The ability to deal with a conflict situation is related to the level of moral development.

An attempt to determine the understanding of moral concepts by country children aged 6 to 10 was made by Renata Pasik (Pasik, 1999). Her study concerned 10 concepts: lazy, jealous, friendly, theft (stealing), lying, fair, brave, forgiving, obedient, hurt. 64 children for one rural school were interviewed. The analysis of what they said shows that the understanding of moral concepts among country children aged 6 to 10 is at a level of images and concrete. The most common way of explaining those notions is by giving examples, where the word is associated with one or several instances of specific behavior covered by the notion. The understanding of the concepts is descriptive. Children's moral notions are shaped, the author emphasizes, by their personal experience in their social milieu. Usually a certain type of behavior is associated with a particular concept. Those associations are not always correct. The limited life experience, problems with generalizing and imperfect use of language mean that the understanding of moral concepts among children from rural areas is decidedly low.

Problems of Educational Reform

As part of the public debate on the reform of education in Poland, several diagnoses and studies were carried out related to the state of education, threats posed by unequal access to education, and changes regarding curricula, syllabuses and teaching methods. In the area of early primary education, as part of a monitoring project run by the independent Institute of Public Affairs (Instytut Spraw Publicznych), Roman Dolata studied the functioning of the system of evaluation in primary school, including descriptive evaluation. (Dolata, 2001). 20 teachers of year 2 from a random sample of primary schools were interviewed. In each of the schools one teacher with between 6 and 12 years of experience was selected. The interview concerned first the teacher's understanding of the essence of descriptive evaluation and the principles of current and classifying evaluation, moving form current to final evaluation and communicating results to students and parents. Teachers were also asked about their opinions of descriptive evaluation. In the second, most important part of the interview the teacher was asked for a detailed description of the performance of two students: a good one and a weak one. Another source of information about evaluation were the school records. Parents of the children taught by the interviewed teachers were also interviewed. They were asked to fill in a questionnaire concerning their views on descriptive evaluation. Among many interesting observations made by the author of the study, the following are most noteworthy: the understanding of descriptive evaluation was mostly gained through contact with short, practical guideline brochures, which did not contain any critical discussion of the different contexts of innovation. Although most teachers admit that descriptive evaluation eliminates the element of selection and is oriented towards emphasizing the student's achievements in a positive way, in practice, an alarmingly large number of teachers see descriptive evaluation as a mere change of form. Most have a negative emotional attitude to it because of the drastic workload it involves. In this respect, changes are certainly necessary to rationalize the teachers' work. The language of descriptive evaluation is strikingly uniform, which means the informative value of those descriptions is limited.

Parents' opinions regarding descriptive evaluation vary. Generally, however, the prevailing view is that evaluation in the form of a grade was better. Interestingly, this opinion is more often expressed by parents with higher education, whose children have a better chance of succeeding at school.

The idea of correcting educational inequality, which was one of the basic ideas of educational reform in Poland, is not being realized, as research findings show. Research by Barbara Murawska indicates that segregation begins at the start of primary education (Murawska 2003). The aim of the study was to get to know the enrolment procedures and procedures for sorting pupils into classes, as it is possible to suppose that those procedures are the beginning of the process producing social inequality in education. Enrolment in public schools in Poland is by district: a school is required to accept all children from its district; after that, it can fill the remaining places with children from outside. This allows schools to pick children according to their own criteria. Information regarding entrance procedures in primary schools and the procedures for dividing first-year pupils into classes was obtained from three sources: parents, teachers and head teachers The study was conducted in 40 randomly chosen state primary schools in Warsaw. The "segregation effect" was calculated for 38 of them because in two there was only one first-year group in each. Information was gathered regarding 130 first-year classes. 104 teachers teaching such classes responded to a questionnaire. 1824 parents filled in a questionnaire, most of them mothers. Interviews were conducted with 36 heads and deputy heads of primary schools. The research was carried out in 2001.

The analysis of the data showed that the division of pupils among schools explains 7% of the variance of the SES indicator. The division of pupils into classes explains 15% of the variance of the SES indicator. This means that the schools and the procedures used by them in sorting pupils into classes are responsible for 8% of the segregation effect. Those procedures differ and depend on a schools ideology. There are schools with active anti-segregation policies, where the segregation effect is close to zero. In other schools, the procedures used lead to considerable differences in the social set-up of classes. Those differences are usually a secondary effect of the school's actions. There are also schools that apply procedures that are bound to increase the segregation indicator.

Supporting Local Educators

In the mid-1990s a cooperation between academic centers and local educators began. One example of such collaboration is the support given to the educators in the town of Kwidzyn by a team from the Department of Pedagogy, Warsaw University, consisting of Elzbieta Putkiewicz, Barbara Murawska and Roman Dolata, (Dolata, Murawska, Putkiewicz 2001). Since 1996 that team has conducted annual diagnoses of primary school students' academic achievement. After each monitoring a report was produced, addressed to the town authorities, teachers and head teachers. Each report consisted of three parts. Part one contained a discussion of all the test questions and an analysis of errors made by the children. Part two presented results achieved by children form different schools in the town. Part three, which contained the results of each particular class, was treated as confidential and given directly to the teachers working with that class. The results always took into account the students' socio-economic status (SES).

A diagnosis of the skills of students beginning year 1 of primary school was carried out in 1998 using the (already mentioned) questionnaire "Get to Know Your Students". The results were comparable with those obtained from children from a large city. It turned out that more than a half of the children had already acquired basic reading, writing and arithmetic skills. The diagnosis of children's skills at the beginning of school education was a starting point for the introduction of individualized teaching. We tested its efficiency by monitoring the skills of second-year pupils. To have a point of reference, we first carried out the test with second-year students in 1998. Linguistic and mathematical skills were tested. The questions were not strictly matched to the requirements of the curriculum. Some went beyond the curriculum, some appeared quite banal. This was done in order to obtain information about the whole range of students' achievements, from the poorest to a level that we might consider impossible to achieve for children at this age. Mathematical skills were tested by three blocks of problems: decimal notation, basic arithmetic, descriptive mathematical problems, and mathematics in everyday life, fractions and elements of geometry. Language skills were diagnosed through nine types of tasks: error correction, composing sentences, matching opposites, matching similar words, understanding clichés, recognizing inappropriately used words, recognizing the correct meaning if words, composing a description. In 1999 we diagnosed the children who were taught using the individualized method. It turned out that second-year students' skills had only improved in some areas. The children did decidedly better at reading mathematical texts, solving problems of the type "mathematics in everyday life", geometry and producing words with similar meanings. There were no significant differences in arithmetic, error correction, matching opposites and composing a story.

Third-year pupils' skills were diagnosed in 1996. As in the other diagnoses, linguistic and mathematical skills were tested. In building the tests, the authors started with the analysis of the curriculum for early primary education and the requirements children would have to meet in further education in order to identify the main aims of teaching. Then questions and problems were developed to test the realization of those aims. The result was a test covering: in mathematics, basic arithmetic, descriptive problems, solving equations; in linguistic skills, reading comprehension (tested in three ways: following instructions, filling gapped sentences and understanding a text) and composing a story. The results of the maths test indicated that children rarely displayed what might be called mathematical resourcefulness; they achieved better results when applying algorithmic procedures than when required to use flexible, critical thinking. That conclusion came as no surprise to the teachers. Although the reasons are complex, the teachers agreed that the main cause is lack of individual effort and self-reliance in solving problems. In the course of the discussion of third-year students' test results the authors of the study wonder how to abandon traditional lessons and have children face mathematical problems individually. The tested students also displayed a certain helplessness when faced with descriptive mathematical problems. They had problems reading and understanding their content. It is a consequence of difficulties with learning reading comprehension, reading instructions, discovering the relationship between colloquial language and the formalized language of mathematics, and grasping the role of the latter in understanding a text. A relatively low level of achievement was also noted in reading short, popular texts on scientific subjects.

Another example of collaboration between academics and practitioners in the field of education is the private primary school in Olsztyn. It was founded in cooperation with the University of Warmia and Mazury and maintains constant cooperation with it. The observation of school practice inspired Dorota Klus-StaŁska to reflect on ways in which students structure their school knowledge (Klus-StaŁska 2002). The purpose of the study was to form a theoretical basis for the interpretation of events occurring in the classroom in the context of cultural change. In order to achieve that aim, other objectives had to be set, such as selecting terms which are particularly meaningful from the point of view of school knowledge, discovering the relations between those terms and events in the classroom, interpreting the classroom events from the selected perspective. The research consisted in observing lessons in more than ten state schools and the private school already mentioned. An analysis of the observation material led the author to describe two different models of lessons, which she called dialogue and monologue education. Each of those models has a different structure, which makes students build their own knowledge in different ways. Monologue education, although it serves many functions, is not sufficient. Only dialogue education establishes a relationship between the student and the teacher and between the student and the knowledge he or she is acquiring. The features of that relationship are: increasing the student's responsibility for his of her own knowledge, the opportunity to discover the sense of what one is doing, replacing an imposed order of meanings with one created by oneself, elimination of cognitive dependence on the teacher and replacing feigned emotions and values with authentic ones.

Research Prospects

As the review of the research shows, the research topics concern selected issues and do not form a well-thought-over field of analysis. They rather reflect the interests of certain individuals than pursuing a defined research policy. The majority of then have little chance of influencing the shape of education at national level. They are rather a stimulus to the revision of teachers' opinions and a demonstration of ways of proceeding methodologically in contacts with children. In the present economic situation of the country there is no sign that this situation is going to change. Research funds—compared to those in other countries are very limited and their distribution is linked with the prestige of a given area of knowledge. Still neither the state nor local authorities recognize the importance of an early education for children's development so the research funds are extremely difficult to obtain. All the efforts were put into the preparation of educational reform in 1999 and its implementation.

The publishing market is full of manuals for teachers dealing with the problem of work with the young child and for heads of schools, showing how to be a good manager. Most of those publications use the research results from others countries or include a set of speculative opinions.

Relationships with concrete pieces of research are rare. I hope that research policy will be changed. Lately, there has been increasing public interest in young children's education, influenced by the activity of people appreciating the significance of that stage of education.

REFERENCES

Arciszewska E. (2002). *Czytajace przedszkolaki: mit czy norma?* (Kindergarten readers: Myth or a standard?) Warszawa, ZAK.

Bielen, B., Zegadlo-Malkowska H. (1998). Developmental achievements of 7-year-old children in Poland in the light of international tests and requirements of the Polish Language School Programme. International Journal of Early Years Education, 6, 2, s. 177-185.

Blumsztajn A. (2002). Dostep dzieci wiejskich do jakosciowej edukacji przedszkolnej w Polsce. W: Ogrodzinska T. (red.) Koncepcja wyrównywania szans edukacyjnych mlodszych dzieci poprzez upowszechnienie wychowania przedszkolnego i obnizenie wieku obowiazku szkolnego do szesciu lat. (The access of rural school children to qualitative kindergarten education in Poland. In: OgrodziŁska T. The concept of evening-out of educational opportunities of young children by spread of kindergarten education and lowering the age of school duty to 6). Warszawa,

Bokus B. (2000). *Swiaty fabuly w narracji dzieciecej* (The world of plot in children's narration). Warszawa, Energeia.

Branska E. (2002). Szanse i zagrozenia edukacji przedszkolnej. (Opportunities and dangers of pre-school education). "Wychowanie w Przedszkolu", 2, 67 - 71.

Cywinska M. (1996). Dziecko piecio- i szescioletnie w sytuacjach konfliktu z rówiesnikami- relacja z badan (The 5-6-year old child in the situation of conflict with peers). "Kwartalnik Pedagogiczny", 1, 119-131.

Dolata, R. (2001). Reforma wewnetrznego oceniania osiagniec uczniów uczniów szkole podstawowej. W: Konarzewski K. (red.) Szkolnictwo w pierwszym roku reformy systemu oswiaty (The reform of internal evaluation of pupils' achievement in primary school. In: Konarzewski K. The school system in the first year of educational reform). Warszawa, Instytut Spraw Publicznych.

Dolata, R., Murawska, B., & Putkiewicz, E. (2001). *Monitorowanie osiagniec szkolnych jako metoda wspierania lokalnego srodowiska edukacyjnego.* (School achievement monitoring as a method of endorsing the local educational community). Warszawa, Wydawnictwo Akademickie ZAK.

Oswiata i wychowanie w roku szkolnym 2001/2002. (Education in the school year 2001/2002) GUS 2002.

Filipiak E. (1996). *Aktywnosc jezykowa dzieci w wieku wczesnoszkolnym.* (Language activity in early education children). Bydgoszcz, Wydawnictwo Wyzszej Szkoly Pedagogicznej.

Frymark W. (1996). *Rozwiazywanie problemów przez analogie u dzieci szescioletnich.* (Analogical problem solving in 6-year-old children). "Kwartalnik Pedagogiczny", 3-4, 59-76.

Grzelak, Sz. (2003). Akademia Rodzinna w Kobylce. W: Zahorska M. (red.) Edukacja przedszkolna w Polsce—szanse i zagrozenia. (Family academy in Kobylka. In: Zahorska M. Pre-school education in Poland—opportunities and dangers). Warszawa, Instytut Spraw Publicznych.

Kaminska, K. (2003). Upowszechnienie edukacji przedszkolnej w Polsce—stan i prognozy na przyszlosc. W: Zahorska M. (red.) Edukacja przedszkolna w Polsce—szanse i zagroğenia. (The spread of kindergarten education in Poland—current state and future forecast. In: Zahorska M. Pre-school education in Poland—opportunities and dangers). Warszawa, Instytut Spraw Publicznych.

Karwowska-Struczyk, M. (1998). Childrens' activities and their effect on child development: The results if the IEA Pre-primary Project in Poland. International Journal of Early Years Education, 6, 2, s. 207-243.

Karwowska-Struczyk, M. (1999). Summary and implications of the IEA Pre-primary Project phase 2 study in Poland. In: The IEA Preprimary Project. Poland phase 2 study findings, a report prepared for the World Bank, Washington, D. C., USA, High Scope Educational Research Foundation, Ypsilanti, MI, s. 1-14.

Karwowska-Struczyk M. (2000). *Nisze ekologiczne a rozwój dziecka.* (Ecological niches and child development). Warszawa, Wydawnictwo Instytutu BadaŁ Edukacyjnych.

Key data on education in Europe—2002 edition. Euridice 2002.

Klus-Stanska D. (2001). Integracja i dezintegracja wiedzy szkolnej. Uwagi na marginesie koncepcji Basila Bernsteina. (School knowledge integration and disintegration. Some remarks concerning Basil Bernstein theory). "Kwartalnik Pedagogiczny", 3-4, 87-103.

Klus-Stanska, D. (2002). *Konstruowanie wiedzy szkolnej.* (Constructing school knowledge). Olsztyn, Wydawnictwo Uniwersytetu Warminsko-Mazurskiego.

Konarzewski, K. (red.) (2001). *Szkolnictwo w pierwszym roku reformy systemu oswiaty.* (The schooling system in the first year of educational reform). Warszawa, Instytut Spraw Publicznych.

Kostynowicz J., & Kuklinska Z. (2003). Male dziecko w reformie oswiaty. W: Zahorska M. (red.) Edukacja przedszkolna w Polsce—szanse i zagrozenia. (The young child in educational reform. In Zahorska M. Pre-school education in Poland—opportunities and dangers). Warszawa, Instytut Spraw Publicznych.

Lotys, M. (2003). Gmina Barciany. W: : Zahorska M. (red.) Edukacja przedszkolna w Polsce—szanse i zagrozenia. (Barciany commune. In: Zahorska M. Pre-school education in Poland—opportunities and dangers). Warszawa, Instytut Spraw Publicznych.

Lubowiecka J. (2001). Szanse edukacyjne dzieci przedszkolnych. (Educational opportunities of pre-school children). "Wychowanie w Przedszkolu", 7, 392-397.

Minimum programowe przedmiotów ogólnoksztalcacych w szkolach podstawowych i srednich obowiazujace od 1 wrzesnia 1992. (Minimum programme of general subjects in primary and secondary schools binding since 1. 09. 1992). (1992) Warszawa, Fundacja Rozwoju Edukacji Narodowej.

Murawska B. (2003). Social segregation at the start of primary education. Kwartalnik Pedagogiczny, 1-2.

Murawska B. (2003). Training teachers to diagnose students' skills at start of primary education. W: Putkiewicz E., Wilkomirska A. (red.) Problems of teacher education in the rolling changes of education systems all over the world. Warszawa,Wydawnictwo UW. (in press)

Ogrodzinska T. (red.) (2002). *Koncepcja wyrównywania szans edukacyjnych mlodszych dzieci poprzez upowszechnienie wychowania przedszkolnego i obnizenie wieku obowiazku szkolnego do szesciu lat.* (The concept of evening-out of educational opportunities of young children by spread of pre-school education and lowering the age of school duty to 6). Warszawa,

Pasik R. (1999). Z badan nad rozumieniem pojec moralnych przez dzieci wiejskie w wieku 6-10 lat. (Of research on moral issues comprehension by country children aged 6-10). "Kwartalnik Pedagogiczny", 1, 143-150.

Podstawa programowa dla szkól podstawowych i gimnazjów. (Programme base for primary and junior high schools) (1999). www.men.waw.pl

Podstawa programowa wychowania przedszkolnego dla przedszkoli i oddzialów przedszkolnych w szkolach podstawowych. (Programme base for pre-school education for kindergartens and kindergarten group in primary schools) (2000). www.men.waw.pl

Program nauczania poczatkowego. (Early school curriculum) (1979). Ministerstwo Oswiaty i Wychowania Instytut Programów Szkolnych. Warszawa, Wydawnictwa Szkolne i Pedagogiczne.

Program wychowania w przedszkolu. (Pre-school curriculum) (1973). Ministerstwo Oswiaty i Wychowania Instytut Programów Szkolnych. Warszawa, Wydawnictwa Szkolne i Pedagogiczne.

The education system in Portugal. Eurybase 2001.

Reforma systemu edukacji. Projekt. (The reform of the educational system in Poland). (1998). MEN. Warszawa, Wydawnictwa Szkolne i Pedagogiczne.

Rozporzadzenie Ministra Edukacji Narodowej z 19 kwietnia 1999 r. w sprawie zasad oceniania, klasyfikowania i promowania uczniów i sluchaczy oraz przeprowadzania egzaminów i sprawdzianów w szkolach publicznych. (The order of the Minister of National Education of 19. 04. 1999 on the rules of evaluation; classification and promotion of pupils and studentsand conducting examinations and check-ups).

Sutkowska, M. (2000). *Male przedszkole wiejskie—praca z grupa z róznym wieku.* (The small country kindergarten—working with a group of mixed age children). Warszawa, "Male dziecko", TRIO.

Ustawa o rozwoju systemu oswiaty i wychowania w Polsce Ludowej. (Act of development of school system in the Polish People's Republic) (1961). Warszawa, PaŁstwowe Zaklady Wydawnictw Szkolnych.

Ustawa o systemie oswiaty z 7 wrzesnia 1991 roku. (Act of education system of 7.09.1991). Dz. U. 1996, nr 67.

Ustawa z 8 stycznia 1999 roku, przepisy wprowadzajace reforme ustroju szkolnego. (Act of 8.01.1999—regulations introducing the reform of school system). Dz. U. 1999, nr 12.

Wilgocka-Okon B. (1993). Przedszkole. (Kindergarten). W: Encyklopedia Pedagogiczna. Warszawa, Fundacja Innowacja.

Zytko M. (1999). Opinie nauczycieli o edukacji jezykowej dzieci w wieku 6-9 lat. (Teachers' opinions on language education of children aged 6-9). "Kwartalnik Pedagogiczny", 2, 118-129.

Zytko M. (red.) (2002). *Ksztalcenie zintegrowane. Problemy teorii i praktyki.* (Integrated education. Theoretical and practical problems). Warszawa, Wydawnictwo Akademickie Zak.

CHAPTER 9

RESEARCH IN EARLY CHILDHOOD EDUCATION IN PORTUGAL

Teresa Vasconcelos

Presently, I look at children as my masters. I don't think that I have much to teach them. Instead of making them depend upon me, I follow them. I do not have the aim of turning them into esthetic, moral or wise people. I let them work, I let them enjoy. They have so many inner resources!

—Irene Lisboa (1942)

INTRODUCTION

These words, written by the distinguished Portuguese pedagogue and writer, Irene Lisboa—one of the first women primary school teachers trained to become a public pre-school teacher—suggest a *romantic view* of young children, so common in the beginning of 20th century in Portugal and abroad. Yet these words also highlight the bulk of Irene Lisboa's practice as a pedagogue, because she questioned traditional academic primary school practices. In her travels throughout Europe she researched some of the most innovative programs for young children at the time: from Montessori to Décroly, *La Maison des Petits* in Geneva—and even described

International Perspectives on Research in Early Childhood Education, 259–291
Copyright © 2005 by Information Age Publishing
All rights of reproduction in any form reserved.

what was then-called the *Project Method* by Kilpatrick, Dewey's disciple (Lisboa, 1942). Despite her *romantic views*, we now find very *modern* the importance she gives to actively listening to young children and respecting their inner resources. Irene Lisboa was ahead of her time, looking at children as *meaning makers* (Bruner & Haste, 1990).

Despite the work of eminent, innovative pedagogues such as Irene Lisboa, the development of early childhood education in Portugal is a history permeated by contradictions and backlashes, where economic, political, and cultural constraints sometimes prevented the field from evolving at the same pace as in other European countries.

This chapter attempts to describe the "state of the art" of research in a field that, in Portugal, we call *educação de infância* (early childhood education): the care and education of children under 6, which is the age the child begins compulsory schooling. Birth to six, therefore, will be the focus of this work. A brief introduction will present the organization of the educational system in Portugal. The second section of the chapter will provide a historical overview of the development of early childhood education. The third section will describe the present state of early childhood education. The fourth section will reflect on research and policy issues related to early childhood education in Portugal. Finally, a critical review of current research in early childhood will be provided, along with a discussion of trends and issues that require further research. It is important to highlight that this review should be considered incomplete and partial. Our ability to gather data was limited and available information scarce and scattered. Later in the chapter we will explain how the *corpus* of analysis was created.

The current Portuguese educational system (Figure 9.1), according to Law 6/86 with the changes introduced by Law 115/97,[1] starts when the child is 3-years-old, in what legislators call *preschool education*—the first stage of basic education. Compulsory education age starts at the age of 6, with the so-called *first cycle of basic education* (previously called primary school). The *second cycle of basic education* is then followed by the *third cycle of basic education*. If children do not fail a grade, they will complete nine years of compulsory education by the age of 14-15. They then may take three years of *secondary education*, which will give them access to higher education: As an alternative, they may choose to attend vocational schools which will prepare them to enter the work force at the age of 18. They may also enter the work market directly at age 16, after completing the last two years of compulsory schooling with a training component recognized by the Ministry of Labor. This last program provides them with credentials that give them access to the job market. Future changes in legislation are slated to make completion of secondary education compulsory.

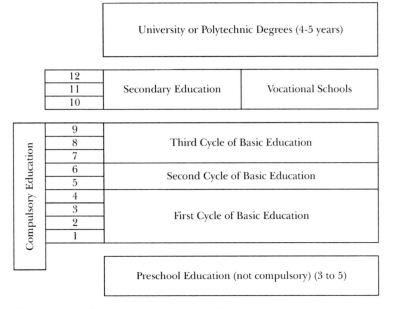

Figure 9.1.   The educational system in Portugal.

Despite the drive to prolong compulsory education a high percentage of children (up to 10 %) do not complete nine years of compulsory education and drop out of school, or only finish it after several years of repeated failure. Yet despite the work of eminent and innovative pedagogues such as Irene Lisboa, and the efforts put into adult in-service training, and although formal recognition is given to acquired skills, the rate of illiteracy among the adult population is still around 11%, and a significant percentage of the population (47.3%) has a low level of literacy.[2]

The development of Portuguese society since the April 25, 1974, Revolution, which re-established democracy in Portugal, has been remarkable, but it has not been consistent, due to economic and cultural constraints. Women's rights, immediately recognized in the 1976 Constitution, have only gradually been acknowledged in practice, even though women continue to be the main caretakers for very young children. Portugal is one of the countries in Europe where most women work outside the home on a full-time basis: 80.3% of all Portuguese women aged 25-34 years work full-time (1999 data) and families need support services for their children. Despite the hardship, in 1997, 59.7% of the population with college-level degrees were women. However, old cultural models, traditional division of tasks, and salary disparities still prevail and ultimately lead to limited opportunities, injustice and inequity. This fact is relevant if one is

to understand the extent to which the history of early childhood education is connected with women's struggle for freedom and equity.

HISTORY OF EARLY CHILDHOOD EDUCATION IN PORTUGAL

We can trace the beginnings of early childhood institutional care and protection in Portugal to 1485 when Queen Leonor created the *Misericórdias*,
charitable organizations and establishments developed and run by the
Catholic Church, to provide shelter and food to abandoned children, the
elderly and the sick. Poor children, at that time, were kept at home until
the age of 7 and then sent to work. By the 18th century, the *Misericórdias*
had fulfilled the role of protecting abandoned children until that age, giving them training—including instruction in reading and writing—then
sending them into the labor market. Only much later, with the liberaliza-
tion of the Monarchy in the beginnings of 19th century (Liberal Revolution of 1820), and the separation of power between the State and the
Catholic Church, was there a concern for compulsory and free elementary
education for all children. The first two Normal Schools for teacher training were created in 1835 and, simultaneously, King Pedro IV created the
Sociedades das Casas da Infância Desvalida (Asylums for Deprived Children)
all over the country for the protection of poor and abandoned children.
The management of these asylums was given to private secular boards.
We may conclude that the issue of "care" and "custody" for young children in Portugal, as well as a vision of early education mainly as a "social
problem " permeated by principles of Christian charity was, since the
beginning, aimed at overcoming poverty, abandonment and infant mortality. Such a vision strongly influenced the development of the field.

Liberal ideas coming from Northern Europe brought the influence of
the kindergarten movement from Germany and the concern for educating young children through play. The first Froebelian public kindergarten
(*jardim de infância*) was established in 1882 by the municipality of Lisbon
in a public garden: Froebelian materials and activities (gifts and "occupa-
tions") were imported, and a few young ladies received training in Germany to become kindergarten teachers. The requirements demanded
they be "healthy, strong, dedicated" and possess a "missionary vision." By
the end of the 19th century, several writers and intellectuals, including
João de Deus, António Feliciano de Castilho, Joaquim de Vasconcelos,
Carolina Michaelis de Vasconcelos, Adolfo Coelho and others, had developed readers or children's books containing traditional tales to help to
raise the level of literacy among the Portuguese population. Almost simultaneously, it was mandated that every factory with more than 50 women-
workers create a crèche, 0 to 3, according to the principles of the "hygien-

ists" (Ferreira, 2000), meaning that the primary concern, in those early years, was to be the safeguarding of children's health.

On October 10, 1910, Portugal became a republic and successive but unstable governments declared the importance of education for a country that was then 75% illiterate. It was believed that raising consciousness through education, meaning an awareness of one's potential for self-improvement, was an important condition for a more fair, free and humane society. A new law[3] created a public system of what was then called "pre-primary education for children of both sexes" and, in August of the same year, a curriculum was introduced that was based on play, but encouraged reading and writing as well. It was thought that teachers "should have the most complete pedagogical, moral and professional training". At least one specialized course trained 11 former primary school teachers (among them Irene Lisboa) to work in pre-primary class-rooms near laboratory primary schools attached to Normal Schools. Yet between 1912 and 1926 very few public kindergartens were created (only serving 1% of children from 3 to 6 years of age). In 1911, João de Deus Ramos, son of the poet João de Deus, created the first João de Deus private *jardim de infância*, which was influenced by Froebelian ideas, as well as by republican and humanitarian ideals of citizenship and education for all. These kindergartens accepted children from 3 to 8 and were aimed at combating the high levels of illiteracy among the Portuguese population. They therefore introduced reading and writing at an early age, using the readers (*Cartilha Maternal*) created by the poet, João de Deus. The architecture of these kindergartens was typically Portuguese and all the class-rooms opened onto a large space resembling a Portuguese *praça* or town square. João de Deus also created *itinerant schools* to promote adult literacy.

By then, two systems coexisted in the field of early childhood: a system of welfare and social services (day care), connected to the Ministry of Social Affairs which supported private charities, whose strong ideology of dependency was closely linked to charitable practices; and an emerging system of *jardins de infância* (kindergartens) aimed at preparing all children for public schooling. However, the latter system was less capable of becoming universal, due to the instability of governments during the First Republic.

In 1926 a coup d'état installed the dictatorship of António de Oliveira Salazar. This dictatorship had a strong ideological concern with religion and the preservation of traditional family values. Women were meant to stay at home taking care of their children; the existing public kindergartens were closed in 1937, and compulsory school was reduced to 4 years for boys and 3 years for girls. Between 1936 and 1942, Normal Schools, which were then centers for innovation and research in pedagogy, were closed. Irene Lisboa, one of the leading pedagogues of the time, was forced into early retirement. The now-defunct pre-school educational system, was replaced by the *Obra das Mães pela Educação Nacional* (Mothers' Movement for National Education). It was a movement controlled ideologically by the State, and aimed at better preparing women for their role as mothers and providers of "children for the nation". Yet between 1940 and 1960 women in the work force increased by 80% due to industrial development, massive male emigration to other countries created by endemic poverty, and the outbreak of war in Portugal's overseas colonies. The need for services for young children increased, but they were services connected with the Ministries of Health and Social Affairs. Public pre-school education remained non-existent until the new rise of parliamentary democracy in April, 1974. Social sciences, such as psychology, sociology, and anthropology, were considered "dangerous" and subversive. Only didactics prevailed, as well as traditional subjects such as Mathematics, Science, and the Portuguese language. The arts were also undervalued in all public schools.

Yet there was some resistance in civil society, especially in private colleges where teacher-education was taking place. In the 1940s the João de Deus Movement of Kindergartens was allowed to start its own training of teachers, called the *educadoras do povo* (people's educators). Later, in the fifties, two private schools training early childhood educators (*educadoras de infância*), which were closely connected with the Catholic Church, were created in Lisbon. Then, in the 1960s, two other schools were created in Oporto in the north and Coimbra in the center of the country. The philosophy of these teacher training schools was based on Christian and humanistic values. They introduced Montessori's and Décroly's methods into Portuguese pedagogy and were responsible for some of the country's most progressive pedagogical innovations during those days. During the early 1960s the *Movimento da Escola Moderna* (Modern School Movement), which introduced Portugal to Freinet's[4] Pedagogy (Niza, 1992), created an underground organization of teachers (there was no freedom of assembly or right to organize labor unions) which promoted pedagogical innovation in private settings and also linked schooling to the student's introduction to democratic life and the cooperative reconstruction of culture (Niza, 1992; 1996).

In the 1960s the Portuguese *educadoras de infância* worked within the social services that had been set up for young children (day care, crèches, hospitals, boarding centers, and summer camps) or in emerging private schools and kindergartens for well-off families. For many young women, it was an acceptable and fulfilling profession until—at least in most cases—it came time to marry and raise their own families. Primary school teacher training (Normal Schools), by then reduced to two years, was totally controlled by the State.

The 1971 educational reform of Minister Veiga Simão declared the need to re-institute the preschool educational system; however, only in 1974, with the coup d'état that established democracy, were those intentions acted upon. By then only 10% of Portuguese young children from 0 to 6 had access to social service settings funded by the Ministry of Social Affairs, and a minority had access to pre-primary classrooms in private schools under limited supervision of the Ministry of Education. With the implantation of democracy, a very strong popular movement, led mostly by working-class and rural women, emerged and demanded *jardins de infância* for their young children. The movement promoted the occupation of empty houses, manors and buildings so that they might be used as pre-schools. It was during this period of the mid- and late seventies that public early childhood education developed "not essentially through laws and decrees planned in central offices, but more as a result of the enactment of citizenship and participatory democracy. This enactment meant the capacity and the power of the people—and specifically the parents—to press the Government to develop quality preschool experiences for young children" (Vasconcelos, 1995, p. 117).

In 1977 the public system of pre-school education was created by law and, in 1979, a Statute for Kindergartens *(Estatuto dos Jardins de Infância)* was published.[5] The public education system legalized all kindergartens created during the popular movement and, until 1985, enlarged the public kindergarten system until 12% of all eligible children were enrolled. This included a significant increase in kindergartens in rural areas. A parallel system still existed, run by the Ministry of Social Affairs which had a "care-based" vision of early childhood education and tried to compensate for social inequalities by specifically dealing with children "at risk". The network of crèches for children 0 to 3 was limited to 10%. The reduced number of crèches meant that working women had to rely on extended family or childminders. Most of these childminders had no training or any kind of supervision. Formosinho suggested that "a residual societal perception remains from earlier times when it was considered that all early childhood education is a private affair that only concerns the family" (Formosinho, 1996, p. 3).

The following quote highlights the strong connection between the developments of early education in Portugal and the struggle for democracy and for women's liberation:

It is a history that, like the destiny of children and their education, will swing between the private and the public; a history written in close connection with the history of the family and the history of women; a history

involving both the family and the school; a history that swings between protection and emotionality on one side, and scientific and technical rationality
on the other; a history that exists somewhere between intuition and "know-
how" on one side, and a theoretical-practical normativity on the other; a
postponed history marked by underdevelopments, but one that is also
impregnated with utopia and dreams. (Magalhães, 1997, p. 115).

RECENT DEVELOPMENTS IN THE FIELD

Expanding and developing early childhood education was the aim of
educational policies enacted by the Socialist Party Government which was
in office from 1995 to 2001. A *Program for the Expansion and Development of
Preschool Education* was launched by the Government in 1996 in coordination with local authorities, private nonprofit institutions (charities), and
private for-profit institutions. All these initiatives were led by the Ministry
of Education and involved the Ministry of Work and Social Affairs, the
Ministry of Justice, and the Ministry of Regional Development (Ministério
da Educação, 1996). This Program aimed to create a national network of
kindergartens (3-6 years olds) with the following guidelines:

- To establish program-contracts with municipalities, charities, and
  private entities with a view to expanding and developing pre-school
  education;
- To consider all pre-school centers as fulfilling both an educational
  and a social role;
- To promote a unified system of pedagogical supervision under the
  responsibility of the Ministry of Education;
- To guarantee flexibility of the different types of organizational
  models, according to the social needs of each region;
- To compensate for social and regional inequalities that exist in the
  country.

The attempts to democratize early childhood education became possible because of a political agenda for the field. A remarkable process of
expansion took place. From 36% of coverage in 1988 and 57.5% in 1996/
97, coverage rose to its present figure of 72.7%. This figure represents
84.2% coverage for children of 5, 72.4% for 4-year olds, and 58.3% for 3
year olds (2000/01 data). Forty-seven percent of the schools belong to the
public network, 34% are private nonprofit, and 19% are private for
profit.[6] The Law for Pre-school Education[7] (DEB 1997a, 1998b) considers
preschool as "the first stage of basic education" and, among its goals, aims
at "contributing to equal opportunities in access to education and success-

ful learning" (article 10). The law also considers that "the state has to provide support to areas in most need" (article 5). Preschool education is considered both an educational service for children and a social service for working families, which implies after-school activities, and meals and transportation, according to each family's needs. Further legislation (Decree-Law 147/97) clarified what is understood by equality of opportunities: "equality of opportunities implies that families, independently of their economic possibilities, should have equal access to any pre-school setting" (article 7). Areas in most need were described as: "a) areas where the offer of pre-school settings (both public and private) covers less than 50% of children 3-5 years old; b) areas at risk of school exclusion or social exclusion; c) areas affected by high degrees of school failure; d) urban areas with large populations" (article 23).

Despite the recommendations of specialists, professionals in the field, and researchers, the care and education of children under 3 was left to the Ministry of Social Affairs. Coverage rates for 0-3 year olds are much lower than for 3-5 year olds, and are not more than 13%: 11% of children have access to creches; 0.8% are cared for by childminders. Childminders are women from the community who care for one or more children whose parents are at work. Two other kinds of services may be used by families: mini-creches which are small contexts providing family-like environments (covering 0.05% of all children) and family-creches which are groups of childminders (not less than 12 or more than 20), living in the same geographic area who are given technical and financial support, under the supervision of technical services (charities or nonprofit organizations). 0.70% of children are entrusted to this latter type of service which is becoming the most common day-care model for children under three.

For all teachers, including early childhood educators, a four-year university degree is now required and each classroom of 25 children was required to have at least one licensed *educadora de infância* (early childhood educator). A set of *Curriculum Guidelines* (DEB, 1997b) was developed to enable the Ministry of Education to pedagogically supervise the country's network of kindergartens (3 to 6 years olds). A two year consultation process involving early childhood educators, teacher trainers, administrators, parents, and researchers (Silva, 1997) took place before the final publication of the *Curriculum Guidelines*. The document was considered to be a *Vygotskyan document* (Gaspar, 1998b) by Portuguese researchers, since it outlined the principles of social construction that form the basis for knowledge; and since it was organized around content areas and not, as had traditionally been done, around development areas. The content areas were defined as: personal and social development; creativity and communication (including art, language and literacy, and mathematics); and knowledge of the world (DEB, 1997b, 1998b; Silva,

1997). Autonomy was given to teachers as "curriculum constructors and managers" (Vasconcelos, 1997b). The curriculum guidelines were considered to have the potential to become "a scaffold" for teaching practice, provided educators with the possibility of constantly re-construct them with a critical eye." (Vasconcelos, 2003, p. 206).

Since the eighties, itinerant provision and CAIC's (Centers for community animation) were made available in sparsely populated zones and areas with specific demographic features where it would be difficult to maintain a formal *jardim de infância*.

RESEARCH AND POLICY ISSUES RELATED TO EARLY CHILDHOOD EDUCATION IN PORTUGAL

In 1995, in their critical analysis of research into education in Portugal, Correia and Stoer describe the status of research being done into early childhood education. In their work they make a strong appeal for contributions by sociologists and anthropologists. They point out that to date, most research has been conducted by psychologists and that a multidisciplinary approach to research in the field is required.

Because of the historical developments described earlier, early childhood education was, for many years, a minor field of research, although systematic research had been done into child health and infant mortality. Only during the late 1970s was funding made available for research, but this financial support was largely geared toward issues in developmental psychology and children with special needs. Because of its contribution to the area of early childhood we would like to acknowledge the systematic and thorough research done by Bairrão Ruivo and his team from the late 1970s to the present in Lisbon, and in the early 1980s at Oporto University (Bairrão et al., 1997, 1994, 1989). In his work he introduced the ECERS scale (Early Childhood Environment Rating Scale, Harms & Clifford, 1980) which used a nationwide sample, and provided useful information on the quality of early childhood education throughout the country.

A great deal of pedagogical experimentation and innovation took place in the late 1970s and early 1980s with pioneering projects that were primarily conducted in rural or socio-economically deprived urban areas. These projects coordinated early childhood educational initiatives with family and community development activities, using an action-research approach (for a in-depth study of these projects, see Silva, 1996). Without imposing a single organizational or developmental model, the projects shaped the field of early childhood education by involving local communities and resources and creating synergies which emphasized child development that was rooted in traditional cultural contexts. Given the limited public funding available for research in early childhood education, most of the projects were funded by private entities such as the Gulbenkian, Van Leer, and Agga Khan Foundations. Thus, in the absence of public policies, the role of private entities was crucial to research and innovation in the field. The *Instituto das Comunidades Educativas* (Institute for Educational Communities), founded in 1992 and sponsored both by private foundations and public subsidies, has been involved in the ongoing development of projects and programs in rural or sparsely populated zones and areas with specific populations such as Roma children or migrant workers (D'Epinay & Canário, 1994).

In 1997, using European Community funding, the *Fundação para a Ciência e Tecnologia* (Foundation for Science and Technology) joined several public entities together under the common banner of "continually promoting the advancement of scientific and technological knowledge in Portugal". This public Foundation provides scholarships for advanced training and education and funding for research projects. Another public Institute, the *Instituto de Inovação Educacional* (Institute for Educational Innovation), which has supported key research and innovation programs in schools since 1987, has been recently terminated. This Institute was responsible for the research journal *Inovação* (Innovation) which published a significant number of works on early childhood and primary education.

Yet other entities in civil society are consistently lending support to the field. APEI, the Association of Early Childhood Educators, founded in 1976, has been consistently turning out significant work of interest to involved professionals. A specialized professional journal, *Cadernos de Educação de Infância*, subscribed to by a substantial number of early childhood educators, was created in 1986.

The *Associação Criança* (Childhood Association) founded by researchers from the Minho University in 1996, promotes research and innovation around curriculum models for early childhood education (Oliveira-Formosinho, 1996), and has been involved in adapting and experimenting in Portugal with scales such as the ECERS (Harms & Clifford, 1980), COR, PIP (High/Scope, 1989), the Louvain Involvement Scale (Laevers, 1994) that measure early childhood environments. These scales would provide teachers with tools for self-assessment. Aside from the work described above, the *Associação Criança* has, in general, been working towards a significant improvement of preschool settings in the northern region of Portugal (Oliveira-Formosinho & Formosinho, 2001).

In 1998 an association of early childhood researchers, the Study Group for the Development of Early Childhood Education (GEDEI), was formally created. For several years it had been an informal support group of researchers connected with different universities and polytechnics. The GEDEI, currently an association with individual and institutional associates, organizes one international research symposium per year on relevant issues in the field and edits the only specialized early childhood research journal in the country, *Infância e Educação—Investigação e Práticas* (Infancy and Education—Research and Practices).

The developments that have taken place since the 1970s show that organized civil society and research centers in universities and polytechnics have steadily started assuming responsibility for the conception and development of research into early childhood education.

CURRENT RESEARCH IN EARLY CHILDHOOD EDUCATION

The OECD study on Portuguese early childhood education and care (DEB/OECD, 2000) quoted Portuguese researchers who affirmed that "the present status of data collection is a legacy inherited from the past, and [is] in need of more precision and clarification, since during the dictatorship, data collection was considered, in general terms, one of the means of control used by the State" (p. 225) and that "a cultural change [was] needed." The OECD recommendations point to the need for collecting more reliable and consistent statistics on the situation of young children in Portugal. A later work, the OECD's *Comparative Report*, supplied a more complete picture of the status and situation of young children that was enhanced by the use of comparative figures and charts.

Table 9.1 presents some of the most important research carried out in the field of early childhood education since the eighties. The corpus of analysis consisted of published research (books, journal articles), major research reports and PhD dissertations, and some conference proceedings. It was impossible to analyze a significant number of masters' theses unless the research results were published in scientific journals.[8] We have organized the information according to level. By *macro-level* we mean specifically research on the general history of the field and research at the macro-political, national, and regional level as well as research dealing with early childhood teacher training. The term *meso-level* indicates research carried out at the school and community level, as well as studies dealing with programs for professional development. Curriculum and assessment issues were placed at this level because, despite the fact that there is a set of curriculum guidelines defined centrally, curriculum is redefined and reconstructed at the local

Table 9.1.   Major ECE Research in Portugal (1980-2003)

Levels	Content	Authors
Macro-level	History of ECE	Ferreira Gomes, 1977 Cardona, 1997 Vilarinho, 2000 Ferreira, 2000 Leandro, 2000 Magalhães, 1997 Bairrão & Vasconcelos, 1997
	Policies in ECE	Formosinho, 1994; 1996; 1997 Formosinho & Vasconcelos, 1996 Formosinho & Sarmento, 2000 Bairrão et al. 1989. 1990, 1994, 1997 Bairrão & Tietze, 1994 Vasconcelos, 1997b; Vasconcelos et al., 2003 DEB/OECD, 2000 OECD, 2001
	Comparative Policies	IEA Study (Bairrão et al. 1989, 1990, 1994) Vasconcelos, 1990 Bairrão & Tietze, 1994 OECD, 2001
	Teacher Education	Estrela et al. 2002; Afonso, 2002 Oliveira-Formosinho 1997, 1999, 2002 Formosinho 2000, 2002 Simões, 1993 Cró, 1998, 1990 Seco, 1993
	Regional Studies	Cardona 1995, 2000 O-Formosinho & Formosinho, 2001 Vasconcelos et al. 2003
	Nonformal programs	Vasconcelos, 1980, 1983 Silva 1996 Cruz, 1994 D'Epinay & Canário, 1994 Paiva, 1998
Meso-level	Professionals	Moita, 1992 Vasconcelos, 1995, 1997a, 2002 Oliveira-Formosinho ,2001, 1999, 1997 Sarmento Pereira, 2002 Cardona, 2002 Seco, 1993
	Supervision in ECE	Oliveira- Formosinho 2002, 1999, 1997 Oliveira-Formosinho & Formosinho, 2001
	Curriculum Models	Nabuco, 1996, 1997 Oliveira-Formosinho, 1996 Niza, 1996 Folque, 1998; Folque & S.-Blatchford, 2003

(Table continues)

Table 9.1.   Continued

Levels	Content	Authors
Meso-level (continued)	Curriculum Guidelines	Silva, 1997 Gaspar 1998b Leite, 1999 Vasconcelos, 2003
	Specific Curriculum Areas;	Sim-Sim 2001 Viana, 2001 Formosinho Simões 1988 Martins,1996 M.L Vasconcelos, 2002 Barros & Palhares ,1997 Botelho, 1995 Gaspar, 2001, 1998a Coquet, 1997 Esteves, 1998
Meso-level	Transitions	Nabuco, 1992, Nabuco & Lobo, 1997 Portugal, 2002b
	Working with the under 3	Portugal, 2000a, 1998 Aguiar, Bairrão & Barros, 2002
	Parent Involvement	Folque & Siraj-Blatchford, 1996 Gaspar, 1998a Homem, 2001 Mata, 2002 Silva, 2002
	Quality Evaluation;	Bairrão, 1998 Nabuco, 1996, Nabuco & Prates 2002 IGE, 2002, 2001 O.Formosinho, 2001 O-Formosinho & Formosinho, 2001 O-Formosinho & Araújo, 2001 Sá & Saraiva, 1998
Micro-level	Classroom ethnography	Vasconcelos, 1995, 1997a Vasconcelos & Walsh, 2001
	Ethnography with children	Iturra, 1996a&b, 1997 Ferreira, 2002a & b, 2001, Ferreira & Rocha,2000 Ferreira, Rocha & Vilarinho, 2000 Saramago, 2002, 1994 Vieira, 1992

level. *Micro-level* research indicates studies conducted at the classroom level (mainly ethnographic), as well as children's ethnographies or ethnography with children. The terms *macro, meso, micro* have been adopted from Bronfenbrenner's work (1979), but are far from being a rigorous application of his ecological framework.

The Macro-Level

For many years the only history of the field of early childhood was to be found in the work of Ferreira Gomes (Gomes, 1977), an educational historian. Recently, relevant studies by four specialists in early childhood education brought new information and critical insights into the development of the field. Cardona (1997a) makes an exhaustive analysis of the official discourse (1834-1990) around early childhood education, specifically the legislation produced and its implication for government policies. Her work confirms that from the early 1800s to the present, two concepts of early childhood education- the social and the educational- have coexisted.

In her work *Policies for Pre-school Education (1977-1997)* Vilarinho (2000) reflects on the process of constructing the idea of pre-school education by analyzing 20 years of legislation using an interdisciplinary approach: educational sociology, sociology of children, educational administration, educational policies, history of education and psycho-pedagogy. She discusses the conflicts inherent in "the process of constructing the consensus needed to legitimize policies" (Vilarinho, 2000: 16).

Ferreira (2000) also makes a critical contribution to the history of the field by comparing the social-medical discourse—"saving bodies" - with the psycho-pedagogical discourse—"developing minds"—found in a number of sources dating from 1880 to 1940. A specific study of Irene Lisboa as a pedagogue (Leandro, 2000) highlighted the outstanding contribution of this woman—a practitioner, researcher, writer and intellectual— to the development of the field. Other works also bring specific insights to the study of early childhood education, such as Magalhães's description (1997) which links early childhood education with the status of women and cultural issues, and the work of Bairrão and Vasconcelos (1997) which analyzes the development of the field after the April 1974 revolution, a time when democracy was being implemented.

The first studies developed in Portugal to have policy implications, were connected with the international IEA study (Olmstead & Weikart, 1987, 1994) and were carried out by Bairrão and his team at Oporto University, starting in the mid-eighties (Bairrão et al., 1989, 1990, 1994, 1997). In 1990, Vasconcelos wrote a Comparative Report for the Ministry of Education on European Union policies in early childhood education, highlighting the under-development of the field in Portugal (Vasconcelos, 1990). Using the European IEA Study as a basis, Bairrão and Tietze wrote a new comparative study of European Union policies (Bairrão and Tietze, 1994). This study highlights the need for an ecological dimension in analyzing and evaluating quality in early childhood settings throughout Europe.

In 1994 João Formosinho presented an important study to the *National Council of Education* (Formosinho, 1994). In the work, which discussed the status of the field, he criticized the absence of clear policies on the part of the government and strongly urged that clear policies on early childhood education urgently be put into place. The published report of his study was highly publicized, and had such a political impact that the three opposition parties of the time included the issue in their election campaigning. As a result, the urgent need to develop a well-functioning system of early childhood education was placed on the political agenda. In 1995, the newly-appointed socialist government asked Formosinho and Vasconcelos for a *Strategic Report* (Formosinho & Vasconcelos, 1996) with a plan with the priorities for the development of the field to take place within the following few years. This plan would be used to orient the Ministry of Education policies described earlier (Ministério da Educação, 1996).

In 2000, the above mentioned report of the OECD on *Education and Care for Young Children* (DEB/OECD, 2000) provided a new description of the status of early childhood education, and highlighted some of the contradictions that had arisen within the recently-instituted expansion plan, specifically the absence of clear policies for 0-3 years olds, and the absence of supervisory follow-up on the policies implemented, which were also outlined by the *Comparative Report* of the 12 countries studied (OECD, 2001).

After 1996, a number of detailed studies were carried out. The studies centered primarily on organizational issues involved in the expansion of early childhood education in Portugal (Formosinho, 1997; Formosinho & Sarmento, 2000). An exemplary study by Cardona (1995, 2000) depicted the developments of early childhood education in a district to the north of Lisbon (Santarém).

Under the aupices of the *National Council of Education* Vasconcelos et al. (2003) studied issues of *equity* in the development of early childhood education. After an in-depth study of the expansion process in a borough of Lisbon, the team carried out a multiple case study of four early childhood settings, which had been developed by different sponsoring agencies. The study showed that even a seemingly exemplary, very progressive borough, where 90% of the children had access to services, full day programs and free meals, showed significant inequities in access to quality services when in-depth qualitative data were analyzed. These inequities were not specifically caused by a lack of physical and financial resources but by organizational problems and limited supervision which resulted in poor educational outcomes. This problem was aggravated by teacher turnover in the public school system, which did not allowed for in-depth pedagogical work. It is important to emphasize that anthropological and ethnographic research, along with new trends in childhood sociology (such as allowing children to voice their own feeling and perspectives) were extremely instrumental in highlighting some of the contradictions inherent in the recent political efforts to develop the field.

The training of early childhood teachers, specifically the importance of quality supervision during their practicum has also been object of research. The most consistent work in this field has been done by Oliveira-Formosinho (1997, 1999, 2002) who studied the supervision processes, pairing students/classroom teachers, and supervision aimed at implementing preschool curriculum models. Two other studies (Estrela et al, 2002 and Afonso, 2002) done under the auspices of the former Institute for Accreditation of Teacher Education summarize research into childhood teacher education (1990-2000). These studies show that teacher education curricula are fragmented. Other studies (Cró, 1998, 1990; Seco, 1993; Simões, 1993) suggested strategies of intervention in teacher training that stem from developmental psychology. Formosinho has produced some of the most thought-provoking reflections on preschool teacher education for the early years (2002, 2000) and specifically the crucial role of the practicum in early childhood teacher education.

The Meso-Level

At the *meso-level*, in addition to studies carried out in formal settings, there have been studies dealing with informal programs aimed at educating young children and fostering parent involvement.

Non-formal programs for young children—alternatives to the traditional kindergarten—virtually began in the 1970s, with the pioneering work of the Grail Movement[9] which conjointly sponsored rural women's literacy programs, adult educational actions, and non-formal initiatives for young children (Vasconcelos, 1980, 1983). Several studies were described by Silva (1996) exploring the crucial connection between the education of young children and the overall development of rural or deprived communities. Conducted between 1976 and 1986 (a time of emerging grass roots movements), these studies challenged blind, across-the-board, egalitarian practices and explored specific community, adult and child development models that had come about on their own. In 1994 Cruz came out with an in-depth study of itinerant preschool practices which resulted in positive developmental outcomes for both children and mothers (Cruz, 1994). Paiva (1998) did pioneer work with Roma children and their families and described specific techniques and philosophies for working with itinerant populations.

Studies centered on the practice of early childhood professionals are also very important if one is to gain a better understanding of certain facets of the field. A pioneer study by Moita (1992) contains interviews with three early childhood teachers and provides an in-depth description of their experiences, showing how the public and private dimensions of their lives intersected. Vasconcelos (1997a) carried out an ethnographic study on the life and work of an early childhood teacher in the public school system. At the *meso-level*, this study demonstrated the close relationship between the teacher's life and her political and humanistic beliefs, as well as the democratic and empowering manner in which she dealt with young children (Vasconcelos, 2002; Vasconcelos & Walsh, 2001). Another study, by Sarmento Pereira (2002), recounted the lives of five early childhood teachers in the north of Portugal. Sarmento found common trends in these professional's teaching philosophy. She described how these teachers constructed their life stories based on identities that stemmed from their childhoods and how these identities were constantly reconstructed throughout their lives. Sarmento's research also highlighted the importance of the interaction among these teachers' various social roles.

Cardona (2002) published a study of early childhood public school teachers in a specific area of the country (Ribatejo, northeast of Lisbon) and described how they constructed a sense of their own profession despite the hardships of their working conditions. All of these studies, centered on personal experiences, portray a professional group that is highly committed to their work, strongly influenced by humanistic values, and devoted to the idea that children should be exposed to a wide range of experiences beyond those that are aimed merely at preparing them for elementary school.

Still at the *meso level*, it is important to mention the consequences of studies on quality that were developed by Bairrão et al. (1998, 1997). The national sample studied by these authors showed that Portuguese preschool education was of *average* quality. This means, in practical terms, that at the local level, the development of children in most need (from poor socio -economic backgrounds, at "risk", or with special needs) was not affected by their attending preschool educational institutions.

Oliveira-Formosinho (1999) and her associates (Oliveira Formosinho & Araújo, 2001; Oliveira-Formosinho & Formosinho, (2001) and Nabuco and Prates (2002) have been using and adapting well known scales such as the ECERS, COR, PIP, and the Laevers Involvement Scale, for training and supervising early childhood teachers, involving them in evaluating and improving their own practices.

The most consistent study of curriculum models for early childhood education has been developed under the umbrella of the *Projecto Infância* (Childhood Project) of Minho University and the *Associação Criança* (Childhood Association) in the north of Portugal (Oliveira-Formosinho, 1996; Oliveira-Formosinho and Formosinho, 2001). Niza (1996) described the *Modelo do Movimento da Escola Moderna* (Modern School Movement), a progressive model inspired by Freinet's pedagogical approach, which views classroom life as an opportunity to foster citizenship. Further studies have explored the scope of this model (Folque, 1998; Folque and Siraj-Blatchford, 2003). Oliveira-Formosinho (1996) describes the High/Scope Model and discusses its implementation in Portugal. Nabuco (1996) carried out a comparative study of three preschool curricula. The study showed that "formal" approaches (academically-oriented) were counterproductive, had negative consequences on children's self-esteem, and were apt to hinder children's learning.

An important research-based work was the set of *National Curriculum Guidelines* (DEB, 1997b[10]). As was mentioned above, the *Curriculum Guidelines* were a set of general principles to be re-constructed by teachers within their pedagogical teams. The process of developing this document was considered a practice of excellence by OECD (2001). Silva, the researcher in charge, with a core team in the Ministry of Education, described the process of collectively developing the document and also the wider consultation process that took place (Silva, 1997). Silva is presently doing research on the implementation process. Gaspar (1998b) studied the document from a Vygotskyan standpoint and found a clear socio-constructivist perspective in its philosophy. Leite (1999) studied it from a multicultural perspective. Vasconcelos (2003) queried a group of early childhood teachers in the field about the importance of the curriculum guidelines. She found that the *Curriculum Guidelines* had assumed a clear role in the field. Three themes emerged from the feedback given by teachers: that the *Guidelines* had political significance ("Our work is more visible."); professional meaning ("The curriculum guidelines are part of our identity."); pedagogical meaning ("It is a written text that orients our work.").

Recently, the General Inspection of Education (IGE, 2001; 2002) has started publishing annual reports from a national sample of early childhood settings. These reports show that, despite the presence of a general nurturing climate, the curriculum areas of Reading and Math need to be improved as does parental involvement and the transition to primary school.

Research is still sparse in specific curriculum areas, suggesting the need for more research. However, a few researchers have taken a more in-depth look at certain curricular areas, to whit: Sim-Sim (2001) and Viana

(2001) in the area of language development and reading, Formosinho Simões (1998) in the area of children's communication, M. L. Vasconcelos (2002) in the area of story telling and oral language, Martins (1996) in the area of emergent literacy, (Botelho, 1995) Barros and Palhares (1997) and Gaspar (2001, 1998a) in the area of Math education, and Esteves (1998) in the area of Environmental education for young children. Some research has been done on children's drawing (Coquet, 1997). Unfortunately, systematic research in other specific curriculum areas has been limited. However, significant work has been done for masters' theses which are not included in the scope of this work.

We would now briefly like to address research in settings for children under three. Aguiar, Bairrão and Barros (2002) applied an adapted version of ITTERS (Infant and Toddler Environment Rating Scale, Harms, Clifford & Cryer, 1980) to a set of 37 infant care facilities in the urban Oporto area and found the quality of the teaching in these facilities to be poor. Portugal (1998) researched crèches from an ecological standpoint (Bronfrenbrenner, 1979) and has also published work on 0 to 3 year-olds and family involvement in crèches (Portugal, 2000a, 2000b). The scarcity of research in this area shows how crucial social and political investment in the under-three group is.

Some studies are currently being carried out on parental involvement. An ethnographic study of parent involvement in an urban early childhood setting (Homem, 2001) demonstrated how teachers, despite their positive discourse, kept parents only superficially involved in order to maintain their power. Previously, Folque and Siraj-Blatchford (1996) had polled a nation-wide sampling of parents with regard to their expectations for early childhood education. Gaspar (1998) showed how parents can be involved in their children's Math education. Mata (2002) studied literacy practices in families of preschool age children. An ethnographic study in three rural kindergartens (Silva, 2002) showed the importance of the role of the teacher in parent involvement and highlighted how mothers become involved in different ways than fathers.

The issue of the transition from *creche* to kindergarten has been researched by Portugal (2002b) and from kindergarten to primary school by Nabuco (1992) and Nabuco & Lobo (1997). These studies highlight the need for clear-cut pedagogical initiatives such as providing teachers with more information and inviting primary school teachers to learn about the work being done in kindergartens.

The Micro-Level

At the micro-level research using standardized scales has been used since the eighties as we mentioned above. This research, which provides information about the overall quality of early childhood education, has also been used by professionals to improve the quality of their teaching. Research describing classroom practices in depth, such as the ethnographic case-study referred to above (Vasconcelos, 1995, 1997; Vasconcelos and Walsh, 2001), with classroom vignettes and interviews with the teacher, bring to light detailed information of a more in-depth nature. The metaphor of a "large table", symbol of democratic life in the classroom emerged from the study showing how rich intellectual life is generated in the classroom when the teacher carefully nurtures social interactions among the children.

A recent, major ethnographic study of young children by Ferreira (2002a) written from the perspective of childhood sociology and anthropology, shows how important the pre-school classroom setting is to social interactions among children. Several works around gender and play (Ferreira, 2002b), the socio-construction of the celebration of birthday parties (Ferreira, 2000) and the need for children's participation and listening to children (Ferreira, Rocha and Vilarinho, 2000) emerged from this study and have contributed toward listening to the children's voices in this field of research. Finally, Saramago (1994, 2001) has been doing research with young children on the construction of identities in peer groups.

In conclusion, even though it is still early, we can clearly see that a new field of research is emerging that has veered away from the mono-disciplinary line of research based primarily on developmental psychology. The current trend is now toward multi-disciplinary research that makes use of contributions from childhood anthropology and sociology, pedagogy, and even economics (Sá & Saraiva, 1998). We can also see a shift from quantitative methods to a variety of interpretive methods that provide us with a much richer, more profound and more detailed picture of the field.

FUTURE TRENDS

The OECD (2000) study of early childhood education and care in Portugal suggested the need "to make differentiated investments in order to reduce inequalities and establish equality of opportunities." According to OECD, "in order to provide for children in most need" (ibid., p. 36) there is a need for a broader approach that also strives to lower poverty and unemployment rates and reduce wage inequalities. Among other recommendations the OECD focuses on:

- Improving coherence in policy-making and implementation;
- Pre-service and in-service training of staff, including teacher education;
- Strengthening inspection and self-evaluation;

- Improving standards and accountability;
- Addressing gender issues and the needs of children under three years;
- Keeping records of children and their transfer into other settings;
- Improving implementation, monitoring and consultation;
- Providing reliable statistics and an independent supervisory board for children;
- Developing research on the quality of diverse forms of provision (2001, p. 217).

These recommendations directly address some of the problems described earlier and call for early childhood education that is closely connected to adult development and the regeneration of local communities (Vasconcelos, 1997b). They also demonstrate the need for research developed around assessment and evaluation issues, at different levels of the system, including school and classroom levels.

However, despite all the limitations highlighted in the OECD study (2000), which followed a remarkable expansion of the pre-school system (1996-2000), we feel it is safe to say that the beginning of this new century will bring a boom in research in the field. This is not only because the field has received public attention and recognition, but also because a substantial number of former early childhood educators have pursued academic careers and done masters and PhD degrees. These educators will ultimately contribute with their skills and expertise- not only in the administration and decision making arenas- but in the formal academia and research fields as well. Many of the studies mentioned earlier were developed by former early childhood practitioners out of their graduate work. They bring into the larger field of scientific research, the voices and concerns of professionals. Since universities and polytechnic institutes have become institutions for training early childhood teachers, these nascent researchers may now be challenged to serve the public by producing research connected to the "local" and "situational". There is an urgent need to apply research at the *macro level* to initiatives to change classroom life in a manner that will positively impact the lives of young children and families, while lending dignity to the work of classroom professionals.

We would like to add a word about the contribution of interpretive studies and ethnographic approaches and research. As a rather recent form of conducting inquiry, interpretive studies provide a holistic and comprehensive panorama seen from the subject's point of view. The first anthropological studies of the nineteenth century have only recently gained respect in educational sciences as a unique approach to doing research. From the perspective of childhood sociology, these phenomenon-based approaches may help policy and decision-makers connect with "the change of political and social structures, transforming institutions and guaranteeing cultural renovation " (Pinto and Sarmento 1997: 19) in order to contribute toward:

- a clear social inclusion of all children;
- institutions that are respectful of the best interests of children; and
- the acceptance of children's voices as a legitimate expression of participation "in the life of the city" (ibid., p. 19).

Pinto and Sarmento (1997) insist that southern European countries need to work more systematically on the image of the child as a subject of rights in order to:

> verify and recognize present social insertion of young children, by research-ing their words and by bringing to daylight the factors that prevent a clearer assumption of children as full social actors. (p. 19)

This perspective calls for more ethnographic studies about the life of children such as the studies centered on children from rural backgrounds that were pioneered by the well-known anthropologists Iturra (1996a, 1996b, 1997) and Vieira (1992). In addition, more detailed study of chil-dren and families from minority backgrounds must also be carried out, as well as studies involving children whose first language is not Portuguese. This last point will become a crucial social and political issue in years to come and will challenge educational researchers to provide relevant research and information.

International and national data show that only high quality programs have an impact on the reduction of inequalities (Bairrão, 1998). There-fore, there is much to be done, not only in helping families and communi-ties to understand that quality does matter, but also that those who need to demand higher quality are, in general, those who are less informed, and those most in need of empowerment.

Promoting high pedagogical quality in daily curriculum activities appears to be an important issue and standardized scales are not enough to effect changes. Quality needs to be defined by the most direct actors in the field (children, parents, community members and teachers). These actors need to put their energies together to strive for better quality. Some efforts has been done to adapt very important programs to the Por-tuguese context (Pascal & Bertram, 1997; DEB, 1998a), but more work needs to be developed on a broader, more well-organized, nation-wide scale. More research needs to be done around initial teacher training. Leadership and supervision are emerging issues of crucial importance

(Vasconcelos et al, 2003). Studies of best practices in training for supervision and leadership need to be developed, as well as in-depth studies showing how high quality supervision generates educational quality. In attempting to gather information for this work, we encountered a lack of research in specific curriculum areas as well as a lack of reliable statistics and statistical studies on specific groups of children (special needs, minority children, immigrant children, etc.)

Early childhood education in Portugal is a field of opportunities, of immense possibilities, and of promise. The challenge is to re-appropriate our rich past as *explorers, navigators and discoverers*[11] and develop research that is constantly reconstructing and reinventing itself, producing innovation and creating new knowledge, systematically re-assessing its overall aims. It should be research that actively lends an ear to its own era. Portuguese poet Sophia de Mello Breyner wrote, referring to Portugal's famed discoverers:

> He commanded them to navigate
> Always further, to discover what there was
> Ever south and to inquire
> The sea, the land, the wind, the quiet
> The people, the stars
> And to enter each day into the unknown.
> (Sophia de Mello Breyner Andresen)

ACKNOWLEDGMENT

This paper was written under a research grant SFRH/BPD/9363/2002 by FCT—Fundação para a Ciência e Tecnologia (Portuguese Foundation for Science and Technology). The author is deeply indebted to Isabel Lopes da Silva from IIE (Institute for Pedagogical Innovation) for her useful comments and insights in different phases of the preparation of this manuscript.

NOTES

1. Law 46/86, of October 14, Comprehensive Law of the Educational Systhem, with changes introduced by Law 115/97, of September 19. Presently a new draft law for education is under public discussion.
2. National Literacy Study, 1996, by Benavente, Rosa, Firmino da Costa & Ávila. Lisbon: Calouste Gulbenkian Foundation.
3. Decree-Law of March 30, 1911

4. Freinet (1896-1966), a progressive French Pedagogue, was responsible for introducing the principles of cooperativism into schools. He used active methodologies, activity centers, the printing press and cooperation among schools.

5. Decree-Law 542/79

6. 2000/01 data from DAPP (Department of Prospective Evaluation, Ministry of Education).

7. Law 5/97 of February 10.

8. There is no centralized department which could provide us with reliable information. Therefore this work may contain omissions. This is just a first attempt to organize highly dispersed and scattered information. For this fact the author apologizes in advance to her colleagues.

9. The Grail is an international women's movement which, in the Portuguese context, has been working consistently in raising the status of women through educational programs.

10. There is an English abbreviated version of the Curriculum Guidelines as well as the framework Law for Preschool Education published by the Department of Basic Education in Portugal (DEB, 1998b).

11. I mention here the outstanding work done by Portuguese discoverers and navigators in the XVI and XVII centuries as an inspiring metaphor.

REFERENCES

Afonso, N. (2002). A Avaliação da formação de educadores de infância e professores do 1º e 2º ciclo do ensino básico (The evaluation of early childhood teacher education). In N. Afonso & R. Canário (Ed.), *Estudos sobre a Situação da Formação Inicial de Professores*. Porto: Porto Editora/INAFOP.

Aguiar, C., Bairrão, J., & Barros, S. (2002). Contributo para o estudo da qualidade em contexto de creche na área metropolitana do Porto (A contribution for the study of quality in creches in Oporto). *Infância e Educação: Investigação e Práticas, 5*, 7-28.

Bairrão, J. (1998). O que é a qualidade em Educação Pré-Escolar? Alguns resultados acerca da qualidade da educação pré-escolar em Portugal (What is quality in pre-school education? Some results about quality in Portugal). In DEB (Ed.), *Qualidade e Projecto na Educação Pré-Escolar*. Lisbon: Departamento da Educação Básica.

Bairrão, J., Leal,T., Abreu-Lima, I., & Morgado, R. (1997). Educação Pré-Escolar. In DAPP (Ed.), *A Evolução do Sistema Educativo e o PRODEP* (The evolution of the Portuguese educational system) (Vol. II, 17-110). Lisbon: Departamento de Avaliação Prospectiva e Planeamento.

Bairrão, J., & Tietze, W. (1994), *A Educação Pré-Escolar na União Europeia* (Pre-school education in the European Union). Lisbon: Instituto de Inovação Educacional.

Bairrão, J., Barbosa, M., Borges, I, Cruz, O., & Pinto, I. M. (1989). Care and Education for Children under the age of six in Portugal. In: Olmsted, P.P. e D.P.

Weikart (Ed.). *How Nations Serve Young Children: Profiles of Childcare and Education in 14 Countries.* Ipsilanti, MI: The High/Scope Press.

Bairrão, J., Barbosa, M., Borges, I, Cruz, O., & Pinto, I. M. (1990). *Perfil Nacional dos Cuidados Prestados às Crianças com Idade Inferior a Seis Anos* (National profile of care under 6). Lisbon: Gulbenkian.

Bairrão, J., Barbosa, M., Borges, I., Cruz, O., & Pinto, I. M. (1994). Kindergartens and grandparents. In P. P. Olmsted & D. P. Weikart (Ed.), *Families speak: early childhood care and education in 11 countries.* Ipsilanti, MI: The High/Scope Press.

Bairrão J., & Vasconcelos, T. (1997). A educação pré-escolar em Portugal: Contributos para uma perspectiva histórica (Preschool education in Portugal: contribution towards a historical perspective). *Inovação, 10*(1), 7-19.

Barros, G., & Palhares, P. (1997). *Emergência da Matemática no Jardim de Infância* (Emergent math in kindergarten). Oporto: Porto Editora.

Benavente, A., Rosa, A., Firmino da Costa, A., & Ávila, P.(1996). *A Literacia em Portugal: Resultados de uma pesquisa extensiva e monográfica* (Literacy in Portugal: Results of an extensive research). Lisbon: Gulbenkian.

Botelho, D. (1995). *Resolução de problemas e procedimentos de descoberta em colaboração em crianças dos 4 aos 10 anos* (Problem solving and discovery processes in children 4 to 10). Unpublished doctoral dissertation, Coimbra University, Portugal.

Bronfenbrenner, U (1979). *The ecology of human development: Experiments by nature and design.* Cambridge, MA: Harvard University Press.

Bruner, J., & H. Haste (1990). *The child's construction of the world.* London: Routledge.

Cardona, M. J. (2002). Modelos de formação inicial e desenvolvimento profissional: Um estudo sobre os educadores de infância portugueses (Models of initial and in-service training: A study about Portuguese early childhood teachers). *Infância e Educação: Inovação e Práticas, 5*, 43-61.

Cardona, M. J. (2000). *Um Estudo sobre a Educação de Infância no distrito de Santarém* (A study of early childhood education in the Santarém district). Lisbon: ESE Santarém/Fundação Gulbenkian.

Cardona, M. J. (1997). *Para a História da Educação de Infância em Portugal: O discurso oficial (1834-1990)* (Towards the History of Preschool Education: The official discourse). Oporto: Porto Editora.

Cardona, M. J. (1997). *Os Educadores de Infância Portugueses: Formação e caracterização do grupo profissional* (Portuguese early childhood educators). Proceedings of 6th National Meeting of AFIRSE. University of Lisbon: 265-275.

Cardona, M. J. (1995). *A Educação de Infância no distrito de Santarém* (Early childhood education in the Santarém district). Lisbon: ESE Santarém/Fundação Gulbenkian.

Carneiro, R. (Ed.) (2000) *O Futuro da Educação em Portugal: Tendências e Oportunidades* (The Future of Education in Portugal: Tendencies and opportunities) (4 Volumes) Lisbon: *DAPP.*

Coquet, M. E. (1997). *A narrativa gráfica de crianças dos cinco aos dez anos de idade* (Graphic narratives of children from 5 to 10). Doctoral Dissertation. Lisbon: Technical University.

Correia, J. A., & Stoer, S. (1995). Investigação em Educação em Portugal: Esboço de uma análise crítica (Research in Education in Portugal: A critical analysis). In: B. P. Campos, (Ed.). *A Investigação Educacional em Portugal*. Lisbon: Instituto de Investigação Educacional.

Cró, M.L. (1998). *Formação Inicial e Contínua de Educadores/Professores* (Initial and In-service Training of Teachers). Porto: Porto Editora.

Cró, M.L. (1990). *Actividades de educação pré-escolar e activação do desenvolvimento psicológico: Contributo para a formação contínua de educadores de infância e professores do 1º ciclo* Preschool activites and psychological development activation). Unpublished PhD dissertation. Aveiro: Aveiro University.

Cruz, I (1994). *The evaluation of a home-visit education program in Portugal*. Doctoral Dissertation. Cardiff: University of Walles.

D'Épinay, R. & R. Canário (1994). *Uma Esacola em Mudança com a Comunidade* (A school changing with the community). Lisbon: Instituto de Inovação Educacional.

DEB/OCDE (2000). *A Educação Pré-Escolar e os Cuidados para a Infância em Portugal* (The Education and Care for children under six in Portugal) Relatório do Exame Temático da OCDE (bilingual edition). Lisbon: Departamento da Educação Básica.

DEB (1998a). *Avaliação e Desenvolvimento da Qualidade nos Estabelecimentos de Educação Pré*-Escolar: Um programa de desenvolvimento profissional (EEL Project/Projecto QAI). Lisbon: Departamento da Educação Básica.

DEB (1998b). Early Childhood Education in Portugal. Lisbon: Departamento da Educação Básica.

DEB (1997a). *Legislação* (Legislation). Lisbon: Departamento da Educação Básica.

DEB (1997b). *Orientações Curriculares* (Curriculum Guidelines). Lisbon: Departamento da Educação Básica.

Esteves, L. M. (1998). *Da Teoria à Prática: Educação Ambiental em Crianças Pequenas* (From Theory into Practice: Environment Education with young children). Porto: Porto Editora

Estrela, M.T., M. Esteves & A. Rodrigues (2002). *Síntese da Investigação sobre Formação Inicial de Professores em Portugal (1990-2000)* (Synthesis of Initial Teacher Training Research). Oporto: Porto Editora/INAFOP.

Ferreira, M. (2002a). *A gente aqui o que gosta mais é de brincar com os outros meninos! - As crianças como actores sociais e a (re)organização social do grupo de pares no quotidiano de um Jardim de Infância* (Children as social actors and the social (re)organization of peer group in the daily life of a kindergarten). Unpublished PhD dissertation. Oporto: Faculdade de Psicologia e Ciências da Educação.

Ferreira (2002b). O trabalho de fronteira nas relações entre géneros em espaços de "brincar ao faz-de-conta" (Relationship of work and gender in early childhood) *Ex aequo*, 7: 113-130.

Ferreira, M (2000). *Salvar Corpos, Forjar a Razão: Contributo para uma análise crítica da criança e da infância como construção social em Portugal. 1880-1940* (Saving bodies, building reason: Contribution towards the critical analysis of childhood as a social construction, 1880-1940) Lisbon: Instituto de Inovação Educacional.

Ferreira, M e C. Rocha (2000). *Vou fazer seis anos! Queres vir à minha festa?". A construção sócio-cultural do aniversário: valores, práticas sociais em contextos de Jardim de Infância e famílias de meio rural e urbano* (Social construction of aniversaries) Proceedings of Internacional Congress "Mundos Sociais e Culturais da Infância". Braga, January, 19-21: 356-372.

Ferreira, M, C. Rocha & E, Vilarinho (2000). *Changing professional practice. The sociology of childhood for the right of partcipation of children.* In: Ross, A. (2000) (Ed) Developing identities in Europe: citizenship education and higher education, Proccedings of the second Conference of the Children's Identity and citizenship in Europe Thematic Network, CiCE Second European Conference, University of Athens, London, Cice publication, pp: 287-294.

Folque, A. & I. Siraj-Blatchford (2003). *Children and pedagogues learning together in the early years: The collaborative process of MEM pedagogy.* Paper presented at the 13th EECERA Conference. Glasgow, Scotland: 3-6 September.

Folque, M. A. (1998) - The influence of Vygotsky in Movimento da Escola Moderna Early Childhood Education Curriculum in Portugal. *Journal of Early Childhood Teacher Education, 19* (2).

Folque, M. A. & Siraj-Blatchford, I. (1996). Parents views of quality in early childhood services in Portugal. *International Journal of Early Childhood*. OMEP.

Formosinho, J. (2002). A academização da formação dos professores de crianças (The academization of training teachers for early childhood). *Infância e Educação: Investigação e Práticas, 4*, 19-35.

Formosinho, J. (2000). *Teacher education in Portugal: Teacher training and teacher professionality.* Proceedings of the Conference on Teacher Education Policies in the European Union and Quality of Lifelong Learning. Lisboa: Portuguese Presidency of the Council of the European Union.

Formosinho, J. (1997). O contexto organizacional da expansão da educação pré-escolar (The organizational context of the expansion of pre-school education). *Inovação, 10*, 1: 21-36.

Formosinho, J. (1996*). Portuguese Preschool Education: Policy issues and the quality debate.* Keynote Speech at the 6th EECERA Conference. Lisbon: September 1996.

Formosinho, J. (1994). *Parecer nº 1/94. A Educação Pré-Escolar em Portugal* (Rulling: Pre-school Education in Portugal). Lisbon: Conselho Nacional de Educação.

Formosinho, J. e T. Sarmento (2000). *A escola infantil pública como serviço social: A problemática do prolongamento de horário* (Public preschool as a social service: the problem of full-day attendance). *Infância e Educação: Investigação e Práticas, 1:* 7-27.

Formosinho, J. e T. Vasconcelos (1996). Relatório Estratégico para a Expansão e Desenvolvimento da Educação Pré-Escolar (Strategic Report for the Expansion of Preschool Education). Lisbon: Ministério da Educação.

Formosinho Simões, M.D. (1988). *Comunicação entre Crianças: investigação empítica precedida de um estudo sobre linguagem e comunicação* (Communication among children: an empirical and theorectical study). Phd dissertation. Coimbra: Universidade de Coimbra.

Gaspar, M.F. (2001). O desenvolvimento numérico de crianças em idade pré-escolar: O Projecto Mais-Pais (Numeracy development in pre-school children:

The project More-Parents). *Infância e Educação. Investigação e Práticas, 3*: 115-150.

Gaspar, M. F. (1998a). *O Projecto Mais-Pais: envolvimento dos pais num projecto curricular no domínio numérico na educação pré-escolar* (More Parents Projects: parental involvement in numeracy in pre-school education). Unpublished Doctoral dissertation. Coimbra: Coimbra University.

Gaspar, M. F.(1998b). (Re)conciliar o (irre)conciliável: As orientações curriculares para a educação pré-escolar e a teoria de Vygotsky. (To reconcile the impossible? Curriculum guidelines and Vygotsky's theory). In Núcleo de Análise e Intervenção Educacional (Ed.). *Ensaios em homenagem a Joaquim Ferreira Gomes* (pp. 347-354). Coimbra: Núcleo de Análise e Intervenção Educacional, Faculdade de Psicologia e de Ciências da Educação da Universidade de Coimbra.

Gomes, J. F. (1977). *A Educação Infantil em Portugal* (Early Childhood Education in Portugal). Coimbra: Almedina.

Harms, T. and R.M. Clifford. (Ed.) (1980). *Early Childhood Environment Rating Scale*. New York: Teachers College Press.

Harms, T.; R.M. Clifford, and D. Cryer. (Ed.) (1980). *Infant and Toddler Environment Rating Scale*. New York: Teachers College Press.

High/Scope (1989). *Program Implementation Profile (PIP)*. Ipsilanti, MI: High/Scope Educational Research Foundation.

Homem, L. F. (2001). *A relação escola-família: As fronteiras da cooperação* (Relationship School-family: the frontiers of cooperation). Lisbon: Instituto de Inovação Educacional.

Inspecção Geral da Educação.) (2002). *Avaliação Integrada das Escolas. Relatório Nacional 2000-2002.* (Integrated Evaluation of Schools: National Report, 2000-2002). Lisbon: Inspecção Geral da Educação.

Inspecção Geral da Educação. (2001). *Avaliação Integrada das Escolas. Relatório Nacional 1999-2000* (Integrated Evaluation of Schools: National Report, 1999-2000). Lisbon: Inspecção Geral da Educação.

Iturra, R. (1997). *O Imaginário das Crianças. Os silêncios da cultura oral* (Children's Imagination: The silences of oral culture). Lisbon: Fim de Século Edições.

Iturra, R. (Ed.) (1996a). *O Saber das Crianças* (Children's Knowledge). Cadernos ICE. Setúbal: Instituto das Comunidades Educativas.

Iturra, R. (1996b). Gosto de ti por seres mulher. Ensaio de Antropologia da Educação (I like you because you are a woman: an essay on Anthropology of Education). In: Iturra, R. (Ed.). *O Saber das Crianças*. Cadernos ICE (pp. 13-26). Setúbal: Instituto das Comunidades Educativas.

Laevers, F. (1994). *The Leuven Involvement Scale for Young Children Experiential Education Series*. N. 1. Leuven: Center for Experiential Education.

Leandro, M.E. (2000). Irene Lisboa: Educadora: Construção da Identidade Pessoal e Profissional. Processos de Auto-formação (Irene Lisboa: Processes of Self-Formation). *Infância e Educação: Investigação e Práticas, 1:* 29-60.

Leite, C. (1999). Perspectivas multiculturais nas Orientaçõs Curriculares para a Educação Pré-Escolar (Multicultural perspectives in Preschool Curriculum Guidelines). *Perspectivar Educação, 6:* 56-61.

Lisboa, I (1942). *Modernas Tendências da Educação* (Modern Education Tendencies). Lisboa: Cosmos.

Magalhães, J.P. (1997). Um contributo para a história da educação de infância em Portugal (A contribution for the history of early childhood education in Portugal). In: M. Pinto e M.J. Sarmento (Ed.). *As Crianças: Contextos e Identidades.* Braga: Universidade do Minho. Centro de Estudos da Criança.

Martins, M.A. (1996). *Pré-História da Aprendizagem da Leitura* (pre-history of learning how to read). Lisbon: Instituto Superior de Psicologia Aplicada.

Mata, M.L. (2002). *Literacia Familiar: Caracterização e Práticas de Literacia em Famílias com Crianças em Idade Pre-escolar e Estudo das suas Relações com as realizações das Crianças* (Family Literacy). Unpublished PhD dissertation. Braga: Instituto de Estudos da Criança. Universidade do Minho.

Máximo-Esteves, L. (1998). *Da Teoria à Prática: Educação ambiental com as crianças pequenas ou O Fio da Navalha* (Environment Education with Young Children). Oporto: Porto Editora.

Ministério da Educação (1996, March). *Plano para a Expansão e Desenvolvimento da Educação Pré-Escolar* (Plan for the Expansion and Development of Pre-school Education). Lisbon: Ministério da Educação (Ministry of Education).

Moita, M.C. (1992). Percursos de Formação e Trans-formação (Paths of formation and trans-formation). In: A. Nóvoa (Ed.) *Vidas de Professores* (Teachers' Lifes). Oporto: Porto Editora.

Nabuco, M. (2000). Assessing Quality in Early Childhood Education and Care with the Early Childhood Environment Rating Scale (ECERS). In Airi Hautamäki (Ed.). *Emergent Trends in Early Childhood Education - Towards an Ecological and Psychohistorical Analysis of Quality.* Faculty of Education. University of Helsinki.

Nabuco, M. (1997). Três Curriculos de Educação Pré-Escolar em Portugal (Three preschool curricula in Portugal). *Inovação, 10,* 1: 73-87.

Nabuco, M. (1992). Transição do Pré-Escolar para o Ensino Básico (Transition from pre-school to primary). *Inovação. 5,* 1: 81-93.

Nabuco, E. M. & S. Prates. (2002). Melhoria da Qualidade em Educação da Infância "a partir de dentro" (Improving quality from "inside"). *Infância e Educação. Investigação e Práticas, 5:* .29-42.

Nabuco, M., & Lobo, M. (1997). Articulação entre o Jardim de Infância e o 1º Ciclo do Ensino Básico (um estudo comparativo) (Transition preschool to primary: a comparative study). *Saber Educar, 2* :.31-42.

Niza, S. (1996). O modelo curricular de educação pré-escolar da Escola Moderna Portuguesa (The prechool curriculum model of Modern School Movement in Portugal) .In: J. Oliveira-Formosinho (Ed.). *Modelos Curriculares para a Educação de Infância.* Oporto: Porto Editora.

Niza, S. (1992). Em comum assuminos uma educação democrática (In commom we assume a democratic education). In: MEM (Ed.) *Vinte e Cinco Anos do Movimento da Escola Moderna.* Lisbon: MEM. Cadernos de Formação Cooperada.

OECD (2001, June). *Starting Strong: Early Childhood Education and Care. Education and Skills.* A Report of an International Comparative Study. Paris: OECD.

Oliveira-Formosinho, J. (2002). A supervisão pedagógica da formação inicial de professores no âmbito de uma comunidade de prática (Pedagogical Supervision of teacher initial education within a community of practice). *Infância e Educação: Investigação e Práticas, 4,* 42-68.

Oliveira-Formosinho, J. (1999). *O Desenvolvimento Profissional das Educadoras de Infância* . (Professional Development of Early Childhood Teachers). PhD dissertation. Braga: Minho University.

Oliveira-Formosinho, J. (1997). Em direcção a um modelo ecológico de supervisão de educadoras de infância (An ecological model for supervision of early childhood teachers). *Inovação, 10*, 1: 89-109.

Oliveira-Formosinho, J. (1996). O Currículo Highscope (Highscope Curriculum). In: J. Oliveira-Formosinho (Ed.) *Modelos Curriculares em Educação de Infância*. Oporto: Porto Editora.

Oliveira-Formosinho,J.and Formosinho, J.(Org) (2001) *Associação Criança: Um contexto de Formação em Contexto.* (Childhood Association: A context for context training. Braga: Editora Minho.

Oliveira-Formosinho, J., & Araújo, S. B. (2001). Estudo psicométrico PIP-ECERS: Implicações ao nível dos instrumentos e da amostra (Psychometric study of PIP-ECERS). *Infância e Educação: Investigação e Práticas, 3*, 97-113.

Olmsted, P.P. e D.P. Weikart (Ed.) (1989). *How Nations Serve Young Children: Profiles of Childcare and Education in 14 Countries.* Ipsilanti, MI: The High/Scope Press.

Olmsted, P.P. e D.P. Weikart (Ed.) (1994). *Families Speak: Early Childhood Care and Education in 11 Countries.* Ipsilanti, MI: The High/Scope Press.

Paiva, M. (1998). *Ciganos e Educação* (Roma children and education). Setúbal: Instituto das Comunidades Educativas.

Pascal, C. e Bertram, T. (1997). *Effective Early Learning: Case studies in improvement.* London: Hodder & Stoughton.

Pinto, M. e M.J.Sarmento (Eds.) (1997). *As Crianças: Contextos e Identidades* (Children: Contexts and Identities). Universidade do Minho: Centro de Estudos da Criança.

Portugal, G. (2000a). Educação de Bebés em Creche - Perspectivas de Formação Teóricas e Práticas (Educating babies in crèches: Theorectical and Practical perspectives). *Infância e Educação. Investigação e Práticas. Revista do GEDEI, 1:* 85-106.

Portugal, G. (2000b). Subsídios para a compreensão das interrelações criança-família-creche (Contribution to understanding the interaction family-crèche) (pp. 31-54). In: Anne Marie Fontaine (Ed.) *Parceria família-escola e desenvolvimento da criança.* Oporto: ASA

Portugal, G. (1998).*Crianças, famílias e creches, uma abordagem ecológica* (Children, Families and Crèches: An ecological framework). Oporto: Porto Editora.

Sá, P. and P. Saraiva (1998). Aplicação de metodologias de planeamento e qualidade na concepção de um jardim de infância (Applying quality methods to kindergarten). *Qualirama*, Nov/Dec: 27-31.

Saramago, S. (2001). Metodologias de pesquisa empírica com crianças (Methods for research with children). *Sociologia, Problemas e Práticas, 35*: 9-29.

Saramago, S. 1994). As identidades da infância: Núcleos e processos de construção das identidades infantis. (Childhood identities). *Sociologia, Problemas e Práticas, 16:* 151-171.

Sarmento, M.J. and M. Pinto (1997). A criança e a infância: definindo conceitos, delimitando um campo (Children and Childhood: defining concepts and structuring a field). In: Pinto, M. e M.J.Sarmento (Eds.). *As Crianças: Contextos e Identidades* Braga, Universidade do Minho: Centro de Estudos da Criança.

Sarmento Pereira, M. T. (2002). *Percursos Identitários de Educadoras de Infância em Contextos Diferenciados: Cinco histórias de vida* (Identity Pathways of Early Childhood Teachers: Five life stories). Lisboa: Instituto de Inovação Educacional.

Seco, G. (1993). O auto-conceito escolar em educadoras de infância: Um estudo transversal (Self-concept in early childhood teachers). *Revista Portuguesa de Pedagogia, 27,* 1: 119-139.

Silva, A. (2002). Os pais e o jardim de infância em meio rural: um estudo de caso (Parents and the rural kindergarten: A case study). *Infância e Educação: Inovação e Práticas, 5:* 89-113.

Silva, I.L. (1997). Construção participada de orientações curriculares para a educação pré-escolar(Participated construction of curriculum guidelines). *Inovação, 10,* 1: 37-53.

Silva, I.L. (1996). *Prática educativas e construção de saberes. Metodologias da investigação-acção* (Educational Practices and Knowledge Construction: Research-action methods). Lisbon: Instituto de Inovação Educacional.

Sim-Sim, I. (Ed.) (2002). *A Formação para o Ensino da Língua Portuguesa na Educação Pré-Escolar e no 1º Ciclo do Ensino Básico* (Training for teaching Portuguese Language in pre-schools and primary schools). Oporto:Porto Editora/ INAFOP.

Simões, M.H.R. (1993). Estádios do ego e competência educativa como vectores do desenvolvimento do professor: Uma experiência no contexto da formação inicial de educadoras de infância (Ego stages and educational competency in early childhood initial training). *Unpublished PhD dissertation. Aveiro: Aveiro University.*

Vasconcelos, M.L. de M. (2002). *Contar histórias: análise da produção oral de crianças pré-escolares em contextos educativos diferentes* (Sory telling: analysis od pre-school children's productions). PhD Dissertation. Braga: Minho University.

Vasconcelos, T. (2003). Co-constructing curriculum guidelines for early childhood education in Portugal: A bottom-up perspective. *Researching Early Childhood* (Journal of the University of Gottembourg). *Special Issue: Play, Care and Education. Curricula for Early Childhood Education. Vol 5:* 193-210.

Vasconcelos, T. (2002). "I am like this because I just can't be different..." Personal and Professional Dimensions of Ana's Teaching: Some implications for teacher education. In: D. Rothemberg (Ed.). *Issues in Early Childhood Education. Curriculum, Teacher Education and Dissemination of Information.* Champaign, IL: ERIC Clearinghouse on Elementary and Early Childhood Education.

Vasconcelos, T. (1997a). *Ao Redor da Mesa Grande: Prática educativa de Ana* (Around the Large Table: Ana's educational practice). Oporto: Porto Editora.

Vasconcelos, T. (1997b). Planting the field of Portuguese Preschool Education: Old roots and new policies. *European Early Childhood Research Journal, 5,* 1: 5-15.

Vasconcelos, T. (1995). Houses and fields and vineyards shall yet be bought in this land – The story of Ana, a public kindergarten teacher in Portugal. Ph.D. Dissertation. IL: The University of Illinos at Urbana-Champaign.

Vasconcelos, T. (1990). *Situação da Educação Infantil nos Estados Membros da CEE*(Situation of Early Childhood Education in EU countries). Lisbon: Gabinete de Estudos e Planeamento (Unidade Eurydice).

Vasconcelos, T. (1983). Animação Infantil em Meio Rural: uma história do passado ou um projecto de futuro? (Children's animation in rural areas). *Jornal da Educação, 65:* 10-12.

Vasconcelos, T. (1980). Projecto de Animação Infantil em Meio Rural: uma alternativa na nossa educação pré-escolar (Project for Children's Animation in Rural Areas). *Escola Democrática, 33-34:* 8-16.

Vasconcelos, T. & D.J. Walsh (2001). Conversations around the Large Table: Building community in a Portuguese Public kindergarten. *Early Education and Development, 12,* 4: 499-522.

Vasconcelos, T., I. D'Orey, L. Homem. & M. Cabral (2003). *Educação de Infância em Portugal: Situação e contextos numa perspectiva de promoção de equidade e combate à exclusão* (Early Childhood in Portugal: Situation and contexts from an equity viewpoint). Lisbon: Conselho Nacional de Educação.

Viana, F.L.P. (1998). *Da linguagem oral à leitura: Construção e validação de testes de competências linguísticas* (From oral language to reading: tests construction and validation). PhD dissertation. Braga: Minho University.

Vieira, R. (1992). *Entre a Escola e o Lar: O curriculum e os saberes da infância.* (Between school and home: childhood curriculum and knowledge). Lisbon: Escher.

Vilarinho, E. (2000). *Políticas de Educação Pré-Escolar em Portugal (1977-1997)*(Policies for Pre-school Education in Portugal, 1977-1997). Lisbon: Instituto de Inovação Educacional.

CHAPTER 10

EARLY CHILDHOOD EDUCATION RESEARCH IN SPAIN

Miguel A. Zabalza

AN INTRODUCTION TO SPAIN'S EDUCATIONAL SYSTEM

Spain is a democratic country organized into 17 autonomous regions. It follows the federal model with power shared between the national government and the regional governments. The principal responsibility of the autonomous regions is to legislate on affairs within their region.

This sharing of responsibilities between national and regional governments clearly affects the organization of the education system. The national government establishes the general framework of the Spanish educational system that is common to the whole country, including the national curriculum, but educational planning and management is the responsibility of each autonomous region. As a result, the Spanish educational system is not homogenous throughout the country. While common elements can be found, each autonomous region has created its own legislation and has made different decisions about particular aspects of education, such as curriculum development, school organizational system, teacher training, and financing.

International Perspectives on Research in Early Childhood Education, 293–333
Copyright © 2005 by Information Age Publishing

In this two-headed structure it is not infrequent that conflicts arise between the national government and the autonomous regions' governments regarding the legitimacy to legislate and/or to regulate different aspects of education. This is what has happened in the education acts promulgated in recent years: from the General Ordination Law of the Educational System (LOGSE)[1] in 1990 to the Quality on Education ACT (passed in December, 2002).[2] In those acts there are issues regulated by the national government, which the autonomous governments demand as their own responsibility.

Generally, the national government has the responsibility to establish the general structure of the educational system (the different phases or levels of teaching and their essential characteristics, including the basic contents to be taught in each of them) and the conditions to accredit the studies (see Appendix I). The national government also establishes the basic conditions of the teachers' professional qualifications. But the policies on the selection and in-service training of teachers (including salary), the syllabuses and the conditions under which students progress inside the system, the development and time organization of syllabuses (with the possibility of including contents beyond the *minimum requirements* established by the national curriculum) and the organization of schools, including financing, depend on the educational administrations of the autonomous regions.

To understand the dynamics of the educational system, it is important to understand this distribution of responsibilities. Although the Spanish experience of decentralisation is still recent, one can notice differences in the approach that the individual autonomous governments follow when establishing their educational priorities, their investment in education, the measures used to assure the quality of the system, and the way to meet the educational needs of all their students.

In this distribution of duties and educational responsibilities, municipalities play a relatively small role. Compared to the important role they play in other European countries, especially in early childhood education, their involvement is marginal in Spain. And with few exceptions, they limit themselves to the physical maintenance of public schools. Hence municipal educational policies have focused on developing out-of-school activities, such as leisure, extracurricular activities and job training.

To this dichotomous political structure (national versus autonomous), another double category must be added: *public* versus *private*. In the Spanish tradition, there have been two main forms of educational provision: schools dependent on the national government or *public schools*, and those linked to private enterprises or associations, the *private schools*. Normally, public schools are widespread at the compulsory education levels (primary school and first part of secondary school) and share its presence in

**Table 10.1.   Public vs. Private Provision in
Early Childhood Education (3- to 6-year-old-children)**

Years	93-94	94-95	95-96	96-97	97-98	98-99	99-00	00-01	01-02	02-03
% Public	64.9	66.0	67.2	67.6	67.6	67.7	67.0	66.2	65.5	65.8
% Private	35.1	34	32.8	32.4	32.4	32.3	33	33.8	34.5	34.4

Source: Ministry of Education (2004).

the noncompulsory levels (nursery and postcompulsory secondary schools (see Table 10.1). In the last quarter of the century, a new type of school has been developed, the *state assisted schools,* financed with public funds though managed by private companies or associations.

A LOOK BACK AT THE HISTORY OF CHILDHOOD EDUCATION IN SPAIN

Despite the fact that education and initiatives in favor of infancy are as ancient as the history of humanity, institutional attention for young children has a short history. In Spain, it goes back a little more than 150 years, to the mid-nineteenth century. It is, on the other hand, a history that is very much linked to the development of *services for infants* in the rest of Europe. In fact, many pioneers were people who had to go into exile from Spain due to their liberal ideas. This in turn gave them the opportunity to get to know the experiences of other countries, which they tried to introduce in Spain when they returned.

The beginnings of childhood education in Europe go back to the end of the eighteenth century. Spodek and Brown (1996) refer to Oberlin's *knitting houses* in Alsatia (1767); Owen's *infant school* in Scotland (1816); Fröebel's *kindergartens* in Germany (1873); Montessori's *casa dei bambini* in Italy (1907) and McMillan's nursery schools in London (1911). Lucchini (1997) refers to the *five musketeers* who acted as predecessors to the modern infant school: Owen, Fröebel, Agazzi, Montessori and Ciari. He also adds other relevant names: Pestalozzi in Switzerland; Aporti, the initiator of the first infant schools in Italy, and Decroly in Belgium. All those names had an ample influence on the introduction of childhood education in Spain, which was delayed until the mid-nineteenth century. To the previous names we should add Monlau with his *casas cuna* (cradle houses) in Barcelona (1840), Montesino with his *escuela de párvulos* (schools for children) in Madrid (1840) and Manjón with his *escuelas del Ave María* in

Granada (1889). Monlau was a catalan doctor exiled in France due to his liberal ideas in 1837. There, he had the opportunity to get to know the French educational institutions. When he returned to Barcelona in 1840, he promoted the casas cuna for the children of poor workers. He suggested that the casas cuna should have a timetable that coincided with the working timetable, that mothers should be able to freely go there to feed their babies and that there should be two rooms, one for resting with cribs and the other for playing with a patio next to it. The casas cuna were run by nuns and ladies dedicated to charity. Montesino (1791-1849), was also a doctor and pedagogue who exiled to London because of his liberal political ideas. This gave him the opportunity to get to know the English experience with regard to infant care. When he returned from exile, he carried on with his political activity and created a commission to support infancy in Madrid and, through it, the first escuela de párvulos (1838). In his case, due to the proximity of the court and the middle class, his schools acquired more of an instructive orientation than one of assistance from the start. Later, worried about the training of his educators, he wrote a manual for childhood educators and turned his escuela de párvulos into the first Spanish normal school, which was a specialized training center for professionals in childhood education. On the other hand, the experience of Father Manjón (1846-1923) in Granada, is clearly one of assistance. His *escuelas del Ave María* (1889) emerged initially to look after children from poor neighborhoods in Granada.

The origins of the concern for infancy are mixed with variables of different types. It was basically an urban phenomenon linked to the industrial revolution and the impact that the revolution had on employment, the family structure and the new life conditions of the different social groups. The rural world and its values were in crisis. The new distribution of resources among the different social strata gave rise to great marginalization and poverty as well as to a new mentality, which was less stuck to the traditional values that had been promoted by families. Emigration to cities and big production centers made the guardianship that traditional rural families had over education and the socializing process of their children disappear. The collapse of traditional social values and the crisis in previous life and cohabitation systems gave rise to a double social feeling:

1. Fear and insecurity due to the loss of traditional values, which in turn made political and religious institutions worry about childhood education as a way to control the progressive collapse of the structure of beliefs that was considered of great value. Arnau, Rector of the University of Barcelona and one of the most important persons responsible for Catalan public education in the mid-nineteenth century, supported the escuelas de párvulos because he con-

sidered them very useful be it for their educational function or their moralizing task.

2. The awareness of the appearance of new layers of social marginalization with a vast number of groups lacking resources. This situation especially affected young children who in many cases ended up begging in the streets, malnourished and lacking hygienic care. This provoked the charitable reaction of social groups (mainly of a religious nature or laymen/women dedicated to charity) who wished to help by assisting children. To this double circumstance, common to different European countries, we can add a third one in Spain:

3. The appearance of nationalistic feelings (defending a local point of view regarding the power of the state) linked to the educational proposals. In some regions of Spain, the defense of values entrusted to childhood education, was linked to the very values of the region such as language, traditions, culture, and so forth. The local authorities entrusted the school to make the values of the region prevail. To do this they looked for educational models and authors that would serve as a doctrinal point of reference. As a response, the institutions belonging to the central state promoted and imposed opposite approaches. That gave rise to vast doctrinal controversies between regionalists who defended Froebel and Montessori (whom they used as a symbol for their defense of the autonomy and educational value of all that was local) compared to those supporting the centralism that followed Montessino and Giner de los Ríos. In this section we must also include the brutal antinationalist reaction provoked by the Franco regime after the Spanish civil war which made many interesting *Froebelian* and *Montessorian* experiences disappear, calling them *foreignizing*, *activators of separatism* and promoters of a *school without God*.

From a historical point of view, we could say that the history of childhood education in Spain has always oscillated around two axes: the *care* versus *education* axis and *naturalism* versus *instruction* axis. The first is a sociopolitical axis, which marks the orientation of the services for children, and the second is a technical axis, which marks the content of the services and intervention modalities postulated. Each of the mentioned axes constitutes a continuum with two extreme poles and intermediate positions. In this way, we could say that attention given to young children has gone through moments in which there was an orientation based more on the care and attention of poor children and their families (assistential view) and other moments in which education and development of individual capacities were more predominant. In the same way, we have gone through moments in which there has been a prevalence of more liberal views (based on autonomy and free play) compared to other approaches, which focused more on direct instruction.

THE CARE VERSUS EDUCATION AXIS
(CARE VS. EDUCATION)

The controversy between some services for children that focus on care and protection compared to some services with a focus that is clearly more educational, has been with us since the mid-nineteenth century. Some of the Spanish pioneers in attention to young children were doctors (Monlau, Montesino) or priests (Manjón) and concentrated on improving hygiene and care for children (especially, poor children and children who begged in cities). But they themselves ended up proposing educational aims and insisted on the importance of training for the professionals who attended to the children's needs. As the services for infants started to concentrate on the children of the middle class, the assistential focus gave way to a more educational and instructive view. In any case, the option to maintain an educational line of action based on *care* or based on *education* affects a group of elements which are part of the action taken concerning small children: addressee, institutions, professionals and type of action to be carried out.

Generally speaking, when the criteria of *assistance and care* for children have been present, the beneficiaries of the services have usually been the families, normally in need. The attention given tends to solve the needs of the family or their difficulties to attend to their children. In the last few years, this focus has been strengthened as a measure to ease the incorporation of women into the job market. The institutions in charge of granting assistance were private institutions dedicated to charity or public institutions, which depend on the labor, health or social services authorities. Professionals were not demanded for those services. People who simply had some experience with children were recruited, without any specialized training (except for matters concerning child hygiene). At the beginning they were *women who guard children*,[3] a concept that later was added to the term *guardería*, a name which has, until now, included the group of different centers dedicated to looking after children without educational pretensions. With regard to the contents of the attention or service, these were left quite hazy (protection, play, socialization, etc.). The most important thing, in any case, was that the children should be safe from problems and accidents.

On the other hand, when attention to young children was conceived as an *educational action*, the beneficiaries were the very children, independent of their families' social or work situation. The institutions in charge of attending to their needs had similar characteristics to the school centers, they answered to the educational administration and followed their norms. The professionals had to have specialized pedagogical training and the contents of attention were fixed on the official norms (from the 40s onwards, laws started to *orientate* infant education and in the 80s a national curriculum was established).

In any way, institutionalized attention provided for children in Spain has always been marginal and understood as one of the basic tasks of families, that is to say, of women. The existing experiences were scarce and, generally, had nothing to do with the educational system. One had to wait until the arrival of the 60s (Primary Education Act of 1965) for the state to recognize the need to create public infant schools with specialized teachers. From the mentioned act onwards, there is a difference between *maternal schools* and *kindergartens* for children between 2 and 4-years-old and infant schools for children 6 years of age, initiating a dichotomy of the services provided (assistential for the smaller ones, 2-4-years-old; educational for the older ones, 4 and 5-years-old) which was maintained until the 90s when the new socialist act, the LOGSE, establishes an educational sense at all stages, 0-6-years-old. In this process, the new conservative act of 2003 (the LOU act), is a step back in two ways: one goes back to the previous duality (assistential focus for children between 0-2 years of age and educational focus for children between 2-4-years- old) and the term of *preschool* is taken up again for the stage between 0-2-years-old.

The recuperation of the term preschool has been one of the most criticized aspects of the LOU act because it contains two disturbing messages. In the first place, the term had been abandoned in the 90s to express that childhood education was not limited to preparing children for their incorporation to school, instead it had a sense and identity, it was a moment to develop and enrich the child. By adopting once again the expression preschool stage, it seems as if there were doubts as to the educational identity of the attention given to small children. And by calling preschool just this first stage (0-2-years-old), it seems as if one wants to say that the children are already school children when they finish it (3-years-old). This step backwards, is a result, without doubt, of the conservative mentality of that current Spanish government. But, it arises also from the incapacity of public infant schools and their professionals to offer the families real help. A model that is so excessively scholarly in nature (timetables, resources, professionals, etc.) loses flexibility and does not find an adequate solution to the needs that children and families have nowadays. There is a need for a network of polyvalent services that provide it with the flexibility to attend to the different demands (assistential and educational).

THE NATURALISM VERSUS INSTRUCTION AXIS
(PLAY VS. LITERACY)

The second axis around which attention to young children has evolved in Spain, is the one which refers to the very content of the attention provided, what one supposedly does with the young children while they are in the institutions or services dedicated to looking after them. The aim is to control their development and imbue them with cultural and social guidelines or, on the other hand, to create an atmosphere that promotes the natural development of the child. This is what Genishi, Ryan, Ochsner and Yarnall (2001) have proposed as a contrast between a Lockian focus (to treat the child *tamquam tábula rasa*, as if he/she were an empty recipient that has to be filled) and a Rousseaunian focus of the small child (consider him/her as someone that has to be left to develop autonomously).

In this way, attention given to young children in Spain was never exclusively assistential. Even the initiatives in favor of poor children used to be completed with the formal and hardly systematic education of the first letters and notions of religion and morality. This aim to overcome the mere assistential function of infant schools started to appear from the beginning. In 1866, Julián López, Director of the Infant Schools in Barcelona, wrote that "our infant schools have nothing in common with the infant schools found in some foreign countries where children are instructed memoristically," and invited everyone to follow in Montesino's steps "proposing childhood education as a development of intelligence, the senses and the body" (Opening lesson of the academic year, 1866).

Froebel's influence at the dawn of Spanish early childhood education was very important, especially because it filled the vague and indefinite idea of childhood assistance envisaged by the pioneers with content. Froebelian influence on the importance of hygiene, paying attention to the children's psychological and intellectual needs as well as those of affection, games as promoters of development, the importance of the training of educators, and so forth, turned into the basic ideas of initiatives in favor of childhood. But, Froebel was introduced in Spain by liberal pedagogues and was adopted as an ideological framework by the nationalist movements. This provoked a rejection on behalf of the conservatives and supporters of a more traditional idea of education. The conservatives stated that Froebel had made three big mistakes: "to affirm that a child is good by nature, to consider that education is the natural development of people as rational beings and to foment and always respect the child's freedom" (González, 1991). As one can see, official Spain rejected Rousseaunian influences. Education was conceived as a process destined to transform the child, to overcome innate weaknesses. Conservative pedagogues believed that Froebel's idea that educating is leaving the child to grow and facilitate his/her autonomous development, was simply "the negation of all pedagogical system"[4] (Garcia Navarro, 1913, p. 35)

Froebel's influence carried on with María Montessori, who lived in Barcelona from 1918. Many schools, generally elite ones, adopted the Montessori system. Great value was given to the scientific focus they gave to their educational program and the variety of material used. The importance she gave to the education of the senses, the manipulation of objects, children's' free experimentation, and so forth, was soon adopted by the most advanced schools.

The first Spanish pedagogues drank from those same fountains: Dewey, Rousseau, Pestalozzi and Froebel. The fact that some of them were doctors and the assistential sense given to childhood attention, made them give a lot of importance to the health of children, their eating habits and cleanliness. It was only father Manjón who developed a proposal with his own pedagogical characteristics: open-air lessons, use of games as a teaching resource, handcrafts, use of drama by the children as a learning tool. His pedagogical proposal had a lot of success and when he died, in 1923, there were already 400 Ave María schools all over Spain, some of which are still with us today.

During the twentieth century, Spanish childhood education progressed in an uncertain way, with some model experiences and quite a lot of low quality. However, the currents of pedagogical innovation which followed (the modern school movement; new Freinetian, Montessorian and Decrolinian schools; the Institución Libre de Enseñanza [the free institution of education], the pedagogical renovation movements, and so on) were a breath of fresh air to childhood education: games and free activities for children were given great value, intense contact with nature was promoted, didactic and sensorial experimentation resources for children were improved.

The arrival of the Franco regime meant a sudden halt in the pedagogical progress reached up until then. Traditional Spanish pedagogy was revived and everything that came from abroad was rejected. A councilor from the town hall of Barcelona wrote the following in the *La Vanguardia* newspaper on 17-IX-39,

> We must achieve the transformation of the education that was called Spanish, albeit it was Spanish only by its residence...and which looked to be the reflection of the foreign orientations of the Pestalozzi and the Froebel, the Decroly and Montessori ... which took inspiration, exclusively, from the notions of the French Revolution of liberty, equality and fraternity, through which one arrived at the school without God.

Many teachers were purged, if not simply annihilated. The basic Franco regime idea, *fatherland, religion, family,* together with the great influence of the Catholic Church, constituted a perfect setting to return to an idea of childhood education that was very much linked to the family, to instructional and moralistic ideologies, and of course, to an authoritarian style of education. Boligas wrote in 1943,

> With regard to pre-school education ... educational action is limited to the family sphere and that of the Church.... We must not neglect these years: it would be like giving our children's formation over to strange influences; during these years, children belong nearly exclusively to the family. The family is the only one responsible and its action can save its children. (p. 43)

The arrival of democracy meant a new turn to the pedagogical approaches of childhood education. European influence, especially Italian, was strong and Spanish society assumed the importance of early education to strengthen infant development and enrich his/her experiences, be it intellectually, emotionally or socially. That is why, more and more, educational attention provided for young children is conceived as an action which creates enriching contexts where all the children can develop their capacities in a balanced way and feeling happy. That is the mission of the national curriculum of childhood education that I will refer to next.

CURRENT ORGANIZATION AND CURRICULUM OF CHILDHOOD EDUCATION IN SPAIN

As mentioned earlier, since LOGSE conferred an educational feature to the whole period of nursery education (from 0-6 years), while the New Education Act of December 2002 (hyperbolically called the Quality Act) distinguishes between preschool education (0-3 years) and infant education (3-6 years). The first part has a care nature, as support to families. The second part maintains the educational approach. As far as nursery education is concerned, early childhood services are optional. The national government (through autonomous regions) is obliged to offer the necessary resources and devices so that all children, from the age of three may have a place in the public system of education. Still, families may opt whether or not to send their children to nursery schools.

The First Stage of Early Childhood Services: Preschool Education (0-3-Year-Old Children)

In the new Quality Act this period lost its previous educational orientation and it is now intended to guard children, enabling families to find a balance between working life and family life. It is considered as a care service provided by *professionals with a proper qualification* (interesting blurred denomination just to avoid the condition of an educational competence for people caring for young children). This first period will not be organized by the education authorities, but by regional family, labor or social security authorities. So the big effort of teachers' unions and families during the last decade to preserve the idea that young children should be taught by education professionals with the proper teaching qualifications has vanished.

Despite the official care nature and the lower training level required of professionals, the Quality Act establishes important targets for this stage, intended for the development of children such as the following: (a) language development as a learning focus; (b) knowledge and progressive control of their body; c) play and movement; (d) environment discovery; (e) meeting with peers; (f) development of sensory skills. These are no simple issues at all. Their development involves a strong formative commitment and requires that the professionals working with children should have higher qualifications. And these qualifications have educational connotations that go beyond the fact of just *taking care of them*.

The Second Stage of Early Childhood Services: Infant Education

Three- to 6-year-old children are enrolled in infant education. This is a proper educational stage with specialist teachers with a 3-year university degree and governed by education authorities. Though voluntary for families, infant education is practically universal in the whole country, with an attendance of almost 100%. Tables 10.2 and 10.3 show the progressive spread of schooling that took place in recent years.

The act emphasizes its prelearning stage nature with the purpose of approaching early childhood education to school parameters. The targets for nursery education are: (a) knowing their own body and its movement possibilities; (b) observing and exploring the family, social and natural environment; (c) acquiring progressive autonomy in daily routines; (d) establishing relationships and learning the main aspects of meeting with

Table 10.2.   Schooling Rates in Spain (3-5 Years)

	Years							
	90-91	*94-95*	*97-98*	*98-99*	*99-00*	*00-01*	*01-02*	*02-03*
Percent	75.9	87.2	91.4	93.7	94.8	96.4	98.4	100

Table 10.3.   Schooling Rates by Age

	3-Year-Old Children	4-Year-Old Children	5-Year-Old Children
1994-95	57.4%	100%	100%
1999-00	84.1%	99.3%	100%

Source: Ministry of Education.

others; (e) developing oral and writing communicative skills and an introduction to reading and writing; (f) introduction to basic numeracy. The act explicitly establishes reading and writing techniques and basic numeracy as the main priorities for this period. The introduction of a foreign language (in the last year) and initiation to information and communication technology as well as religion education is included.

School attendance for 3-6-year-old children is envisaged as free in the act *as far as the available budget funds may allow for it.* On the one hand, this is a great step forward, since free education was not guaranteed in the past. However, by making it conditional on the available budget funds, there is always an excuse to resort to this exception. On the other hand, these free services will be provided by private nursery schools with official grants, which created great controversy among those social sectors, which would prefer a commitment to improve public education. Since places in public or supported institutions are not guaranteed for all the existing demand at present, many families have to resort to private institutions for nursery schools and pay for them.

There are curriculum guidelines for early years education. Assuming the idea of the potential of young children to learn from the earliest stage within a clear educational framework, these official guidelines determine general minimum goals for children to attain at a given stage, defined as a series of abilities and broad curricular areas. The curriculum at this stage is structured around five large areas of experience related to children's development: *Body and personal autonomy* (includes body knowledge and control; play and movements and personal care); *Life environment* (includes interpersonal relationships; knowledge, care and respect of the living beings and objects; life in society); *Communication* (includes linguistic and communicative skills); *Number representation; Artistic expression* (includes plastic and pictorial arts; musical expression; drama and body expression); *Religious studies* (includes symbols, celebrations and traditions of different religious believes). Since the curricular guidelines are designed to ensure that the experiences provided for young children are global and not fragmented, these five areas are to be addressed systematically throughout the 3 years in all schools.

Nursery schools are intended to enrich children's everyday life as far as relationships with others (adults and children), play, language and experimenting with different materials are concerned. The curricular proposal does not determine specific levels of achievement for each area or when each area has to be worked with. Teachers and schools decide on such issues which are usually recorded in the educational and curricular projects elaborated by schools, adapting official curricular regulations to their own context. Those curricular proposals have a double structure: an educational project (showing the master lines of the education model to be performed by this institution) and a curricular project (describing the curricular contents and activities to be developed and its distribution along the different years).

Preeparation of Spanish Nursery School Teachers

The teacher training degree is a 3-year one (though nowadays the credit system is used). There are seven specialties in that degree: nursery school, primary education, music, physical education, foreign language, special education and hearing and language. Each specialty has its own requirements (although some of the subjects may coincide). Future nursery school teachers will have to study three different types of university subjects:

Main or Basic Subjects

These are compulsory and common subjects for all universities in the country established by the ministry of education through the university board. These subjects are a condition for the degree to be recognized by the national government and account for 40% of the total subjects. Some of the following contents are common for all future teachers: Psycho-pedagogical basis of special education; general didactics; school organization; psychology of child education and development; sociology of education; contemporary education theories and institutions; new technologies applied to education. Others subjects are specific for the specialty of nursery education: knowledge of natural, social and cultural environment; music expression and its didactics; artistic expression and its didactics; linguistic skills and its didactics; mathematics and its didactics; psychomotor development; child literature. A long period (320 hours) of practicum (a placement period in a nursery school under the supervision of a tutor teacher) is required.

In addition to that, each university may introduce additional required subjects for the students at that university. They usually cover about 30% of the degree requirements.

Elective Subjects

Students may choose different subjects according to their particular interests and professional expectations. They may cover about 15-20% of the degree requirements.

Free Curriculum Subjects

Spanish regulations allow students to take 10% of their subjects as free choice among different cultural or scientific activities not necessarily related to their degree. They can choose subjects from other specialties, such as foreign languages, attending conferences, or participating in different cultural initiatives.

The training of nursery school teachers does not finish with completion of their university degree. There are different kinds of in-service training for the teaching staff: courses, seminars, continuous working groups, training programs at schools, 1-day meetings, and direct advice from the educational administration advisors. Every 6 years teachers must demonstrate that they have completed at least 100 hours of training activities, which entitles them to a salary increase. This incentive has led to a great increase in training initiatives but also to a loss of intrinsic motivation. Sometimes it is hard to say if participants are interested in the activity or simply need to complete the required amount of hours.

Teacher centers, institutions where selected teachers acted as advisers for their colleagues, initially coordinated in-service training activities. These centers have gradually disappeared or have been modified due to lack of transparency in the selection process, lack of credibility for advisors or operating difficulties. Nowadays each regional government organizes the system differently.

Issues Related to the Nursery Schools in Spain

The following are important issues regarding the need for improvement of Nursery Education in Spain:

The Double System Organization (and Conception) of Small Children's Education

The copresence of two cycles, the first addressed to 0-3-year-old children and focusing on family and care policies (labor or family ministry), the second addressed to 3-6-year-old children with an educational approach and regulated by the ministry of education causes a lack of continuity in early childhood services and the educational value during the first three years is lowered.

The problems arising out of this division in nursery education are:

- The day care center approach differs significantly from the educational approach focused on fostering children's development.
- The different qualifications of teachers (vocational training at secondary school level in day care centers versus university training in kindergarten) create a double category of professionals and makes communication among them problematic.
- The lack of national government's financial involvement in the first cycle where parents, companies or care associations must pay for the services.

The Debate Between Private and Public Education in Nursery Schools

Public schools are financed by the regional governments, private schools or services operate as particular business. A strong discussion is taking place on whether private education (in the first period of nursery school) should be subsidized with public funds or not. Those in favor of subsidizing public and private education (the right-wing party) mention the citizens' right to equality. Those against it (left-wing parties) state that the public provision should be improved first for poor social groups who cannot afford to pay for nursery schools; otherwise inequality is fostered from the beginning. Religious centers and private companies mainly run this period of nursery education. The accreditation of schools and its supervision poses a big unsolved problem, since until now the only requirement for those schools is to be acknowledged as a business activity. One can still find nursery schools not meeting the necessary safety measures and located in unhealthy sites or in high flats.

The Virtual Priority for Politicians Regarding Attention Given to Young Children and the Real Contradictions

Each political party states that education is one of its priorities. However, such electoral promises are not reflected on budget or organizational measures. The situation has improved considerably in Spain, but there are still important problems regarding nursery education such as:

- *Child/teacher ratio:*   Researchers suggest that the *ratio* children/ teacher should be a maximum of 12 children per adult in the 3-6-year-old-children classes, and not more than 8 in the 0-3 cycle. The ratio in Spain is around 20 children per adult (19 in the public schools and 21 in the private ones).

- *Number of adults in each classroom:*   Generally, the only adult in classroom is the teacher who is responsible for all the work and the children's care. Thus, they cannot carry out rich initiatives or provide an individualized attention to children.
- *The real investments:*   The real investments in education are lower than the average in developed countries. There has been some improvement, but mainly regarding buildings and infrastructures rather than regarding professionals and everyday work resources.
- *The teacher training program:*   The 3-year teacher training program is not adequate. It is being requested that future nursery and primary school teachers take a 4-or 5-year university degree in order to improve training in arts, technology, special educational needs, and so forth, and to equal the status of teachers at the other levels.

The Problem of Continuity in the Transition to Primary Schools

The transition between nursery schools and primary schools is important. Nursery schools are focused on playing and children's autonomy. Early childhood education is oriented to development. Primary schools are focused on academic learning using student's books and on the development of regulated activities. At present time, there is a strong clash of cultures that need to be resolved, though several initiatives have started.

The Problem of Quality and Quality Assurance

Quality is a requirement, but quality policies in Spain are mainly centered on results. This criterion cannot be applied to nursery education since it is focused on the individual development of children. A nursery school is not better if the children can read and write at the age of five, since it should not prepare children for primary school as was thought in the past. The quality issue in nursery education is highly important but proper criteria should be used (Zabalza, 1997).

Current New Doctrinal and Practical Approaches

Some new issues have appeared in the Spanish nursery education context:

- Progress in *Neuroanatomy* have introduced important changes in the work carried out with early childhood. The experiences of early brain stimulation show unbelievable levels of *child development* such as: children able to distinguish two different brands of cars, kinds of plants, to identify a specific painting among others, to solve problem situations at the age of two or three. Many nursery schools (especially private ones) are including these procedures in their work. They offer it as a marketing strategy: "your children will be almost extremely gifted". But the question is: Is this the right way? What are the effects? Much more research is needed on this issue.

- *Multiculturalism* (linguistic competence, different family, religion, cultures) poses an important question that has been growing in the last few years (in some classes there are children from 7 or 8 different cultures, speaking at least the same number of different languages). More than 10% of young children in nursery classrooms are foreigners, but Spanish nursery schools do not have consolidated experience to face this challenge and, on many occasions, lack the necessary resources to do it adequately.

- The *integrated formative system*, as suggested by Italians, that is the opening of schools to the environment and the necessity of external supports to solve those problems schools cannot face on their own, is very difficult to achieve in Spain. The incorporation of social workers to schools, shared work with families, development of educational projects involving the whole city are some examples.

RESEARCH IN EARLY CHILDHOOD EDUCATION

Spain has traditionally been more focused on the development of practical procedure for children's care than on research. The late introduction of professional training in nursery education at the university was a disincentive to research initiatives. Research on early childhood had been mainly conducted in university areas, other than education, such as psychology, sociology, medicine, music, sciences and languages. In recent years, papers focused on the specific study of teaching practices started to appear.

A few considerations regarding the topics, the authors and the limitations they face should be made before analyzing the research papers in nursery education made in Spain.

- The area of nursery education has been a frequent object of short-term studies by researchers. With a few exceptions (for example, the paper by Palacios, Lera, & Moreno in 1994), there is no continuity between existing studies. Most of them were doctoral dissertations or related publications instead of longitudinal research.

- In Spain there is no research information storage and retrieval system. The few systems available (for instance, the International Bulletin of Bibliography of Eduacation) are inadequate to reflect the studies and papers on social sciences comprehensively. That is the reason why there are no papers in Spain about systematic reviews of scientific production on this topic, except the bibliometric analysis done by Perea Riquelme in 1996. To carry out this review of papers it has been necessary to directly contact the different research teams asking them to provide updated information on their publications.

- Literature specializing in nursery education is extensive in Spain. But most of the existing magazines, documents and books refer to experiences or analysis of different aspects of activity with young children, lacking the precision research demands. The literature, in general, has a more didactic and professional nature.

Papers can be organized around topics, which are similar in content and ideas to those made in other countries (e.g., Genishi et al., 2001). We may also establish three categories in nursery school research:

- Generic papers about nursery education or any of its basic components: child rearing environment, institutions taking care of young children, families, legislation, child learning and development, general children pedagogy.
- Papers focused on the study of curricular areas or young children development in areas such as language, writing, music.
- Papers about teachers or papers made by teachers expressing their opinions.

Generic Reports about the Basic Components of Nursery Education and Child Development

This section refers to general topics regarding work with young children, which can be divided into the following sections:

Childrearing Contexts

Some papers analyze different child rearing contexts and their effects on development. We may note the paper by Palacios, Lera and Moreno (1994) assessing the impact of the family and school context on child development. Using the ECERs and HOME scales they made a longitudinal study analyzing the family context of children when their mothers were pregnant and the family and school context when children were 5 years old (including the ideas of teachers).

The family is the focus of most of the papers regarding child rearing context, (Fernández de Haro, 1988; González, Hidalgo, & Moreno, 1998; Oliva & Palacios, 1992, 1998; Toorio López, 2001). However schools have also been analyzed as social contexts for child life and development (Lera & González, 1998; Luque & Candau, 1998). Other papers have analyses the influence of the social context on school work with young children (Gómez Salas, 1997; Jiménez Raurell, 1996, regarding poorer areas; García Huerta, 1994, in rural environments). Finally, Riera (2003a) has studied the differences produced in childhood development as a consequence of having gone to different social and educational services for young children

Child Learning and Development

The subject of child development, including learning processes, has been a recurrent theme in the scientific production under analysis. Some papers show a psychological approach (Ceacero Cubillo, 1996; García Fernández, 1997), and others show a more pedagogical one (Granada Azcárraga, 1999; Marchena, 1997; Mérida Serrano, 1999; Roz, 1998; Zabalza, 2002;).

Didactic Aspects
Papers describing the educational action in the classrooms are included in this group. Some papers study the educational activities in nursery schools in a general descriptive way (Elizalde, 1997; Méndez Cevallos, 1996; Pérez Montero, 2002; Riera, 2003b) others study applicable methodology (Almenar, 1997; Alonso, 2000, 2001; Viciana, 2000) or the way to develop certain skills or values (e.g. *cooperative learning*: Sánchez Blanco, 1993). We may find papers addressing general problems of children care such as "personal tutorial classes" (Gutierrez Tapas, 2001).

Space
The discovery of the value of space and its educational power became one of the pillars of the child education transformation over the last years. Working in centers and a flexible organization of rooms spread until it became one of the identifying marks of nursery schools compared

to primary and secondary schools. This aspect has been thoroughly studied in some papers (Elizalde, 1997; Iglesias Forneiro, 1996).

Social Interaction

The particular interaction among children and adults and among children themselves is another relevant aspect of the education of young children. Some papers analyze the interactive dynamics itself (Álvarez Núñez, 1998; Prieto Laina, 1997), other papers associate interaction with the learning of rules and values (Escorza Subero, 1994; Sánchez Blanco, 1993; López González, 1991) or with the learning of some school skills (Díez Vegas, 2001; Poveda, 2000). Other papers deal with the relationship between parents and teachers (Barcia & Rodríguez, 2002).

Assessment

Some research papers refer to the assessment of certain nursery education programmes (Ferradás, 1998; Garagorri, 1994). We should note the small number of papers on assessment (of program, contexts, resources) in a country with so many educational initiatives and proposals for young children. Other papers have focused assessment on the analysis of what happens in the classroom, in the way teachers manage children education (Mir Pozo, 1999; Iglesias Forneiro, 1996; Palacios & Lera, 1992). Some papers have focused on the analysis of how child assessment and observation is carried out (Giner, 2000).

Special Educational Needs

The policy of integration for boys and girls with special educational needs in ordinary classrooms is generalized in Spain and researchers have addressed it (Gervilla, 2002; Carrión, 1999; Parrilla, 1999; Piqué Simón, 1996). The special learning characteristics and/or the development of children with disabilities have also been analyzed (Fernández Rey, 1998; Martínez Abellán, 1994). The role of external support services to teachers in charge of children with special needs has also been dealt with (López Sánchez, 2000; Parrilla, 1997).

Organization and Administration of the Nursery Education Centres

The teaching and managing function are associated in Spain. School principals are teachers chosen by the teaching staff to carry out managing functions for a period of time. Therefore, the study of organization and administration in schools has always been associated with the study of the teaching actions and profession.

Some papers deal with legislative or political issues of school administration (Alonso Santamaría, 1992; Calvo Rueda, 1994; Granell, 1999). Other papers focus on requirements of that managing function, such as democratic participation or innovation (Castro Quiñones, 1998; Soler, 1998). Others on the configuration of the school curricular project (Martínez Mínguez, 2000). Other papers study the existing external counselling system for centres teaching young children (Cordero Arroyo, 1995). Some papers have dealt with the study of the principals' professional profile and their satisfaction level with it (Caballero Martínez, 1999; Armas, 1995).

Economic Aspects

The studies about the economic dimension of child services are not very frequent in Spain, except for official statistics. That is the view offered by Fuenmayor (1993) on the financing of children's education.

Gender

The emergence of papers on the relationship between gender and education is very recent in Spain. In general, papers are essays dealing with global topics rather than research papers on nursery education. However, some papers deviate from this tendency. The work carried out by Arenas Fernández (1995) is a case study dealing with gender construction in children. Other authors address this topic regarding how children build their gender identity according to the type of games and activities offered at infant school (Lera, Ganaza, Gutiérrez, & García, 2000) or according to whether their teachers are men or women (Lera, 1999).

Global and Local Views

Some papers deal with the analysis of nursery education either providing a generic analysis on several issues (concepts, history, authors, programmes) in the Manual or Encyclopaedia format (Gallego, 2003) or with specific analysis on concrete questions such as quality (Palacios et al., 1995; Zabalza, 2001). Some papers compare the Spanish nursery education with other European countries (Lera, 1996; Tietze, Cryer, Bairrao, Palacios, & Wetzel, 1996; Tietze et al., 1997). Other papers provide local views, studying the development of nursery education in a region or a specific city (Vicente Villena, 1999; Zabalza, 1998; Rueda Parras, 1999; Escarihuela Monreal, 1991).

Papers Focusing on Curriculum Areas or Child Development

Many papers refer to curriculum contents, dealing with different topics regarding the education of young children such as the following:

Arts and Creativity

Papers under the title *artistic development* deal with child artistic development through basic studies on *children artistic abilities* and the analysis of the impact education has on the development of child artistic skills. Some researchers deal with creativity in a generic way (Barcia Moreno, 2001, 2002; López Martinez, 2001; Fernández Rey, 1998); others focus on some of the arts: plastic art and drawing (Guerra Cabrera, 2002; Segurado, 1992), drama (Cantos, 1996), music (Cabanelas, 2001; Bernal Vázquez, 1996).

Language

Researchers in the field of nursery education have been attracted by the study of child language. In fact, language is usually considered as a basic ability for development and it greatly influences development at school. Studies deal with language from three different views: as a basic individual ability (Defior, 1994; Ruesga, 2000; Acosta & Ramos, 1998; Aguado Alonso, 1994), as a skill to be developed at school (Morales Núñez, 1999; O'Shanahan, 1995; Mendizábal Ituarte, 1994) as a function which may undergo alterations and needs a special educational attention (Massa Gutiérrez, 2000; Romero, 1999; Moreno, 1998; Gallego Ortega, 1996; Bustos Barcos, 1993)

Due to the Spanish bilingual situation in many regions, we find papers dealing with the process of second language learning in bilingual contexts (Sotes Ruiz, 1996). In other cases, papers focus on the use of literary texts and popular tales in the didactic work with young children (Aller García, 1993; Sotes Ruiz, 1996; Barcia Mendo, 1998)

Literacy

Literacy is another field where pedagogic and psychological research has made remarkable progress lately. There are numerous papers on this topic dealing with literacy from a general view (Garcia Vidal, 1998; Gómez Castillejo, 1995) and as a school learning process (Ribera Argüete, 2001; Ruiz Jiménez, 1999; Carlino Cantis, 1995; Lozano Martínez, 1993; Dominguez Gutiérrez, 1992) and as a resource for the cultural immersion of the children who come from other countries and cultures (Clemente Linuesa, 1992).

Mathematics

Many studies address the development of numeracy in young children. The researchers have focused on the basic aspects of logical mathematical thinking (Fernández Escalona, 2001) and on its didactic approach in the classroom (Rochera Villach, 1996).

Motor Functions

The recognition of young children's bodies and their motor functions are two important curricular fields in nursery schools. Some studies have analyzed motor functions as a basic ability of individuals (Aguirre Zabaleta, 1996) and other papers dealt with motor function didactics for young children (Bolarín Martínez, 1998; Mendiara Rivas, 1996; Justo Martínez, 1996; Vaca Escribano, 1994; Fernández Nares, 1990).

New Technologies

The presence of computers and new technologies in nursery classrooms is a recent phenomenon in Spain but causing a deep impact. National and regional programmes intended to providing centres with resources and training teachers in their use have been established. There is still much to do, but nowadays most schools have added new technologies to the resources available to help children develop their experiences.

Researchers have addressed this topic regarding nursery schools making descriptive studies (Urbina Ramírez, 2000; Martínez Lobato, 1998), analyzing and submitting specific proposals for the incorporation of new technologies in the education of young children (Barrio Valencia, 1994). Some papers focus on the cultural analysis of underlying discourses in TV and in the multimedia products offered to young children (Licona Vega, 2000; Bernal Bravo, 1998).

Social Sciences

The wide range of activities under the name *social sciences* is a basic curricular field in Spanish nursery schools. Some studies focus on the cross-thematic issues such as health (Garcia Vale, 1998; Terronteras Muñoz, 1995) or on interpersonal relationships (Quintero Rodríguez, 1996). Others address more academic issues such as the way children know and represent their life environment (Nadal Perdomo, 1998) or natural phenomena (Vega Navarro, 2001).

Papers About Teachers or Papers Made by Teachers Expressing Their "Opinions"

In the 1980s and the first part of the 1990s, taking into account the importance of the new qualitative approaches, educational research was focused on the study of teachers. Papers on *teachers' thinking*, on the processes of class planning and development, on diaries and autobiographies, on the living and professional cycles and on gender differences regarding the profession date back to this time. Teachers were the main subjects of research papers. The intensity of that concern has decreased now, though it is a strong and interesting research line, with one new feature: there are more and more teachers acting as researchers. Many research papers about the teachers' role have adopted a horizontal and democratic approach. Researchers and teachers form teams to develop study projects to make the sense of teaching and the factors affecting its development clear. And there are teachers who conduct and write their own research.

The studies on this section can be subdivided into several groups:

Professional Profile

The changing nature of the work developed on child services and nursery schools led to studies about the teacher profile in nursery education. Spain is a country where we do not find the variety of services other countries have. The model of care services (for 1–3-year-old children) or the model of nursery schools (preferably for 3–6-year-old children) are practically the only option available for families. The functions professionals in nursery education must perform are very wide and variable (for instance, the incorporation of 3-year-old children to public schools involved a real professional shock as teachers were not used to attend so young children who required a very special care).

As a result, research papers on the profile of nursery school teachers appeared. Some studies dealt with the global functions teachers developed (Gil Molina, 1995); others addressed specific functions, such as oral language (Pérez Montero, 2000); authority (Vega Morán, 1999). In other cases the topic under study is the process through which teachers built their professionalism (Martínez & Saureda, 2002).

Training

The question of professional profile is closely related to teacher training. Teacher training has undergone great changes in Spain, what was reflected on research. Researchers have dealt with the topic of teacher training as regards to preservice training (Torrecilla Jareño, 1995) to inservice training (Fernández González, 2000; Rodríguez Pulido, 1996). Some of the training models with special success, like *Formación en Centros (training in schools)*, have also been studied (Martínez Olmo, 1999; Rodríguez Fernández, 1999; Sola Martínez, 1992). Teacher training has been analyzed from a global point of view (Alonso, 2002) and from the point of view of carrying specific functions (e.g. for innovation: Sousa Guerreibo, 2002; for supervision: Pérez García, 2001)

Teachers' Thinking

Though common in the 1980s in Spain, there are still research papers on the way of thinking of nursery school teachers. In some cases, the so-called *practical knowledge* is studied (Argos González, 1996), or *personal theories* (Reyes Santana, 2000), the *views* (Fuentes, 1998) or the *ideas* and their relationship with practice (Lera, 1994) or an overall view of all them (Quinza Segura, 1994).

Biography

Those research papers focused on recovering the teachers' *opinions* are based on the same ideas stated at the beginning of the section. Teachers tell their lives and their activities and manage their process of decoding and study. Studies based on *diaries* (Zabalza, 1991), on *biographies* (Fernández Cruz, 1994) or on *narratives* (Martínez & Saureda, 2002) belong to this kind of research.

SOME FINAL CRITICAL REMARKS ON EARLY NURSERY EDUCATION RESEARCH IN SPAIN

This generic and descriptive view of the recent Spanish research in early childhood education may be completed by a final remark on its characteristics. The following issues reflect my opinion about this situation:

Though there has been a great increase lately, research on early childhood education is still scarce. And it would be even more, if we apply strict criteria to distinguish what can be classified as research and what not. On the other hand, potential researchers find enormous difficulty to get financial aids for their projects. The different calls for financial aids to carry out research projects do not usually include the specific field of nursery education as a priority.

Existing researches show an approach more oriented to the *application* than to the *basic* or *evaluative* research. Almost all the research is qualitative and/or ethnographic and is based on descriptions or plain statistical analyses. Experimental research or research including causal analysis models is almost nonexistent. There are not longitudinal or laboratory studies either.

As we have seen in the review of papers carried out, the subjects are very varied. Those addressing development and learning of different curricular areas such as language, motor functions, arts, and so forth, are predominant. Unlike other countries, in Spain there is not a significant concern to assess the efficiency of the different educational models or to compare one method with the others. There are no studies with such a purpose.

The resources used in research are very varied: observation, interviews, questionnaires, tests, different scales. Except in those studies in collaboration with international teams, work is normally carried out with *ad hoc* tools and scales more than with standard tools. Thus, any comparison of the results among different researches or any attempt to generalize the results is almost unfeasible.

A new ethical and participative trend regarding research processes has become established. A kind of research more committed to schools and teachers has replaced strictly academic research. An active involvement of teachers in research projects has been achieved: research is not carried out on schools and teachers, but rather research is carried out with teachers.

Despite the fact that research topics are very close to classroom themes and to real problems in nursery education, research has had a low impact on the educational practice. The only clear exception to this situation has been the field of *reading-writing*, where research results have been successful in modifying teachers' performances. But, in general, educational practice is said to work with its own logics and distant from research results. Even when some kind of link is made explicit (e.g. the incorporation of the *constructivism* approach to teaching), the way how it comes into practice is more based on intuition and personal view of teachers than on research data.

However, this lack of connection between research and educational practice has not had dramatic effects. Spanish nursery education is undergoing one of the most successful moments in its long history. The way young children are cared is innovative, flexible and playful. It may also be said that the quality of the real educational practice at the present moment is higher than that of research about this field. In our case, research tends to go behind the practice (to be able to study it, analyze it and make it a doctrine) instead of showing the way to be followed. The probable reason for this is that teachers working with small children are highly qualified and very motivated.

APPENDIX: STRUCTURE OF THE SPANISH EDUCATION SYSTEM

There are four main educational levels in Spain: nursery education, primary education, secondary education and university education. The second level and part of the third one are compulsory and embody the right of all Spanish citizens to receive education. However, despite not being compulsory, nursery education, especially for children 3-6-years-old, has become almost universal as the beginning of the schooling process. The new Quality in Education Act for 2002 includes as an innovation a widespread and free education at the level of nursery education for 3-to-6-year-old children living in Spain.

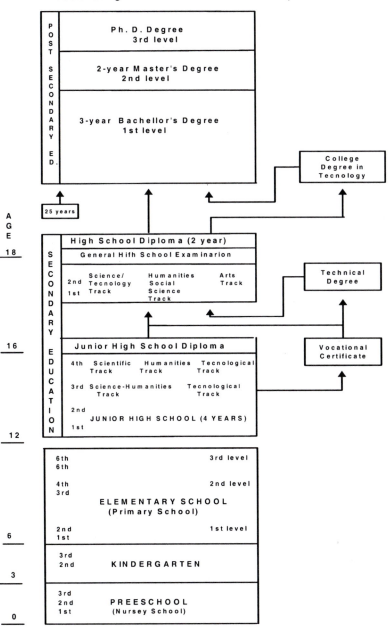

Figure 10.1.

Apart from university education and upper vocational studies, all students up to 16-years-old follow the same educational scheme. They go through the three common *stages*: nursery education (0-6 years), primary education (6-12 years) and compulsory secondary education (12-16 years). At this stage, (16-18 years), they can choose between staying in the baccalaureate (where different modalities are offered) and going to university, or transfer to middle vocational studies to continue further upper vocational studies. Figure 10.1 shows this educational itinerary.

NOTES

1. General Act on the Education System, January, 1990.
2. Ley de Calidad de la Enseñanza. Quality in Education Act, November, 2002.
3. Dones d'aguantar criatures (women who put up with children), was what the women who looked after children were called in nineteenth century Catalonia. They were frequently elderly women who were no longer in condition to carry on working.
4. Las fundamentales teorías de aquel alemán ilustre, el espíritu de sus doctrinas, lo que podríamos llamar froebelianismo, son, a nuestro modo de ver, la negación de todo sistema pedagógico (The fundamental doctrines of that honorable German, the spirit of his doctrines, what we might call Froebelianism, are, in our opinion, the negation of all pedagogical system).

REFERENCES

Acosta, V., & Ramos, V. (1998). *Estudio de los Procesos del Habla Infantil desde la Perspectiva de los Procesos Fonológicos* [A study of childhood speaking processes from a phonological point of view]. Málaga, Spain: Aljibe.

Aguado Alonso, G. (1994). *El Lenguaje del Niño de Dos Años y Medio* [The language of a two and a half year old child]. Navarra, Spain: Universidad de Navarra. CC. Educación.

Aguirre Zabaleta, J. (1996). *Desarrollo de la Inteligencia Motriz como Base Para la Evolución y Capacitación* [Development of motor intelligence as a base for evolution and capacitation]. Zaragoza, Spain: Universidad de Zaragoza. Medicina.

Aller García, C. (1993). *Los Cuentos Infantiles de Camilo Jose Cela. Su Aplicación Didáctica en la Educación Infantil y Educación Primaria* [Children's tales by Camilo Jose Cela: Their didactic application in childhood education and primary education]. Seville, Spain: Universidad de Sevilla. CC. Educación: Didáctica Lengua y Literatura.

Almenar Rodríguez, Ma. L. (1997). *Propuesta De Un Modelo Didáctico Innovador De Educación Infantil Para La Comunidad Autónoma De Andalucía* [Proposal for an innovative didactic model in childhood education for the autonomous community of andalucia]. Madrid, Spain: Universidad Nacional de Educación a Distancia. CC. Educación.

Alonso Santamaría, A. (1992). *Estudio sobre la Reforma de la Educación Infantil en España: 1985-1992* [Study on the childhood education reform in Spain]. Santiago, Spain: Universidad de Santiago. CC. Educación.

///Alonso, A. (2000). La Imprenta al Servicio de la Metodología para la Educación Infantil Actual. Una Experiencia Innovadora en el C.E.I. "Madre de Dios de Begoña", *Anuario de Pedagogia No. 2* [Printing at the service of methodology for current childhood education: An innovative experience at "Madre de Dios de Begoña" childhood education centre]. *Yearbook on Pedagogy No. 2.* Zaragoza, Spain: Universidad de Zaragoza. CC. de la Educación.

Alonso, A. (2001). Una Experiencia Educativa Innovadora con Niños de 3-6 Años. Escuela Madre de Dios de Begoña, Zaragoza. *Anuario De Pedagogía No. 3* [An innovative educational experience with 3-6 year-old children: Madre de Dios de Begoña School, Zaragoza]. *Yearbook on Pedagogy No. 3.* Zaragoza, Spain: Universidad de Zaragoza. CC. de la Educación.

Alonso, A. (2002). Funciones del Educador, del Equipo Docente y de los Padres en la Educación Infantil. *Anuario de Pedagogía No. 4* [Functions of the educator, the teaching team and the parents in childhood education] *Yearbook on Pedagogy No. 4.* Zaragoza, Spain: Universidad de Zaragoza. CC. Educación.

Álvarez Nuñez, Q. (1998). *A Pragmática da Comunicación e a Interacción Profesor-Alumno na Aula. Análise da Evolución do Control Relacional* [The pragmatics of communication and teacher-student interaction in the classroom: Analysis of the evolution of relational control]. Santiago de Compostela, Spain: Universidad de Santiago. CC. Educación.

Arenas Ferández, Ma. G. (1995). *La Construcción del Género en la Escuela Infantil. Estudio de un Caso* [Gender building at infant school: A case study]. Málaga, Spain: Universidad de Málaga. CC. Educación.

Argos González, J. (1996). *El Pensamiento del Profesor de Educación Infantil: Estudio de Casos sobre el Conocimiento Practico de Docentes en Ejercicio* [How infant school teachers think: Case studies on the practical knowledge of teachers in practice]. Oviedo, Spain: Universida de Oviedo. CC. Educación.

Armas, M. (1995). *As Necesidades Formativas dos Directores Escolares no Contexto da Reforma* [The training needs of school principals in the reform context]. Santiago, Spain: Universidad de Santiago. CC. Educación.

Barcia Mendo, E. (1998). *Los Cuentos Populares Extremeños. Su Aplicación Didáctica en Educación Infantil y Primaria* [Popular tales from extremadura. Their didactic application in childhood and primary education]. Badajoz, Spain: Universidad de Extremadura. CC. Educación.

Barcia Moreno, M. (2001). *La Creatividad En El Niño De Educación Infantil. Incidencia Del Contexto Familiar* [Creativity in the child in childhood education: Incidence of the family Context]. Sevilla, Spain: Universidad de Sevilla. CC. de la Educación.

Barcia, M. (2002). *Familia y Creatividad: el Binomio Perfecto* [Family and creativity: The perfect binomial]. In A. Gervilla (Ed.), *Creatividad Aplicada* [Applied creativity] (pp. 171-189). Madrid, Spain: Dykinson.

Barcia, M., & Rodríguez, M. (2002). *Formas de Participación-Colaboración Padres y Maestros en Educación Infantil* [Ways for parents-teachers to participate-collaborate in childhood education]. Màlaga, Spain: HUM205.

Barrio Valencia, L. (1994). *La Utilización del Ordenador como Ayuda para la Enseñanza y Aprendizaje de la Escritura: Estudio de Casos* [The use of the computer as an aid for teaching and learning writing: Case studies]. Valladolid, Spain: Universidad de Valladolid. CC. Educación: Didáctica de la Lengua.

Bernal Bravo, C. (1998). *Análisis de los Discursos Subyacentes en la Programación Televisiva y su Reconstrucción en la Educación Infantil* [Analysis of underlying discourses in television programmes and their reconstruction in childhood education]. Almería, Spain: Universidad de Almería. CC. Educación.

Bernal Vázquez, J. (1996). *Implicaciones de la Música en el Curriculum de Educación Infantil y Formación de Educadores* [The implications of music in the childhood education curriculum and teacher training]. Málaga, Spain: Universidad de Málaga. CC. Educación.

Bolarín Martínez, Ma. J. (1998). *Elaboración de una Guía de la Observación de los Parámetros Psicomotores* [Elaboration of an observation guide for psychomotor parametres]. Murcia, Spain: Universidad de Murcia. CC. Educación

Bohigas, F. (1943). Orientación pedagógica. ¿La educación a quién corresponde? [Pedagogical counselling. Who is in charge of education?]. *Consigna, 34(3)*, 23.

Bustos Barcos, Ma. C. (1993). *Logopedia Escolar: Niños con Alteraciones del Lenguaje Oral en Educación Infantil y Primaria* [School logopaedia: Children with oral language alterations in childhood and primary education]. Barcelona, Spain: Universidad de Barcelona. CC. Educación.

Caballero Martínez, J. (1999). *Nivel de Satisfacción Personal y Profesional de los/as Directores/as de los Centros de Educación Infantil, Primaria y Secundaria en Andalucía* [Level of personal and professional satisfaction of female/male directors of childhood, primary and secondary education centres in Andalucia]. Granada, Spain: Universidad de Granada. CC. Educación.

Cabanellas, I. (2001-2003). *Proyecto Investigación: Procesos Rítmicos Espacio-Temporales en el Primer Año de Vida* [Research project: Space-temporal rythmic processes in the first year of life]. Pamplona, Spain: University of Pamplona.

Calvo Rueda, Mercedes. (1994). *La Educación Infantil en España. Planteamientos Legales y Problemática Actual* [Childhood education in Spain: Legal issues and current problems]. Madrid, Spain: Universidad de Complutense. CC. Educación.

Cantos Ceballos, A. M. (1996). *La Expresion Dramática en el Aula: Una Metodologia Creativa Fundamentada en el Legado Historico-Cultural de la Antigüedad* [Drama in the classroom: A creative methodology based on the historical-cultural heritage of ancient times]. Málaga, Spain: Universidad de Málaga. CC. Educación.

Carlino Cantis, P. C. (1995). *Desarrollo de las Estrategias de Lectura y Escritura* [Development of reading and writing strategies]. Madrid, Spain: Universidad de Autónoma. Psicología.

Carrión Martínez, J. J. (1999). *Integración Escolar y Escuela para Todos. Estudio de Caso* [School integration and a school for all: A case study]. Almería, Spain: Universidad de Almería. CC. Educación.

Castro Quiñones, S. (1998). *La Innovación a través de la Revisión Colaborativa de la Acción Directiva en Centros Escolares de Educación Infantil y Primaria. Pautas para la Elaboración de una Guía de Análisis* [Innovation through the collaborative review of the directive action in school centres for childhood and primary education]. Barcelona, Spain: Universidad de Barcelona. Pedagogía.

Ceacero Cubillo, J. (1996). *Procesos de Transferencia Positiva y Negativa en el Razonamiento Analógico* [Positive and negative processes of transfer in analogical reasoning]. Madrid, Spain: Universidad Nacional de Educación a Distancia. Psicología.

Clemente Linuesa, M. (1992). *La Lectura en la Escuela Infantil: Una Perspectiva Cultural* [Reading in infant school: A cultural perspective]. Salamanca, Spain: Universidad de Salamanca. CC. Educación.

Cordero Arroyo, D. (1995). *El Asesoramiento Externo en los Centros Educativos de Educación Infantil y Primaria. Situación, Perspectivas y Debates en el Contexto de la Formación Permanente del Profesorado en Cataluña* [External assessment in educational centres for infant and primary education: Situation, perspectives and debates within the permanent teacher training context in Catalonia]. Barcelona, Spain: Universidad de Barcelona. Pedagogía.

Defior, S. (1994). *La consciencia fonológica y el aprendizaje de la lectoescritura* [Phonological awareness and literacy learning]. *Jufancia y Aprendizaje, 67-68*, 90-113.

Díez Vegas, C. (2001). *La Interacción Social y la Construcción del Conocimiento en el Inicio Lectoescritor. Un Estudio Longitudinal* [Social interaction and building awareness at the beginning to read and write: A longitudinal study]. Madrid, Spain: Universidad Nacional de Educación a Distancia. Psicología.

Domínguez Gutiérrez, A. (1992). *La Enseñanza de Habilidades de Análisis Fonológico en el Aprendizaje de la Lectura y de la Escritura. Programas para Educación Infantil* [Teaching phonological analysis skills when learning to read and write: Childhood education programmes]. Salamanca, Spain: Universidad de Salamanca. CC. Educación.

Elizalde Alcayaga, L. M. (1997). *El Trabajo Cotidiano En Dos Escuelas Infantiles (0-3 Años). Análisis Descriptivo Y Simbolización* [Daily work in two infant schools (0-3 years old): Descriptive analysis and symbolization]. S. Sebastián, Spain: Universidad de País Vasco. CC. Educación.

Escorza Subero, Fco. J. (1994). *El Inicio de la Comprensión Autónoma de las Normas y Valores Sociales. Una Intervención Educativa* [Beginning of autonomous comprehension of norms and social values: An educational intervention]. Zaragoza, Spain: Universidad de Zaragoza. Psicología.

Esarihuela Monreal, A. (1991). *La Planificación de la Educación Preescolar y Primaria en la Provincia de Alicante* [Planning in pre-school and primary education in the province of Alicante]. Valencia, Spain: Universidad de Valencia. CC. Educación.

Fernández Cruz, M. (1994). *Una Aproximación Biográfica al Desarrollo Profesional de Maestros de Educación Infantil: Ciclo Vital, Identidad, Conocimiento y Cultura* [A biographical approximation to the professional development of teachers in childhood education: Vital cycle, identity, knowledge and culture]. Granada, Spain: Universidad de Granada. CC. Educación

Fernández De Haro, E. (1988). *Análisis y Medición de la Influencia de la Participación de Padres en el Proceso de Maduración del Niño, en el Periodo de Educación Infantil* [Analysis and measurement of the influence of parent participation in the process of child maturing, in the childhood education period]. Granada, Spain: Universidad de Granada. Psicología.

Fernández Escalona, C. (2001). *Relaciones Lógicas-Ordinales entre los Términos de la Secuencia Numérica en Niños de Tres a Seis Años* [Logical-Ordinal relationships between the numeral sequence terms in children from three to six years old]. Málaga, Spain: Universidad de Málaga. CC. Educación: Didáctica Matemáticas.

Fernández González, Ma. P. (2000). *Los Cefocops y su Función en la Formación Permanente del Profesorado de Educación Infantil en Galicia* [Teacher Training Centres and their Function in the Permanent Training of Teachers in Childhood Education in Galicia]. Madrid, Spain: Universidad Nacional de Educación a Distancia. CC. Educación.

Fernández Nares, S. (1990). *La Educación Física en el Sistema Educativo Español: Curriculum y Formación Del Profesorado* [Physical education in the Spanish educational system: Curriculum and teacher training]. Granada, Spain: Universidad de Granada. CC. Educación.

Fernández Rey, E. (1998). *Desarrollo de la Creatividad Analógica en la Educación de los Niños Deficientes Visuales y Ciegos: Un Estudio de Casos* [Development of analogical creativity in the education of children with visual deficiencies and blind: Case studies]. Santiago de Compostela, Spain: Universidad de Santiago. CC. de la Educación.

Ferradás Blanco, L. (1998). *Avaluación da Calidade do Programa "Preescolar na Casa"* [Evaluation of the quality of the programme "Preschool at home"]. Santiago, Spain: Universidad de Santiago. CC. Educación.

Fuenmayor Fernández, A. (1993). *La Educación Infantil: Financiacion e Incentivacion* [Childhood education: Funding and incentive]. Valencia, Spain: Universidad de Valencia. CC. Económicas.

Fuentes, E. (1998). *Ensinar en Educación Infantil: Perspectivas do Profesorado* [Teaching in childhood education: Teachers' views]. Santiago de Compostela, Spain: Tórculo.

Gallego Ortega, J. L. (1996). *Disfunciones en la Articulación y la Morfosintaxis: Diseño, Desarrollo y Evaluación de un Programa de Intervención Didáctica* [Malfunctions in articulation and morphosyntax: Design, development and evaluation of a didactic intervention programme]. Granada, Spain: Universidad de Granada. CC. Educación.

Gallego, J. L. (2003). *Enciclopedia de la Educación Infantil* [Childhood education encyclopaedia]. Granada, Spain: Alfaguara.

Garagorri Yarza, X. (1994). *Proyecto "Haurtxoa". Evaluación de un Proyecto de Renovación del Segundo Ciclo de Educación Infantil* [The "Haurtxoa" Project: Evaluation of a renovation project of the second cycle of childhood education]. San Sebastián, Spain: Universidad de País Vasco. CC. Educación.

García Fernández, J. M. (1997). *Validación de Tres Formas del Inventario de Miedos Escolares* [Validation of three forms of the school fears inventory]. Murcia, Spain: Universidad de Murcia. Psicología.

García Huerta, A. (1994). *La Educación Infantil en el Medio Rural: Problemas, Perspectivas. Su Adaptación Metodologiíta en la Reforma Educativa* [Childhood education in the rural context: Problems, views. Its methodological adaptation in the educational reform]. Madrid: Universidad Nacional de Educación a Distancia. CC. Educación.

García Navarro, P. A. (1913). *Manual teórico-práctico de educación de párvulos según el método de los Jardines de Infancia de F. Froebel* [Theoretical and practical handbook of infant education according to the method of F. Froebel's kindergartens]. Madrid, Spain: Imprenta Hernando. .

García Vale, Ma. C. (1998). *Análisis de Conductas Manifiestas de Educación para la Salud Mediante Observación Sistemática de Actividades de Educación Infantil (3-4 Años)* [Analysis of manifest conduct in health education through systematic observation of childhood education activities (3-4-years-old)]. Santiago, Spain: Univeridad de Santiago. Psicología.

García Vidal, J. (1998). *La Evaluación Predictiva de la Iniciación Lectora* [Predictive evaluation of reading initiation]. Sevilla, Spain: Universidad de Sevilla. CC. Educación

Genishi, C., Ryan, S., Ochsner, M., & Yarnall, M. M. (2001). Teaching in early childhood education: Understanding practices through research and theory. In V. Richardson (Ed.), *Handbook of research on reaching* (4th ed., pp. 1175-1210). Washington, DC: AERA.

Gervilla, A. (2002). *Necesidades Educativas de la Infancia ante el Nuevo Milenio* [Educational needs in childhood facing the new millennium]. Málaga, Spain: Universidad de Málaga. Grupo de Investigación de Educación Infantil y Formación de Educadores.

Gil Molina, Pilar. (1995). *Los Profesionales de Educación Infantil. Su Perfil Profesional Hoy en Guipúzcoa. Una Propuesta Formativa* [Childhood education professionals. Their professional profile today in Guipuzcoa: A formative proposal]. San Sebastián, Spain: Universidad de País Vasco. CC. Educación.

Giner, T. (2000). *La Tarea de Evaluar en la Educación Infantil. Algunos Problemas Relacionados con la Lectoescritura* [The task of evaluating in childhood education: Some problems related to reading and writing]. In A. Calatayud, J. Jorba, A. Parcerisa, N. Sanmarti, M. Ballester, J. M. Batallosa, J. Córdova, J. Diego, M. Fons, T. Giner, B. Mir, J. Moreno, L. Otero, T. Pigrav, & J. Pitalúga: *Evaluación como Ayuda al Aprendizaje [Evaluation as an Aid to Learning]*. Barcelona, Spain: Graó.

Gómez Castillejo, A. (1995). *Análisis de los Factores Implicados en el Aprendizaje de la Lectoescritura y su Tratamiento en el Sistema Educativo* [Analysis of the factors implied in the learning of reading and writing and its treatment in the educational system]. Madrid, Spain: Universidad de Complutense. CC. Educación.

Gómez Salas, F. (1997). *La Importancia del Entorno Social en el Desarrollo Curricular del Segundo Ciclo de Educación Infantil* [The importance of social surroundings in the curricular development of the second cycle in childhood education]. Madrid, Spain: Universidad de Complutense. CC. Educación

González Agápito, J. (1991). Educación Infantil e Industrialización en Cataluña [Childhood Education and Industrialization in Catalonia] *Revista Interuniversitaria de Historia de la Educación* [Interuniversity review on the History of Education], *10*, 135-154.

González, M. M., Hidalgo, V. Y., & Moreno, M. C. (1998). La Vida en Familia [Family life]. *Cuadernos de Pedagogía, 274*, 50-55.

Granada Azcárraga, M. (1999). *Análisis Comparativo del Proceso Educativo desde la Perspectiva del Aprendizaje Situado y del Aprendizaje en el Aula* [Comparative analysis of the educational process from the point of view of situation learning and classroom learning]. Doctoral dissertation. Madrid, Spain: Universidad de Complutense. CC. Educación.

Granell Pérez, R. (1999). *Vales Educativos: El Caso De Valencia* [Educational vouchers: The case of Valencia]. Valencia, Spain: Universidad de Valencia. CC. Económicas y Empresariales.

Guerra Cabrera, J. (2002). *La Plástica y el Medio Ambiente: Propuesta de Instrumentación Metodológica de la Educación Artística en Infantil y Primaria y su Interacción en el Desarrollo Curricular* [Art and the Environment: Methodological instrumentation proposal of artistic education in childhood and primary education and its interaction in curricular development]. La Laguna, Spain: Universidad de La Laguna. Bellas Artes

Gutiérrez Tapas, M. (2001). *Elaboración, Aplicación y Evaluación de un Modelo de Acción Tutorial para el Desarrollo Socio-Personal del Alumnado de Educación Infantil y Primaria en el Ámbito de un Colegio Rural Agrupado* [Elaboration, application and evaluation of a model of tutorial action for the socio-personal development of the students in childhood and primary education in the grouped rural school context]. Madrid, Spain: Universidad Nacional de Educación a Distancia. CC. Educación

Iglesias Forneiro, L. (1996). *Deseño e Manexo de Espacios na Aula de Educación Infantil. Analise do Pensamento e Actuación dos Profesores/as* [Design and management of spaces in the childhood education classroom: Analysis of the thoughts and actions of the teachers]. Santiago, Spain: Universidad de Santiago. CC. Educación.

Jiménez Raurell, M. M. (1996). *Educación Infantil (Ciclo 0-3) en un Barrio Marginal* [Childhood education (cycle 0-3) in a marginal neighbourhood]. Madrid, Spain: Universidad Nacional de Educación a Distancia. CC. Educación.

Justo Martínez, Eduardo. (1996). *La Intervención Psicomotriz en Educación: su Influencia sobre el Esquema Corporal y el Autoconcepto en Niños de 5 Años* [Psychomotor intervention in education: Its influence on the body scheme and self-concept in 5-year-old children]. Granada, Spain: Universidad de Granada. Psicología.

Lera Rodríguez, Ma. J. (1993). *Ideas de los Profesores y su Practica Educativa. Un Estudio en Preescolar* [Teachers' ideas and their educational practice: A study of pre-school]. Sevilla, Spain: Universidad de Sevilla. Psicología.

Lera, M. J. (1994). *Las Ideas de los Profesores y su Práctica Educativa. Un Estudio en Preescolar* [Teachers' ideas and their educational practice: A study of pre-school]. Sevilla, Spain: Universidad de Sevilla. Psicología.

Lera, M. J. (1996). Education under five in Spain: A study of pre-school classes in Seville, Spain: *European Journal of Psychology of Education, XI*(2), 139-151.

Lera, M. J. (1999). Maestras y Maestros, ¿Iguales o Diferentes? [Female and male teachers, the same or different?]. *Infancia, 57,* 26-28.

Lera, M. J., & González, M. M. (1998). La Vida en las Aulas [Life in the classrooms]. *Cuadernos de Pedagogía, 274,* 62-66.

Lera, M. J., Ganaza, I., Gutiérrez, M., & García, S. (2000). *A jugar...que de todo aprenderás* [To play...you will learn from everything]. Sevilla: Consejería de Educación. Junta de Andalucía e Institutolicona Andaluz de la Mujer.

Licona Vega, A. L. (2000). *Videojuegos, Juego Simbólico y Educación Infantil: Adaptación del "Sistema Esar" para una Propuesta de Modelo de Análisis y Selección de Videojuegos Destinados a Niños y Niñas de 3 A 7 Años de Edad* [Video games, symbolic games and childhood education: Adaptation of the "Esar System" for a proposal of an analysis and selection model of video games destined for children of 3 to 7 years of age]. Palma de Mallorca, Spain: Universidad de Illes Baleares. CC. Educación.

López González, C. (1991). *La Emigración Española y la Educación Infantil-Juvenil en el Marco de la C.E.E. Hacia una Política Educativa Intercultural* [Spanish emmigration and childhood-youth education in the framework of the EEC: Towards an intercultural educational policy]. Santiago, Spain: Universidad de Santiago. CC. Educación.

López Martínez, O. (2001). *Evaluación Y Desarrollo De La Creatividad* [Evaluation and development of creativity]. Murcia, Spain: Universidad de Murcia. CC. Educación.

López Sánchez, M. (2000). *La Percepción de los Tutores/as de Educación Infantil y Educación Primaria como Usuarios/as de los Equipos de Orientación Educativa en la Comunidad Autónoma Andaluza* [Views of tutors in childhood education and primary education as users of the educational orientation teams in the autonomous community of Andalucia]. Granada, Spain: Universidad de Granada. CC. Educación.

Lozano Martínez, J. (1993). *Un Modelo Integrado de Practica Psicomotriz y Acceso a la Lectoescritura en Niños Socialmente Desfavorecidos* [An integrated model of psychomotor practice and access to reading and writing in socially impaired children]. Murcia, Spain: Universidad de Murcia. CC. Educación.

Lucchini, E. (1997). "La pedagogia Dell'infanzia, oggi" [Current childhood pedagogy]. In F. Frabboni (Org.): *Scienze dell'Educazione e scuola dell'infanzia* [Educational sciences and early childhood school] (pp. 61-100). Roma: La Nuova Italia Científica. Pgs. 61-100.

Luque, A., & Candau, X. (1998) Contextos Educativos y Desarrollo Infantil [Educational contexts and childhood development]. *Cuadernos de Pedagogía, 274,* 68-73.

Marchena Consejero, E. (1997). *Un Programa de Control de Estímulos y Formación en Conceptos en Niños de Educación Infantil* [A programme for stimuli control and concept training for children in childhood education]. Cádiz, Spain: Universidad de Cádiz. CC. Educación.

Martínez Abellán, R. (1994). *El Desarrollo Psicomotor del Niño Ciego. Influencia en su Evolución General y en la Adquisición de los Aprendizajes Básicos* [Psychomotor development in blind children: Influence on their general evolution and acquisition of basic learning]. Murcia, Spain: Universidad de Murcia. CC. Educación.

Martínez Lobato, E. (1998). *Estudio de la Integración de los Medios Informativos en los Currículos de Educación Infantil y Primaria: sus Implicaciones en la Practica Educativa* [Study of the integration of news in childhood and primary education curriculums: Its implications in educational practice]. Madrid, Spain: Universidad de Complutense. CC. Educación.

Martínez Mínguez, L. (2000). *El Proyecto Curricular de Centro como Documento de Cambio y de Innovación en los Centros Educativos de Primaria* [A centre curricular project as a document of change and innovation in primary educational centres]. Barcelona, Spain: Universida de Autónoma, CC. Educación.

Martínez Olmo, F. (1999). *La Formación en Centros. Un Estudio de Caso en la Educación Infantil* [Training in centres: A case study in childhood education]. Barcelona, Spain: Universidad de Barcelona. CC. Educación.

Martínez, A., & Saureda, N. (2002). *La Constitución de la Profesionalidad de los Profesores* [The constitution of the professionalism of teachers]. Alicante, Spain: Club Universitario.

Martínez, A., & Saureda, N. (2002). *La Narrativa de los Profesores: una Perspectiva Situada* [Teacher narrative: A situated perspective]. Alicante, Spain: Club Universitario.

Massa Gutiérrez, Ma. L. (2000). *Las Dificultades en la Adquisición del Lenguaje y su Relacion con los Hábitos en la Primera Infancia: Aspectos Educativos y Preventivos* [The difficulties in language acquisition and its relation with habits in first infancy: Educational and preventive aspect]. Madrid, Spain: Universidad de Complutense. CC. Educación.

Méndez, L. (1996). *Educar a los más Pequeños. Una Experiencia en Educación Infantil* [Educating the youngest: An experience in childhood education]. Córdoba, Spain: Universida de Córdoba. CC. Educación.

Mendiara Rivas, J. (1996). *Educación Física y Aprendizajes Tempranos. Contribución al Desarrollo Global de los Niños de 3 a 6 Años y Estudio de sus Estrategias de Aprendizaje en Espacios de Acción y Aventura* [Physical education and early learning: Contribution to the global development of children of 3 to 6 years of age and a study of their learning strategies in spaces for action and adventure]. Zaragoza, Spain: Universida de Zaragoza. CC. Educación.

Mendizábal Ituarte, A. (1994). *Factores Relevantes en la Enseñanza-Aprendizaje del Euskera en la Educación Infantil* [Relevant factors in the teaching-learning of Euskera in childhood education]. Madrid, Spain: Universidad Nacional de Educación a Distancia. CC. Educación.

Mérida Serrano, R. (1999). *Los Mapas Preconceptuales como Estrategia para el Desarrollo Sociocognitivo Infantil* [Preconceptual maps as a strategy for child sociocognitive development]. Córdoba, Spain: Universida de Córdoba. CC. Educación.

Mir Pozo, Ma. L. (1999). *Adaptación de un Instrumento (Cgc) sobre la Gestión de Clase en Educación Infantil* [Adaptation of an instrument (Cgc) to classroom management in childhood education]. Palma de Mallorca, Spain: Universida de Illes Baleares. CC. Educación.

Monlau, P. F. (1840). *De la instrucción pública en Francia* [About public instruction in France]. Barcelona, Spain: A. Bergnes.

Montesino, P. (1840). *Manual del maestro de párvulos* [Handbook of an infant teacher]. Madrid, Spain: Imprenta Nacional.

Morales Núñez, Fernando. (1999). *El Vocabulario de los Niños en el Segundo Ciclo de la Educación Infantil (Area:Sanlucar-Chipiona)* [Children's vocabulary in the second cycle of childhood education (Area: Sanlucar-Chipiona)]. Sevilla, Spain: Universida de Sevilla. CC. Educación.

Moreno, M. (1998). *El Desarrollo Morfosintáctico en Niños con Retraso de Lenguaje: Evaluación e Intervención en el Contexto Escolar* [Morphosyntactic development in children with language deficiencies: Evaluation and intervention in the school context]. La Laguna, Spain: Universida de La Laguna. CC. Educación.

Nadal Perdomo, I. (1998). *La Concepción del Espacio Próximo y Lejano. Justificación de una Propuesta Alternativa para el Estudio del Medio en Primaria* [The conception of near and far spaces: Justification of an alternative proposal for the study of the medium at primary level]. Las Palmas, Spain: Universida de Las Palmas. Geografía e Historia.

Oliva, A., & Palacios, J. (1992). *Ideas de los Profesores sobre la Educación y el Desarrollo* [Teachers' ideas on education and development]. Sevilla, Spain: Universida de Sevilla. Psicología.

Oliva, A., & Palacios, J. (1998). I*deas y Valores sobre la Educación Infantil* [Ideas and values on childhood education]. *Cuadernos de Pedagogía, 274*, 46-49.

O' Shanahan, J. I. (1995). *La Enseñanza del Lenguaje Oral y las Teorías Implícitas del Profesorado* [Teaching oral language and the implicit theories of teachers]. La Laguna, Spain: Universida de La Laguna. Pedagogía

Palacios, J., & Lera, M. J. (1992). *Observación de las Actividades de Preescolar (OAP)* [Observation of pre-school Activities (OPA)]. Sevilla, Spain: Universida de Sevilla. Psicología.

Palacios, J., Lera, M. J., & Oliva, A. (1995). Quality of child care in Spain. In W. E. Fthenakis & M. R. Textor (Eds.), *Quality of child care: International perspectives* (pp. 91-199). Berlin, Germany: Beltz.

Palacios, J., Lera, M. J., & Moreno, M. C. (1994). Evaluación de los Contextos Familiares y Extrafamiliares en los Años Preescolares: escalas HOME y ECERS [Evaluation of family and extrafamily contexts in pre-school years: HOME and ECERS scales]. *Infancia y Aprendizaje, 66*, 72-78.

Parrilla, A. (1999). Educational innovations as a school answer to diversity. *International Journal of Inclusive Education, 3*(2), 93-110.

Parrilla, A., Hernández, E., & Murillo, P. (1997). Developing a shared approach to support: A support group case study. *European Journal of Special Need Education, 12*(3), 209-224.

Perea Riquelmen, S. (1996). *Análisis Bibliométrico de la Producción Española sobre Educación Infantil (1976-1994) a través de la Base de Datos Isoc* [Bibliometric analysis of Spanish production on childhood education (1976-1994) through the Isoc database]. Murcia, Spain: Universida de Murcia. Psicología.

Pérez García, Ma. P. (2001). *La Tarea Supervisora en la Formación del Profesorado de las Etapas de Educación Infantil y Primaria: Un Modelo Reflexivo de Supervision* [The supervisory task in the teacher training of teachers for the childhood and primary stages: A reflexive model of supervision]. Granada, Spain: Universida de Granada. CC. Educación.

Pérez Montero, C. (2002). *Las Tareas de Educar en 0-6 Años* [The tasks of teaching 0-6 year-olds]. Madrid, Spain: CEPE.

Pérez Montero, Ma. C. (2000). *Perfil del Nuevo Profesor de Escuela Infantil de Acuerdo con las Exigencias de la Nueva Ley de Educación. Su Formación en Lenguaje Oral para la Enseñanza de Niños 18 Meses a 4 Años* [Profile of the new infant school teacher according to the demands of the new education act: His/her training in oral language to teach children from 18 months to 4 years old]. Madrid, Spain: Universidad de Complutense. CC. Educación.

Pique Simón, B. (1996). *Individualización y Curriculum en la Educación Infantil. La Actividad en el Aula y la Atención a La Diversidad. Estrategias Didácticas* [Individualisation and curriculum in childhood education. Activity in the classroom and attention to diversity. Didactic strategies]. Barcelona, Spain: Universida de Barcelona. Pedagogía.

Poveda Bicnell, D. (2000). *Un Análisis Etnográfico de la Interacción en el Aula en Relación con la Alfabetización* [An ethnographic analysis of the interaction in the classroom in relation to literacy]. Madrid, Spain: Universida de Autónoma. Psicología.

Prieto Laina, J. L. (1997). *Análisis de la Interacción Educativa en el Aula de Educación Infantil desde la Perspectiva Socio-histórico-Cultural* [Analysis of educational interaction in the childhood education classroom from a socio-historical-cultural perspective]. Córdoba, Spain: Universida de Córdoba. CC. Educación

Quintero Rodríguez, S. (1996). *La Educación para la Convivencia en el Marco de la Didáctica de las Ciencias Sociales* [Education for cohabiting in the didactic framework of social sciences]. La Laguna, Spain: Universida de La Laguna. CC. Educación: Didáctica CC. Sociales.

Quinza Segura, F. (1994). *Conocimientos, Actitudes y Hábitos Relacionados con la Salud en los Estudiantes de Magisterio* [Knowledge, attitudes and habits related to health in students studying to be teachers]. Valencia, Spain: Universida de Valencia. Medicina.

Reyes Santana, M. (2000). *Teorías Personales de los Profesores en Formación sobre las Organizaciones Educativas* [Personal theories of teachers being trained on educational organisations]. Huelva, Spain: Universidad de Huelva. CC. Educación.

Ribera Aragüete, P. (2001). *La Producción de Géneros Escritos en Alumnos de Cinco Años. Una Perspectiva desde la Enseñanza* [The production of written material in children of five: A view from teaching]. Valencia, Spain: Universidad de Valencia. Filología.

Riera, M. (2003a). *Implementación de Nuevos Servicios Socio-Educativos Destinados a la Primera Infancia y Familias: Espacios Familiares* [Implementation of new socio-educational services destined for first infancy and families: Familiar spaces]. Palma de Mallorca, Spain: Gobern Balear.

Riera, M. (2003b). *Estudio sobre la Gestión de la Clase. Identificación y Evaluación de Dificultades con los Alumnos que Cursan Estudios de Magisterio en Educación Infantil* [A study on classroom management. Identification and evaluation of difficulties with students taking the teaching course on childhood education]. Palma de Mallorca, Spain: Universida de les Illes Baleares. CC. Educación.

Rochera Villach, Ma. J. (1996). *Interactividad e Influencia Educativa: Análisis de Algunas Actividades de Enseñanza y Aprendizaje de los Primeros Números de la Serie Natural en Educación Infantil* [Interactivity and educational influence: Analysis of some teaching and learning activities of the first issues of the natural series in childhood education]. Barcelona, Spain: Univeresida de Barcelona. Psicología.

Rodríguez Fernández, A. (1999). *Valoración de la Estrategia de Formación Permanente del Profesorado en Centros* [Evaluation of the permanent training strategy of teachers in centres]. Almería, Spain: Universida de Almería. CC. Educación

Rodríguez Pulido, J. (1996). *La Evaluación de la Formación Permanente del Profesorado en la Comunidad Autónoma de Canarias: Merito del Programa de Formación Permanente del Profesorado de Educación Infantil en la Provincia de Las Palmas de Gran Canaria* [Evaluation of the permanent training of teachers in the autonomous community of the Canaries: Merit of the permanent training programme of childhood education teachers in the province of Las Palmas of Gran Canaria]. Las Palmas, Spain: Universida de Las Palmas. CC. Educación.

Romero, Ma. (1999). *Los Trastornos del Desarrollo del Lenguaje: Diseño de un Programa de Intervención* [Language development disorders: Design of an intervention programme]. Madrid, Spain: Universidad de Complutense. CC. Educación.

Roz Concha, S. (1998). *Investigación-Acción. Perspectivas Innovadoras Del Aprendizaje Infantil* [Investigation-Action: Innovative perspectives on childhood learning]. Madrid, Spain: Universidad Nacional de Educación a Distancia. Cc. Educación.

Rueda Parras, C. (1999). *Atención Prestada a la Infancia en la Ciudad de Jaen (1940-1995)* [Attention given to childhood in the city of Jaen (1940-1995)]. Jaen, Spain: Universidad. de Jaen. CC. Educación.

Ruesga, P. (2000). *Influencia del Lenguaje Afirmativo-Negativo en el Uso de Conectores Lógicos* [Influence of affirmative-negative language in the use of logical connectors]. Madrid, Spain: Universidad de Complutense. CC. Educación.

Ruiz Jiménez, S. (1999). *La Lecto-Escritura: Un Modelo de Aprendizaje Significativo a Partir de Unidades Didácticas en el Segundo Ciclo de Educación Infantil* [Reading-writing: A model for significant learning through didactic units in the second cycle of childhood education]. Murcia, Spain: Universida de Murcia. CC. Educación

Sánchez Blanco, C. (1993). *El Desarrollo de la Cooperación en el Segundo Ciclo de Educación Infantil. Análisis de la Práctica Educativa* [Development of cooperation in the second cycle of childhood education. analysis of educational practice]. Madrid, Spain: Universidad de Complutense. CC. Educación.

Segurado Cortés, Ma. B. (1992). *Análisis de los Elementos Plásticos del Dibujo Infantil Espontáneo y sus Implicaciones Educativas* [Analysis of the artistic elements in spontaneous children's drawings and its educational implications]. Valencia, Spain: Politécnica. Bellas Artes.

Sola Martínez, T. (1992). *La Formación del Profesorado de Educación Infantil en Zaep* [Teacher training in childhood education in Zaep]. Madrid, Spain: Universidad Nacional de Educación a Distancia. CC. Educación.

Soler Santaliestra, J. R. (1998). *La Participación Democrática de la Comunidad Educativa en la Administración y Gestión del Centro Escolar: El Consejo Escolar* [The democratic participation of the educational community in the administration and management of the school centre: The school council]. Barcelona, Spain: Universida de Autónoma. CC. Educación.

Sotes Ruiz, J. P. (1996). *La Comunicación Profesor/Alumnos al Comienzo de un Programa de Inmersión al Euskera* [Teacher/student communication at the beginning of an Euskera immersion programme]. Barcelona, Spain: Universida de Barcelona. Psicología.

Sousa Guerreibo, M. (2002). *Innovación Educativa y Formación de Profesores de Educación Infantil* [Educational innovation and teacher training in childhood education]. Sevilla, Spain: Universida de Sevilla. CC. Educación.

Spodek, B., & Brown, P. C. (1996). Alternativas curriculares na Educaçâo de Infancia: Uma perspectiva histórica [Curriculum alternatives for early childhood education: An historical perspective]. In J. Formosinho (Ed.), *Modelos curriculares para a Educaçâo de Infancia* [Models of curriculum for early childhood education] (pp. 13-50). Porto, Portugal: Porto Editora.

Terronteras Muñoz, A. (1995). *Aspectos Preventivos de la Medicina Escolar: Análisis Valorativo en una Comunidad Educativa Andaluza* [Preventive analysis of medicine in school: Evaluating analysis in an Andalucian educational community]. Sevilla, Spain. Universida de Sevilla. Medicina.

Tietze, W., Cryer, D., Bairrao, J., Palacios, J., & Wetzel, G. (1996). Comparisons of process quality in five countries. *Early Childhood research Quartely, 11*, 447-475.

Tietze, W., Hendertmark-Mayser, J., Rossbach, H. G., Kumm, V., Wetzel, G., Palacios, J., & Lera, M. J. (1997). *Cross national analysis of the quality and effects of different types of early childhood programs on children's development*. Brussels, Belgium: European Union DGXII.

Toorio López, S. (2001). *Estudio Socioeducativo de Hábitos y Tendencias de Comportamiento en Familias con Niños de Educación Infantil y Primaria en Asturias* [Socioeducational study of habits and behavioural tendencies in families with children in childhood and primary education in Asturias]. Oviedo, Spain: Universidad de Oviedo. CC. de la Educación.

Torrecilla Jareño, Ma. T. (1995). *La Formación Psicológica del Profesorado de Educación Infantil en La Universidad de Valencia: Análisis de la Situación Actual y Propuestas de Futuro* [Psychological training of teachers in childhood education in the university of Valencia: Analysis of the current situation and future proposals]. Valencia, Spain: Universida de Valencia. Psicología.

Urbina Ramírez, Santos. (2000). *Análisis del Uso del Ordenador en el Segundo Ciclo de Educación Infantil. Estudio de Caso* [Analysis of the use of the computer in the second cycle of childhood education. A case study]. Palma de Mallorca, Spain: Universida de Illes Baleares. CC. Educación.

Vaca Escribano, M. (1994). *Tratamiento Pedagógico de lo Corporal en Educación Infantil: Propuesta de un Modelo de Intervención a través del Estudio de un Caso de Segundo Ciclo* [Pedagogical treatment of all related to the body in childhood education. Proposal of an intervention model through a case study of the second cycle]. Madrid, Spain: Universidad Nacional de Educación a Distancia. CC. Educación.

Vega Morán, M. (1999). *La Autoridad del Maestro en el Aula. Su Estudio Concreto en Los Centros de Educación Infantil y Primaria de Ponferrada (Leon)* [Authority of the teacher in the classroom: Its concrete study in childhood and primary education centres of Ponferrada (Leon)]. Madrid, Spain: Universidad Nacional de Educación a Distancia. CC. Educación.

Vega Navarro, A. M. (2001). *Sol y Luna, Una Pareja Precopernicana. Estudio del DIA y la Noche en Educación Infantil* [The sun and the moon, a precopernican couple: A study of day and night in childhood education]. La Laguna, Spain: Universida de La Laguna. CC. Educación.

Vicente Villena, Ma. P. (1999). *Educación Infantil: de la Accion Social a la Accion Educativa. Una Aproximación a La Realidad en la Comunidad Autónoma de la Región de Murcia* [Childhood education: From social action to educational action. An approximation to the reality of the autonomous community of Murcia]. Murcia, Spain: Universida de Murcia. CC. De la Educación.

Viciana Garofano, V. (2000). *Efectos de un Programa Metodológico Lúdico para la Mejora de los Contenidos Curriculares en Niños/as del Segundo Ciclo de la Etapa de Educación Infantil* [Effects of a methodological entertaining programme for the improvement of curricular contents for children in the second cycle of the childhood education stage]. Granada, Spain: Universida de Granada. CC. Educación

Zabalza Beraza, M. A. (2001). *La Calidad de la Educación Infantil* [The Quality of Childhood Education]. Madrid, Spain: Narcea

Zabalza Beraza, M. A. (Ed.). (1998). *A Educación Infantil en Galicia* [Childhood education in Galicia]. Santiago de Compostela, Spain: Consejería de Educación. Xunta de Galicia.

Zabalza, M. A. (1991). *Los Diarios de Clase: Documentos para Estudiar Cualitativamente los Dilemas Prácticos de los Profesores* [Class diaries: Documents for the qualitative study of teachers' practical dilemmas]. Barcelona, Spain: PPU.

Zabalza, M. A. (Ed.). (1997). *La calidad en la educación infantil* [The quality of childhood education]. Madrid, Spain: Narcea.

Zabalza, M. A. (Ed.). (2002). *Proyecto de Investigación: Prendizaje Eficaz en la Infancia* [Research project: Effective early learning]. Santiago de Compostela, Spain: Xunta de Galicia.

CHAPTER 11

EARLY CHILDHOOD EDUCATION IN TURKEY

An Overview

Sevda Bekman

Early childhood education had been largely side lined in the first decades of the new Turkish Republic(1923), mostly due to the prioritization of primary education. In the 1960s it began to be articulated again largely with a social service understanding for children who for various reasons did not receive adequate care from their mothers. It is only in the 1990s that we can say early childhood education began to receive the attention it deserved and a large number of studies, projects and programs have been conducted since then. In terms of institutional development, a preschool education general directorate was established within the Ministry of National Education (MONE) in 1992 to meet the increasing needs in the community and standardize early childhood education institutions in Turkey .

Turkey does not have a standardized widespread system of early childhood education programs. Services in early childhood education programs either belong to or are under the supervision of MONE or general

International Perspectives on Research in Early Childhood Education, 335–353
Copyright © 2005 by Information Age Publishing

directorate of Social Welfare and Child Protection Agency (SSCPA). In addition to public or government supervised services there are a number of services run by a few non governmental organizations (NGO) in the country. Nearly all the public services as well as services under the supervision of the government are centre based and located in the large cities. The services provided by the NGOs can be described as largely alternative services to centre based early childhood education and include as home-based programs, TV programs or summer schools for preschool age children.

According to 2002-2003 figures there are 11,324.000 schools and 19,849 classes in the early childhood education system in the country. Hence, only 14% of 5-6-year-olds and 11% of 4-6 year-olds benefit from any form of services. When the entire target population of 0-6 years is considered, the coverage is indeed very low (Ministry of National Education, 2003).

The existing early childhood education services fall into the following three categories: nursery classes (kindergartens) which cater to children between 5-6 years of age before they begin formal schooling; preschool centres (day care centres, children's houses) which cater to children aged between 3-6 years; and creche and day care centres which cater to children from 0-6 years of age.

Turkey has undergone rapid social change involving mass migration from rural to urban areas. The number of women, including mothers of young children, employed in nonagricultural jobs outside the home has increased rapidly. This has created a demand for centre-based education and a consequent increase in the number of such centres. The combination of rapid increase in the number of centres, inadequate supervision and control by the government agencies, low expectation on the parts of parents, and diffusion of responsibility in the government agencies has led to the development of both a qualitatively poor early childhood education programs and of a quantitative gap between the services that are available for different sectors of the society. The present services are distinctly divided into two with respect to their aims: custodial and educational. Unfortunately, the number of custodial centres far outweigh the number of educational ones.

Although the current research in the area is limited in coverage, it has addressed some of the significant concerns in the area.

This chapter aims to provide an overview of the early childhood education (ECE) programs and policies in Turkey, tracing its historical development, critically examining the contemporary status, and presenting a review of current research in the area.

HISTORY OF THE DEVELOPMENT OF EARLY CHILDHOOD EDUCATION IN TURKEY

Development of early childhood education in Turkey dates back to the prerepublic era of 1923. At the establishment of the republic in 1923, there were 80 nursery schools in 38 cities with 5,880 children enrolled. With the reformation of the script in 1928, replacing the Arabic with the Latin alphabet, primary education—rather than early childhood education—became a priority for the government in a quest to increase the literacy rate. Many early childhood education institutions were either reassigned as primary schools or shut down in order to create more resources for primary education. Consequently, early childhood education was left to the responsibility of families and local administrations. The remaining institutions could only be used by women in poverty who had to work; this situation continued until the late 1940s (Okay, 1983).

Early childhood education was articulated as a means to family education for the first time in 1949 at the fourth National Education Conference. In 1961, the primary education law was passed, followed by the 1962 preschool regulations. Soon after, early childhood education appeared in the second 5-year development plan of 1962, but it was still seen as the education of 5 to 6 year-old-children whose mothers had no education. In the period between 1968-1972, decisions were made to establish and improve independent preschools, nursery classes within preschools, and preschools within girls vocational schools. The third and the fourth 5-year development plans duly considered the importance of a widespread early childhood education program targeting the needs of the country and recommended the expansion of programs for the children of blue-collar workers, who are generally deprived of their mothers' care and education. Finally in the fifth 5-year development plan of 1977, it was decided that public and private resources should be maximized in order for at least 10% of the 5-6-year-old children population to benefit from early childhood education (State Planning Organization, 2003).

In terms of institutional structures, a number of ministries and agencies in Turkey have responsibilities in supporting the development of children of working mothers, including the MONE, Ministry of Health, Ministry of Employment and the SSCPA in Turkey. The responsibilities of the SSCPA have been defined as primarily establishing institutions for the care and education of children aged 0-5 years.

In national education conferences over the past 2 decades, early childhood education has been a more prominent part of the agenda in that subcommittees have been established and studies conducted on the importance of early childhood education, the extension of early childhood education, early childhood education models, early childhood education teacher training and recruitment, and so forth (Ministry of National Education, 2003).

In 1996, the XVth national education conference made two important commitments: the first, to increase the years compulsory education from 5 years to 8 years, and the second, to make at least 2 years of preschool education compulsory in the future (Ministry of National Education, 2003).

To summaries, early childhood education had been largely side lined in the first decades of the new Turkish Republic, mostly due to the prioritization of primary education. In the 1960s it began to be articulated again largely with a social service understanding for children who for various reasons did not receive adequate care from their mothers. It is only in the 1990s that we can say early childhood education began to receive the attention it deserved and a large number of studies, projects, and programs have been conducted since then. In terms of institutional development, a preschool education general directorate was established within the MONE in 1992 to meet the increasing needs in the community and standardize early childhood education institutions in Turkey (Oktay, 1999). Most recently, the 8-year compulsory education law enacted in 1997-1998 seems to be a promising step towards compulsory preschool education.

Demographic Information and Cultural Practices

Turkey is a country with a population of about 67,633.000. Of the 67,633.000 population, 9% are under 5-years-old. According to 2001 figures for the population under five, there are 43 deaths for every 1000 children (United Nations Children's Fund [UNICEF], 2003). In the descending order of mortality rates for under fives in the world, Turkey is 79th. The same decreasing trend is also observed in infant mortality rates. While the number of infant deaths was 163 for every 1000 infant in 1960, this number decreased to 36 in 2001 (UNICEF, 2003). Of the adult population, 85% is literate and while the 94% of the males are literate, the percentage drops to 77 for females. The schooling percentage of 8 years of compulsory education is 88% for the population of 6-14-year-olds (UNICEF, 2003).

Kagitcibasi and Sunar (1992) describe Turkish family both closely knit and independent and hierarchical. Socialization practices in the family are tuned for children to learn relations and social skills so as to function in a close knit context in which power and authority differences are clear cut. Family culture of relatedness exist in the context of social change. This dynamic existence of relatedness and social change characterises the

Turkish family. Parents see education of children as an important means to help them become successful in life. A difference in their aspirations and expectations regarding their children's education is articulated. The reason for this difference is always mentioned as their economic and life situation. For young children, play is observed as something children engage in naturally. Mostly it is observed as a mean to pass time.

Current Status of ECE in Turkey

Turkey does not have a standardized widespread system of early childhood education programs. Services in early childhood education programs either belong to, or are under the supervision of MONE, or SSCPA. In addition to public or government supervised services, there are a number of services run by a few NGO in the country. Nearly all the public services, as well as services under the supervision of the government, are centre based and located in the large cities. The services provided by the NGOs can be described as largely alternative services to centre based early childhood education, and include, as home-based programs, TV programs or summer schools for preschool age children.

According to 2002-2003 figures from the MONE there are 11,324.000 schools and 19,849 classes in the early childhood education system in the country. Hence, only 14% of 5-6-year-olds and 11% of 4-6- year-olds benefit from any form of services. When the entire target population of 0-6-year-olds is considered, the coverage is indeed very low (Ministry of National Education, 2003).

The existing early childhood education services fall into the following three categories: nursery classes (kindergartens) which cater to children between 5-6 years of age in the year before they begin formal schooling; preschool centres (day care centres, children's houses) which cater to children aged between 3-6 years, and creche and day care centres which cater to children from 0-6 years of age. In addition, children between the ages of 0-18 months and up to 25 months, who are under the protection of the state by court order, are cared for in children's homes or training institutions appropriate for their age group.

While the MONE is largely responsible for the development and education of the age group 4-6 years, SSCPA is responsible for the age group 0-6 years. The public preschools, under the responsibility of MONE, mainly fall into the category of nursery classes since nursery classes, are a part of primary education institutions. There are few public preschool centres, which belong to MONE. Institutions which are under the supervision of MONE but belong to the private sector, are mainly preschools or nursery classes of private elementary schools. On the other hand, the public institutions, which belong to SSCPA, are mainly creche and day care centres. The private institutions, which are under the supervision of SSCPA, cater to children between the ages of 3-6 or 0-6 years and fall within the creche and day care centre categories. The institutions, which serve children who are under the protection of the courts, are governmental services and belong to SSCPA. In addition to these facilities there are creche and day care centres which belong to other public organizations (ministries, universities) and private (factories, trade unions) (Oktay 1983).

POLICY AND TRAINING CONCERNS IN EARLY CHILDHOOD EDUCATION

Turkey has undergone rapid social change involving mass migration from rural to urban areas. The number of women, including mothers of young children, employed in nonagricultural jobs outside the home has increased rapidly. This has created a demand for centre-based education and a consequent increase in the number of such centres. The combination of rapid increase in the number of centres, inadequate supervision and control by the government agencies, low expectation on the parts of parents, and diffusion of responsibility in the government agencies has led to the development of both a qualitatively poor early childhood education programs and of a quantitative gap between the services that are available for different sectors of the society. The present services are distinctly divided into two with respect to their aims: custodial and educational. Unfortunately, the number of custodial centres far outweigh the number of educational ones (Bekman, 1993, 2002; Kagitcibasi, Sunar, & Bekman, 2001).

As with any developing country, public resources are scarce and in the education sector, the government allocates the greatest portion of funds to compulsory primary education. The funds allocated to early childhood education from the general budget of MONE less than the 1% of the amount allocated to primary education.

At the same time, the MONE maintains the position of trying to expand early childhood education services with a singular centre based education model. This position is reflected in the eighth 5-year development plan, which has specified plans to increase the coverage of early childhood education to 25% of the child population by 2005 through an expansion of preschool centres. Centre based early childhood education is only one among several models of early childhood education. This limits diversity within the system and results in a narrow definition of the target age group for early childhood education. The age range of the target population for early childhood education is also defined narrowly by the policies. There is hardly any mention of a target population of 3-6-year-olds or 0-6-year-olds in any policy or programming. Policy decisions in recent years have therefore tended to result in—albeit limited—single model services for only the group 5-6-years-old of age.

Centre based models are also the most expensive, requiring large infra-structural investment which makes it difficult to implement on a large scale over a small period of time. The dominance of the centre-based model also tends to ignore the diversity of needs within different target groups. This narrow definition of possible services indicates that the per-centage of the population reached will always be unsatisfactory. Under present conditions, this shortcoming is even more critical for children from unstimulating environments since a large number of available facili-ties are privately owned and charge tuition. We can therefore conclusively state that the present system does not target those children who are most in need of early childhood support.

For countries like Turkey, which have very large young populations who are urgently in need of early intervention, it may in fact be easier as well as more beneficial to implement different models for different segments of the population rather than expanding one model for all the segments (Myers, 1992). If the aim is to reach a large number of children, priority should also be given to cost-effective programs that can be applied on a large scale.

Similarly, if the policy priority is to overcome social and gender based inequalities and provide a fair start to formal schooling for all children, programs should priorities those who are most in need of early interven-tion. The policies of expansion have resulted in growth of early childhood education centres in big cities largely by private institutions rather than public. Under these conditions children most in need of early support mechanisms have difficulty in accessing the services both economically and geographically.

In terms of the aim of early childhood education policies, MONE has favoured a preparation for school approach. This is reflected both in the target group for services (5-6-year-olds) and the content of the curricu-lum. However, even a cursory review of the literature will reveal that prep-aration for school is only one aim of early childhood education programs. Intervention approaches to reach groups under developmental risk may be more important for developing countries with large social inequalities. Present public policy does not target or priorities such groups for inter-vention.

Institutionally, early childhood education does not have a standardised policy of supervision, accreditation, or licensing. The diffusion of respon-sibility in early childhood education among the government agencies

(MONE and SSCPA) has created a number of differences in policies of implementation. For example, regulations regarding curriculum and teacher status are different for the two agencies. The curriculum of MONE early childhood programs are centralized whilst the curriculum of the SSPCA centres are largely developed by the staff members themselves. Also teachers employed by MONE are required to have a 4-year university degree in preschool teaching, while teachers employed by SSCPA are not. This requirement by MONE (which is by far the largest employer of preschool teachers in the country) has increased the scarcity of teachers. As a result MONE has had to modify this regulation by employing students from child development departments of the Open University as temporary teachers. These policies and practices have led to variations in the quality of the teachers in the system.

The development of the early childhood education as an academic discipline has also undergone certain changes. For a long period departments of child development and education were the only departments training teachers and educators in the area of early childhood education. These were few in number. In 1998 the Commission of Higher Education took a decision to increase the teacher training departments in the country. As a result, now there are 33 teacher training departments of early childhood education in the country. While the graduates of child development and education departments can not be certified as teachers, the graduates of teacher training departments are. As expected, the newly developed departments are in their infancy, while the former are well established. Thus one can observe distinct differences between these departments regarding quality of teaching, number of research as conducted and the number of well trained teaching staff.

CURRENT RESEARCH IN EARLY CHILDHOOD EDUCATION

The overview of the current research shows that several topics have been examined in the area through research but one cannot talk about a research policy or a main debate around specific questions. Existing research indicate a trend very similar to the state of the field of early childhood education as a whole, namely limited in coverage and still in a stage of infancy. The present review primarily deals with research carried out by early childhood educators. As the review illustrates, the studies are either descriptive in nature or small scale comparison studies.

Efficacy of the Early Childhood Education Programs

The effectiveness of the programs has been the subject matter of a number of studies. While some of the researchers examine the issue from the perspective of *quality* and the appropriateness of factors like curriculum, teacher behaviour, physical arrangement of the classroom, others have approached the subject from the perspective of *effectiveness* and have studied the effects of the program on the development of the child.

Research examining the quality of early childhood education centres (Bekman, 2002, 1993; Kagitcibasi, 1996; Kagitcibasi, Sunar, & Bekman, 2001) evaluated preschool centres on various dimensions such as objectives of curriculum, physical arrangement, number and nature of the available materials, equipment and activities, and staff-child ratio. Studies have found that educational centres in comparison to custodial (care oriented as opposed to development and education) centres are superior in: physical arrangements directed towards facilitating the overall development of the child; the quantity and the quality of materials and equipment; class size and staff/child ratio (Bekman, 1993, 2002; Kagitcibasi, 1997; Kagitcibasi, Sunar, & Bekman, 2001). The behavior of teachers in educational as opposed to custodial centres are cognitively oriented and aim to enrich the child's overall development (Bekman, 2002). These studies have confirmed that the aim of a centre (educational vs. custodial) affects all components of preschool education: physical arrangement, materials and equipment, program, teacher behavior, staff/child ratio, parent-teacher relationship, and whether or not there is an evaluation of the programs, as well as the overall development of the child. It has also been found that the enriching environment in educational centres overcome expected developmental differences due to social class (Bekman, 1982). A very striking finding was that working class children in educational centres engaged in play behavior which was cognitively more complex and held higher levels of social participation than that of the middle class children in centres with similar aims.

Studies investigating the effects of preschool education on child development indicate positive outcomes (Gürkan,1979; Zembat & Tokol, 1996). Children who attend a preschool program have better cognitive, language, and motor development skills, are better adapted to primary school, display healthy emotional development, are academically advanced, and have special interests and skills compared to children who do not attend any type of preschool. Preschool attendance has also been found to improve the level of class performance and promote better self-help skills (Başal, 2000; Dinçer & Demiriz, 2000).

Physical Conditions of the Preschool Centers

Research on the physical conditions of centre-based educational institutions have revealed conflicting results. Dincer (2000a) conducted a study in 88 preschool centres in Istanbul and used the physical environment rating scale developed by Lovell and Harms (1985). It is reported that one-third of the centres were rated low with respect to items of safety, appropriateness of texture, functionality of the play area, and ease of observing children. In another study Oktay, Zembat, Onder, Guven and Fathi (1994) conducted a survey to examine the physical arrangement of 25 preschool centres in Ankara. It was observed that the physical facilities were well equipped in that there were various activity corners in the group rooms and the materials were located at a level that children could reach independently. The physical arrangement was found to be developmentally appropriate for preschool aged children. These two studies also highlight that the assessment criteria used and the locations of the preschools can result in different findings.

Curriculum in the Preschool Centers

Some of the research studies have examined the curricula in the early childhood education programs from different perspectives. In a study which investigated the types of curricula, data was collected from 280 schools selected randomly from the 522 registered schools in Istanbul. It was found that centres under the control of MONE tend to follow the centralized curriculum while centres under the control of the SSCPA implement curricula developed by teachers at each centre. Developmental levels of children were taken as the main factor and individual differences had a secondary role in preparing the curriculum of SSCPA centres (Oktay et al., 1994). Available toys and materials at hand also determined the design of the curriculum, as some teachers would confine activities in the curriculum to these materials. Many teachers mentioned *holistic development of the child* as the main objective of curriculum development.

The use and role of computers in the curriculum has always been a controversial issue in early childhood education. In Turkey, it is observed that centres use computers both for fun and education (Zembat, 1997). A survey was conducted with 50 administrators and 132 teachers from different preschools in Istanbul. Fifty percent of the respondents found computers as appropriate tools for education while the other 50% respondents did not. This represents a very small sample of preschool staff in Turkey and cannot be interpreted as general is able representative finding.

There have been some attempts to improve the preschool curriculum. Such attempts have included development of curriculum in specific areas and studies of their efficacy. These remain largely at an experimental stage. In line with such an attempt, Dincer and Guneysu (1997) designed and implemented a problem solving training for children and later evaluated the effects of the training on interpersonal problem solving skills. Interpersonal problem solving skills with peers and with mothers were studied separately and the results indicate a significant difference in that children in the experimental group did better in interpersonal problems solving with peers than did the control group. Furthermore, it was observed that the experimental group of subjects did better with their peers than with their mothers. Onder and Kamaraj (1998) studied the effects of an 8 week pedagogical drama activity program on social—emotional development of children who attend preschool centers and found that social emotional performance of children were positively effected by the program. More recently Oktay and Aktan-Kerem (2001) evaluated the *School Readiness Program* which mainly included activities of reading readiness, linguistic competence, and acquisition of concepts administered for 4 days a week, for 60-90 minutes per day, and lasted 6 weeks. The program was found to enhance skills like phonological awareness, print concept, usage of vocabulary, auditory and visual discrimination.

The school-parent-child education program developed by Senocak, Erdogan, Unver, Sucuka and Bekman (1998) aimed to help children prepare for formal schooling and to facilitate parent involvement, and was implemented as a part of the curriculum of MONE preschool centres. Work sheet activities for children designed to improve literacy and numeracy skills were carried out as a part of the daily curriculum. In addition, parents were expected to attend group meetings to empower them in contributing to the development of their children. Parents were also expected to carry out literacy and numeracy activities at home similar to those implemented in the centres. Evaluations immediately after the program was completed indicated that those children who had been in the program had better preliteracy and numeracy skills compared to those who had not attended the program (Bekman & Topac, 1999). Moreover, mothers who participated in the program were found to use more positive and less negative child rearing practices. The evaluation of the program 1-year later, when the children had completed their first year of primary school, indicated better academic achievement in the first year of schooling for the children who were in the program compared to other children. Teachers perceived the children who were in the program as socially and cognitively ready for school, attentive and easily adapted to school requirements, curious, attentive and easily adapted to the school requirements. Parents were also more satisfied with what their children were learning at school and felt that the school met their expectations. Teachers of the children participating in the program also felt that the school and home environment worked in coordination with each other for the development of the child. Over 11,000 mothers and children have participated in this program in six provinces of Turkey.

Behavior and Attitudes of Teachers

A number of studies have examined the difference in attitudes and behaviors of teachers in early childhood education programs with respect to certain variables such as type of institution they worked in, age, marital status, years of experience, job satisfaction, class room density and the age of the children they worked with, educational level, level of satisfaction with job, and salary.

Among these studies an investigation of 248 university students from four universities revealed that although training to be a preschool teacher was not the first choice that many had selected in the university entrance application forms, once they began their education they were pleased with their choice (Dincer, 2000b). In a study by Turla, Tezel and Avci (1997) it was found that teachers with more years of experience and lower levels of education have difficulty in both adapting to new techniques and more prone to mention problems. Investigating the attitudes of teachers with respect to various factors such as age, marital status, years of experience, number of children in the class and job satisfaction, Zembat and Bilgin (1996) found that young teachers, married teachers, teachers working for more than 15 and less than 5 years, and teachers who had low job satisfaction had more autocratic attitudes. They did not pay any attention to child's wishes or ideas, exhibited dominating behaviors and enforced a large number of rules for children. The working conditions were also found to be indicative of attitudes: teachers working with smaller groups of children and for only half a day were found to be more democratic than teachers working a full day and with larger groups (Zembat & Bilgin, 1996).

In-service training for teachers is an important part of the Turkish early childhood education system. Oktay and Zembat (1997) have studied the effects of in-service training programs on teachers and found these programs to be effective in improving relations with colleagues, and these relationships to evaluate their own work, improve knowledge and change views regarding program development, program evaluation, the importance of creativity, and the role of the child in the learning environment.

Studies on Children Attending Preschool Centers

Studies conducted with children who attend preschool centres have focused on the development of children's environmental awareness, self-concept, perception of caregivers and family concepts and school readiness. In a study by Haktanir and Cabuk (2000), environmental awareness of children between 4-6 years of age was examined. Environmental awareness was defined as having interest in the environment and environmental problems, being able to recognize the importance of behaviors such as leaving garbage in picnic areas, spitting, reusing plastic bags and the like. Children from high socioeconomic backgrounds with fathers in executive positions, mothers with university education, and with no siblings were found to have more environmental awareness.

In the study of the family concept of preschool children, Haktanir and Darica (2000) found that irrespective of gender, 5-6-year-olds had poor family concepts (defined as legal, social, biological, and kinship dimensions of the family). Haktanir and Dogan (1996) also found that 5-6 year-olds perceived their mother as equipped to take care of their children, but girls believed their fathers and grandmothers were better equipped for child care than did boys. In another study, socioeconomic status has been found to be positively related to 4-5-year-olds' self-concept, where self-concept was defined as cognitive, social and physical competence (Haktanir & Aktas, 1994; Onder, 1999). Oktay (1980) examined factors affecting school readiness and found that Turkish children who were between 5.6 to 6 years of age, from high socioeconomic status, and stimulating environments, have better emerging literacy skills.

Parent Involvement and Child Rearing Practices

Parent involvement is considered one of the main components of quality in centre-based early childhood education. A study by Ensari and Zembat (1996) set out to examine how much the teachers and administrators foster parent involvement in 55 centres. In almost all of the schools studied there were no procedures or mechanisms for the parents to contribute to the administrative and educational programs in the preschool centres. While families claimed the attitudes of school administrators were an important barrier to parent involvement, administrators claimed that parents lack interest. Schools are increasingly finding that programs to improve parent involvement are necessary and one such intervention in this regard is the preschool parent child education program described in the curriculum section.

Other studies have examined child rearing practices of parents with different characteristics such as working status and educational level. Such studies of child rearing practices serve an important role in understanding development of children and individual differences (Dincer & Demiriz, 2000). Findings indicate that children of working mothers and mothers with high school and university education have better self-help skills than children of nonworking mothers and mothers with primary school diplomas. Attitudes of mothers in the teaching profession and mothers with administrative jobs have been compared and it was found that both groups value hard working, active and independent children and maintain a protective attitude but mothers in the teaching profession were found to be more democratic and did not display disciplinary or dominating attitudes (Mangir & Haktanir, 1990).

Studies on Home-Based Early Childhood Education Programs

As discussed so far, the early childhood education programs in the country is predominantly center based. One of the most well documented models of home based programs in Turkey is the mother child education program. This program began in 1982 as the Turkish early enrichment project, a home based early childhood education program to increase the coverage of early chiildhood programs in the country and is one of the longest running research projects in Turkey. It has been the subject of several qualitative and experimental researches (Bekman, 1998, 2003; Kagitcibasi, 1996, 1997; Kagitçibasi, Sunar & Bekman, 2001; Kagitcibasi, Bekman & Goksel, 1995; Kocak, 2000). The program is a 25 week home based parent education and pre-school program, aiming to both sensitize the mother to the needs of the child and to enhance the cognitive development of the child in order to better prepare him/her for school. Although only 90 children participated in the program in the original research project, the program has to date reached 135,000 mothers and children. Both short and long-term results have indicated positive effects on children's overall development, commitment to schooling and school achievement. Better quality of interaction between family members and the child, better family adjustment, and a better perception of the child by the parents have been reported in the comparison of the research groups. Further studies of the program have been conducted after it became a national, state run program and results have revealed significant improvements in preliteracy and prenumeracy skills illustrating clearly that children in the program are more prepared to deal with the expectations of formal schooling than their counterparts not in the program. Children were also followed up in their first year of schooling and the effects of the program were found to be sustained in that the experimental children had better literacy and numeracy skills, began to read earlier than the control group and had higher end-of-year academic grades. These positive effects are also reflected in mothers in that they had better child rearing practices. The change reflects the presence of certain mother-child interactions which lead to more adequate growth and development of children (Bekman, 1998).

CONCLUDING COMMENTS

Programs for early childhood education in the country remains at a preliminary stage of development and there is an urgent need to improve both the coverage and the quality of the system. Since this is of course very much dependent on the policies enacted by the government, it has been necessary to review what has been done to date and how effective we have been in meeting the specific needs of young children in Turkey.

The current status of early childhood education in Turkey calls attention primarily to the low level of access to early childhood programs in the country. The pursuit of a single model of centre based programs may not be viable in this case, if we are to concentrate efforts on increasing access in the shorter term. Instead, it would make sense to embrace different models that are low cost, require less investment, and are capable of reaching significant populations. The well documented and promising results of the home based mother child education program indicates the relevance and viability of such alternative programs.

It has been well established in the literature that early childhood education programs can overcome the unfavorable conditions of the home environment and thus have an important role in the advancement of human development. For countries with large social and economic inequalities and diverse populations, early childhood education programs become even more important. However, to be truly effective in improving social inequalities, a multiprogram approach targeting the needs of specific populations would need to be employed. This would require an aim of intervention that is beyond the *preparation for school* focus of current public policies. Unfortunately, in Turkey, the system does not provide adequate access to children living under *risk* of development nor does it allow for intervention programs targeting linguistic or cultural differences. Programs with contextual relevance are often the most effective for such target groups, since programs which empower both the child and family are not only important in the development of early childhood but can also be significant in community development.

Finally, the issue of quality early childhood education is of paramount importance in Turkey. Since the field is still at an early stage of development, there are a number of concerns regarding accreditation, training, and curriculum, all of which are directly related to the effectiveness of the system. Research in the field indicate attempts to improve the quality of early childhood education, with evaluations of experimental models of curricula or programs as well as an assessment of existing practices. We believe that an increase in the number of children benefiting from early childhood education in Turkey will have a bearing on the number and quality of research in the area.

REFERENCES

Basal, H. A. (2000, September). *İlköğretim birinci sınıf öğrencilerinin sınıf içi etkinlik düzeylerinde okulöncesi eğitim, sosyo-ekonomik düzey ve cinsiyetin etkileri* [The effects of preschool education, socio-economic status and gender on the level of class performance]. Speech given at the XI. Ulusal Eğitim Bilimleri Kongresi, Erzurum.

Bekman, S. (1982). *Preschool education in Turkey: A study of the relations between children's behaviour, the aims of the program, and the sex and social class of the child.* Unpublished doctoral dissertation, University of London, London.

Bekman, S. (1993). Preschool education system in Turkey: Revisited. *International Journal of Early Childhood, 25*, 13-19.

Bekman, S. (1998). Long-term effects of the Turkish home-based early enrichment program. In U. P. Gielen & A. L. Comunian (Eds.), *The family and family therapy in international perspective* (pp. 401-417). Trieste, Italy: Legoprint-Lavis.

Bekman, S. (2002). Does day care centre experience and it's aim matter? *European Early Childhood Education Research Journal, 10*(1), 123-135.

Bekman, S. (2003). From research project to nationwide program: The mother-child education program of Turkey. In T. S. Saraswathi (Ed.), *Cross-cultural perspectives in human development theory, research and applications* (pp. 287-325). New Delhi, India: Sage.

Bekman, S., & Topac, B. (1999). *III. Okulöncesi Veli Çocuk Eğitimi Programı İstanbul Pilot Projesi değerlendirme araştirmasi* [III. Preschool parent child education program Ýstanbul pilot project evaluation research.]. Retrieved March 17, 2003, from http://www.acev.org/arastirma/arastirma/ovcep_istanbul.doc

Dincer, C. (2000a, August). Okulöncesi eðitim kurumlarindaki diþari oyun alanlarinin deðerlendirilmesi [Evaluation of the outdoor play areas in preschool education institutions]. In Z. Gökçakan (Ed.), *VIII. Ulusal Eğitim Bilimleri Kongresi Bilimsel Çalışmaları* (1-3 Eylül 1999, Cilt-1, pp. 423-432). Trabzon, Turkey: Karadeniz Teknik Üniversitesi Basimevi.

Dincer, C .(2000b, September). *Okulöncesi öğretmenliği anabilim dalı öğrencilerinin mesleğe yaklaşımları* [Approaches of the preschool education department students towards the occupation]. Speech given at the XI Ulusal Eğitim Bilimleri Kongresi, Erzurum.

Dincer, C., & Demiriz, S. (2000). Okulöncesi dönem çocuklarýn öz bakim becerilerinin annelerinin çalışıp çalışmama durumlarýna göre incelenmesi [Inspection of the self help skills of preschool age children according to employement status of their mothers]. *Hacettepe Üniversitesi Eğitim Fakültesi Dergisi, 19*, 58-66.

Dincer, C., & Guneysu, S. (1997). Examining the effects of problem solving training on the acquisition of interpersonal problem solving skills by 5-year-old children in Turkey. *International Journal of Early Years Education, 5*(1), 37-46.,

Ensari, H., & Zembat, R. (1996, May). Ailelerin Okulöncesi eðitim programlarýna katýlýmýnda karþýlaþtýklarý engeller. In *II. Ulusal Eðitim Sempozyumu Bildirileri* (pp. 1-8). Ýstanbul, Turkey: Marmara Üniversitesi Atatürk Eðitim Fakültesi.

Gurkan, T. (1979). Okulöncesi eðitimin ilkokuldaki etkileri üzerine bir inceleme [An inspection of the effects of preschool education on primary education]. *Eğitim ve Bilim, 22*, 16-26.

Haktanir, G., & Aktas, Y. (1994, May). 3-4 yaş çocuklarının motor gelişim özelliklerinin incelenmesi. [Inspection of the motor development of 3-4 year old children]. *10. YA-PA Okulöncesi Eğitimi ve Yaygınlaştırılması Semineri* (pp. 139-146). Ankara, Turkey: Ya-Pa Yayınları.

Haktanir, G., & Cabuk, B. (2000, September). Okulöncesi dönemdeki çocukларýn çevre algýlarý.

[Environment concept in preschool aged children]. *IV. Fen Bilimleri Eğitimi Kongresi Bildiri Kitabı* (pp. 76-81). Ankara, Turkey: Hacettepe Üniversitesi Eğitim Fakültesi.

Haktanir, G., & Darica, N. (2000). 5-6 Yaş Çocuklarinin Aile Kavrami [Family concept in 5-6 year olds]. *S.D.Ü. Burdur Eğitim Fakültesi Dergisi, 1* (1), 105-122.

Haktanir, G., & Dogan, S. (1996). Çocukların bebekler ve bakımlarına ilişkin düşünceleri [Children's thoughts on babies and baby care]. *Milli Eğitim, 132*, 33-34.

Kagitcibasi, C. (1996). *Family and human development across cultures: A view from the other side.* Mahwah, NJ: Erlbaum.

Kagitcibasi, C. (1997). Parent education and child development. In M. E. Young (Ed.), *Early child development: Investing in our children's future* (pp.243-272). New York: Elsevier.

Kagitcibasi, C., Bekman, S., & Goksel, A. (1995). A multipurpose model of nonformal education. *Coordinator's Notebook, 17*, 24-32.

Kagitcibasi, C., & Sunar, D. (1992). Family and socialization in Turkey. In. J. L. Roopnarine & D. B. Carter (Eds.), *Parent-child relations in diverse cultural setting: socialization for instrumental competency: Annual advances in applied developmental psychology* (Vol 5. pp 75-88). Norwood, NJ: Ablex

Kagitcibasi, Ç., Sunar, D., & Bekman, S. (2001). Long-term effects of early intervention: Turkish low income mothers and children. *Applied Developmental Psychology, 22*, 333-361.

Kocak, A. A. (2000). Mothers speaking: A study on the experience of mothers with mother-child education program. Unpublished master's thesis, Bogazici University, Istanbul, Turkey.

Lovell, P., & Harms, T. (1985). How can playgrounds be improved? A rating scale. *Young Children, 40*, 3-9

Mangir, M., & Haktanir, G. (1990). *A.Ü. Ziraat Fakültesi'nde çalışan annelerin çocuk yetiştirme tutumları üzerine bir araştırma* [A research on the child rearing practices of the mothers employed at the A. U. Faculty of Agriculture]. Ankara Üniversitesi Ziraat Fakültesi Yayınları: 1177, Bilimsel Araştırma ve İncelemeler: 649, s: 1-87, Ankara, Turkey.

Ministry of National Education. (2003). Available from Ministry of National Education Web site, http://w.w.w.meb.gov.tr

Myers, R. (1992). *The twelve who survive.* London: Routledge.

Oktay, A. (1980). *Okula başlama olgunluğunu etkileyen sosyo-ekonomik ve kültürel faktörlerin incelenmesi* [An inspection of the socio-economic and cultural factors that affect school readiness]. Ýstanbul, Turkey: Ýstanbul Edebiyat Fakültesi Pedagoji Enstitüsü.

Oktay, A. (1983). Türkiye'de okul öncesi eğitimin dünü ve bugünü [Preschool education in Turkey yesterday and today]. *Marmara Üniversitesi Atatürk Eğitim Fakültesi Eğitim Bilimleri Dergisi*, 7.

Oktay, A. (1999). *Türkiye Cumhuriyeti'nin 75. yılında okul öncesi eğitim ve ilköğretim* [Preschool and primary education at the 75th anniversary of the Turkish Republic]. Ankara, Turkey: TÜBA.

Oktay, A., & Aktan-Kerem, E. (2001). Okulöncesi dönem çocuklarýnda okuma geliþimi ve okumaya hazırlık programının etkisinin değerlendirilmesi [Development of reading in preschool children and an evaluation of the reading readiness program]. Unpublished doctoral dissertation, Marmara University, Ýstanbul, Turkey.

Oktay, A., & Zembat, R. (1997). Okulöncesi eğitimcisinin yetiştirilmesinde yeni eğilimler [New tendencies in training of the preschool educator]. In G. Haktanır (Ed.), *Okulöncesi Eğitim Sempozyumu Okulöncesi Eğitimde Yeni Yaklaşımlar (pp. 24-32)*. Ankara, Turkey: Ankara Üni. Ziraat Fak. Ev Ekonomisi Yüksek Okulu Çocuk Gelişimi Ana Bilim Dalı Türkiye Okul Öncesi Eğitimi Derneği.

Oktay, A., Zembat, R., Onder, A., Guven, Y., & Fathi, L. (1994, April). İstanbul'daki okulöncesi kurumlarında uygulanan programların özelliklerinin tespiti araştırmasi [A research on the features of the programmes that are applied in preschool education institutions in İstanbul]. In *1. Eğitim Bilimleri Kongresi Bildirileri* (Cilt 2, pp. 805-814). Adana, Turkey: Çukurova Üniversitesi Basımevi.

Onder, A. (1999, October). *Preschool children's self-concept in relation to socio-economic status, age and gender.* Speech given at the ESSOP 1999-Annual Congress of the European Society for social pediatrics school health, Ýstanbul, Turkey.

Onder, A., & Kamaraj, I. (1998, August). *Social emotional effects of pedagogical drama in Turkish preschool children.* Paper presented at the 22nd World Congress of OMEP Child's Rights to Care, Play and Education, Copenhagen, Denmark.

Senocak, D., Erdogan, D., Unver,S., Sucuka, N., & Bekman, S. (1998). School-parent-child program. Istanbul, Turkey: ACEV.

State Planning Organization. (2003). Available from State Planning Organization Web site, http://w.w.w.dpt.gov.tr

Turla, A., Tezel, F., & Avci, N. (1997). Okulöncesi öğretmenlerinin fiziksel şartlar, program, yöntem, teknik, sinif ve davranış yöntemi sorunlarının bazi değişkenlere göre incelenmesi [Inspection of the physical conditions, programme, method, techniques, classroom and behaviour method problems according to some variables]. *Milli Eğitim Dergisi, 151,* 95-101.

UNICEF. (2003). The state of the world's children. NewYork: Oxford University Press.

Zembat, R. (1997, May). Okulöncesi eðitim kurumlarında bilgisayar kullaniminin mevcut durumu nasýldýr? Nasil olmalidir? [How is the current situation about computer use in preschool education institutions? How should it be?]. In *1. Ulusal Çocuk Gelişimi ve Eğitimi Kongre Kitabı* (pp. 380-389). Ankara, Turkey: Hacettepe Üniversitesi.

Zembat, R., & Bilgin, H. (1996, September). Okulöncesi eğitim kurumlarında çalişan öğretmenlerin öğretmenlik tutumlarinin incelenmesi [Inspection of the teaching attitudes of the teachers who work in preschool education institutes]. In *II.*

Ulusal Eğitim Sempozyumu Bildirileri (pp.108-118). Ýstanbul, Turkey: Marmara Üniversitesi Teknik Eğitim Fakültesi Döner Sermaye Saymanlığı.

Zembat, R., & Tokol, O. (1996, September). Okulöncesi eğitim kurumlarına devam eden ve etmeyen 3-6 yaş çocuklarının gelişim özelliklerinin incelenmesi [Inspection of the developmental features of 3-6 years children who attend to preschool education institutions and who do not]. In N. U. İnan & O. Aydın (Eds.), *II. Ulusal Eğitim Sempozyumu Bildirileri* (pp. 50-61). İstanbul, Turkey: Marmara Üniversitesi Atatürk Eğitim Fakültesi Matbaa Birimi.

CHAPTER 12

EARLY CHILDHOOD EDUCATION

An International and Contemporary Perspective

Bernard Spodek and Olivia N. Saracho

For many decades education programs for young children have been developed all over the world. These early childhood programs in different countries have encountered many challenges and concerns. Many of these programs have been based upon historical models of early childhood education created by such pioneers as Freidrich Froebel, Maria Montessori, Margaret MacMillan and John Dewey, as noted in the introduction to this volume. Most of the approaches to early childhood education that existed during the past century have continued, although they have been revised, modified and reconceptualized. Other historical approaches to early childhood education have faded from the scene, however. Additionally, each country has developed its own organizational arrangements to provide education to young children. This has made early childhood education both a universal international phenomenon as well as a very local one.

International Perspectives on Research in Early Childhood Education, 355–360
Copyright © 2005 by Information Age Publishing
355

The chapters in this volume describe the international roots of early childhood research and practice, as they are manifested in a number of countries. The chapters present a brief history and describe the current status of early childhood education in selected countries. There are also descriptions of the issues that face early childhood educators there. Finally, each chapter presents a review of current research being conducted in these countries.

In essence, the volume presents a glimpse of the intellectual base of early childhood education in many parts of the world. There are many issues that can be identified in early childhood education around the world. These include the issues that follow.

INTERNATIONAL CONCERNS

Early childhood education and care services for young children from birth to 8 years of age are organized in a number of ways in the countries presented here. Generally, the education of children is split into two or possibly three levels of organization. Infants and toddlers, those below the age of three -- are served by crèches or home day care settings. Preschool children -- between the age of 3 and 6 or 7 years of age are served in preschools, nursery schools or kindergartens. Older young children are educated in the first three grades of the elementary school. The education of children below the age of six or seven tends to be less formal than that for older young children.

In most countries the care and education of young children are seen as separate functions. Separate institutions provide these distinct functions. The differences extend beyond the names of these institutions, but include different regulatory agencies, different policies, different staff qualifications, different programs, different ways of operating, and different funding sources. However, child care programs offer some degree of education, whether provided explicitly or implicitly.

Changes in the political structures of countries have also impacted on early childhood education in recent years. Not only is the availability of programs and services influenced by the political structure of a country, but also the content and method of instruction at both the preschool and elementary school level. In each case there was a change from heavily structured teacher directed activities to more open child-responsive practices as countries moved towards democracy.

There is also a concern about the availability of resources to support early childhood education in various countries. As economies expand, additional resources may be provided for early childhood education programs in a country. Unfortunately, when economies contract, there is often a press to reduce these resources.

Most countries have a mix of state supported and independent early childhood education institutions. The independent programs may be operated by not-for-profit agencies or they may be operated by profit making institutions. In some cases government subsidies are provided to nonstate supported programs in a variety of ways. In other countries such programs must depend entirely on fees from families alone. This situation places limits on the quality of services provided since these institutions do not wish to price themselves out of the market. Staff salaries represent the largest expense of these programs. As a result, there is pressure to maintain low salaries. This causes less qualified persons to be more likely to be hired as teachers. It also leads to a high rate of teacher turnover.

The role that early childhood education plays in a country reflects not only the children's level of development but also the different cultural values. Historical developments, recent changes in society and changes in family structures have influenced early childhood policy making. As families have become smaller and as more mothers of young children enter the work force, early childhood education takes on increased importance in a number of countries. Not only do these programs provide care for young children during their parents working hours, but they also serve as another socializing agency for children.

These are some of the issues that face early childhood education programs in various countries. Another issue relates to the quality of preschool education. The question of how one defines quality in early childhood education programs, as well as how one assesses the level of quality of programs, is one that is being addressed in many countries. This issue, along with others, has generated a need for greater research in early childhood education. Other significant issues relate to the role of play in early childhood education, the nature of social interactions between adults and children and among children within these programs, and the relationship of early childhood special education to the education of more normally developing young children. In addition, there is the challenge of the transition from home to school and between the preschool or kindergarten and the primary school.

LOOKING AT RESEARCH IN EARLY CHILDHOOD EDUCATION FROM AN INTERNATIONAL PERSPECTIVE

These chapters have provided a sample of activities in early childhood education programs in the different countries. They describe a vibrant intellectual community concerned with improving the quality of services for young children and with the acquisition of knowledge related to early childhood education. Research activity is being conducted with great vigor in many countries around the world. Only a selected few of them have been included here; others could have been explored and may be explored in a future volume. There is much that can be learned from this volume, however. Let us suggest the following:

- **There are differences in the levels of maturity of early childhood programs in the various countries represented here as well as in the level of research activity.**

  Early childhood education programs have only recently been developed in some of these countries, while in other countries programs of early childhood education have a history that is almost a century long. Additionally, early childhood education programs are more positively viewed and have greater public and financial support in some countries than in others. Similarly, there is a greater development of early childhood education research activities in some countries than in others.

- **While research in early childhood education is a relatively new activity in general, it is growing steadily as individuals in various countries seek greater knowledge of the field.**

  In many countries, such as Greece and Turkey, the research enterprise is relatively young. It can be expected that as this enterprise matures and as more early childhood educators are trained as researchers and scholars, research activities will increase. What is especially important is that the conditions that support early childhood education research are continuing to improve.

  There needs to be a greater commitment on the part of all countries to support not only the practice of early childhood education, but inquiry into that practice as well. Universities, departments of education and social service and research and development agencies need to increasingly focus on the education of young children and its consequences. Already there is an increase in the avenues for the dissemination of research. National and regional conferences with a focus on early childhood education are developing. New journals on early childhood education are appearing, both nationally and internationally. National and regional organizations supporting conferences that focus on research in early childhood education are growing stronger.

- **There are common concerns that drive early childhood education in many countries.**

  The need to clarify the relationship between care and education is a common issue that is facing many nations. Definitions of what constitutes early childhood education is important here as well as the issue of whether one can reasonably provide for the care of young children without offering them some educational experiences. The term *educare*, describing a common service in which child care and early education are provided within the same institution, has had some popularity in the United States and elsewhere. There are some nations in which this joint service is actually the norm. In many more, however, these two elements of early childhood education are provided in different institutions, under the supervision of different government agencies, with different regulations applying, and different standards existing remains the norm. Unfortunately, in many cases bureaucratic petrifaction supports the status quo.

- **Newer approaches to research in early childhood education can be found in some of the countries with more mature early childhood education paradigms.**

  In some countries a range of newer paradigms drives early childhood educational research. These include an increased attention to constructivist research and other forms of qualitative research, feminist research, and postmodernist research. Early childhood educators seem to be moving increasingly beyond surveys of existing practices and positivist approaches to research in early childhood education

  All this suggests that research activity in early childhood education is vigorous and alive in many places in the world. As we continue our work, increasing numbers of people will be involved in inquiries stimulated by the many puzzlements regarding early childhood education. As individuals meet and share their work, either through face-to-face contacts, through the printed work or through the electronic media, the field will grow richer and stronger. As a result, in years to come we expect to see additional volumes sharing research in early childhood education on an international basis, with more countries represented and more ideas being shared within the field and around the globe.

FUTURE EXPECTATIONS

Although it is more difficult to predict the future of early childhood education at an international level than at a national level, a number of alternatives exist. It seems evident that conditions that support the development of early childhood education in many countries have improved and will continue to improve. Similarly, conditions that support the development of research in early childhood education can also be expected to improve.

Early childhood researchers and educators will continue to have opportunities to create new educational environments for young children and to study them. Early childhood programs will continue to respond to the social context in which they are implemented. Early childhood education issues in more developed countries can provide lessons for program sponsors in less developed countries. Assessment of these programs within the appropriate cultural context can support program dissemination and development. Research evidence on the importance of the early years of life suggests that programs of early childhood education and development are an important avenue for social change. The needs of young children, their families, and their communities can be integrated programmatically. The twenty-first century can offer early childhood education a bewildering assortment of alternatives to meet these needs.

At the beginning of the twenty-first century, developments in all countries offer many possibilities for the future of early childhood education. Threats to peace seriously affect early childhood education programs in many places. Additionally, societies may feel the need to reallocate resources when threatened and lose their flexibility in responding to social concerns. Individuals may reject some early childhood education programs or ideas that they perceive as threatening, whether because they have developed in foreign soils or because the programs are seen as too open and thus threatening to the status quo. On the other hand, governments may also assist international efforts to support early childhood education programs during periods of crises.

Early childhood education leaders need to prepare for the future of early childhood education by becoming flexible so that their plan can be modified with ease in response to internal conditions or world events. Early childhood education researchers, scholars, educators, advocates, and leaders need to identify educational goals in relation to a transforming society. Early childhood education both in the United States and in other nations need to be able to respond to the changing social, cultural, technological, and economic conditions. The thoughts and work of early childhood researchers, scholars, and leaders can influence the disposition of international early childhood education programs. This presents a challenge and a responsibility to early childhood education advocates, including researchers, scholars, and educators among others.

ABOUT THE AUTHORS

Sevda Bekman completed her masters and doctoral study at the University of London. She is a professor and chair of the Department of Primary Education of Boazçi University. Dr. Bekman's academic work concentrates on early childhood intervention. She has contributed to the development of various programs such as the Mother-Child Education Program, the Father Empowerment Program, the School-Parent Child Program, and the accelerated preschool Summer Program for South-East Turkey for multilingual populations. Under the scope of these projects, she has conducted various evaluation studies on the effectiveness of home and center-based early childhood education programs that target children in poverty,

Hara Cortessis-Dafermou is a researcher at the Center for Educational Research, Ministry of Education, Greece. Her doctoral thesis was on the construction of the written language of pupils with low performance, when serving as a teacher of secondary education. She taught at the Department of Early Childhood Education, University of Thessaly, 2001–2003. Her research interests focus on approaching written language in early childhood and planning educational interventions to promote school achievement.

Demetra Evangelou is an associate professor of early childhood education at the University of Thessaly, Greece. Prior to that she was with the Department of Child Development and Family Studies at Purdue University. She has taught and conducted research in Greece and the United States. Dr. Evangelou completed her graduate studies at the University of Illinois. Her research interests include teacher training and early childhood curriculum.

Jane Harper is a Senior Lecturer in Educational Psychology within the School of Education at the University of South Australia. She has extensive experience in teaching and the management of initial and postgraduate teacher education programs. Her current interests include management and policy development in higher education and the educational applications of information and communication technologies.

Sachiko Kitano is an associate professor of early childhood care and education at Fukuoka University of Education. She received her PhD in education from Hiroshima University. She is interested in the professionalism in early childhood education and her most recent research interests are in the areas of function of professional organizations, in-service training, and policy. She is examining the positive and negative consequences of the systematization and institutionalization of early childhood education.

Young-Ja Lee is a professor of early childhood education at Duksung Women's University, Seoul, Korea. She received her EdD in early childhood education from Boston University. Her research interests include development and evaluation of early childhood educational programs, young children's language development, teaching-learning strategies of language and literacy for young children, and young children's emotional intelligence development. Her publications include *Language Education for Young Children, Development of Infant/Toddler Program Based on Play and Exploration,* and *A Program to Increase the Emotional Intelligence of Young Children.*

Ole Fredrik Lillemyr, after completing teacher training, studied music, and holds the degree of Magister Artium of Education. He worked in secondary school and at the university. He was a visiting professor at University of Illinois 1980/81. Since 1997 he has been a professor of education at Queen Maud's University College, Trondheim (formerly rector at QMC). He has written several articles, research reports, and published textbooks. Research interests are self-concept, motivation, play, and sociocultural influences on learning.

Barbara Murawska is a member of the faculty of education in Warsaw University, Poland. She is the head of post-graduate studies for early education teachers and a collaborator of the Institute of Public Affairs. She deals with social problems in education, first of all in early education, and educational measurement and testing. Among her more important publications are: *Social Segregation in Primary School* (2004), with R. Dolata and E. Putkiewicz and *School Achievement Monitoring as a Method of Endorsing the Local Educational Community* (2000).

Mikko Ojala is a professor in preschool and early elementary education at the University of Helsinki, Finland. He has the diploma for primary school teacher and developmental psychologist. For his doctoral theses he studied how to develop and teach memory strategies for children between 7-12 years old. He is currently the head of kindergarten teacher training and has a position at the research center for Early Childhood and Elementary Education. Serving as a national leader for the IEA Preprimary project, he has published several cross-cultural studies about children's learning and development. Since 2000 he has studied the effects of preschool education for 6-years old children. Dr. Ojala has published and edited several textbooks and has served as an expert for EU, OECD and OMEP.

Unhai Rhee is a professor of child and family studies at Yonsei University, Seoul, Korea. She received her PhD in education from the Ohio State University in 1974. Her research interests include evaluation of early childhood programs, developing assessment scales, and social development of children and adolescents. Her publications include *Research Methods in Child Study* and *Psychological Assessment for Children*.

Won Young Rhee is a professor in the Department of Early Childhood Education at Chung-Ang University, Seoul, Korea. She is a former Kindergarten teacher. She received her PhD from Ewha Women's University. Her research interests include parent education, child-rearing culture and curriculum and teaching methods for young children.

Olivia N. Saracho is a professor of education in the Department of Curriculum and Instruction at the University of Maryland. Her areas of scholarship include family literacy, cognitive style, teaching, and teacher education in early childhood education. Dr. Saracho was coeditor of the *Yearbook in Early Childhood Education* Series (Teachers College Press). Currently she is coeditor of the Contemporary Perspectives in Early Childhood Education series (Information Age Publishing). Dr. Saracho's most recent books are *Contemporary Perspectives on Play in Early Childhood Education*, *Studying Teachers in Early Childhood Settings* and *Contemporary Perspectives on Language Policy and Literary Instruction in Early Childhood Education*, coedited with Bernard Spodek (Information Age Publishing).

Wendy Schiller is a writer, researcher and teacher. Professor Schiller has worked in Canada, South Africa, Papua New Guinea, and Australia with indigenous populations and has taught at the tertiary level in Canada and Australia. Wendy has edited and authored 11 books, 25 book chapters and over 35 journal articles. She is currently director of research in the de

Lissa Institute of Early Childhood and Family Studies at University of South Australia. She was recently been awarded an Order of Australia Medal (OAM) for service to early childhood education.

Yoko Shirakawa is a professor of early childhood education at Konan Women's University and Professor Emerita at Kobe University where she taught early childhood education for 24 years. She has published several books and articles on early childhood education in Japan. . Her areas of scholarship are the contents and methods in early childhood education.

Bernard Spodek is professor emeritus of early childhood education at the University of Illinois. He began in 1952 as an early childhood teacher in the New York City area. He received his doctorate from Teachers College, Columbia University. His research and scholarly interests are in the areas of curriculum, teaching, and teacher education in early childhood education. He was president of the National Association for the Education of Young Children (1976-78) and is currently president of the Pacific Early Childhood Education Research Association. Bernard Spodek was coeditor with Olivia N. Saracho of the *Yearbook in Early Childhood Education* Series (Teachers College Press). They are currently coeditors of the Contemporary Perspectives in Early Childhood Education series (Information Age Publishing).

Teresa Vasconcelos is a professor of early childhood education at the School of Education of the Lisbon Polytechnic, Portugal. She was director for basic education at the Ministry of Education and responsible for the development and expansion of the preschool system in Portugal. She received her PhD at the University of Illinois in Urbana-Champaign. She is a specialist in case studies and ethnographies widely published. She has been consultant for OECD, Bernard Van Leer and Soros Foundations.

Ann Veale has been an early childhood teacher in New Zealand and Australia. She has made a career as an academic at the University of South Australia. At the time of her retirement she was head of school of the de Lissa Institute of Early Childhood and Family Studies. She continues to be a commentator and researcher in the arts for young children, and reflects on international perspectives and development within the profession.

X. Christine Wang is an assistant professor of early childhood education at the State University of New York at Buffalo. A native of the Peoples' Republic of China, she completed her bachelors and masters degrees at Beijing Normal University. She obtained her PhD from the University of Illinois at Urbana-Champaign in 2003. Her research interests include technology in early childhood education, sociocultural, and international issues. She is also interested in qualitative research methods and video ethnography in particular, and research related to international issues. She is also interested in qualitative research methods and video ethnography in particular.

Miguel A. Zabalza is doctor in psychology and pedagogy since 1979. He is a professor of didactics and school organization at the University of Santiago de Compostela (Galicia-Spain). His current research lines are the school curriculum, early childhood education and teacher education. His best know books are: *Curriculum Design and Development*, *Didactics for Early Childhood Education*, *Quality in Early Childhood Education*, *Universities: The Scenario and the Actors*, and *Professional Competences of the University Teachers*.

Jiaxiong Zhu is a professor of early childhood education at East China Normal University (ECNU), Shanghai, P. R. of China. He is head of Early Childhood Education Institute of ECNU. He obtained his MEd from the University of Massachusetts at Amherst. His research interests include curriculum development and policy making in early childhood education, and sociocultural research.

Printed in the United States
207121BV00004B/10-12/A